D1221378

Exploring Three Approaches to Psychotherapy

Exploring Three Approaches to Psychotherapy

Leslie S. Greenberg, Nancy McWilliams,
and Amy Wenzel

American Psychological Association • Washington, DC

Published by
American Psychological Association
750 First Street, NE
Washington, DC 20002
www.apa.org

To order
APA Order Department
P.O. Box 92984
Washington, DC 20090-2984
Tel: (800) 374-2721; Direct: (202) 336-5510
Fax: (202) 336-5502; TDD/TTY: (202) 336-6123
Online: www.apa.org/pubs/books
E-mail: order@apa.org

In the U.K., Europe, Africa, and the Middle East, copies may be ordered from
American Psychological Association
3 Henrietta Street
Covent Garden, London
WC2E 8LU England

Typeset in Meridien by Circle Graphics, Inc., Columbia, MD

Printer: United Book Press, Inc., Baltimore, MD
Cover Designer: Mercury Publishing Services, Inc., Rockville, MD

The opinions and statements published are the responsibility of the authors, and such opinions and statements do not necessarily represent the policies of the American Psychological Association.

Library of Congress Cataloging-in-Publication Data

Greenberg, Leslie S.
 Exploring three approaches to psychotherapy / Leslie S. Greenberg, Nancy McWilliams, and Amy Wenzel.
   pages cm
 Includes bibliographical references and index.
 ISBN 978-1-4338-1521-8 (hardcover) — ISBN 1-4338-1521-4 (hardcover) — ISBN 978-1-4338-1520-1 (paperback) — ISBN 1-4338-1520-6 (paperback) 1. Psychotherapy. 2. Psychotherapy—Practice. 3. Psychotherapists. I. McWilliams, Nancy. II. Wenzel, Amy. III. Title.
 RC480.G728 2014
 616.89'14—dc23
                                    2013007814

British Library Cataloguing-in-Publication Data
A CIP record is available from the British Library.

Printed in the United States of America
First Edition

http://dx.doi.org/10.1037/14253-000

Contents

Preface

This book was created as a follow-up to two successful DVDs, *Three Approaches to Psychotherapy With a Female Client* and *Three Approaches to Psychotherapy With a Male Client* (American Psychological Association [APA], 2012). These programs showed guest experts representing three distinct approaches to psychotherapy: Judith Beck demonstrating cognitive therapy, Leslie Greenberg demonstrating emotion-focused therapy, and Nancy McWilliams demonstrating psychodynamic therapy. The process of creating the DVDs was a long one. It began with research on what approaches we would include, and we chose these three as representative of the initial major schools in psychotherapy—behavioral, humanistic, and psychoanalytic, respectively—and chose these specific guest experts for their standing in the field.

We knew from years of experience filming psychotherapy demonstrations that to capture more than an initial session with a client whom the therapist has not met before, we needed to provide the therapist with information about each client. For this reason, we asked Jon Carlson, the cohost for these DVDs and host of many APA videos, to record an intake session with each client participant. We sent the guest experts these recorded sessions, so each therapist went into the demonstrations with the same information about each participant.

Actual production of the DVDs took several months. Each guest expert flew into Chicago on separate occasions to meet with our two client participants, and then returned again for a roundtable discussion of their collective efforts. I cohosted the roundtable discussions with Jon Carlson, and we spent several interesting and busy days with the guest experts, in and out of the studio, creating the opening segment for the videos as well as the roundtable.

The therapist's work was discussed and analyzed in an atmosphere of collegiality and a spirit of genuine curiosity about how the approaches could be compared. It is one thing for an expert in psychotherapy theory to discuss abstractly the differences or the common factors across approaches. It is an entirely different thing to sit three therapists side by side to discuss their work with the same clients. The resulting discussions were lively and enlightening, providing insight into the nature of therapy as it is practiced today.

The idea for this book was born during the studio sessions in which we recorded the two 75-minute roundtable discussions. For all the richness, depth, and length of those roundtables, I think everyone involved felt that we could have talked for hours more (and we did, actually, off camera). Not long after production ended, I proposed that we continue our roundtable in the form of a book about the sessions, a book that could be read in two ways: First, as a commentary on the DVD programs, an extension of the roundtable discussion; and second, as a stand-alone introduction to three distinct theories of psychotherapy practice, one that features extensive case examples integrated into the discussion of the approaches. We feel that the book has fulfilled that original vision.

I would like to thank all those involved in the DVDs and this book: The client participants, who made the brave choice of allowing the camera to record their genuine thoughts and responses during a therapy demonstration; each guest expert, who gamely put him- or herself up for comparison with two other guest experts as exemplars of their particular approaches; and Jon Carlson, my cohost. Of course, those of us on screen were only the visible portion of the final product: Months of planning by APA Books and the Department of Digital Learning at Governors State University went into creating the programs. The quality of the final programs stands as a testament to the hard work done by all—client participants, guest experts, Jon, myself, and staff.

I also want to thank the authors, both Leslie Greenberg and Nancy McWilliams, who further commented on their own work on the DVDs, and Amy Wenzel, a scholar and practitioner who agreed to write on Judith Beck's therapy demonstration. Their willingness to pore over the sessions and uncover the workings of these disparate approaches will prove valuable to students of psychotherapy—which I hope all practitioners continue to be throughout their careers.

Gary R. VandenBos, PhD
APA Publisher

How to Use This Book

This book is intended as an aid for comparing and contrasting three distinct approaches: emotion-focused therapy, psychodynamic therapy, and cognitive therapy. Chapters 2 through 4 were each written by one of the book's authors, each a prominent practitioner of the approaches: Leslie S. Greenberg wrote Chapter 2 ("Emotion-Focused Therapy"), Nancy McWilliams authored Chapter 3 ("Psychodynamic Therapy"), and Amy Wenzel contributed Chapter 4 ("Cognitive Therapy"). The book may be used alone or in conjunction with the DVDs *Three Approaches to Psychotherapy With a Male Client* and *Three Approaches to Psychotherapy With a Female Client*. Following is a step-by-step guide on how to use the book, with or without the DVDs. These are only some suggested ways to do so.

How to Use the Book With the DVDs

1. Read Chapter 1: Introduction.
2. Watch the introductory part of the DVD.
3. Read the opening part of Chapters 2 through 4, in which each therapist explains his or her approach (i.e., everything except the case applications on the demonstration sessions with Chi Chi and Kevin).
4. Reread "Questions to Consider Before Watching the DVD" in the "Questions for Classroom Use" at the end of the Introduction.
5. Review the client summaries at the end of the Introduction, which feature background on each client.

6. Watch the therapy session for each therapist with each client.
7. Reread "Questions to Consider After Watching the DVD" in the "Questions for Classroom Use" at the end of the Introduction.
8. Read the therapist's case applications on the demonstration session you watched.
9. After watching all sessions and reading all case applications, watch the therapist roundtable discussion.

How to Use the Book Without the DVDs

The book may be read straight through, as one would read any book, or the reader may use the following steps:

1. Read the Introduction, except for the questions at the end of the chapter ("Questions for Classroom Use").
2. Read the first part of Chapter 2 on emotion-focused therapy.
3. Review the client summaries at the end of the Introduction, which feature background on each client.
4. Read "Questions to Consider Before Watching the DVD" in the "Questions for Classroom Use" at the end of the Introduction.
5. Read "Questions to Consider After Watching the DVD" in the "Questions for Classroom Use" at the end of the Introduction.
6. Read the therapist's case applications.
7. Read the first part of Chapter 3, then repeat Steps 3 through 6.
8. Read the first part of Chapter 4, then repeat Steps 3 through 6.

Exploring Three Approaches to Psychotherapy

Introduction 1

P sychotherapy in practice is both an art and a science. A student can read and commit to memory every available empirically validated technique, become immersed and grounded in a specific theory of practice, and still not truly understand psychotherapy as it is practiced. True understanding will only come with real-time exposure to therapist–client interactions.

For many years, the only way to develop a real sense of how psychotherapy worked was to practice it. However, a continuing project in training mental health practitioners over the past 50 years has been to provide demonstrations of psychotherapy to them before they actually come face to face with a client. The American Psychological Association (APA) Psychotherapy Video Series was developed as just such an educational and training tool. Part of why we created the Psychotherapy Video Series of demonstrations (and have created PsycTHERAPY, an entire database of such demonstrations) is that there is no practical way to demonstrate a theory except through its corresponding techniques, and

http://dx.doi.org/10.1037/14253-001
Exploring Three Approaches to Psychotherapy, by L. S. Greenberg, N. McWilliams, and A. Wenzel

there is no better way to demonstrate a technique—its timing, how it looks—than to capture it in video.

Techniques of psychotherapy are rational and systematic procedures designed to produce an amelioration of the client's mental health, and in best practice psychotherapy techniques are applied within a theoretical framework or approach. Therefore, these videos demonstrate applied theory. In the same way that books and lectures about theory and technique are necessary, but not sufficient, to understanding psychotherapy practice, the video demonstrations are best viewed with some grounding in the theory being demonstrated. The videos in the APA Psychotherapy Video Series begin with a brief introduction to the therapeutic approach used in the video, and many may be paired with companion texts from APA Books to further ground a student in the approach.

Brief History of the Gloria Psychotherapy Demonstrations on Video

The video demonstrations discussed in this book have a historic precedent after which the DVDs are named: the original *Three Approaches to Psychotherapy* (Shostrum, 1965), commonly known as "the Gloria tapes." This classic training film has been viewed by many counselors and psychologists, and it contains three demonstrations with a single client—Gloria—with three world-renowned psychotherapists: Carl Rogers, demonstrating his approach, client-centered therapy; Frederick Perls, demonstrating Gestalt therapy; and Albert Ellis, demonstrating rational emotive behavior therapy. The film was created by Everett Shostrum in 1964 in California with a volunteer client named Gloria, who agreed to be filmed talking with each psychotherapist about current problems in her life.

This film for decades was the most prominent and influential video demonstration of psychotherapy in practice. It was the first time complete filmed psychotherapy sessions were made widely available for training use. It was translated into many languages and became a regular part of psychology curriculums in the United States and internationally. Additional demonstration tapes were created after this, but none were as influential as this seminal tape.

The original *Three Approaches* film was the inspiration for the practice of taping psychotherapy sessions. Because the original filmed sessions were so influential, both on the field as a whole and on APA's own psychotherapy demonstration series, it seemed time to revisit the idea of comparing three major approaches side by side with one client. Thus began the development of the DVDs *Three Approaches to Psychotherapy With a Female Client* and *Three Approaches to Psychotherapy With a Male Client.*

The Next Generation
of Three Approaches

Three Approaches to Psychotherapy With a Male Client and *Three Approaches to Psychotherapy With a Female Client* present three distinguished psychotherapists from three orientations demonstrating their distinct approach in entire 50-minute sessions with the same single male and female clients. The sessions are spontaneous and unrehearsed, with volunteer clients who work with each therapist to help demonstrate the different approaches. The new DVDs feature Judith S. Beck, demonstrating cognitive therapy; Leslie S. Greenberg, demonstrating emotion-focused therapy; and Nancy McWilliams, demonstrating psychodynamic therapy. Beck, Greenberg, and McWilliams define and illustrate their individual approaches, engage in a roundtable discussion about their work, and provide voiceover commentary for their respective sessions. Their spirited presentation demonstrates the shared features and key differences of three leading contemporary approaches, allowing the viewer a chance to compare and contrast the techniques and qualities of three master psychotherapists who demonstrate examples of therapy from three very different theoretical perspectives.

By using this book, in conjunction with the DVDs, the student will learn how experienced practitioners translate theoretical concepts into practice, gain a firsthand look at what happens in live sessions, observe how therapists deal with specific critical incidents in treatment, and illuminate specific therapeutic interventions. In the next few pages, we build on this concise introduction by reviewing the approaches and purposes of the *Three Approaches* and by summarizing the objectives and content of this book.

The three chosen psychotherapists practice what are frequently identified as representative of the three major theoretical systems and clinical styles in psychotherapy (Nelson-Jones, 2011): cognitive–behavioral, psychodynamic/psychoanalytical, and humanistic. Our intent is to expose readers and viewers to these approaches without judgment or bias toward one approach or another. Neither the contributors nor APA is endorsing any particular approach.

We do hope, however, that the video demonstrations and this book will enhance the critical analysis of these three psychotherapy systems. The DVD and book illustrate the differences and similarities between the three approaches, and thus between the three main theoretical schools of which they are representative. Such a general understanding of the three major theoretical systems will serve readers well as they encounter new approaches, whether they are students of theory, practitioners, or professors of psychotherapy.

Selecting the Approaches: Why These Three?

There are many different types of psychotherapy in existence today, many of them with strong empirical support for their effectiveness. Viewers and readers may ask: Why choose these three approaches? What makes them so special? The answers to these questions require a brief look at the history of psychotherapy.

Psychotherapy developed in the past century from the original psychoanalytic approaches such as psychoanalytic and Adlerian therapy—commonly referred to as the "first wave" of psychotherapy theory—through successive waves of theoretical schools. The second wave were the learning theories, such as cognitive–behavioral and behavioral therapy; the third wave were the humanistic theories, such as Gestalt and person-centered or Rogerian therapy; and the more recent approaches—feminist, multicultural, and constructivist therapies—would be considered part of the fourth wave, the postmodern theories. For some definitions of the three main theoretical schools, please see Exhibit 1.1. Although currently psychotherapy practice includes many approaches, the three original waves are still strongly represented in the field (Nelson-Jones, 2011).

There are variations of approaches from among these schools: For example, among the learning theories, there are behavioral, cognitive, and cognitive–behavioral therapies; among the humanistic, there are existential–humanistic therapies, person-centered therapy, and emotion-focused therapy; and among the psychoanalytic, there are relational psychodynamic therapy and time-limited dynamic therapy.

In the end, we decided on the current three representatives as strong examples of each major system: cognitive therapy, emotion-focused therapy, and psychodynamic therapy. Our choice is not intended to be an endorsement of any of these approaches, but rather is a reflection of psychotherapy's history, as well as a nod to the original *Three Approaches* film.

EXHIBIT 1.1

Theoretical and Clinical Definitions

cognitive therapy (CT)   a form of psychotherapy based on the concept that emotional and behavioral problems in an individual are, at least in part, the result of maladaptive or faulty ways of thinking and distorted attitudes toward oneself and others. The objective of the therapy is to identify these faulty cognitions and replace them with more adaptive ones, a process known as *cognitive restructuring*. The therapist takes the role of an active guide who attempts to make the client aware of these distorted thinking patterns and who helps the client correct and revise his or her perceptions and attitudes by citing evidence to the contrary or by eliciting it from the client. Developed by U.S. psychiatrist Aaron T. Beck (1921–). See also **cognitive behavior therapy.**

cognitive behavior therapy (CBT)   a form of psychotherapy that integrates theories of cognition and learning with treatment techniques derived from cognitive therapy and behavior therapy. CBT assumes that cognitive, emotional, and behavioral variables are functionally interrelated. Treatment is aimed at identifying and modifying the client's maladaptive thought processes and problematic behaviors through cognitive restructuring and behavioral techniques to achieve change. Also called **cognitive behavior modification; cognitive–behavioral therapy.**

emotion-focused therapy   an integrative individual therapy that focuses on emotion as the key determinant of personality development and of psychotherapeutic change. In sessions, the therapist helps the client to become aware of, accept, make sense of, and regulate emotions as a way of resolving problems and promoting growth. Techniques are drawn from client-centered therapy, Gestalt therapy, and cognitive behavior therapy. A principal proponent of this approach is South African–born Canadian psychologist Leslie S. Greenberg (1945–).

humanistic therapy   any of a variety of psychotherapeutic approaches that reject psychoanalytic and behavioral approaches; seek to foster personal growth through direct experience; and focus on the development of human potential, the here and now, concrete personality change, responsibility for oneself, and trust in natural processes and spontaneous feeling. Some examples of humanistic therapy are client-centered therapy, Gestalt therapy, existential psychotherapy, and experiential psychotherapy.

psychotherapy   any psychological service provided by a trained professional that primarily uses forms of communication and interaction to assess, diagnose, and treat dysfunctional emotional reactions, ways of thinking, and behavior patterns of an individual, family, or group. There are many types of psychotherapy, but generally they fall into four major categories: psychodynamic (e.g., psychoanalysis, client-centered therapy), cognitive–behavioral (see cognitive behavior therapy, cognitive therapy), humanistic (e.g., existential psychotherapy), and integrative psychotherapy. The **psychotherapist** is an individual who has been professionally trained and licensed (in the United States by a state board) to treat mental, emotional, and behavioral disorders by psychological means. He or she may be a clinical psychologist, psychiatrist, counselor, social worker, or psychiatric nurse. Also called **therapy; talk therapy. —psychotherapeutic** *adj.*

psychodynamic psychotherapy   those forms of psychotherapy, falling within or deriving from the psychoanalytic tradition, that view individuals as reacting to unconscious forces (e.g., motivation, drive), that focus on processes of change and development, and that place a premium on self-understanding and making meaning of what is unconscious. Most psychodynamic approaches share common features, such as emphasis on dealing with the unconscious in treatment, emphasis on the role of analyzing transference, and the use of dream analysis and interpretation.

Purpose of This Book

We have prepared this book to assist the viewer in comparing and contrasting the approaches as demonstrated in the DVDs. The core of this book is the three chapters on the three approaches. In developing these chapters, we asked the authors to include

- an explanation of the theoretical model,
- principal techniques of each approach, and
- a discussion of both the male client and female client demonstration.

The combination of the brief theoretical discussion and overview of the major techniques is intended to augment the basic information that the viewer will gather from each therapist's opening interview. The discussion of the demonstrations provides another window into the therapists' work with the clients. Although the chapters may stand alone and be read without watching the DVDs, the optimal use of this book is to read it in conjunction with viewing the client sessions on each DVD.

The goal of each clinical demonstration on these DVDs is to create an unrehearsed therapy session that captures the theoretical approach and style of the particular psychotherapist. We arranged for each therapist to see the same client in each DVD so as to allow viewers, as much as possible, to see how three different approaches look when working with the same person and the same material. This allows viewers a unique opportunity to compare and contrast the specific techniques and qualities of the approaches.

More specifically, the *Three Approaches to Psychotherapy* DVDs were designed for clinical training and continuing education. Among the anticipated uses are (a) learning how three prominent practitioners, representing the three major schools of psychotherapy, work with a client; (b) concretely illustrating the three approaches' theoretical concepts in psychotherapy practice; (c) gaining a firsthand look at what occurs in psychotherapy; (d) comparing the technical interventions and relationship stances associated with the three major schools of psychotherapy; (e) learning how the therapists deal with particular critical incidents in treatment; (f) training in specific therapeutic interventions; and (g) providing material for psychotherapy process research.

This book augments the framing material on the DVDs so as to further enhance the educational power of the video material. By reading this book in conjunction with a review of the DVDs, viewers and readers will develop a keen understanding of the three different approaches demonstrated and a sense of not only how they look in practice but also *why* they look the way they do from one moment to the next.

The combination of book and DVD, reading and watching, is a unique learning opportunity that we hope will provide a fascinating introduction to the three main schools of psychotherapy practice.

Questions for Classroom Use

Each DVD features a wealth of material in addition to the actual therapy demonstrations, including an introductory interview and a discussion among the three psychotherapists. However, it might be useful to begin viewing an educational program such as this with some questions planned out. To this end, as viewers watch either of the *Three Approaches to Psychotherapy* DVDs, they may want to consider the following questions.

QUESTIONS TO CONSIDER BEFORE WATCHING THE DVD

- On the basis of the therapists' description of the orientation, what do you know about the orientation that is demonstrated?
- What topics and issues do you think the therapists will address in their demonstration?
- What are your impressions of each therapist's work on the basis of published material, conversations with or about him or her, or any other sources of information?
- What are your expectations of each therapist's style and behavior in conducting psychotherapy? What types of clients, disorders, or circumstances would be most suited to each of these forms of psychotherapy?
- What do you expect of Drs. Greenberg, McWilliams, and Beck? Will he or she be active or passive? Will he or she be structured or unstructured? Will the focus be on the past or the present? Will the session focus on behaviors, on thoughts, or on feelings? What do you expect to be the relative balance between attention to technique versus interpersonal interaction?

QUESTIONS TO CONSIDER AFTER WATCHING THE DVD

- Is each session a good or bad representation of the theoretical model as described by the therapists?
- Did the session progress as you anticipated? Was the client as you expected? Was the therapist?

- What are your general reactions to the session? What do you feel was effective? What do you think are the strengths and weaknesses of this approach?
- If you had not been informed that it is "X approach," what would you have called it? What makes this a distinctly emotion-focused, psychodynamic, or cognitive approach?
- Did the operations of the therapist proceed in accordance with the theoretical precepts to which the therapist claims allegiance?
- What are the strengths of each approach?
- What empirical research supports the efficacy of the approaches?
- What are the similarities and differences in these three approaches?
- How did these differences translate to action?
- How did watching three therapists from different orientations help make you a better therapist?

About the Clients: Background and Precipitating Events

Several months before we taped the sessions on the DVDs, the two clients sat before a camera for interviews not included on the two *Three Approaches* DVDs. These were what are commonly referred to as *intake interviews*: Both clients were asked a series of questions meant to elicit information about their lives, including facts about their jobs, their families of origin, their current families, and any issues or problems they were currently experiencing. This intake was intended to provide each therapist with as much background information about the clients as possible. This was meant to allow the therapists to immediately begin working on the client's current presenting problems without as many of the frequently used intake-type questions that many initial sessions include.

In the interest of providing readers with some of the same information that the therapists had, what follows are brief descriptions of the intakes. We include a transcript of the entire intake in Appendixes A and B, should readers want additional background information.

KEVIN SUMMARY

Age: 43
Gender: Male
Race/ethnicity: Caucasian, Irish, and Lithuanian descent
Marital status: Single
Education: BA
Occupation: Music teacher and performer

Current status and presenting issues: Kevin has been experiencing fear and anxiety and is currently in psychotherapy. He admits to using recreational drugs and alcohol in the past but has been substance free (including caffeine) for a year. He is self-employed, but his income is unstable, as he relies on money from individual music students as well as performance opportunities. He reports that "getting food on the table is a struggle—we don't have all that we need." He was raised as a Catholic, but he does not practice any religion, although he identifies himself as "spiritual based." He describes himself as creative, orderly, and having a sharp mind. He also says he has trouble showing affection. He has had one long-term relationship of 4 years, which ended when another woman with whom he had relations, the mother of his daughter, became pregnant. He has had a number of shorter relationships (1–8 months) in the succeeding 17 years, but nothing long term, and is currently involved at a distance with a person who is partnered with someone else. They communicate by e-mail and phone and provide some emotional support to one another. On a scale of 1 to 10, with 10 being the highest, Kevin identifies his current interpersonal relationship quality as a 1.

Parents: His father (deceased, Catholic, Irish descent) died when Kevin was 9 years old. Kevin's mother (age unknown, Catholic, Lithuanian descent) remarried 1.5 years after the death of Kevin's father.

Kevin talks about the strong impression his birth father made on him and how he was and continues to be a role model. He describes him as strong, honest, a dedicated person, and a strong Catholic. He was also a heavy smoker who lived a fairly stressful life and who was a weekend drinker and susceptible to depression. His mother and father were married for 19 years.

Kevin says his mother is sweet, "mom-ish," but can also be ferocious. Kevin described himself as having a good relationship with his stepfather—he says he is fun and has a lot of "cool" interests. He mentions that he clashed with his stepdad when he was a teenager. Kevin views his mother and stepfather as a big support. He and his daughter lived with them for 10 years and now visit them, as they recently moved out of state. His mother and stepfather have been married for 33 years.

He reports that both his maternal and paternal grandparents had unstable families: Maternal grandmother had six children by four different men, and the paternal grandfather abandoned the family.

Siblings: Kevin is the third child in a family of four. He has an older sister (51 years old), an older brother (46 years old), and a younger brother (40 years old). His sister has been married several times, one brother is divorced, and the younger brother has never married.

Children: Kevin has a 17-year-old daughter. He has been solely responsible for raising her since she was 2 years old. Kevin says that on a scale of 1–10, with 1 being low, he would describe his relationship as an 8 or 9. However, he says that he feels the relationship will improve even more when she turns 18 because "a lot of the legal obligations are going to be relieved," and right now he feels a lot of pressure to provide for her. When that pressure is relieved, he will relax, and their relationship will be even better. When she was 14–15 years old, she went to live with her mother for a year but returned to Kevin after some traumatic incidents. She and Kevin have been in family counseling, and the daughter is on medication for emotional disorders.

Daughter's mother: Kevin and his daughter's mother lived together when she was pregnant and for some time after she had the baby. Kevin has had custody of the daughter since she was 2 years old. The mother now lives out of state.

CHI CHI SUMMARY

Age: 47

Gender: Female

Race/ethnicity: Caucasian, Italian, and Mexican descent. Her father was an Italian American and her mother is from Mexico. Chi Chi was bilingual, English and Spanish, as a child, but she identifies more strongly with her Italian descent. She also speaks Italian.

Marital status: Single

Education: Some college

Occupation: Unidentified professional office work; part-time bartender

Current status and presenting issues: Chi Chi describes herself as a very good writer, a good actress, and a good talker. She has a small circle of good friends; she is generally outgoing and social. Her hobbies include gardening, reading, writing, and playing board games. She enjoys drinking alcohol, but she does not drink to excess, although she reports that she has in the past. While she has tried many illegal drugs, she never "got into them."

Chi Chi has previously been in individual and group therapy in which she was working on anger management and processing her sadness over the loss of a 6-year relationship. She feels that the therapy helped her greatly with her anger. In her previous therapy, she felt that having directed behavioral interventions was most helpful, whereas she did not feel that talking about her emotional state was productive. She reports that she became "too upset and could not go on with it."

Chi Chi would like to work with the three therapists on her motivation and self-direction. She feels that she continually starts activities but is unable to bring them to a successful conclusion. She would like to be able to set goals and follow through with them, from career plans, to exercise and weight management, and to writing. She feels that her life is adrift, and she wants to gain control and establish clear direction.

Parents: Chi Chi's parents were married for 35 years. Her mother is living, and Chi Chi describes her as "very dramatic." Her mother was both verbally and physically abusive to her children, with Chi Chi "getting the worst of it." Her father has been dead for 10 years. He died at 65 from a heart attack. Chi Chi describes her father as "the calm type." Chi Chi's father worked for the U.S. State Department, and the family lived outside of the United States for the majority of her life in a variety of countries: the Dominican Republic, Hong Kong, and Italy.

Siblings: Chi Chi has one sister who is 10 months older than her and is mildly developmentally disabled. Her sister lives with her mother. Chi Chi describes her sister as being just like her father, calm and quiet, whereas she describes herself as being much more like her mother. She has a brother who is 2 years younger than her. She says her brother "has issues" and has had some difficult times. He is divorced and has two children.

References

Nelson-Jones, R. (2011). *Six key approaches to counseling and therapy* (2nd ed.). Thousand Oaks, CA: Sage.

Shostrum, E. L. (Producer/Director). (1965). *Three approaches to psychotherapy* [Motion picture]. (Available from Psychological and Educational Films, 3334 East Coast Highway, Suite 252, Corona Del Mar, CA 92625)

Leslie S. Greenberg

Emotion-Focused Therapy 2

E motion-focused therapy (EFT) is an approach informed by an understanding of the role of emotion in human functioning and psychotherapeutic change. EFT is founded on a close and careful analysis of the process of emotional change in actual sessions of psychotherapy. This focus on emotion leads both therapist and client toward strategies that promote the awareness, acceptance, expression, use, regulation, and transformation of emotion as well as to corrective emotional experience with the therapist. The goals are strengthening the self, regulating affect, and creating new meaning.

EFT grew out of client-centered, Gestalt, experiential, and existential therapies, viewed through the lens of modern emotion theory. These humanistic/experiential approaches saw people as having resources and being capable of awareness, growth, and choice. Subjective experience was seen as influencing behavior, and people were seen as having the potential for both agency and creativity. EFT has developed beyond its origins in the third force by drawing on advances in affective

http://dx.doi.org/10.1037/14253-002
Exploring Three Approaches to Psychotherapy, by L. S. Greenberg, N. McWilliams, and A. Wenzel

neuroscience and research and theory on emotion and cognition coupled with research on change processes in psychotherapy (Greenberg, 1986).

EFT is based on two major treatment principles: the *provision* of an empathic therapeutic relationship and the *facilitation* of therapeutic work on emotion (Greenberg, Rice, & Elliott, 1993). The empathic relationship is seen both as a curative factor in and of itself and as providing a facilitative environment for therapeutic work on particular EFT tasks that reoccur across people and across therapy. This forms an approach in which empathic following, with high degrees of therapist presence, plus process directive guiding, in which the therapist facilitates clients to engage in different forms of emotional processing at different times, combine synergistically into a sense of flow. Therapy is seen as involving a coconstructive process in which both client and therapist influence each other in nonimposing ways to achieve a deepening of client experiencing and exploration and the promotion of emotional processing. EFT therapists are not experts on what clients are experiencing or the meaning of their behavior, but rather are experts on methods to help clients access and become aware of emotions and needs.

EFT has been shown to be effective in both individual and couples forms of therapy in a number of randomized clinical trials (Elliott, Greenberg, & Lietaer, 2004; Johnson, Hunsley, Greenberg, & Schindler, 1999). EFT was found to be highly effective in treating depression in three separate clinical trials (Goldman, Greenberg, & Angus, 2006; Greenberg & Watson, 1998; Watson, Gordon, Stermac, Kalogerakos, & Steckley, 2003) and complex trauma (Greenberg, Warwar, & Malcolm, 2008; Paivio & Nieuwenhuis, 2001; Pavio & Pascual-Leone, 2010). In addition, EFT has been found to be highly effective in preventing relapse in depression (77% nonrelapse; Ellison, Greenberg, Goldman, & Angus, 2009). Emotion-focused couples therapy also has been shown to be effective in reducing marital distress and increasing marital satisfaction, trust, and forgiveness (Greenberg, Warwar, & Malcolm, 2010; Johnson, Hunsley, Greenberg, & Schindler, 1999).

In this chapter, the theory of EFT treatment is discussed briefly, followed by a discussion of the phases of treatment, main markers, and tasks. An EFT approach to case formulation is then presented, and finally both the cases on the DVDs are discussed.

Theory of Functioning

Emotions have been found to be connected to our most essential needs (Frijda, 1986). They rapidly alert us to situations that are important to our well-being, giving us information about what is good and bad for us by evaluating whether our needs are being met. They also prepare and guide us in important situations to take action toward meeting our needs. EFT views emotion as setting a basic mode of processing in action (Greenberg, 2002, 2011). For example, fear sets fear processing in motion and organizes us to search for danger, and anger sets anger processing in motion, focusing us on violation.

Emotional experience is formed into internal organizations (emotion schemes) that influence our future experience of that emotion. Lived experiences are associated with representations of the bodily states they created and are thus given affective meaning. In this way a somatic state, a visceral experience, becomes a marker for a specific experience and is stored in memory (Damasio, 1999). These somatic markers can then be accessed by present cues that evoke the emotion scheme. Any previous outcome that has been bad for you will be experienced as an unpleasant gut feeling (Damasio, 1994), and you will tend to make decisions not leading to this kind of unpleasant event. In this way, the body is used as a guidance system, and it is emotions that guide our decisions by helping us to anticipate future outcomes on the basis of previous experience stored in emotion schemes that activate gut feelings.

EFT proposes that emotions themselves have an innately adaptive potential that if activated can help clients reclaim unwanted experience, change problematic emotional states, and change interactions. EFT is designed to help clients become aware of and make productive use of their emotions. Clients are helped in EFT to better identify, experience, accept, explore, make sense of, transform, and flexibly manage their emotions. As a result, clients become more skillful in accessing the important information and meanings about themselves and their world that emotions contain, as well as more skillful in using that information to live vitally and adaptively. Clients in therapy are also encouraged to face dreaded emotions in order to process and transform them. A major premise guiding intervention in EFT is that if you do not accept yourself as you are, you cannot make yourself available for transformation. Emotional change is seen as the key to enduring cognitive and behavioral change.

A core feature of EFT is that it makes a distinction between conceptual and experiential knowledge, and people are viewed as wiser than their intellects alone. Rather than "I think, therefore I am," EFT is based on the idea that "I feel, therefore I am" and that in any significant personal experience we think only inasmuch as we feel. Experiments in directed awareness are used to help concentrate attention on as yet unformulated emotional experience to intensify its vividness and symbolize it in awareness. In therapy, emotion is focused on as a visceral experience and is accepted as well as worked with directly to promote emotional change. Finally, it is the articulation of emotion in narratives of ways of being with self and others that provides the story of our lives (Angus & Greenberg, 2011).

At the center of the approach is helping people, when they need to use emotion as a guide and be changed by its urgings, to discern when they need to change emotions and when they need to regulate them. A key tenet of therapy is that a person needs to experience emotion in order to be informed and moved by it and to make it accessible to change. People do not change their emotions simply by talking about them, by understanding their origins, or by changing beliefs. One changes emotions by accepting and experiencing them, by opposing them with different emotions to transform them, and by reflecting on them to create new narrative meaning.

Changing emotions is seen as central to the origins and treatment of human problems, but this does not mean that working with emotions is all that is focused on in EFT. Most problems have biological, emotional, cognitive, motivational, behavioral, physiological, social, and cultural sources, and many of these need attention. EFT adopts an integrative focus on motivation, cognition, behavior, and interaction; it's just that in EFT, the focus is on people's emotions as a primary pathway to change.

EMOTION SCHEMES AND A DIALECTICAL CONSTRUCTIVIST VIEW: INTEGRATING BIOLOGY AND CULTURE

As well as simply having emotion, people also live in a constant process of making sense of their emotions. Reason and emotion are thus integrated via an ongoing circular process of making sense of experience by symbolizing bodily felt sensations in awareness and articulating them in language, thereby constructing new experience (Greenberg & Pascual-Leone, 1995; Greenberg, Rice, & Elliott, 1993). How emotional experience is symbolized influences what the experience becomes in the next moment. Therapists therefore need to work with both emotion and meaning making and facilitating change in the emotional experience and the narratives in which they are embedded (Greenberg & Angus, 2004).

Two fundamental levels of emotion generation are seen as important. One level involves the automatic processes that produce primary responses following simple perceptual appraisals. These emotions are seen as occurring from birth and as the generative source of much of our initial emotional experience both developmentally and in adulthood. As individuals have more lived experience and develop more cognitive/linguistic capacities, these automatic processes are followed by a second fundamental level of emotion, a more complex processing activity in which sensory, memorial, and ideational information is combined to form emotion schemes. These are mental organizations that represent our emotional experience plus the activating situation and form our emotion schematic memories.

These emotion schemes are seen as the primary source of experience and at the base of the adult emotional response system. They are defined as internal memory structures that synthesize affective, motivational cognitive and behavioral elements into internal organizations that are activated rapidly out of awareness by relevant cues (Greenberg, 2011; Greenberg & Safran, 1987). In contrast to cognitive schema, they consist largely (or sometimes entirely) of preverbal and affective elements (e.g., bodily sensations, action tendencies, visual images, and even smells). They are internal networks represented as wordless narratives consisting of beginnings, middles, and ends, agents, objects, and intentions (Angus & Greenberg, 2011; Greenberg, 2011). They are built from lived experience that when activated produces higher order organizations of experience and forms the foundation of the self (Greenberg, 2002, 2011).

It is important to note, however, that according to EFT, experience is not generated by a single emotion scheme or a single level of processing. Greenberg and colleagues (Greenberg, 2011; Greenberg & Pascual-Leone, 2001; Greenberg & Watson, 2006) proposed that experience is generated by a tacit synthesis of a number of schemes and a number of levels of processing that are coactivated and that coapply. This synthesis of multiple schemes forms the basis of our current self-organizations in any one moment—the self I find myself to be in a situation—and it provides the bodily felt referent of experience (Greenberg, 2011) to which I need to attend to experience myself. The EFT perspective is that conscious experience and personal meaning derive from attending to, exploring, and making sense of these implicit bodily felt self-organizations by a process of attention and reflection. Given the internal complexity from the synthesis of many schemes and levels of processing, experience is always multidetermined and multifaceted. Thus, we are always in a process of constructing the self we become in the moment by a dialectical process of symbolizing our bodily felt feeling in awareness, reflecting on it, and forming narratives that explain it.

In this dialectical constructivist view, EFT theory takes emotion as the fundamental datum of human experience and recognizes the importance of meaning making and narrative change and ultimately views emotion and cognition as inextricably intertwined (Greenberg, 2011; Greenberg & Pascual-Leone, 2001; Greenberg & Watson, 2006). Ultimately, feelings are not facts. Rather, they are a process of informing us of what is significant to us in the moment and forming a disposition to act, so we always need to live in a process of using this information to orient to the world and construct meaning. We need to make sense of the information and action tendency provided by emotion and decide what to do.

EMOTION ASSESSMENT

An important feature of EFT is the distinction between primary and secondary emotion on the one hand and adaptive and maladaptive emotion on the other (Greenberg, 2002, 2011; Greenberg & Safran, 1987). *Primary* emotions are defined as a person's core first immediate gut response to a situation, such as sadness about loss or fear at threat. *Secondary* emotions, in contrast, are responses to preceding emotional reactions, often obscuring or interrupting these more primary emotional reactions (e.g., depressed hopelessness covering shame at not being good enough, rage covering shame at loss of self-esteem). They can also be secondary to more cognitive processes (e.g., anxiety in response to catastrophic thinking). Most secondary emotions are symptomatic feelings, such as phobic fear, feelings of depletion, and hopelessness in depression. Although secondary emotions are generally maladaptive, primary emotions can be either adaptive or maladaptive. Primary adaptive emotions serve a person's goals, needs, and concerns in the world and prepare the individual for adaptive action. Examples are fear at threat, preparing the individual to escape or avoid a dangerous situation, or anger at a violation, preparing the individual to reassert his or her boundaries. Primary maladaptive emotions are core painful emotions that are more a reflection of past unresolved issues and unmet needs (based often on traumatic learning) than an adaptive response to current circumstances. Consequently they don't prepare the individual for adaptive action in the world. Examples are fear in response to human intimacy that stems from experiences of childhood abuse or feeling the shame of inadequacy when one is criticized, which stem from invalidation by one's peers or parents.

It is important to note that from an EFT perspective, it is the activation of primary emotion that is therapeutic. Primary adaptive emotions need to be accessed in order to extract the adaptive information they contain and to use them in problem solving. Primary maladaptive emotions need to be activated and accessed to make them amenable to transformation by bringing them into contact with more adaptive emotional responses (Greenberg, 2002, 2011). EFT works on the basic principle that people must first arrive at a place before they can leave it. Secondary emotional experiences, including symptomatic emotions, in contrast, are best bypassed or explored to get to their underlying primary generators. EFT introduces a concept of deepening of emotion, which involves not simply arousal but also moving from secondary to primary emotion. In addition, symptomatic emotional experiences are not viewed as the primary targets of intervention; rather, they are explored in order to gain access to their primary generators.

Underlying emotion schemes and the subsequent meaning-making process, by which we make sense of our experience, are the primary targets of intervention and change in EFT. Clients need to arrive at their core painful emotions to make them accessible to new input and to activate new adaptive experience in therapy in order to transform their maladaptive experience. Furthermore, clients need to develop new narratives that assimilate experience into existing cognitive structures and generate new ones. As we see it, no important story is significant without emotion, and no emotions take place outside of the context of a story. Therapy thus involves changing both emotional experience and the narratives in which it is embedded (Angus & Greenberg, 2011; Greenberg & Angus, 2004).

TYPES OF DYSFUNCTION

From an EFT perspective (Greenberg, 2011), dysfunction results from four major different emotional processing problems: (a) lack of emotion awareness, that is, the inability to symbolize bodily felt experience in awareness, often resulting from the avoidance or disclaiming of primary experience; (b) maladaptive emotional responses, generated by emotion schemes, often resulting from traumatic learning in interpersonal situations with primary care givers; (c) emotion dysregulation, involving the under- or overregulation of emotion, often resulting from failures in the early dyadic regulation of affect; and (d) problems in emotion/narrative construction and existential meaning, stemming from people's inability to make sense of their experience and their narrative accounts of self, other, and world (e.g., incoherent narrative, problematic narratives of violation or loss). In addition, people are seen as struggling with both self–self and self–other relational problems, and either or both of these form additional foci of treatment.

PRINCIPLES OF EMOTIONAL CHANGE

EFT theory proposes six major principles of emotional change in therapy: emotion awareness, expression, regulation, reflection, transformation of emotion, and corrective emotional experience. These are all seen as best facilitated in the context of an empathic therapeutic relationship that facilitates these processes.

Awareness

Increasing awareness of emotion is the most fundamental principle. Knowing what one feels provides access to the adaptive information and the action tendency in the emotion and reconnects people to their motivation to meet the needs and goals embedded in the emotions. Emotional awareness is not thinking about feeling; rather, it involves experiencing the feeling in awareness. What is disowned or split off cannot change. When that which is disclaimed is felt, it changes. The goal of awareness is acceptance of emotion. Self-acceptance and self-awareness are interconnected.

Expression

Expression differs from awareness. It involves saying or showing what one feels using words or actions. Expression is a manifestation that represents or embodies something else. Expressing emotion in therapy does not involve the venting of secondary emotion but rather overcoming avoidance to experience and express previously constricted primary emotions.

Regulation

Regulation involves managing emotional intensity. An important issue in any treatment is what emotions need to be regulated. Emotions that require down-regulation generally are either secondary emotions, such as despair and hopelessness, or anxiety or primary maladaptive emotions, such as the shame of being worthless, traumatic fear, and panic.

Reflection

In addition to recognizing emotions and symbolizing them in words, promoting further reflection on emotional experience helps people make narrative sense of their experience and promotes its assimilation into their ongoing self-narratives. What we make of our emotional experience makes us who we are. Reflection helps to create new meaning and develop new narratives to understand experience (Goldman, Greenberg, & Pos, 2005; Greenberg & Angus, 2004; Greenberg & Pascual-Leone, 1997; Pennebaker, 1995).

Transformation

The most novel and important principle is the transformation of emotion by emotion. This applies most specifically to transforming primary maladaptive emotions such as fear, shame, and the sadness of lonely abandonment (Greenberg, 2002, 2011). Often these withdrawal emotions are transformed by access to adaptive approach emotions of empowering anger that sets boundaries and overcomes obstacles and a contact-seeking form of the sadness of grief that promotes compassion for the self and soothing by self and other. This principle of emotional change suggests that a maladaptive emotional state can be undone by activating another, more adaptive emotional state. This involves the client first arriving at a maladaptive emotion to make it accessible to transformation. This process of changing emotion with emotion goes beyond ideas of catharsis, completion, letting go, habituation, or detachment, in that the maladaptive emotion is not purged, nor is it simply attenuated by the person feeling it. Rather, another more adaptive emotion is used to transform or undo it. In addition, it does not involve exposure to feared and avoided internal or external cues, but rather involves transforming emotions, such as feeling worthless or insecure, that are too often felt.

Another important process in transformation is the memory reconsolidation process. The traditional view on memory suggested that once memories have been consolidated and have become part of long-term memory, they are more or less permanent. It was found, however, that every time a memory is retrieved, the underlying memory trace seems to be labile and fragile once again and requires another consolidation period (Nader, Schafe, & LeDoux, 2000). This is called *reconsolidation.* This reconsolidation period allows for another opportunity to disrupt the memory. As memory reconsolidation only occurs once a memory is activated, it follows that emotional memories have to be activated in therapy to be able to change them. Thus, emotional memories can be changed by activating the experience of the memory in a session, and within minutes of this, if a new emotion is experienced, it will be incorporated into the memory and can change the experience of the original memory.

Corrective Emotional Experience

A final way of changing an emotion is to have a corrective emotional experience in the world that changes an old feeling. New lived experiences with another person (often the therapist) are especially important in providing an interpersonal corrective emotional experience. The goal in EFT is for clients, with the help of more favorable circumstances in therapy, to experience mastery in reexperiencing emotions that they could not handle in the past. The client then undergoes a corrective emotional experience that repairs the damaging influence of previous relational experiences. Experiences that provide interpersonal soothing disconfirm pathogenic beliefs or offer new success experience thus can correct interpersonal patterns set down in earlier times. For example, having one's anger accepted by the therapist rather than rejected leads to new ways of being. Overall, the genuine relationship between the patient and the therapist, and its constancy, is also a corrective emotional experience.

METHODS FOR ACCESSING NEW EMOTIONS

A number of ways of helping the client access new emotions to change emotions have been outlined (Greenberg, 2002, 2011). Empathy is continuously helping clients access new feelings, but in addition to empathy, therapists help the client access new subdominant emotions occurring in the present by shifting attention to emotions that are currently being expressed but are only "on the periphery" of a client's awareness or, when no other emotion is present, by focusing on what is needed and thereby mobilizing a new emotion. This is a key means of activating a new emotion (Greenberg, 2002, 2011). These new feelings were either felt in the original situation but not expressed or are felt now as an adaptive response to the old situation. For example, accessing implicit adaptive anger at a violation by a perpetrator can help change maladaptive fear in a trauma victim. When the tendency to run away in fear is transformed by anger's tendency to thrust forward, a new relational position of holding the abuser accountable for wrongdoing is formed.

Other methods of accessing new emotion involve using enactment and imagery to evoke new emotions, remembering a time an emotion was felt, and changing how the client views things, or even the therapist expressing an emotion for the client (Greenberg, 2002, 2011). Once accessed, these new emotional resources begin to undo the psycho-affective motor program that previously determined the person's mode of processing. New emotional states enable people to challenge the validity of perceptions of self/other connected to maladaptive emotion, weakening its hold on them. Accessing adaptive needs acts automatically as disconfirmation of maladaptive feelings and beliefs. In our view, enduring emotional change of maladaptive emotional responses occurs by generating a new emotional response, not through a process of insight or understanding but by generating new responses to old situations and incorporating these into memory.

Maladaptive emotion schematic memories of past childhood losses and traumas are activated in the therapy session in order to change these by memory reconstruction. Introducing new present experience into currently activated memories of past events has been shown to lead to memory transformation by the assimilation of new material into past memories (Nader et al., 2000). This is called *reconstructive memory* (Nadel & Bohbot, 2001). By being activated in the present, the old memories are restructured by the new experience of being in the context of a safe relationship and by the coactivation of more adaptive emotional responses and new adult resources and understanding to cope with the old situation. The memories are reconsolidated in a new way by incorporating these new elements. The past can in fact be changed—at least the memories of it can be!

BASIC EMOTIONAL PROCESSING
STEPS IN TRANSFORMATION

On the basis of both clinical theory and practice, a model for evoking, exploring, and transforming "bad feelings," which involves moving from secondary emotions through primary maladaptive emotions to primary adaptive emotions, has been proposed and tested (Greenberg & Paivio, 1997; Hermann & Greenberg, 2008; Hermann, Greenberg, & Auzra, 2011; Pascual-Leone & Greenberg, 2007). Transformation of distressed feelings begins with attending to the aroused bad feelings (I feel bad), followed by exploring the cognitive-affective sequences that generate the bad feelings (I feel hopeless, what's the use of trying). Eventually, this leads to the activation of some core maladaptive emotion schematic self-organizations based most often on core painful feelings of fear of abandonment accompanied by sadness or shame ("I'm alone and can't survive on my own," or "I'm worthless"). At this point in the transformation process, something new—an adaptive experience—needs to be accessed.

When clients in states of global distress begin to elaborate and differentiate their thoughts and feelings, they tend to move in one of two directions: into a core maladaptive self-organization or into some form of secondary expression, often of hopelessness or a type of rejecting anger. The maladaptive states generally are based on emotion schemes of fear and the sadness of lonely abandonment or on the shame of feeling worthless. In these core painful states, clients experience themselves as feeling inadequate, empty, lonely, and unable. Transformation of these core maladaptive states occurs when they are differentiated into adaptive needs. Experiencing that one deserves to have one's needs met acts to refute the core negative evaluations about the self that are embedded in core maladaptive schemes. Thus "I need and deserve or deserved to be valued and protected" undoes feelings of shame-based worthlessness, and statements such as "I feel worthless" are transformed into "I am worthy," or statements such as "I feel so alone and unloved" are transformed into "I am lovable." The path to resolution invariably leads to the expression of adaptive grieving for what wasn't and/or to empowering anger or self-soothing. These newly emerging adaptive feelings facilitate a sense of self-acceptance and agency. More resourceful clients often move directly from secondary emotions directly to assertive anger or healthy sadness, but many of the more wounded clients need to work through their core maladaptive attachment-related fear and sadness or identity-related shame (Greenberg, 2002, 2011; Greenberg & Paivio, 1997; Greenberg & Watson, 2006). A refined model of this core change process has been validated on episodes in a group of clients who successfully resolved states of high emotional distress with low levels of meaning to states of high meaning and low distress (Pascual-Leone & Greenberg, 2007).

The essence of this process is that when core adaptive attachment and identity needs (to be connected and validated), embedded in the maladaptive fear/shame/sadness, are mobilized and validated, they help generate the adaptive emotions related to their needs not being met. Thus when one validates that one deserves to be loved or valued, the emotion system, automatically appraising that one's needs were not met, generates anger at having been unfairly treated or sadness at having missed the opportunity of having one's needs met, and these new adaptive feelings undo the more maladaptive feelings. The result is an implicit refutation that the person is not deserving of love, respect, and connection. The inherent opposition of the two experiences—"I am not worthy or lovable" and "I deserve to be loved or respected"—supported by adaptive anger or sadness, in response to the same evoking situation, overcomes the maladaptive state. New self-experience and the creation of new meaning thus lead to the emergence of a new, more positive evaluation of the self.

Within the context of a validating therapeutic relationship, the client then moves on to grieve, acknowledging the loss or injury suffered and recognizing that "I don't have what I need, and I miss what I deserved," and to assert empowering anger and/or self-soothing. Depending on whether the newly owned need involved boundary setting or comfort, clients direct their adaptive emotion expression outward to protect boundaries (i.e., in anger) or inward toward the self (i.e., as compassion or caring). This then often transforms into grieving for what was lost. This grief state is characterized by either sadness over a loss or recognizing that one is hurt (i.e., woundedness), or both. Now, however, the emotional tone is without the blame, self-pity, or resignation that characterized the initial states of global distress. Resolution then involves integrating the sense of loss with the sense of possibility in the new-found ability to assert and self-soothe.

The movement depicted in this process, from secondary emotion through primary maladaptive emotion to primary adaptive emotion, represents a core change process in EFT. Throughout the process of transformation, moderate to high emotional arousal is necessary, but always at a level that remains facilitative of the healing process. Therapists thus need to facilitate optimal emotional arousal sufficiently so that it is felt and can be oriented to as information, but not so much that it is dysregulating or disorienting.

Theory of Practice

The three relationship principles are presence and empathic attunement (Geller & Greenberg, 2011); communication of the Rogerian core conditions of empathy, positive regard, and genuineness; and the creation of a working alliance (Greenberg et al., 1993). EFT is built on a genuinely valuing and affect-regulating empathic relationship in which the therapist is fully present, is highly attuned, and is sensitively responsive to the client's experience. The therapist is respectful, accepting, and congruent in his or her communication. The relationship is seen as being curative in and of itself in that the therapist's empathy and acceptance promotes breaking of the isolation, validation, strengthening of the self, and self-acceptance. In our view the relationship with the therapist provides a powerful buffer to the client's distress by the coregulation of affect. A relationship with an attuned, responsive, mirroring therapist provides interpersonal soothing and the development of emotion regulation. This type of relationship helps clients regulate their overwhelming, disorganizing painful emotions. Over time, the interpersonal regulation of affect becomes internalized into self-soothing and the capacity to regulate inner states (Stern, 1985). When an empathic connection is made with the therapist, affect processing centers in the brain are affected and new possibilities open up for the client. This type of relationship creates an optimal therapeutic environment, which not only contributes to affect regulation but also helps the client feel safe enough to fully engage in the process of self-exploration and new learning. The therapeutic relationship, in addition to being curative, also promotes the therapeutic work of exploration and creation of new meaning.

Another important aspect of a helping relationship is establishing an alliance by collaborating on the goals and tasks of therapy. This promotes the experience that the "two of us" are working together to overcome the problem. Getting an agreement on goals and tasks is dependent on understanding the client and what might be helpful to the client, and thereby it is an enactment of empathy. Goal agreement in EFT often is achieved by capturing the chronically enduring pain with which the client has been struggling and establishing an agreement to work on resolving this pain rather than setting a behavioral change goal.

The three task principles of promoting *differential processing, task completion,* and *agency and choice* are based on the general assumption that human beings are agentic, purposeful organisms with an innate need for exploration and mastery of their internal and external environments. These principles guide therapists in helping clients resolve internal, emotion-related problems through work on personal goals and within-session tasks.

The task principles guide the pursuit of work on therapeutic tasks and facilitate different types of processes at different times, depending on client states. In this process, the emergence of different client in-session problem states are seen as markers of opportunities for differential interventions best suited to help facilitate productive work on that problem state. Therapeutic work involves suggesting experiments, which essentially involves the therapist offering "Try this" followed by "What do you experience?" Experiments in EFT are designed to promote facilitating access to experiencing by the articulation of primary emotions and needs, the acceptance and transformation of painful unresolved emotions, and the explication of implicit feelings and meanings. The work of therapy is not aimed directly at a goal of coping, changing, or fixing, but at the process of allowing and accepting. Change comes as a dynamic self-reorganizing process facilitated first by acceptance and then by moving on, rather than by direct efforts to deliberately change or achieve a specific goal.

EFT thus involves a combination of following and leading, but following is always seen as taking precedence over leading. Over time, with the application of EFT to different populations, it has become clear that the degree of guiding and of providing structure needs to be varied according to the degree of client emotion dysregulation. More distressed and more avoidant clients often benefit from more process guidance and emotion coaching, including a form of emotional reparenting involving soothing and compassion, whereas clients with greater internal locus of control and more reactant styles, or more fragile clients, benefit from more responsive following and less guiding. Clients from different cultural backgrounds often have different expectations of the degree of therapist directiveness, and so this can be varied to match clients' expectations, especially early in therapy.

PHASES OF TREATMENT

EFT treatment has been broken into three major phases, each with a set of steps to describe its course over time (Greenberg & Watson, 2006). The first phase of bonding and awareness is followed by the middle phase of evoking and exploring. Finally, therapy concludes with a transformation phase that involves constructing alternatives through generating new emotions and reflecting to create new narrative meaning. The first phase involves four steps: (a) attending to, empathizing with, and validating the client's feelings and current sense of self; (b) providing a rationale for working with emotion; (c) promoting awareness of internal experience; and (d) establishing a collaborative focus. This second phase also involves four steps: (a) establishing support for emotional experience, (b) evoking and arousing problematic feelings, (c) undoing interruptions of emotion, and (d) helping access primary emotions or core maladaptive schemes. The final phase involves three steps: (a) helping to generate new emotional responses to transform core maladaptive schemes, (b) promoting reflection to make sense of experience, and (c) validating new feelings and supporting an emerging sense of self.

Thus, in EFT it is through the shift into primary emotion and its use as a resource that the deepest change occurs. In some cases, change occurs simply because the client accesses adaptive underlying emotions such as empowering anger and reorganizes to assert boundaries, or the client accesses adaptive sadness, grieves a loss, and organizes to withdraw and recover or reaches out for comfort and support. In these situations, contacting the need and action tendency embedded in the emotion provides the motivation and direction for change and also provides an alternative way of responding. Action replaces resignation, and motivated desire replaces hopelessness.

In many instances, however, once a core primary emotion is arrived at, it is understood to be a complex maladaptive emotion schematic experience, rather than unexpressed primary adaptive emotions such as sadness or anger. Core schemes that are maladaptive result in feelings such as a core sense of powerlessness or being invisible, or a deep sense of woundedness, shame, insecurity, worthlessness, or feeling unloved or unlovable. It is these that often are accessed as being below the secondary bad feelings such as despair, panic, hopelessness, or global distress. Primary maladaptive feelings of worthlessness, weakness, or insecurity have to be accessed in order to allow for change. It is only through the experience of emotion that emotional distress can be cured. One cannot leave these feelings of worthlessness or insecurity until one has arrived at them. What is curative is first the ability to symbolize these feelings of worthlessness or weakness and then to access alternate adaptive emotion-based self-schemes. The generation of alternate schemes is based on accessing adaptive feelings and needs that get activated in response to the currently experienced emotional distress. It is the person's response to his or her own symbolized distress that is adaptive and must be accessed and used as a life-giving resource.

CASE FORMULATION

EFT has developed a context-sensitive, process-oriented approach to case formulation to help promote the development of a focus, which is especially important in briefer treatments (Greenberg & Goldman, 2007). Case formulation relies on process diagnosis, development of a focus, marker identification, and theme development rather than person or syndrome diagnosis. In our approach, process is privileged over content, and process diagnosis is privileged over person diagnosis. In a process-oriented approach, case formulation is an ongoing process, as sensitive to the moment and the in-session context as it is to an understanding of the person as a case, and it takes response to intervention as the best source of information for assessment. The therapist's main concern is one of following the client's process, identifying core pain and markers of current emotional concerns, rather than developing a picture of the person's enduring personality, character dynamics, or a core relational pattern.

Case formulation involves the development of a focus. It also helps fit the therapeutic task to the client's goals, thereby aiding in the establishment of a productive working alliance. To develop a focus, the therapist follows the client's pain, which acts as an emotional tracking device, a compass for following the client's most poignant or painful experience (Greenberg & Watson, 2006), and attends to a variety of different emerging markers. The client's pain and markers guide intervention more than does a diagnosis or even an explicit case formulation.

Distinguishing between primary, secondary, and instrumental emotional responses (Greenberg & Safran, 1987) is also central to case formulation. It is clients' primary emotion that reveals their core need. In addition, it is the clients' presently felt experience that indicates what the difficulty is and whether problem determinants are currently accessible and amenable to intervention. A collaborative focus and a coherent theme develop from a focus on current experience and exploring particular experiences and events to their edges to get to primary emotions rather than on exploring patterns of experience and behavior across situations. Identifying and articulating the problematic cognitive-affective processes underlying and generating symptomatic experience is a collaborative effort between therapist and client and always incorporates identification of the client's chronic enduring pain.

The steps in Exhibit 2.1 have been identified to guide clinicians in the development of case formulations (Goldman & Greenberg, in press; Greenberg & Goldman, 2007).

Perceptual Skills

Treatment is guided by both perceptual skills that guide identification of different types of emotion and problem markers and intervention skills that guide intervention. In this section, some of the general perceptual and intervention skills are outlined first. More specific problem markers and specific interventions for each marker are discussed in the section on markers and tasks.

Accurate assessment of different types of emotion is important because each type of emotion must be worked with differently (Greenberg, 2002; Greenberg & Paivio, 1997). Assessment of different emotion types is a perceptual skill that, once developed, often takes place implicitly as a natural part of the therapist's empathic attunement. The very first emotion assessment therapists probably make is whether clients have too much or too little emotion, and they intervene accordingly, either to access emotion or regulate it. It is important to note that in therapy, all emotion emerges in a relational context and what an emo-

---

EXHIBIT 2.1

Steps to Guide Clinicians in the Development of Case Formulations

---

Stage 1: Unfold the narrative and observe emotional processing style.
  a. Listen to the presenting problem (problem deconstruction and therapeutic relationship building).
  b. Listen for poignancy and painful experience.
  c. Unfold the life story/narrative.
  d. Attend to and observing emotional processing style.

Stage 2: Cocreate a focus and identify the core emotion.
  a. Identify markers for task work.
  b. Identify thematic focus:
    i.   emotion awareness
    ii. emotion regulation
    iii. self–self relations
    iv. self–other relations
    v.   existential meaning creation issues.
  c. Identify underlying core emotion schemes, either adaptive or maladaptive.
  d. Identify blocks to accessing core emotion schemes.

Stage 3: Formulate ongoing markers and tasks related to core issues.
  a. Identify emerging task markers.
  b. Identify micromarkers within tasks.
  c. Assess how new meaning influences or fits in with larger narrative structure and connect back to presenting problems.

---

tion becomes is influenced by the relational context and by the client's cultural rules about emotion expression. A client's inability to regulate or tendency to overregulate emotion thus is an interpersonal and cultural process, not just a function of the client.

EFT therapists never simply assess from their own frame of reference; rather, they collaborate with their client to codetermine how the emotion is functioning at that time for the client. Empathic attunement is essential to sensing what another's emotion is about. Nonverbal cues, especially voice, face, and gesture, are all crucial sources of information as to the nature of the emotion being expressed. The voice or face often tell us if the emotion is primary and sincere or secondary and obscuring other feelings. Therapists' own knowledge and experience of general human emotion responses and sequences of emotion, and their awareness of their own typical emotional responses to situations, informs them as to what is probably primary. Congruence between feeling action tendency and need, such as feeling sad at loss and reaching out for comfort to be close, suggests a primary emotion, whereas being angry and pushing away when hurt and wanting comfort suggests a secondary emotion. In addition, awareness of one's own emotional responses to the client is important in emotion assessment, as people are wired to react emotionally to emotional cues from others, and this provides important information. Thus, we automatically feel compassion for others' primary pain and suffering but are irritated by their secondary whining, and we feel fear or caution at maladaptive, attacking anger, but supportive of empowering, adaptive anger. Knowledge of this specific client's more typical ways of responding and of the kinds of emotional responses often found in specific types of client also is helpful in guiding emotion assessment. Finally, knowledge of the pre- and post-context of the emotional expression is most helpful in understanding the emotion in context. A first-time expression of a new emotion is very different from the same old emotion being expressed for the 20th time, and if the expression of the emotion leads toward more productive processing or adaptive action, or on the other hand to more dysregulation, this informs the therapist's decision as to whether the emotion is primary, adaptive, or not.

Intervention Skills

Intervention is guided by some general strategies, by principles of emotion intervention and an understanding of emotion process, and by descriptions of different specific interventions for different problem markers. The general strategies are described first, followed by principles of emotional change and phases of treatment. This is followed by a discussion of markers and tasks.

GENERAL EFT STRATEGIES FOR WORKING WITH EMOTION

The two major tasks are helping people (a) with too little emotion to access more emotion and (b) with too much emotion to contain their emotions. There are many possible ways of helping clients access feelings, including encouraging their attention to bodily sensations that cue emotions, helping them recall previous emotion episodes or situations that bring up particular feelings, and using vivid emotion cues such as poignant words or images in communicating with them. In addition, therapists can suggest that clients act as if they feel a certain way, or they can exaggerate and repeat phrases or gestures (e.g., speaking in a loud, angry voice or shaking their fist). It is also important to help clients monitor their level of arousal in order to maintain the safety that allows emotion to arise. This last strategy is very important because most people will cut off access to their feelings if they sense that they are losing control.

We have delineated different types of empathy that help clients to access and symbolize their emotions. These range from purely understanding empathic responses, through validating and evocative responses, to exploratory and conjectural responses as well as empathic refocusing (Elliott, Watson, Goldman, & Greenberg, 2004; Greenberg & Elliott, 1997). Empathic exploration is seen as the fundamental mode of intervention in EFT and is a response that is focused on the leading edge of the client's experience—that which is most alive or poignant or implicit—to help it unfold. When a therapist's response is structured in such a way that it ends with a focus on what seems most alive in a client's statement, the client's attention in turn is focused on this aspect of his or her experience and is more likely to differentiate this leading edge of his or her experience. By sensitively attending, moment by moment, to what is most poignant in a client's spoken and nonspoken (nonverbal) narrative, a therapist's verbal empathic exploration can help capture the client's experience even more richly than can the client's own descriptions. This helps the client symbolize previously implicit experience consciously in awareness. Conjecture involves sharing hunches or guesses about what the client may be feeling.

Clients usually begin therapy by telling the story of their problem. EFT therapists start with empathy and attempt to have clients focus inward and deepen their experience. If this does not deepen client experience, they move to focusing guiding attention to the bodily felt sense. This often is followed later by more stimulating interventions such as chair dialogues and imagery work in which affect is heightened to bring it vividly into focal awareness.

Following the use of empathy, the therapist encourages clients to bring their attention to their experiencing as it is bodily felt and to gently ask, "What's problematic for me?" The therapist waits and then helps the client to let words come from the feeling and to focus on the experiential effect this has. The therapist also helps the client to "sense a problem as a whole" and let what is important come up from that bodily sensing. This is the focusing process and represents the basic style of engagement with internal experience that is being encouraged.

EFT therapists also help clients who feel overwhelmed or emotionally flooded develop adaptive strategies for containing emotion by using a range of possibilities including observing and symbolizing the overwhelming feelings (e.g., meditatively creating a safe distance by adopting an observer's stance and describing one's fear, for example, as a black ball located in one's stomach). Offering support and understanding and encouraging clients to seek others' support and understanding are also helpful in regulating emotions, as is encouraging clients to organize their distressing emotions, for example, by making a list of problems. Helping clients to engage in self-soothing is a crucial strategy. Here the therapist encourages relaxation, self-comforting, self-support, and self-care (e.g., "Try telling this other part of you, 'It's OK to feel sad'"). Helping clients in high distress distract themselves by, for example, counting backwards or going in imagination to a safe place is useful for promoting regulation. If clients become overwhelmed in the session, asking them to breathe, to put their feet on the ground, to feel themselves in their chair, and to look at the therapist and describe what they see helps regulate the distress.

Paradoxically, one of the most effective ways of helping clients contain emotion may actually be by helping them to become aware of it, express it, and decide what to do about it, as soon as it arises. This is because suppressing an emotion and doing nothing about it tends to have the effect of generating more unwanted emotional intrusions, thus making it more overwhelming or frightening. One of the dilemmas for clients and therapists alike is knowing when to facilitate awareness and experience of emotion and when to regulate it. A helpful practical guideline, especially for people who experience overwhelming destructive emotions, is to be aware of how intense the feelings are and use this awareness as a guide to coping. Emotional approach and awareness should be used when the emotions are below some manageable level of arousal, say 70%, but distraction and regulation should be applied when they exceed this level and become unmanageable.

In addition to these general strategies for working with emotion, the different types of emotion described previously need to be worked with in different ways. Primary adaptive emotions need to be accessed and more fully allowed to provide information and action tendency. To help clients sort out if what they are feeling is a primary adaptive emotion, therapists respond empathically and act as surrogate information processors, offering symbols to describe feelings that clients can check against their experiences for fit. Therapists' responses that are helpful in assessing if an emotion is primary involve such statements as "Is this what your core feeling is at rock bottom?" or "Check inside; see if this is your most basic feeling." Maladaptive emotions are best handled by helping the client to approach, allow, tolerate, symbolize, regulate, and explore these emotions. Once accessed and accepted rather than avoided, they become amenable to change by accessing different underlying emotions (e.g., undoing maladaptive shame with anger, self-compassion, or pride) and by reflecting on them to make sense of them. Therapists help clients access these emotions by means of empathic exploration of, and empathic conjectures into, clients' deeper experience. In addition, in order to access maladaptive emotions, therapists might ask, "What is your most vulnerable feeling, one you have had from early on, ever since you can remember?" or "Does this feeling feel like a response to things that have happened in the past, or does it feel mainly like a response to what's happening now?" Other questions that are helpful are, "Does this feel like a familiar stuck feeling?" or "Will this feeling help you deal with the situation?"

Secondary reactive emotions are best responded to with empathic exploration to discover the underlying primary emotions from which they are derived (e.g., primary fear under reactive anger). To get beneath the secondary emotions, therapists also might ask, "When you feel that, do you feel anything in addition to what you're most aware of feeling?" or "Take a minute and see if it feels like there is something else underneath that feeling." Finally, instrumental emotions are best explored for their interpersonal function or intended impact on others. The therapist, after conveying an understanding that the person feels sad or angry, might say, "I wonder if maybe you are trying make a point or tell this person something with this feeling?" Thus, people may recognize the intention in their emotional experience, be it their desire for self-protection, or comfort, or an attempt to dominate the other.

MARKERS AND TASKS

A defining feature of the EFT approach is that intervention is marker guided. Research has demonstrated that clients enter specific problematic emotional processing states that are identifiable by in-session statements and behaviors that mark underlying affective problems and that these afford opportunities for particular types of effective intervention (Greenberg et al., 1993; Rice & Greenberg, 1984). Client markers indicate not only the client's state and the type of intervention to use but also the client's current readiness to work on this problem. EFT therapists are trained to identify markers of different types of problematic emotional processing problems and to intervene in specific ways that best suit these problems. Each of the tasks has been studied both intensively and extensively, and the key components of a path to resolution and the specific form that resolution takes have been specified. Thus, models of the actual process of change act as maps to guide the therapist intervention. The following main markers and their accompanying interventions have been identified (Greenberg et al., 1993).

An Unclear Felt Sense

When the person is on the surface of his or her experience, or feeling confused and unable to get a clear sense of his or her experience, the person may say, "I just have this feeling, but I don't know what it is." An unclear felt sense calls for focusing (Gendlin, 1996), in which the therapist guides clients to approach the embodied aspects of their experience with attention and with curiosity and willingness, and to experience them and put words to their bodily felt sense. A resolution involves a bodily felt shift and the creation of new meaning.

Typically, EFT therapists use focusing when clients are willing to explore their inner experience but are unclear about what they are feeling. At these times, an EFT therapist might suggest to clients that they try to focus on the unclear or absent felt sense. This requires that clients identify that place in the body where they usually register their feelings. The therapist then asks them to attend to that inner space and name what comes up. Clients are asked not to reflect on or monitor what they find there but merely to identify it for both themselves and the therapist and then to leave it to one side. Once clients have named all the nuances of their subjective state, EFT therapists ask them to identify one of the feelings or issues on which they wish to focus. Clients are asked to merely attend to and concentrate on the feeling and to try to see what comes up for them. If it is a label, they are asked to check inside to see whether it fits or not. If the label does not fit, clients are asked to search for one that better captures what they are experiencing. Therapists can help in this process by gently and tentatively offering some alternatives to the original label. Together, therapists and clients search until a label that fits the experience is found. Once a label fits, clients may then begin to explore what the feeling means and identify the issue or situation to which it pertains.

Guiding clients through a focusing task involves a number of steps. The essential steps in focusing are as follows: First, the therapist identifies the marker that indicates that the client is vague, stuck, or unclear about his or her feelings. Second, the therapist asks the client to attend to the unclear felt sense. Third, the client is encouraged to describe the quality of the felt sense (the principle of emotion awareness and symbolizing). Fourth, the client is asked to go back and forth between the word (or image) and the felt sense until he or she gets a perfect match (at this stage, clients may experience a shift in their feeling as it becomes clearer; however, this is not always the case). Fifth, clients are encouraged to ask themselves what about the feeling makes them feel what they feel, or what the feeling needs to feel (the principle of reflection on emotion). Sixth, clients are encouraged to appreciate and consolidate any shifts in feeling that have occurred as a result of bringing it into awareness and clarifying what it is about, and they are asked to set aside any critical or negative reactions to the feelings. Seventh, clients are encouraged to receive what came and recognize it as a step in dealing with problem, not the last (Gendlin, 1996). These aspects of a focusing process can be facilitated by the therapist using specific reflections that guide the client's attention inward to bodily felt feelings. The many microprocesses of focusing on a bodily felt sense involved in moving into deeper experiencing can be woven seamlessly into other interventions.

Problematic Reactions and Systematic Evocative Unfolding

Problematic reactions are expressed through puzzlement about emotional or behavioral responses to particular situations. For example, a client saying, "On the way to therapy I saw a little puppy dog with long droopy ears and I suddenly felt so sad and I don't know why." Problematic reactions are opportunities for a process of systematic evocative unfolding. This form of intervention involves vivid evocation of experience to promote reexperiencing the situation and the reaction to establish the connections between the situation, thoughts, and emotional reactions to finally arrive at the implicit meaning of the situation that makes sense of the reaction. Resolution involves a new view of self-functioning.

The sequence of steps in exploring these problematic reactions includes the following. First, the reaction that the client feels is puzzling is identified. Second, the therapist asks the client to provide a vivid description of the scene in which the client was a participant when his or her reaction occurred. Together, the client and therapist work to rebuild and recapture a graphic sense of the situation. Third, once the scene has been vividly recreated by the participants, the therapist guides the client to focus on and symbolize his or her internal reaction (the principle of emotion awareness and symbolizing). Fourth, the client is guided to search for the particularly salient aspect of the situation that triggered the depressed reaction. Fifth, after clients identify what was salient about the situation, they are able to determine how they construed the stimulus so as to arrive at an understanding of its personal meaning (the principle of reflection). This is known as the *meaning bridge*. Sixth, the therapist may then help the client to recognize the emotion scheme that was activated by the problematic situation. The client becomes aware of a personal style and general way of responding that he or she can then examine to understand its origins and determine whether it is still useful (the principle of reflection). Seventh, following the exploration of the emotion scheme, the client is able to come up with new ways of responding emotionally (changing emotion with emotion) or of construing the situation (reflection). The aim of using systematic evocative unfolding is to have clients reexperience as fully as possible the problematic situation to symbolize it more accurately in awareness so as to discover its personal impact or meaning in order to identify alternative needs and action tendencies (Rice, 1974).

There are three markers related to the use of chair work in which the client is invited to engage in dialogues with different parts of the self or with others. I discuss the markers and then go over the interventions in a separate section.

Conflict Splits and Two-Chair Dialogue

In a split, one aspect of the self is in opposition to another aspect. Often this takes the form of one part being critical or coercive. For example, a woman who judges herself to be a failure in the eyes of her sisters quickly becomes both hopeless and defeated but also angry in the face of these criticisms and says, "I feel inferior to them. It's like I've failed and I'm not as good as you." Self-critical splits like this offer an opportunity for two-chair work. In this work, two parts of the self are put into live contact with each other. Thoughts, feelings, and needs within each part of the self are explored and communicated in a real dialogue to achieve a softening of the critical voice. Resolution involves integration between sides.

Self-Interruptive Splits and Two-Chair Enactments

Self-interruptions arise when one part of the self interrupts or constricts emotional experience and expression: "I can feel the tears coming up but I just tighten and suck them back in, no way am I going to cry." In the two-chair enactment, the interrupting part of the self is made explicit by enacting it. Clients become aware of how they interrupt and are guided to enact the ways they do it, be it by physical act (choking or shutting down the voice), metaphorically (caging), or verbally ("shut up, don't feel, be quiet, you can't survive this"), so that they can experience themselves as an agent in the process of shutting down and then can react to and challenge the interruptive part of the self. Resolution involves expression of the previously blocked experience. I go over the intervention task for this marker in a separate section on chair dialogues.

Unfinished Business and the Empty Chair Dialogue

An unfinished business marker involves the statement of a lingering unresolved feeling toward a significant other, such as the following said by a client in a highly involved manner in the first session: "My father, he was just never there for me. I have never forgiven him." Unfinished business toward a significant other calls for an empty-chair intervention. Using an empty-chair dialogue, clients activate their internal view of a significant other and experience and explore their emotional reactions to the other and make sense of them. Access to unmet needs and shifts in views of both the other and self occur. Resolution involves holding the other accountable or understanding or forgiving the other. Unresolved loss and humiliation, centered on unfinished business with a significant other, are usually at the base of the unresolved dependence issues in many interpersonal difficulties. The abandonment/loss process often is even more fundamental than self-criticism. Empty chair dialogue, in which the client expresses unresolved feelings to an imagined other in an empty chair, has been found to be very helpful in resolving unfinished business (Greenberg & Malcolm, 2002; Paivio & Greenberg, 1995).

ADDITIONAL MARKERS AND INTERVENTIONS

A number of additional markers and interventions, such as vulnerability and empathic affirmation/validation, trauma and narrative retelling, alliance rupture and repair, emotional suffering and self-compassion, anxious dependence and self-soothing, and confusion and clearing a space, and more, have been added to the original six markers and tasks identified previously (see Elliott, Watson, et al., 2004; Greenberg, 2002, 2011; Greenberg & Watson, 2006). In addition, a new set of narrative markers and interventions combining working with emotion and narrative have been specified (Angus & Greenberg, 2011). These somewhat self-explanatory markers include markers of the same old story, a repetitive description of difficulties in which the person is stuck, which is best dealt with by promoting reexperiencing specific event memories; the marker of an untold story, in which the emerging story is accessed by empathic exploration; the marker of an empty story, one devoid of emotion and is best enriched by means of empathic conjectures about the implicit feelings; and the marker of a broken story, in which unforeseen outcomes challenge one's security and are best dealt with by promoting coherence.

CHAIR DIALOGUE TASKS

Three of the markers previously mentioned called for different forms of chair dialogues. I would like to expand on these particular intervention tasks, because not only are they complex, they are central to EFT.

The Two-Chair Task for the Self-Critical Marker

In this process, when a self-critical marker such as "I'm not a good enough parent" or "I feel like a failure" appears in the client's presentation, the therapist encourages the client first to visualize him- or herself and to begin criticizing him- or herself and to engage in a dialogue between the critical part and the experiencing part of the self (Greenberg et al., 1993). In the first few dialogues, the goal is to help the client become aware of the constant presence of a self-critical voice and its impact. The critical voice says such things as, "You are too stupid, ugly, fat, selfish, or needy." It is the contempt toward the self that is accompanying these criticisms that evokes the bad feelings, often of powerlessness, helplessness, and hopelessness, and then ultimately of more primary core shame (Whelton & Greenberg, 2005). It is important to capture the feeling and motivation in the critic as well as the critical thought. Clients often do not pay attention to the manner, but only to the content, of their inner dialogues. They concentrate on what is said but not on the relationship between the parts. By paying special attention to the nonverbal elements of the dialogue, the therapist reflects not just content but also the intonation, gestures, posture, and facial expression, thus drawing the client's attention to the affective tone and manner of self talk, as well as to the content.

Second, the critical part is coached to be as specific as possible in expressing its criticisms. This is designed to evoke the client's painful experience more specifically and concretely.

Third, the client is then asked to move to the self chair, which is asked for its affective reaction to the critic. Not just a global reaction of a general malaise like "I feel bad," but a differentiated sense that actually comes alive in the body, in the moment—a feeling, for example, of being paralyzed or of wanting to shrink into the ground (awareness and symbolization). The more the critic can be helped to target concrete instances of experience, for example, of weakness or failure at the meeting yesterday, the more episodic, situational, and emotion memories will be evoked. The experiencing self's initial response is generally characterized by a collapse into a nonresilient state of hopelessness in response to self-criticism. In the session, we want to evoke the secondary hopelessness or despair in order to go through it, to access the core maladaptive state. Often one has to approach and stay with the secondary emotional state in order to differentiate it and arrive at the core feelings. Therapy then needs to go through this secondary, reactive state to a more core level of distress.

Fourth, the crucial step in the dialogue is developing the experiencing self's response to the criticism (principle of emotion expression). Often the core feeling is either shame about the self's deficits or anxiety/fear about the self's ability to survive alone. These dreaded core feelings most often involve a maladaptive feeling of worthlessness or shame-based feelings of inadequacy. We now have to help clients symbolize and express their maladaptive emotions and to access their primary adaptive emotions and needs for survival and well-being. Any client strengths that exist initially lie beyond present awareness.

Fifth, the therapist facilitates access to the need in the maladaptive emotion and the attendant new experiencing and promotes its expression to the critical voice (principle of expression). This leads to an emerging of more adaptive emotions (changing emotion with emotion), assertion of the self, and the combating of the critical voice (Greenberg, 1984). This is the beginning of the emergence of the resilient self. Although it is essential to recognize and affirm the client's underlying feelings, the therapist, when working with splits, also must listen for associated needs and direct the client to express these to the critical side in an assertive manner. Adaptive needs are at the core of the resilient self's tendency to survive and thrive. Needs are associated with action tendencies and direct clients toward attaining goals that are highly relevant to their well-being and that help mobilize new emotions to achieve need satisfaction (changing emotion with emotion). Accessing needs opens pathways in the brain to new emotional states and to pathways to attain those states (Davidson, 2000). Accessing needs is a crucial step in mobilizing resilience. Finally, self-critical splits resolve by a softening of the critical voice into a more compassionate one (changing emotion with emotion), in which the needs are acknowledged and integrated and greater self-acceptance results (see Elliott, Watson, et al., 2004; Greenberg, Rice, & Elliott, 1993).

A possible difficulty in a two-chair dialogue occurs when the experiencing side agrees with the critical voice. Rather than responding to the critic either by agreeing or by trying to dispute the truth of the criticism, or by disagreeing rationally or on the basis of evidence, clients are helped to become aware of the emotional impact on them of the criticism. They are asked what it feels like to be told, "You are worthless," and to speak from the bodily felt experience of shame or hopelessness. The client thus experiences the impact of the criticism rather than agreeing or disagreeing with the validity of the negative thoughts.

Another way of dealing with defeat in the chair dialogue when resilience does not emerge and the person seems stuck is to move the client back into the critic chair. Here the therapist needs to encourage the critic to intensify its critical actions and become more clearly aware of itself as an agent in the creation of the collapse in the self. It is useful to help the client become more aware of the critic's own contempt and hostility, and of the power and superiority the critic feels as it disempowers the self. Such persecutory action also can paradoxically serve to stimulate the "fight back" of the experiencing self. The person then overcomes the resigned, hopeless position by fighting back against the oppressor. In addition, by activating the person as a whole—physiologically, affectively, and cognitively—by being the aggressor in the critical position, the person's overall level of energy is increased. When the person moves back to the persecuted part in the dialogue, the person is already aroused, and this "borrowed" arousal works in the service of self-assertion against the critic, thereby lifting the person out of the hopeless state.

Accepting and staying with the collapsed sense of self is often the most difficult part of this work. First, the client has a tendency to avoid or escape this awful feeling. Next, the therapist has the same tendency and tends to try and "help" or to change the client. However, rather than adopt a modificational stance, the therapist needs to take a stance of acceptance. The therapist's first actions need to promote staying with the present experience and following the process. This requires both therapists and clients to practice an acceptance of "what is." The therapist does not pull for change but rather accepts where the client is, and the client begins to mobilize some resilience. The therapist's goal, then, is to provide a safe and accepting environment, validate the experience, and turn the client's attention inward to the experience. This helps clients begin to differentiate their hopelessness into the constituent components of situation, appraisal, sensation, action tendency, and need/goal/concerns and to develop them into more core feelings. The goal is to help clients ultimately find the sources of strength within themselves by focusing them inward with the help of an empathically attuned, emotion-regulating relationship.

The overall focus when working to evoke adaptive emotion as an antidote to a maladaptive state is always on working at the leading edge of the client's experience. Therapists focus on growth-oriented possibilities that emerge or are implicit in clients' experience. Therapists' responses, however, need to be within people's proximal zone of development, focusing on possibilities within their grasp. This means being neither too far ahead nor too far behind the client. The therapist's response can be a half a step or one step ahead, but it needs to be sufficiently close to where the client is so as to provide a stepping stone that the person can use to step out of their painful state. Two steps ahead is too much and two steps behind is potentially impeding.

Two-Chair Task for Self-Interruptive Splits

The enactment of the interruption of emotion involves a different use of the two-chair dialogue then the one used for self-criticism discussed previously. In comparison with self-critical splits, markers of self-interruptive splits involve actions against the self rather than evaluations of the self and typically have a larger nonverbal, bodily aspect. They sometimes are expressed purely nonverbally, such as with a headache or with tightness in the chest. The therapist's goals in self-interruptive work are both to heighten awareness of the interruptive process and to help the client access and allow blocked or disavowed internal experience.

The most common indicators of self-interruption are resignation, feeling blocked or trapped, or a general inability to feel. This often is accompanied by physical symptoms, such as feeling oppressed, burdened, or blocked, or experiencing tightness in the chest or a pain in the neck. In these cases, the primary feelings or needs have been so efficiently interrupted that they are not in awareness. In trauma, processes such as shutting down, going numb, and dissociating, which were possibly adaptive at the time of the traumatic event, now interfere with the integration of the traumatic experience. These blocks also need to be overcome. In a two-chair enactment, at a marker of self-interruption, clients are encouraged to enact how they stop themselves from feeling, to verbalize the particular injunctions used, or to exaggerate the muscular constrictions involved in the interruption (Greenberg et al., 1993). Eventually, this provokes a response, often a rebellion against the suppression, and the experiencing self challenges the injunctions, restraining thoughts, or muscular blocks and the suppressed emotion bursts through the constrictions. At the beginning of the enactment, the therapist helps clients become aware of how they interrupt and gets them to actually engage in the interruptive action. Having had the client identify with the interruptive process, the therapist then facilitates the expression of what was being interrupted. Having deautomatized the interruptive process by bringing it into awareness and enacting it, and having identified the protective aspect of the interruption and experienced a sense of control, the client now is ready to experience that which has been interrupted. Finally, the therapist guides the client to express some of the suppressed feelings toward a person for whom he has a lot of suppressed anger.

Empty-Chair Task for Unfinished Business

At the beginning of this dialogue, the therapist must first ensure that the client is making contact with the imagined other. Evoking the sensed presence of the other, making sure the person is currently experiencing the real or imagined presence of someone or something in a direct and immediate way is important in evoking the troublesome emotion schematic memory. Second, enacting the other person performing the hurtful behavior also is important in evoking the emotional reaction to the person. The goal of playing the other is to heighten the stimulus value of the other's behavior to in turn evoke the person's affective reaction to it. Once the other has portrayed the negative actions and attitudes, the third step involves accessing the client's affective reaction to this. With the therapist's careful and attuned tracking and reflection, relevant feelings toward the other emerge.

Throughout the dialogue, the therapist focuses on encouraging the expression of the client's concrete experience and emotions toward the other. The fourth step and the main goal of the dialogue is to move beyond these reactions into awareness and differentiation underlying meanings and feelings and encouraging the expression of primary emotional states. Secondary complaint must always be differentiated into its more fundamental components—anger and sadness. Other typical secondary emotions expressed in empty chair work include hopelessness, resignation, depression, and anxiety. These are often expressed in an outer-directed manner in a blaming tone. The therapist acknowledges and helps clients work through these secondary emotions, but maintains the aim of encouraging the "pure" expression of primary emotion: "I resent you" or "I missed having you around" rather than "You were a bastard" or "Why did you neglect me?" Secondary and primary emotions are often first experienced and expressed in a jumbled manner and all mixed together. For example, complaint that is fused anger and sadness often comes out in question form: "Why couldn't you be more . . . ?" or "Why did you . . . ? I just want to know why?" It is important to help clients move beyond the expression of complaint and secondary reactions to expressing their primary emotions to the imagined other, feelings such as sadness, anger, fear, and shame. Anger and sadness are often experienced together, and it is helpful to ensure that these two primary emotional states are experienced, symbolized, and expressed separately. In cases of abuse, combinations of maladaptive fear, shame, and disgust have first to be accessed, regulated, validated (corrective experience), and reprocessed to the point at which the client is ready to access primary anger and sadness (Greenberg, 2002, 2011). For the fifth step, interruptions to the expression of primary emotions need to be worked with to access the core emotion and allow its full expression.

Once emotions have been differentiated and interruptions dissolved, the emotional arousal that is a necessary precondition for resolution of this type of problem emerges. Emotional arousal has been found to be an important precursor of the next step, a change in view of the other. Without arousal, this step is far less probable (Greenberg & Malcolm, 2002). In working with emotions at this stage, therapists need to know that once primary emotions are fully and freely expressed, they move quickly. Anger and sadness tend to follow each other in sequence. Thus, when primary sadness is fully expressed, primary adaptive anger emerges rapidly and boundaries are created (changing emotion with emotion). Conversely, the full expression of adaptive anger allows clients to acknowledge the pain of losses and betrayal and grieve for what they missed.

The sixth step involves facilitating the expression of and validating the client's basic unmet interpersonal needs for attachment or separation or validation. These are needs that were never expressed in the original relationship because people felt that they were not entitled to do so and that the needs would not be met. In order to be productive, the needs must be expressed as belonging to and coming from the self and with a sense of entitlement, rather than as deprivations or accusations of the other. Thus, they are assertions of deserving to be met, rather than expressions of desperate neediness. This step is crucial in helping people establish their sense of the self as an agent, separate from the other, existing in its own right. At this stage, the therapist simply follows the client and encourages the expression of new, experienced emotions and needs (changing emotion with emotion). In addition, the therapist helps clients to symbolize and assert boundaries; to say no to intrusion, for example; or to reassert their rights. Therapists are aware that in early experience people often have found it necessary to disavow their basic needs and that as a result they do not automatically attend to or express those needs. Therapists therefore listen for needs to form and, when they do, quickly validate them (corrective experience) and encourage clients to express them. A thorough exploration of feelings is typically followed by a statement of related needs.

In situations where the need cannot or will not be met by the other, clients must still come to recognize their right to have needs met by the other. This often allows the important seventh step in the process of letting go of the unmet need. At this point in the dialogue, the therapist supports and promotes the letting go of the unfulfilled hopes and expectations. When letting go does not naturally flow from the expression of primary emotions, therapists can help clients explore and evaluate whether the unfulfilled expectations can and will be met by the other, and if not, therapists can help clients explore the effects of hanging on to the expectations. In this situation, therapists can consider asking clients to express to the significant other, "I won't let you go" or "I won't let go of the hope you'll change." Letting go often produces another round of grief work in which the client works through mourning the loss of the possibility of getting the need met from the attachment figure. This is often the most poignant and painful part of the process. Once people truly can grieve for the parent they never had, then they are able to let go and move on.

In the seventh step, through arousal and direct expression of emotions and a strong sense of the legitimacy of their needs, clients begin to let go of previously salient but overly constricted perceptions and to expand their view of the other (reflection). Finally, resolution occurs when clients reach a sense that they are worthwhile and are able to let go of the previously unfinished bad feelings. This letting go is accomplished in one of three major ways: through holding the other accountable for the violation experienced and affirming the self, through letting go of the unmet need, or through increased understanding of the other and possibly forgiving of the other for past wrongs. In nonabuse cases, the client is able to better understand the other and to view the other with empathy, compassion, and sometimes forgiveness. In abusive or trauma-related situations, letting go most often involves holding the other accountable and moving on, but empathy and forgiveness may also occur.

Unfinished business can be worked with by dialoguing in chairs or by using imagery, as discussed previously, without actually having the person speak to an empty chair. Imagery also can be used in a variety of other ways to evoke emotion. The visual system is highly related to emotion, so imagination can be used to evoke an unresolved emotion, to enact dialogues in imagination to experience a new emotion, or to imagine adding people or resources to situations or scenes to help one experience the scene in a new way. Thus, one can ask the client to restructure through imagery an originally damaging scene by expressing what was needed or by bringing one's adult self into a childhood scene. The adult protector can offer the protection that was missing or bring in aids that will empower or protect the person, like a lock and key to secure the room or a cage in which to put the feared person (Greenberg, 2002, 2011).

In this type of imaginal restructuring, the therapist might say,

> Close your eyes and remember the experience of yourself in a situation. Get a concrete image if you can. Go into it. Be your child in this scene. Please tell me what is happening. What do you see, smell and hear in the situation? What is going through your mind?

After a while the therapist asks the client to shift perspectives:

> Now I would like you to view the scene as an adult. What do you see, feel, and think? Do you see the look on the child's face? What do you want to do? Do it. How can you intervene? Try it now in imagination.

Changing perspectives again, the therapist asks the client to become the child:

> As the child, what do you feel and think? What do you need from the adult? Ask for what you need or wish for. What does the adult do? What else do you need? Ask for it. Is there someone else you would like to come in to help? Receive the care and protection offered.

This intervention concludes with the therapist asking the client to

> Check how you feel now. What does all this mean to you about you and about what you needed? Come back to the present, to yourself as an adult now. How do you feel? Will you say goodbye to the child for now?

Unfinished business work, in whatever way it is done, is ultimately about changing emotion schematic memory. Emotions are often embedded in relational contexts. They connect self to other in the memory. Thus, people have memories of feeling shame in the face of a contemptuous parent, anger at an intrusive other, and fear of an abusive other. Therefore, accessing views of others helps evoke emotion, and accessing alternate views of others and mobilizing new responses to others help change emotion memories.

Personally relevant events are stored in memory at their emotion addresses. Therefore, a current disappointment links to other disappointments, a feeling of shame to other losses of face. Present emotional experiences are always multilayered, evoking with them prior instances of the same or similar emotional experiences. If we help people have new lived experience in the session, this helps them restructure their emotion memories. In addition, accessing a new emotion memory is one of the best ways to change an old emotion memory. Once a previously inaccessible emotion memory is evoked, the new memory either dominates (while the old one recedes into the background) or the new one eventually fuses with the old memory and transforms it. New emotion memories, however accessed, help change narratives. The stories people tell to make sense of their experience and to construct their identities are to a significant degree dependent on the variety of emotion memories that are available to them. By changing their memories, or the accessibility of different memories, people change the stories of their lives and their identities.

Case Applications

In this section, I go into some detail about the two clients who appear on the DVDs *Three Approaches to Psychotherapy With a Female Client* and *Three Approaches to Psychotherapy With a Male Client*. It is my intention here to augment my discussion of the clients in the video demonstration sessions with some further thoughts on my work with them.

CHI CHI

First, it is important to comment that as a demonstration session, this session does not parallel an actual first session. The purpose of these videos is to demonstrate a working session, not a first or second session. In a first session, I would adopt a more empathic style throughout and spend the whole session listening to the client's narrative; I would focus on establishing a trusting bond; and I would not engage in marker-guided, process-directive interventions as I did in this session. My general impression of the session, however, was that it was a good enough session and represents what might happen in a third or fourth session of EFT.

I began the session as I normally would, by identifying the client's (Chi Chi's) presenting problem and listening to her story. Early on, I hear that she is self-critical: "I just don't seem to have any self-discipline or self-direction at all" and "I get so angry and disappointed with myself." This is a marker of a self-critical split, but it is a second-level criticism of herself for not being able to get things done. The real problem in her life is that she isn't getting things done, and her reaction to that is that she is angry and critical of herself. So I am aware at this point that she is self-critical but that we will need to get to a more underlying set of processes (possibly self-critical ones) that stops her from getting things done.

I also see that she begins to feel tearful, and so I privilege following her immediate experience over markers by saying, "Yeah, and what do you feel as you say that? I mean, it sounded like it was touching." I hereby set about creating an emotion friendly environment, giving permission for emotion by saying, "But this is really a place where you have permission to be upset," and begin to provide a rationale for working with emotion "because I think somehow, the upset is saying, this is really important to me" (emotion gives you information about what is significant to your well-being).

Because Chi Chi's emotions are accessible, I move quickly, so around the third minute or so I move to facilitating a deepening of her experience when I ask her to focus on her hopeless feeling: "Okay. And as the tears come up, can we stay with them?" An alternate response such as "So what small steps do you try?" would be an undesirable response from my perspective, as it would not deepen experience. We see the emotion-focused nature of this approach exemplified when I say, "What actually happens inside when you feel this tearfulness? If you were to go to your body." I clearly am asking her to focus on her emotion; other approaches generally do not attend directly to emotion in this manner. I then make an exploratory empathic response, saying, "So it's a kind of sense of hopelessness," and I encourage a continued focus with, "But can we try to stay with the hopeless feeling? Where do you feel it in your body?" What is important here is that there is a consistent gentle encouragement to stay with the emotional experience by focusing on her bodily felt experience. By staying with the bodily felt experience—which includes bodily sensations but is more than sensations as it provides the felt meaning of experience—we bring people into the present. Paying attention in this way helps them symbolize in awareness what is happening in themselves in the moment. It is important to note that the meaning of the emotions does not reside fully formed in the bodily experience. Rather, the person is an active organizing agent in the meaning creation process that takes place in a social field. Embodied experience thus both constrains and influences how it is understood, but what people make of their experience also makes them who they are. As the shape of a particular cloud can be formed into a fish or into an arrow but not into a horse, so too is the bodily feeling shaped into what it becomes. There is a bodily felt sense there, but rather than the meaning being in it, the feeling becomes what it is organized into, and some feelings are a better or worse fit for what is there. Therefore, I cannot symbolize bodily feelings of depletion or pain as joy or disgust and be well-oriented in the world. But I can symbolize depleted as feeling hopeless or pain as feeling ashamed. Each symbolization of experience carries different implications. So when Chi Chi describes her current experience as "I'm drowning . . . I can see a light but I can't . . . but I can't reach it and I know that I will never reach it," her way of organizing it in language is pregnant with meaning and implication, both that there is a light, implying possibility, and that she feels she will never reach it, implying hopelessness. Her experience is multifaceted and multidimensional and can be organized in a variety of ways. How it is organized in this dialogue will influence what it becomes. It is a dynamic process. It is important to remember that feelings are not facts but rather current orientations to the world that are in process. Access to this experience makes it amenable to change. Witness that she does not stay stuck in the feelings of hopelessness.

The process of focusing on a bodily felt sense gives people access to their subjective experience at the base of their meaning construction and thereby makes it accessible to development and change. In my view, what is not felt remains the same. However, when it is felt, it is open to change, and the process of attending to it and symbolizing it in awareness is itself a process of change. If there is something that feels bad or unresolved, one needs to allow it and accept it, breathe into it and let it be. Then it can evolve and change, and it often does change into a more adaptive form guided by the organisms drive to survive and thrive. Therapists thus need to have patience and trust in the emotional/experiencing process and understand that one thing leads to another. As Gendlin (1981) said, "nothing that feels bad is ever the last step" (pp. 25–26).

Chi Chi's symbolization then develops into: "Like I'm gonna die without doing anything in my life." She then moves into some self-blame, saying, "Yeah and that's, it's me. It's me. I'm the one who's not moving. Who's not taking any steps and now I don't know how to get myself . . ." This was a complex moment and represented a choice point for me. I ask her when she first remembered having this feeling. I could have asked her to stay with this feeling and to follow where it would go, having faith in her process. An alternate response here would be: "Go to the feeling of not moving. See what it's like in your body. Stay with this feeling and just follow where it goes." This could have led to some further symbolization and differentiation. As I understand my own process, I did not do this in part because of the context. I hardly knew her and did not know how hopeless she felt, although the signs of a "light," albeit one she can't reach, and her motivation for movement are both good indicators of resilience. In the intake interview, she had said of her previous therapy, "I don't think it helped too much to talk about things that were really deeply personally emotional because I would get too upset and then I couldn't go on." So I wanted to ensure we stayed connected to her presenting problem. In addition, having already heard early in our session a marker of self-blame, I saw this as an important aspect of her experience that needed attention. I was strongly influenced here and at later stages by other information from the intake session—that she had had a difficult childhood with her mother, who had been both emotionally and physically abusive, and also that she had had a relationship that ended 6 years ago that still felt emotionally unresolved.

Beginning to Identify Markers

Given that Chi Chi presented with a block to action, I judged this to be her central concern and so decided to move away from focusing to guide her back to her block. Experiences of not being able to get things done generally involve an experience of a split between two parts of self-experience characterized by such feelings as "I want but I can't" or "I want to but I'm afraid." These conflicts are generally involved in presenting issues such as not being able to get things done, writer's block, or decisional conflicts (Greenberg & Webster, 1982) and procrastination. In these blocks, the person is typically identified with the part that wants to do the action and disowns the part that doesn't want to. Chi Chi says, "I want to write, I don't know why I don't write!" She is identified with wanting to write and not aware of any part that does not want to or stops her, which is actually the more powerful part and which succeeds in blocking her behavior. Our studies (Greenberg & Webster, 1982) have shown that in these situations, an internal self-critical process often emerges as the underlying difficulty that needs to be worked on.

In Chi Chi's experience, the dialogue eventually evolves from the one side blaming the self for being unable to act into accessing her deeper level criticism of "You're a fake" and "It won't make a difference." It is important to discriminate between these two levels of criticism. The first level of the self-blaming voice is what I refer to as the "coach critic" because it is trying to coach the self to be better. The coach critic is acting like a not-so-benevolent coach who tries to knock the self into shape with such statements as "You are lazy" and "You never get things done." I work to get beyond this type of coaching and self-blame, which itself is a misguided attempted solution that has now become the problem. Chi-Chi kicks herself for not getting things done in the hope that this will lead to change. She sees her difficulty as a character flaw, and this just makes her feel worse, even hopeless. It is demotivating. Therapeutically I want to move toward the underlying determinant that produces the problem by accessing the deeper level generic criticisms of the self that prevent action, such as "You are stupid, selfish, worthless, or incompetent." These are the type of underlying criticisms we need to get to, as they are involved in evoking the underlying emotion schemes of the shame of worthlessness or the fear of abandonment that block action.

Initiating the Dialogue Task

In this session, I introduce the dialogue by providing some initial structure and support. I name the two parts in conflict and get agreement to engage in the task. The major therapeutic goal in doing this dialogue is to accurately identify the opposing forces in the personality, and this is not always straightforward. I start off the dialogue in a less than ideal way when I say, "But so which part are you more in touch with right now? Is it the part that wants to do things or the part that says, that says let's just drop it?" This is not the best way of introducing the dialogue as it sets up the opposition between "I want to do it" and "I want to drop it" as though it were a decisional conflict. This is not the case, as what she is most in touch with is the critical voice of "You're bad for not doing it"—this is not a decisional conflict. She responds to my query of which side she is most in touch with by saying, "Probably the part that says let's drop it." At this point I self-correct and guide her toward the more self-attacking aspect of that voice when I say, "You're saying to her, what's the use, you're gonna screw it up again."

It takes some work to get at the core negative criticism that produces shame and low self-esteem. Ideally, with more time I would have further explored her experience empathically, to help her get to her more fundamental criticism by saying something like, "Somehow there is a process by which you block yourself. Let's try and understand how that comes about."

Once she gets into the chair dialogue, I try to guide her toward being the voice that blocks her, but her self-blame—"You're going to screw it up"—is quite strong. At one point, however, she does say, "You're just gonna be exposed for the fake that you are." Because we only have a short time, I continually try to guide her toward the underlying criticism rather than the self-blame. It would be possible to work with the "You're a failure for failing" dialogue that she is so involved in, and this would possibly unfold to help her not be so angry at herself for having a problem. Ultimately, however, this is not the level at which it would be most helpful to work. In an ongoing therapy, more exploration would be needed to help her get to her core self-criticism. It is understandably difficult for her to gain access to her automatic internal self-critical processes and to answer questions I put to her such as, "How do you make yourself not committed? Make her not have determination or discipline?" This aspect of her functioning is not readily available to awareness, and because of the single session nature of the video demonstration, I become more active than is ideal, trying to help her get to her core self-critical process that blocks her actions by saying, "Make her not stay committed."

She, however, continues to organize around a second-level critical voice, saying, "It's not gonna make any difference. You're just gonna screw it up again." At this point I decide to ask her to move to the experiencing chair to see if that might help lead to the core split. Access to the core critical process often occurs in the experiencing self chair where she might, for example, respond to her angry voice with something like, "I feel hopeless (secondary emotion). I don't know what happens. I just feel like I can't do it. Somehow I feel like what difference will it make." Or she may say, "I always get in my way." At a point like this she would be closer to the internal process that robs her of her motivation to write. I then might say, "Come over here and say, 'What difference will it make?' or 'Get in her way.' How do you do that?"

Back to the Session

When she moves to the self chair, she first responds with "I feel small and helpless," which suggests that the process is deepening and going in a good direction. She then spontaneously rebels against the critical voice: "That's not true and it's not true and there's . . . I don't know why you're saying it. But we both know that that's not true." This more resilient self-organization, however, doesn't endure, and the self collapses into: "I don't know. I can't . . . I don't have anything to say. I don't . . ." and then, "You're right, I mean . . ." When the self chair agrees with the critical chair, this constitutes a technical crisis in this intervention. The therapeutic task is to separate opposing voices and help them make contact. When there is agreement between the two voices, one loses the contact between opposing voices that drives the dialogue. What therapists need to recognize is that this is a dialogue for evoking core affect and is not about what is true or factual. At this point, the therapist needs to guide the client to the feeling in the self chair. I thus respond to the feeling: "Sort of feels hopeless or you feel like giving up?" She readily identifies with this, and rather than agreement, the dialogue between opposing parts is reconstituted.

In response to me inviting her to tell the critic how it makes her feel, she says, "Well, now I have . . . I feel like I have no reason to make any effort" and "I just go away." We now explore her secondary hopelessness for a while. Her hopelessness is a secondary reaction to her anger at herself but even more so to some core underlying, dreaded feelings of shame, which we catch glimpses of in her tendency to disappear—"It makes me feel small"—in order to run away from her self-attack and her feelings of inadequacy and ultimately her fear from her mother's abuse. These are all experiences that she has been feeling hopeless about changing and copes with by giving up.

We also see here the dialectical tension between following and leading in EFT. I want to stay close to her experiencing—"So make her walk away, disappear"—but I also want to help her get to her more fundamental core critical process that only emerges later. I again try to guide her toward a more core criticism with the response, "That's sort of like a second level (criticism) almost; before you were saying, 'If you expose yourself, you'll be shown to be a fake.'" She again, however, blames herself quite contemptuously: "You have squandered all of your talents, all of your potential. You've just let it all go. So what's the point? You're obviously not anything good with it, you may as well just go crawl off into a hole." A few moments later I try again to get to a more critical process by saying, "But the deeper kind of voice seems to be, you can't do it . . . because you're not good enough—or what do you say to yourself to sort of make her afraid? You don't have the talent or . . .?" She responds with "It's just the talent isn't enough" and then goes back to "You don't have any determination." Continuing to try to get at the more fundamental critical process, I then suggest, "Make her not have determination or discipline—how do you do that?" All the work up to now indicates how difficult it is to get to the implicit process of how she essentially creates the problem of being blocked. She, however, eventually refines her self-blaming voice into "It's not going to . . . it's not gonna make a difference. Nobody else will care." I see this as getting to the more implicit criticisms and therefore ask her to repeat, "Whatever you do won't make a difference, and nobody will care" to heighten the experience that these words represent. Guided by my understanding from the intake of her childhood abuse, I again ask, "And where does that come from in your past?" It is important to understand this is not for insight but to access more emotionally charged memories and the painful experience that is often associated with childhood invalidation. I construe her critical voice as what she says to herself now, but that it is the internalized voice of her mother in her head—an introject—and that having her enact this as her mother will activate more emotion and deepen her experience. At this point, responding to her facial expression and hearing her pause, I empathically conjecture, in an open-ended fashion, that something is happening and then ask if the voice comes from her mother. It is at this point that we enter a more productive phase of our work. Something connects at a deeper level, with greater subjective complexity, and we now catch the mixed quality of the experience of her mother both praising her "very highly for things that I was good at but also conveying that these things were not going to be of value in life."

Enacting her mother helps her first to access her anger at the critical voice. We access the confusion that these double messages from her mother produce in her. We then get to her core critical voice, which is, "Obviously you're not good enough, so maybe at this point you should just give it up." After reflecting how this leaves her confused and deflated, she shifts to feeling her fury at her mistreatment, no longer the hopeless/helpless feelings that dominated the first part of the session. Our search has shown that anger is one of the best antidotes to hopelessness (Sicoli, 2005).

Unfinished Business and Changing Emotion With Emotion

Once we have accessed her more primary critical process, the dialogue begins to shift to more unfinished business with her mother. This is no longer working on the self-critic in her head internalized from her mother. Now we are working with her unresolved emotional memories, her unfinished business with her mother related to unmet attachment and identity needs. She accesses some of her unresolved anger and fury at her mother, which over time we would need to work on to more fully symbolize it in awareness and to get to her assertion of her unmet needs. Aware that time is running out, I attempt to facilitate the emergence of a more agentic sense of self and a new emotional organization by asking her what she needs. I see this as a crucial question to be used after the person has arrived at and accepted a core emotional wound. It would have been ideal here to help her experience and accept more fully what I imagine is the shame and fear of the humiliated and abused self to which the fury is in part a protective reaction, but this would take more time. She replies with, "I needed her to show me how she became such a strong person, I have always admired that about her" and "I needed more guidance." Parenthetically, this also is probably what she now needs from the self-attacking part of her self. The dialogue now proceeds to begin a process of reworking the experience of maltreatment. For a few moments, she feels her fury and rage and connects to her core fear and to the feeling of being hated by her mother, which is probably at the source of her self-blame. I reflect this as feeling rejected and unloved, but this is not perfectly attuned, as it is weaker than hatred. An alternate response would have been, "Tell her how that felt—to be hated."

Ideally, we would have now stayed at this core wound and symbolized some of this experience more fully to create greater coherence of the painful and chaotic experience of hurt, anger, shame, and fear of being hated. Going to the need at this point, however, is helpful in facilitating a reorganization into a more assertive sense of her need to be loved and accepted. This is the self-affirming and self-assertive stance that brings about a corrective emotional experience and helps transform her sense of shame and fear. More work at this level would be needed in an ongoing therapy. She would need to reprocess the intensely painful experience of her childhood, gain greater access to her sense of deserving to have her unmet needs met, and ultimately feel compassion for her wounded self. Change requires some self-compassion for one's own suffering, and without it therapy doesn't occur. Having allowed some of her experience of fury and fear, and having had these validated by the therapist, she spontaneously begins to access a more benign view/experience of her mother and expresses some empathic understanding of her mother's view. One of the ways to facilitate a new view of the mother in unfinished business is to explore her view of her mother's intentions. I do this by asking if she saw the mother as trying to harm her. This crystallizes that although the effect may have been harmful, her mother had good intentions. I then engage in some hot psychoeducation, teaching at a teachable moment when the experience is occurring, commenting on how I think change in this circumstance is possible (by reconsolidating memories, incorporating new experience from the present into the memory, and thereby updating the old memory).

More work would be needed over time to access her implicit experience of not wanting to act, be it for fear or shame, and the implicit self-criticism involved in that experience. Her core negative voice is something like, "No one will care what you do, it won't make a difference," and is a part of her complex self-view of having talent but still feeling inadequate and not good enough. We would, however, need to understand her more fully and work on a variety of issues to get at her core wounded sense of self and her core maladaptive emotion schemes of fear and shame and the ensuing self-organization that resulted from her emotional history especially, but not exclusively, with her mother. What stands out is her lack of compassion for her acting-out child, and I imagine over time she would come to understand and feel more compassion for herself as a difficult child.

Working with the critical voice is a key part of working with blocks to action, because most people use self-criticism to deal with perceived blocks. They attack themselves harshly in a fruitless attempt to get themselves past the block. The critic's admonitions make things worse by evoking resistance to feeling forced. Ultimately, resolution comes from the two parts ceasing the fight and becoming more compassionate, accepting, and listening to each other's underlying feeling. It is useful to note that in self-critical or self-interruptive work, the critical or blocking part often feels that it is protecting the person from some frightening outcome that occurred in the past. So she may tell herself it won't amount to anything to protect against the hope of praise that came from her experience of her mother's mixed message and rage.

Conclusion

We made a good beginning, and in the future sessions, I would be listening for her self-criticism and for her unfinished business with her mother as well as concentrating on building the bond and being attuned to her moment-by-moment experiencing. Other issues, however, arose in her intake that seemed important, especially the unresolved feelings about a relationship with a boyfriend that ended. The focus would be on helping her to become more compassionate to her self and strengthen her sense of self so she could approach her life with a greater sense of self-efficacy and be more able to let go of unresolved feelings toward others—that is, to be more at peace within herself and with others, especially her mother.

KEVIN

In the first 15 minutes or so of the session, I attempted to be empathic but was not as successful as is necessary. In the middle of this session, he begins to talk about his separation from women and loneliness as a problem, and I think here we begin to touch on his yearnings for and his difficulties with closeness. Toward the end of the session, we were able to touch on some of his underlying experience, but even then the process rather rapidly became more conceptual. This is not unusual for a first session, as clients have usually not yet developed sufficient trust to go too deeply into their painful experiences. In the final minutes we began momentarily to contact his fear at his mother's angry outbursts and some of the sources of his dread.

Looking at the session, we see early on that in my eagerness to get to a focus on the underlying determinants of his dread, I say, "I'm aware you said you lost your father when you were nine," and Kevin responds by saying that when psychological issues come up, the fact that his father died when he was 9 is "gonna be an element." This shows me that he is psychologically minded and understands that his father's death impacted him, but the problem is that this is conceptual knowledge and not the reclaiming of the experience of how it affected him. Experiencing what is talked about is one of the main goals of EFT—to reclaim disclaimed experience and action tendencies and not simply to understand that they had an impact. He refers to his "crying and freaking out" when his dad brought him to school, indicating that these experiences were very intense. I empathize and try to evoke the feeling of this by saying, "Even as you say it, it has that kind of almost dramatic quality of, you know, that the dread, but it is. I mean, that scary dread of facing the unknown. I mean it is a scary thing" and "As this young child you had that dread, right, and it was just like unsafe to go out into the world." At this point I thought I noticed a tear, and I asked him about it. Focusing on present emotion when it appears is what it means to be emotion focused. However, as he said, it was more the heat than his sadness that brought the fluid that he was wiping from his eye.

I notice that rather than focusing on the fear or dread, he responds by describing his reaction to the fear, saying that it was "kind of a huge burden . . . to have to deal with that." This feeling of a burden is his secondary emotional reaction. This is an example of his processing style that indicates that it is difficult for him to focus on his primary anxiety and insecurity. He then proceeds to give an external narrative describing what happened in his life, rather than an internal narrative that would relay what he felt during what happened. He says, "Well, interestingly enough, what happened was all the way through fourth grade, I had this dread of going to school, and it didn't come up every day but there were numerous instances. As a matter of fact, the first week of fourth grade I missed the whole week of school 'cause every morning I woke up and I was like mom, can I stay home today and a few months after that is when my father died and that never happened again." His experiencing level at this juncture is at about Level 2, a detached impersonal account, with some Level 3 when his personal reactions are described rather than being focused on exploration of feelings and internal experiences (Level 4 experiencing). At Level 4, clients are in direct contact with their fluid experience and speak from it as opposed to about it. Kevin then continues for some time in a more external narrative at low levels of experiencing. This plus other aspects of his unfolding narrative indicate that his emotional processing style is more external. At this point I attempt to understand him and communicate my understanding to him empathically.

Listening for Poignancy

As we continue, he says that the fear and dread that he had as a child related to going to day care went away after his father died but reemerged again a few years ago when he experienced separation from his partner plus the challenges of a teenage daughter. My efforts at this point are oriented toward following what is most painful to him, not toward trying to understand what caused his problem or unconscious motivations. I believe that this is a surer and quicker way to get at what troubles him at the core than any observation of patterns and hypotheses about his mental models. His emotional experience is presented in the context of a narrative of his childhood and relationships. I attempt to understand this and to follow the thread of his narrative and convey my understanding to him. At times I find it difficult to understand his narrative, so I ask him how he understands that his dread went away after his father died. Rather than asking a question, an alternate intervention would have been to reflect his feeling by saying, "So having to face all these things led you to waking and brought up these awful feelings of dread." After beginning to talk about the dread, Kevin continues to unfold a complex and somewhat incoherent narrative, talking about intuitions of his father's death in a dream and the calming effect his father had on the family when he returned from work. I try to focus him on his grief by saying, "So let's try and talk about that a little bit, get into it and, you know, what's in your intake interview, you talked about this grief, right, and just grieving and sometimes you just feel this sort of deep grief." I think it would have been better to have let his narrative unfold at its own pace and to try and understand him in all his complexity, and over time a coherent focus would develop at a more natural pace on whatever emerged for him as most salient.

The following segment in which he is describing his reaction to a rebuff from a girlfriend sounds highly poignant: "Monday mornings I would wake up and I would feel like somebody died, literally. Like maybe what I should have felt when my father died, but 9 years old, who knows what got into me. And the grief was so deep. The type that, you know, it was hard to breathe, you know." At this point, this situation is a bit unclear; I try to clarify my understanding of it. An alternate response, more focused on his internal experience, could have been "just a deep, deep sense of grief."

At this point, things become somewhat confusing. I again try to clarify whether he felt this grief because he felt rejected by the woman he was referring to. He responds by saying it wasn't mutual, and he goes very external and speaks in the third person. I try to bring it back to his present life situation by saying, "But then it sometimes happens currently? I mean, where you have this—I mean, is it sort of coupled with the dread, the grief and the dread?" He responds by bringing in a situation with another woman friend. I attempt to stay with him and follow his changes in topic, but we lose what seems to have been potentially most painful and poignant—his deep grief.

Basically, in EFT we have three styles of intervention. With empathic symbolizing, we use words mainly to provide understanding and to help clients symbolize their own feelings in awareness. Within this empathic style, we work to balance empathic understanding, which conveys an understanding of what is explicit in what the client is saying, with empathic exploration and evocation to capture what is implicit but not yet articulated and empathic conjecture to offer guesses at what the client may be feeling. If these forms of empathic responding do not seem to help deepen experience, as was the case with Kevin, the option is to move to more guiding styles of intervention—first to directing the client's attention inward using focusing or awareness experiments (paying attention to one's awareness in the moment) and second to an even more guiding style of intervention involving the use of imagery, chair dialogues, and enactments to stimulate more emotional arousal. At this point, with Kevin feeling that my empathic efforts were not succeeding in helping him deepen his experience or move from a more external manner of processing to a more internal one, I decide to use focusing. Later in the session, I introduce a chair dialogue.

Caveat About the Session

The session with Kevin serves to highlight how difficult the synthesizing of following and guiding can be in EFT and how it can become problematic if these are imbalanced, especially in the bonding phase. EFT privileges following over leading, but I think in this session I became too leading too soon as a way of trying to develop a focus in this short-term encounter, and this I think became a hindrance to connecting with him. I also found myself early in the session becoming overly concerned about how to demonstrate my approach with someone as complexly organized as Kevin and losing my ability to be present with him. I was thinking too much about my next steps in the therapy, which took me out of the present moment and led to me not being as empathic as is necessary for successful EFT. Having watched the intake, I entered the session with the awareness that he had a deep well of pain, but this was not an experience he had shared with me directly, so it felt like a type of unspoken secret that we probably would have benefited from by my addressing it more directly.

I sensed that Kevin was hesitant to reveal himself, particularly with a man, something he later confirmed in his exit interview. I met with Kevin twice for this demonstration, and we never really addressed his core concerns, in part because we did not establish a strong empathic connection, which would have led to clearer communication. In an ongoing therapy, I would have needed to address this in the third session by asking him how he was feeling about our sessions and sharing with him that I found myself feeling not as connected to him as I would like to be.

So this session, especially in the first 15 minutes or so, provides a striking example of what not to do in EFT—that is, don't be too goal focused and don't try to get people to feel. Instead, one needs to listen, follow, and connect, especially early on. I believe strongly in *contact before contract,* of forming a bond before setting treatment goals to work on. However, influenced by having seen how conceptual he was in the intake, I moved too rapidly in the first minute, trying to develop a focus by guiding him to his internal experience by saying, "And how are you right now with your anxiety? I mean, are you feeling anxious now?" He responds with the question "This very minute?" and then says, "Not necessarily." I started on the wrong foot and immediately set up a role relationship of me guiding and putting him on the spot and him having to respond, and this set up an undesirable interactional pattern.

Intervention for a Vague or Unclear Felt Sense

Returning to the session, we see that after Kevin talks about a situation with friends and I can't seem to help us develop a focus, I use an experiential focusing intervention (Gendlin, 1996). I use it in an attempt to help him get out of his head and into his body, rather than applying it as a marker of a vague or unclear felt sense to help him symbolize his unclear felt sense. He is quite distant from his own experiencing process, cut off from his emotions, as witnessed by how he jumps from topic to topic, and this makes it difficult to help get to a focus. I guide Kevin with initial focusing instructions:

> Yeah, yeah. So as you talk about even that incident with the friends, with the—I mean what are you feeling inside as you talk about it now or if we actually went to that place where you feel your feelings, what do you feel right now?

Again, a few minutes later, I guide him with:

> Maybe even if you want to close your eyes and to go inside to that place inside where you feel what you feel. You know usually there's some place inside you feel what you feel and maybe you can just go then to see what you're feeling there right now or maybe see what you—you know, what's right now in your life sort of getting in your way of being happy or being okay. You're just trying to sort of get a focus on that which is the most important to you which—but coming from that feeling place in your body [silence] and this sometimes takes some time, you have to clear your mind of other things, you know, of just sort of thinking into yourself.

At this point, in terms of focusing, I think it would have been better to have Kevin clear an internal space by pushing aside all the things that rapidly cross his mind, like the issue with his close acquaintances, and ask him to focus on his bodily felt sense of a central concern. After clearing a space, an alternate response could have been: "Pick a problem that is of most central concern to you and let's focus on that place inside where you feel your feelings and see what you feel about it all." Instead, I try to follow his somewhat heady process in which in response to me asking him to put his hand where he feels his feeling, he in some way accurately represents his process of being in his head as well as in his body. I followed his process to see what emerged, and he gets to some feelings of anger and then to the image of a book. He then goes to: "I'm seeing myself as a child and feeling grief and it's a silent grief that I'm contemplating." Kevin then symbolizes a complex felt meaning: "The world is full of grief and—because of that it's not necessarily the right place for a guy like me. But here I am, so." As indicated by his vocal quality and manner of speech, this has a poignant, existential quality. Then he says, "A lot of it has to do with separation from females." This seems pregnant with meaning. So I invite him to enter into this unclear felt sense with: "So try and actually, if you can, enter that grief and let your words come from it. What's it like? Separating from females from I feel."

This is where the session seems to have the most potential of deepening into something significant. When Kevin moves away from his experience into a more analytic reflection on the complexity of his grief and a core conflict he experiences in relationships—a desire to be close and the disappointment of needs not being met—he says, "I feel—it's complicated. The grief is complicated because it hurts to separate but it's not so much fun dealing with them when they're there either. Because they don't give me what I need. And they give me mental complication." He then says it's frustrating dialoguing with them but it's grief "when they're away." Once again his voice conveys a poignancy when he says, "when they're away" and I respond by empathically conjecturing what he must feel: "I feel lonely or alone when they are away but struggle when I'm with you." An alternate response would be to reverse the order of what I said and thereby to leave the leading edge of my response on his loneliness: "I struggle when I'm with you but feel lonely or alone when they are away." He then picks up on the conflictual aspect and responds with: "Yeah, anger, frustration, disagreement." I guide Kevin back to his body to keep him connected to his current experience and continue a focusing process.

Unfinished Business and Deepening the Session

I note that Kevin's relationship with women represents a core issue for him (notice how he says *females,* which probably is a way of keeping his experience at a distance), and although he states a conflict, I see this as part of the broader, more fundamental issues of separation and loss, and difficulty with closeness and distance, that he is dealing with, and so I suggest a dialogue with his mother, which is more dealing with the unresolved feelings about relational closeness than with the conflict. Kevin enters the dialogue with his mother and readily says he is scared of her blowing up.

When people are engaged in a chair dialogue, I am monitoring what they are in contact with and how in contact they are with both themselves and the other. *Contact* here means what is central or figural in their awareness. I am thereby monitoring whether they are engaged in conceptual or emotional processing, that is, are they in their heads or in their emotional bodies, and are they expressing to the imagined other or more looking at an empty chair but speaking to me? So in response to him saying to his mother, "I'm terrified," I check to see what he is experiencing by asking, "What do you feel as you say that now?" Kevin answers, "That on one hand it's better to not say what I think and feel." He laughs and talks about how it's better to keep a secret and thereby to not hurt anyone. This is clearly conceptual and he is not in contact with his experience, so I guide him back to his experience. I then ask him to move to his mother's chair to attempt to heighten the stimulus of his terrifying mother to help stimulate activation of his emotion schemes to actually generate the experience of fear. I am trying to help Kevin get to his core fear, as in my view the best way to change this fear is first to feel the fear and then to transform it by generating an alternate approach emotion, such as anger at violation to undo the withdrawal.

At this point in the session we seem to be getting a little closer to important material, which over time would need to be worked through. When Kevin enacts the mother, he suddenly bursts into an expression of explosive anger representing his mother. However, he is not quite experientially connected to what he is doing; the expression is more deliberate, done with forethought rather than being a spontaneous experience, but it does serve as an action symbol of what she was like. I then guide him toward his current experience and to his memory of what it felt like with: "What happens inside even now as you get that and then what must have happened? What do you feel when you get that?" His reaction is one of pondering the difference between feeling her feeling and his own feeling. He then goes on to express an understanding of his mother's feelings and of her heavy load as a single parent. In a continued effort to guide him to contact his own experience in reaction to being yelled at, I empathically conjecture into what it must have felt like to receive his mother's anger, and he identifies that he felt shock and fear and guilt. I engage in *hot psychoeducation*, that is, teaching when the experience is alive, by saying,

> So somehow you know that some of the work is to try to
> separate out so that your feelings are felt by you, because it is
> what got ingrained, the fear, the dread, but I understand. I think
> you're also saying, but I also am very compassionate to the other
> one, understanding, but somehow I guess you're saying, I mean,
> I'm imagining you know, just—that was very frightening, right?

Kevin acknowledges this, and so again I ask, "So what did you feel? Just go there and at least name it as a beginning," and later, "When you got that yell, what was it like?" He then identifies the shock he felt, and we begin to approach the small traumatic experience of his childhood with his mother. I work with him to differentiate some of this traumatic experience and he symbolizes in awareness with: "A lot of times it was unexpected . . . I mean you didn't hear the footsteps coming . . . " and "I felt shock through my whole body . . . shock and fear and guilt." I evocatively reflect his experience as a small little kid "that he could just get sideswiped, not know it's coming. I'm scared."

Kevin then symbolizes what it was like for him as a small child: "You're angry but you're powerless, so you can't express your anger because if you do, what are the things that are gonna happen?" After reflecting on how difficult it was as a single parent for his mother and developing his narrative of understanding, I move to end the dialogue by asking him, "What do you want to say to her as a child?" and what he needed. He replies, "I think I got what I needed, but I think there were other things added on that—the shock was an extra that I didn't need." I caught that he was forgiving but also beginning to acknowledge that he did need something; I then end by building a bridge to a next session, suggesting a continuation of this work as a possible focus for future sessions.

We see the potential for Kevin to access a transforming emotion of empowering anger, which would help counteract the maladaptive withdrawal emotions of fear of punishment and the shame of humiliation and powerlessness in abuse. He, however, states the anger in the third person, indicating his manner of distancing from his own experience.

At this point he also seems to be in contact with some understanding and compassion for his mother, although this may be a block to accessing his more painful emotions of pain, anger, fear, and shame that in the future would need to be processed and transformed. So at the end of the session, we seem to be getting a little deeper into his experience. We end by focusing on Kevin's need from her as a child as this is a way to help him self-organize as an active agent who is attempting to survive and thrive. Finally, I end by asking him to come back to himself by symbolizing in awareness what he is feeling in the moment, as being clear on where he is will help him be oriented in the present.

My Understanding of Kevin

Kevin clearly was a highly emotionally sensitive man but one who was protected by a type of false self-organization, which kept him more separate from others and distanced from his experience. My sense was that at core he felt both isolated and anxious about being disconnected. He also had concerns about his image and felt vulnerable to identity shame, and his need to manage his experience and his image were governing his interactions with me in this situation.

Having watched the intake, I entered the session assuming that he was carrying this deep grief and pain and that it would be helpful for him to approach and process this pain, rather than avoid dealing with it, by closing it up again as he had done so remarkably in the intake session. In this session, however, he appeared somewhat hyperrational and self-protective and managed his anxiety by adopting a type of in-charge, all-knowing position. My initial experience, which was based on linguistic, paralinguistic, and facial expressions as well as his narrative and style of relating, felt to me as if I were being kept at a distance. As a result, I felt a little more tension in my body, and I responded by becoming more active in trying to have him enter into a more internal manner of processing.

I inferred from observing his processing style that even though he was talking about fairly painful material that seemed to be troubling him, he found it difficult to experience being vulnerable. This is all highly understandable and representative of a first meeting, especially with men, who often find it harder to open up and experience their feelings. So I saw him as a highly sensitive and anxious man and as distancing from his experience, and this left me feeling a little walled out. It seemed like he was at this time more concerned with telling his story and with his self-presentation than with exploring his problems. My sense was that at core, he felt both isolated and anxious about being disconnected and also felt some identity shame and self-esteem concerns.

Shame often is one of the most important aspects of men's inner experience, and men work hard to appear adequate and in control. Part of what makes treating men challenging in EFT is that they generally don't signal their emotional pain as clearly and straightforwardly as women do. However, it is important to recognize that anger and withdrawal are men's "tears." Men thus often find going to therapy to be a potentially shame-based experience, and so they enter with a need to manage their image in some way to deal with their shame anxiety. They feel vulnerable about opening up to another person who may judge or reject them, and they have a deep fear of being out of control and appearing weak. They go to great lengths to maintain control. This appears to be what is happening with Kevin, and so validation and safety are his first needs, and their provision was my main concern.

So my task as a therapist with Kevin was to create an atmosphere of trust and intimacy with a man who doesn't naturally lean easily toward relationships of this kind, especially not with other men. An additional complexity with Kevin is that he clearly is a highly sensitive man who talks the talk of a sensitive man but is still not able to be open to his own vulnerability, at least not with me. Over time, some self-disclosure by me in carefully calibrated doses, acknowledging that I've experienced some of the same struggles and conflicts, may be helpful in producing more openness in him. I will need to respect Kevin's defenses as necessary protections while honoring his intentions of being willing to be in therapy and not putting too much pressure on him to express emotion.

Conclusion

As I have said, future sessions would need to focus on improving the alliance and developing a focus, and only later using more active methods to stimulate Kevin's emotions. The more fragile the personality, the more the relationship in EFT needs to be central, and so initially I would want to form an empathically attuned relationship with him, one in which I understood his life narrative more fully to establish safety for him and provide a space for us to feel more connected to his struggles. This would need to be a longer term therapy in which over time we would come to deal with Kevin's grief and loss and his identity. The issue of how to work with emotions with people who are emotionally avoidant or alexithymic or more conceptual, or with men who may not be comfortable with their emotions, in my view is best addressed this way: One has to develop the right kind of trusting relationship to reduce their anxiety, and one needs to form an alliance to work on their emotions. Then one needs to explicitly help them pay attention to what they feel. All people have emotions, and so eventually one can work with their emotions. It takes more time with some than with others.

There were a number of points at which we approached his core painful and dreaded emotional experience, although we did not quite manage to get to it. I think Kevin found it difficult to let down his protective defences. I sensed that he was not as open to receiving empathy and compassion from me, and I wondered whether this was a function of a male–male interaction that he found uncomfortable, and I felt validated when he commented, in the exit interview, that it was the first time he had been with a male therapist and that he had found it harder to open up with a man. A safe, trusting relationship with a therapist (possibly with a man—because he lost his father) would, in my view, in and of itself be curative and would also facilitate deeper emotional work. In EFT, the deeper work would occur not in enactments in his relationship with me but by the use of imaginal enactments that would address his insecurities more directly with members of his family and in important peer relationships, in the context in which they occurred.

Future Directions

More research on different populations and on cultural adaptations is needed. Studies of the effectiveness of EFT on anxiety disorders are sorely needed, as well as studies on personality disorders and other clusters of difficulties. In addition, more research on EFT's theory of emotional change is needed. Most pressing is evidence on the effectiveness of changing emotion with emotion and of the effects of moving from secondary through primary maladaptive emotion to adaptive emotion by way of need mobilization. Further work is needed on such central therapeutic processes as experiencing, emotional arousal and expression, and therapeutic presence and empathy. Research on training of therapists addressing such questions as the relative merits of personal work and skill training would also be helpful.

A crucial next step is to introduce EFT training into graduate programs and internships. First, the generic relational, and emotion approach and regulation, skills could benefit all trainees. In training programs committed to teaching evidence-based treatments that have emphasized cognitive–behavioral therapy to the exclusion of other approaches, the evidence is now strong enough to recommend that EFT therapies should be required as part of a training program and offered as an important addition to more symptom-focused, coping-skills acquisition approaches.

The development of preventive programs that train people to become more emotional literate is highly needed. This would involve experientially based psychoeducation programs on how to use, manage, and change emotion. Preventive programs for children, adolescents, young adults, parents, teachers, and managers—programs in which they can learn about their emotions, be encouraged to practice attending to their emotions, become more compassionate toward themselves and others, and learn to regulate emotion and reflect and transform emotions—are crucial steps in applying EFT work more broadly.

References

Angus, L. E. & Greenberg, L. S. (2011). *Working with narrative in emotion-focused therapy: Changing stories, healing lives.* Washington, DC: American Psychological Association.

Damasio, A. R. (1994). *Descartes' error: Emotion, reason and the human brain.* New York, NY: Grosset/Putnam.

Damasio, A. R. (1999). *The feeling of what happens: Body and emotion in the making of consciousness.* Fort Worth, TX: Harcourt College.

Davidson, R. (2000). Affective style, psychopathology and resilience: Brain mechanisms and plasticity. *American Psychologist, 5,* 1193–1196.

Elliott, R., Greenberg, L., & Lietaer, G. (2004). Research on experiential psychotherapy. In M. Lambert (Ed.), *Bergin and Garfield's handbook of psychotherapy and behavior change* (pp. 493–539). New York, NY: Wiley.

Elliott, R., Watson, J. E., Goldman, R. N., & Greenberg, L. S. (2004). *Learning emotion-focused therapy: The process-experiential approach to change.* Washington, DC: American Psychological Association. doi:10.1037/10725-000

Ellison, J., Greenberg, L., Goldman, R. N., & Angus, L. (2009). *Maintenance of gains following experiential therapies for depression, 77,* 103–112.

Frijda, N. H. (1986). *The emotions.* Cambridge, England: Cambridge University Press.

Geller, S. M., & Greenberg, L. S. (2012). *Therapeutic presence: A mindful approach to effective therapy.* Washington, DC: American Psychological Association.

Gendlin, E. T. (1996). *Focusing-oriented psychotherapy: A manual of the experiential method.* New York, NY: Guilford Press.

Goldman, R., & Greenberg, L. (in press). *Case formulation in emotion-focused therapy.* New York, NY: Guilford Press.

Goldman, R. N., Greenberg, L. S., & Angus, L. (2006). The effects of adding emotion-focused interventions to the client-centered relationship conditions in the treatment of depression. *Psychotherapy Research, 16,* 537–549. doi:10.1080/10503300600589456

Goldman, R. N., Greenberg, L. S., & Pos, A. E. (2005). Depth of emotional experience and outcome. *Psychotherapy Research, 15,* 248–260. doi:10.1080/10503300512331385188

Greenberg, L. (1984). Task analysis of intrapersonal conflict resolution. In L. Rice & L. Greenberg (Eds.), *Patterns of change: Intensive analysis of psychotherapy* (pp. 67–123). New York, NY: Guilford Press.

Greenberg, L. (1986). Change process research [Special issue]. *Journal of Consulting and Clinical Psychology, 54,* 4–9.

Greenberg, L., & Angus, L. (2004). The contributions of emotion processes to narrative change in psychotherapy: A dialectical constructivist approach. In L. Angus & J. McLeod (Eds.), *Handbook of narrative psychotherapy: Practice, theory, and research* (pp. 330–349). Thousand Oaks, CA: Sage. doi:10.4135/9781412973496.d25

Greenberg, L., & Elliott, R. (1997). Varieties of emotional expression. In A. Bohart & L. Greenberg (Eds.), *Empathy reconsidered: New directions in theory research and practice* (pp. 209–231). Washington, DC: American Psychological Association.

Greenberg, L., & Goldman, R. (2007). Case formulation in emotion-focused therapy. In T. Ells (Ed.), *Handbook of psychotherapy case formulation* (pp. 379–412). New York, NY: Guilford Press.

Greenberg, L., & Pascual-Leone, J. (2001). A dialectical constructivist view of the creation of personal meaning. *Journal of Constructivist Psychology, 14,* 165–186. doi:10.1080/10720530151143539

Greenberg, L., Rice, L., & Elliott, R. (1993). *Facilitating emotional change.* New York, NY: Guilford Press.

Greenberg, L., Warwar, N., & Malcolm, W. (2010). Emotion-focused couples therapy and the facilitation of forgiveness. *Journal of Marital and Family Therapy, 36,* 28–42. doi:10.1111/j.1752-0606.2009.00185.x

Greenberg, L., & Watson, J. (1998). Experiential therapy of depression: Differential effects of client-centered relationship conditions and process experiential interventions. *Psychotherapy Research, 8,* 210–224.

Greenberg, L. S. (2002). *Emotion-focused therapy: Coaching clients to work through their feelings.* Washington, DC: American Psychological Association. doi:10.1037/10447-000

Greenberg, L. S. (2011). *Emotion-focused therapy.* Washington, DC: American Psychological Association.

Greenberg, L. S., & Malcolm, W. (2002). Resolving unfinished business: Relating process to outcome. *Journal of Consulting and Clinical Psychology, 70,* 406–416. doi:10.1037/0022-006X.70.2.406

Greenberg, L. S., & Paivio, S. C. (1997). *Working with emotions in psychotherapy.* New York, NY: Guilford Press.

Greenberg, L. S., & Pascual-Leone, J. (1995). A dialectical constructivist approach to experiential change. In R. A. Neimeyer & M. J. Mahoney (Eds.), *Constructivism in psychotherapy* (pp. 169–191). Washington, DC: American Psychological Association. doi:10.1037/10170-008

Greenberg, L. S., & Pascual-Leone, J. (1997). Emotion in the creation of personal meaning. In M. J. Power & C. R. Brewin (Eds.), *The transformation of meaning in psychological therapies: Integrating theory and practice* (pp. 157–173). Hoboken, NJ: Wiley.

Greenberg, L. S., & Safran, J. D. (1987). *Emotion in psychotherapy: Affect, cognition, and the process of change.* New York, NY: Guilford Press.

Greenberg, L. S., Warwar, S. H., & Malcolm, W. M. (2008). Differential effects of emotion-focused therapy and psychoeducation in facilitating forgiveness and letting go of emotional injuries. *Journal of Counseling Psychology, 55,* 185–196. doi:10.1037/0022-0167.55.2.185

Greenberg, L. S., & Watson, J. C. (2006). *Emotion-focused therapy for depression.* Washington, DC: American Psychological Association. doi:10.1037/11286-000

Greenberg, L. S., & Webster, M. C. (1982). Resolving decisional conflict by Gestalt two-chair dialogue: Relating process to outcome. *Journal of Counseling Psychology, 29,* 468–477.

Hermann, I., & Greenberg, L. (2008). Emotion types and sequences in emotion-focused therapy. *European Psychotherapy, 7,* 42–60.

Hermann, I., Greenberg, L., & Auzra, L. (2011, June). *Emotion sequences.* Panel presented at the International Meeting of the Society for Psychotherapy Research, Berne, Switzerland.

Johnson, S. M., Hunsley, J., Greenberg, L., & Schindler, D. (1999). Emotionally focused couples therapy: Status and challenges. *Clinical Psychology: Science and Practice, 6,* 67–79.

Nadel, L., & Bohbot, V. (2001). Consolidation of memory. *Hippocampus, 11,* 56–60. doi:10.1002/1098-1063(2001)11:1<56::AID-HIPO1020>3.0.CO;2-O

Nader, K., Schafe, G. E., & LeDoux, J. E. (2000). The labile nature of consolidation theory. *Nature Reviews Neuroscience, 1,* 216–219. doi:10.1038/35044580

Paivio, S. C., & Greenberg, L. S. (1995). Resolving "unfinished business": Efficacy of experiential therapy using empty-chair dialogue. *Journal of Consulting and Clinical Psychology, 63,* 419–425. doi:10.1037/0022-006X.63.3.419

Paivio, S. C., & Nieuwenhuis, J. A. (2001). Efficacy of emotion focused therapy for adult survivors of child abuse: A preliminary study. *Journal of Traumatic Stress, 14,* 115–133. doi:10.1023/A:1007891716593

Paivio, S., & Pascual-Leone, A. (2010). *Emotion-focused therapy for complex trauma: An integrative approach.* Washington, DC: American Psychological Association.

Pascual-Leone, A., & Greenberg, L. (2007). Emotional processing in experiential therapy: Why "the only way out is through." *Journal of Consulting and Clinical Psychology, 75,* 875–887. doi:10.1037/0022-006X.75.6.875

Pennebaker, J. W. (Ed.). (1995). *Emotion, disclosure, and health.* Washington, DC: American Psychological Association. doi:10.1037/10182-000

Rice, L., & Greenberg, L. (Eds.). (1984). *Patterns of change: An intensive analysis of psychotherapeutic process.* New York, NY: Guilford Press.

Rice, L. N. (1974). The evocative function of the therapist. In D. Wexler & L. N. Rice (Eds.), *Innovations in client-centered therapy* (pp. 289–311). New York, NY: Wiley.

Sicoli, L. (2005). *Development and verification of a model of resolving hopelessness in process-experiential therapy of depression.* Unpublished doctoral dissertation, York University, Toronto, Ontario, Canada.

Stern, D. (1985). *The interpersonal world of the infant.* New York, NY: Basic Books.

Watson, J. C., Gordon, L. B., Stermac, L., Kalogerakos, F., & Steckley, P. (2003). Comparing the effectiveness of process-experiential cognitive–behavioral psychotherapy in the treatment of depression. *Journal of Consulting and Clinical Psychology, 71,* 773–781. doi:10.1037/0022-006X.71.4.773

Whelton, W., & Greenberg, L. (2005). Emotion in self-criticism. *Personality and Individual Differences, 38,* 1583–1595.

Nancy McWilliams

Psychodynamic Therapy

3

Compressing more than a century of psychodynamic[1] theory and practice into a short summary is a daunting project, especially at a time when many students of therapy have had scant exposure to, or have been given misinformation about, analytic ideas. Inasmuch as psychoanalysis provided the soil from which most other therapies grew, and was the background against which they originally contrasted themselves, I hope diverse readers will be interested in this synopsis of the evolution of the psychodynamic therapies and the applicability of psychoanalytic ideas to clinical challenges.

Because contemporary analytic thinking can be most easily comprehended in historical context, I begin with a

---

[1]Despite a tendency among some psychologists to make distinctions between "psychoanalytic" and "psychodynamic," the former implying a more classical and extensive type of treatment, I have followed Freud's more embracing use of the term "psychoanalytic," using it interchangeably with "psychodynamic" and simply "analytic."

I am grateful to Kerry Gordon, William MacGillivray, Dolores Morris, Sherwood Waldron, and the members of my consultation groups for their helpful comments on this chapter.
http://dx.doi.org/10.1037/14253-003
Exploring Three Approaches to Psychotherapy, by L. S. Greenberg, N. McWilliams, and A. Wenzel

sympathetic summary of the ideas of Sigmund Freud. But I want to emphasize that despite its debt to him, current psychodynamic thinking cannot be equated with early Freudian notions. The mischaracterization of psychoanalysis as an orthodoxy of Freud worship has deterred many clinicians from considering what may be useful in the psychoanalytic tradition. In the following, I italicize what I see as major and enduring analytic concepts and put dated, colloquial, and ironic terms in quotes.

Theoretical Foundations of the Psychodynamic Therapies

"Psychoanalytic theory" is often construed as one overall body of knowledge, but in fact that theory has constituted an evolving—and somewhat competing—array of theories arising from varying philosophical orientations, shared clinical experience, disciplined naturalistic observation, and scientific research. Even "Freudian theory" is not monolithic; Freud periodically evaluated his ideas and replaced them with models that he felt made better sense of clinical data. Although I cannot cover the whole, vast territory of changing and competing psychoanalytic theories, here are the most influential overall paradigms, in historical order.

EARLY FREUDIAN THEORY AND PRACTICE: DRIVE AND CONFLICT

Psychoanalytic efforts to understand and ameliorate psychopathology began with Freud's work in the late 19th century (Gay, 1988) with people diagnosed with severe "neuroses." At that time, this term connoted all disabling psychopathologies that were not psychotic. The patients who originally captured Freud's attention suffered from what we would now term posttraumatic, borderline, and somatoform disorders. In his era, such problems—ailments like altered states of consciousness, psychogenic loss of body functions, and epileptiform seizures without known physical cause—were labeled "hysterical." Following the charismatic Jean Charcot, Freud first used hypnosis to relieve such symptoms (Breuer & Freud, 1893–1895/1955). Soon, however, influenced by a gifted patient who asked simply to report her stream of consciousness (Freud, 1895/1955), he began valuing *free association,* urging his clients to say whatever came to their minds, no matter how socially inappropriate, irrational, or embarrassing. Thus was born the "talking cure."

The disclosures of Freud's early patients included stories of molestation and incest, leading him to conclude that hysterical syndromes express memories of childhood "seduction" that have been kept out of awareness but are being expressed symbolically by *conversion* into physical illness (Freud, 1894/1962b). He applied concepts from the physics of his day to these narratives, labeling as *repression* the process by which disturbing memories are made unconscious (Freud, 1896/1962a). The idea that there are automatic means of keeping upsetting experiences out of awareness was the germ of the more inclusive concept of *defenses*, that is, unconscious ways we protect ourselves from unbearable thoughts, feelings, and sensations. Freud noted that when his patients would recall painful memories *with their emotional intensity*, their symptoms would diminish. Early psychoanalytic therapy (e.g., Breuer & Freud, 1893–1895/1955) thus emphasized both remembering and emotional expression ("catharsis" or "abreaction").

Soon, Freud ran into problems similar to those encountered a century later by therapists working with trauma victims. For example, some "memories" are not accurate recollections but constructions, affected by complex motives such as trying to say what the doctor wants to hear or simply trying to make sense of symptoms with no known etiology. And remembering and abreacting turned out to be less permanently therapeutic than Freud had hoped. He revised his theory (Freud, 1898/1962c)—never denying that many people with hysterical afflictions have been sexually abused, but stressing the drives, wishes, fantasies, and conflicting feelings that his patients also revealed. Finding similar motives in himself, he concluded that they were universal and looked for them in the other "neuroses" (obsessions, compulsions, phobias, and nonpsychotic depressions). From his patients' free associations, he inferred that many of their symptoms were expressing two contradictory internal attitudes, one or both of which were unconscious— for example, wishes for sexual gratification along with moral rejection of such wishes. Adopting the concept of "dynamism" from physicists such as Helmholtz and Fechner, he began referring to the *dynamic unconscious*, the source of the term *psychodynamic*.

As his patients traced their problems to their early years, Freud began speculating that neuroses are rooted in normal childhood concerns with successive body-centered themes. As a neurologist infused with the Enlightenment faith in science, he drew his models from biology rather than philosophy, the home discipline of prior psychological theory (Sulloway, 1992). He posited that if one's temperament and/or upbringing make it hard to master a normal maturational challenge, one develops an unconscious "fixation" on that stage. He connected depression with the "oral" preoccupations of the child's earliest months, obsessions and compulsions with the "anal" or toilet-mastery issues that peak around age 2 years, phobias with anxieties over gender differences that he saw as appearing around age 3 years (the "phallic" phase, in Freud's male-centered language), and hysteria with the "oedipal" issues of the next couple of years (Freud, 1905/1953b).

Freud was fascinated with the fantasies of 3- to 6-year-old children about competing with one caregiver to win the other, while fearing retaliation for such ideas. Because of its similar themes, he named that phase after the ancient Greek story of Oedipus. The emphasis he eventually put on the oedipal stage, equating its navigation with overall mental health (see A. Freud, 1963), reflects the fact that the capacity to have such fantasies evidences a critical movement beyond egocentrism: The preschooler can imagine relationships between others that are not about oneself. In contemporary terms, he or she has begun to *mentalize* the separate minds of others (Fonagy & Target, 1996). Freud's successors referred to *preoedipal* versus *oedipal* psychologies, the latter seen as healthier. Because it focused on children's drives and their conflicts with realistic and moral limitation, Freud's early thinking came to be called *drive theory* or *drive-conflict theory*.

In daily meetings with his patients, Freud was soon struck with how the therapeutic relationship became suffused with issues from their childhoods. Despite his efforts to be strictly professional, some fell in love with him; others competed or deferred anxiously. Their associations suggested they were experiencing him as if he were an important childhood figure. Initially viewing this *transference* from past to present as a distraction, he eventually came to appreciate its therapeutic potential: If one is given the emotional clout of a parent and is cast in a recurring childhood drama, perhaps one can make the old story come out differently. *Analyzing the transference* became a key feature of analytic treatment (Freud, 1911–1915/1953a). Freud viewed the type of therapy now referred to as *classical psychoanalysis* as suitable only for the clients for whom he had developed it: adults with neuroses (rather than, say, psychoses or addictions or psychopathic personalities). Yet he hoped that what he had learned about unconscious motivation, repetition, conflict, and defense could be adapted to helping a wider range of people.

Freud was an unrepentant generalizer (see Garcia, 1991). If he inferred a dynamic in a patient or in himself, he assumed it existed in everyone. Although problematic, his generalizing set an inclusive, egalitarian tone. Psychoanalysis did not posit a qualitative difference between healthy and sick, normal and abnormal. Analysts see psychological problems as on a continuum, as a matter of degree, as variant aspects and expressions of universal human struggles. Although contemporary analytic therapies have diverged considerably from their

Freudian base, the core ingredients in Freud's early work remain present in one form or another in almost all present-day psychodynamic therapies: an appreciation of dynamic unconscious processes, the assumption of a valence (direction or tilt) to all mental life, a developmental viewpoint, a sense of the ubiquity of conflict and defense, and an attention to transferential processes (Pincus, 2006).

THE EGO PSYCHOLOGY ERA

From roughly the 1930s on, North American analysts developed an approach that became known as *ego psychology*. It drew on Freud's (1923/1961) *structural model,* in which the mind is conceived as an arena of competing demands from the *id* (primitive impulse), *ego* (sense of "I"), and *superego* (conscience and personal ideals). The ego was portrayed as mediating between id, superego, and reality, using both conscious coping skills and unconscious *defenses* such as repression, denial, projection, and displacement. Pathology was understood in terms of defenses that had been adaptive in childhood but that were primitive, inflexible, or ineffectual in later life. Health was equated with *ego strength,* the ability to cope realistically, flexibly, and adaptively with life's challenges (Hartmann, 1958).

Consistent with Freud's Enlightenment-era rationalism, ego psychologists tried to make clients aware of their defenses so that they could consciously choose more adequate ways to cope. To do this, they tried to foster a solid *working alliance* (Greenson, 1967), in which the client experiences the analyst as a warm collaborator. As in any situation that engenders anxiety, the person's defensive patterns would appear in the therapeutic relationship in the form of *resistances* (obstacles to free expression and emotional authenticity). The analyst would comment on the resistances in an effort to interfere with their automatic deployment so that the patient could consider other means of handling anxiety and other painful emotions (Brenner, 1976).

Instead of urging patients to remember, or teaching them about their assumed unconscious conflicts, ego-psychological analysts noted defenses as they appeared as resistances in the therapeutic hour (Fenichel, 1941). Rather than speculating, for example, about a person's probable unconscious childhood hostility, the analyst might remark, "I notice that every time you get close to any negative feelings toward me, you abruptly change the subject. What comes to mind about that?" In an effort to allow transferences to elaborate themselves freely and fully, analysts tried to take a position of *neutrality* (i.e., refraining from advising or exhorting or disclosing their own feelings) and *abstinence* (i.e., not exploiting the patient in any way and not gratifying wishes that could be more usefully understood rather than acted on). *Interpretation* was idealized as the analyst's main therapeutic activity, and *insight* was assumed to be the primary agent of change.[2]

This *exploratory* approach was considered appropriate for people with neurotic conflicts and personality disorders of the hysterical, obsessive–compulsive, phobic, and depressive types (Blanck & Blanck, 1974; Eissler, 1953; Waelder, 1960). For patients with "ego weakness," such as those with psychotic tendencies, *supportive therapy* was considered the treatment of choice. Not well defined until relatively recently (Pinsker, 1997; Rockland, 1992), supportive therapy involved efforts to build ego strength and resilience by such means as active emotional support, educative interventions, and emphasis on the probable outcomes of alternative courses of action. A significant, enduring contribution of ego psychology has been its emphasis on assessing underlying psychic structure before choosing a treatment approach (see Sugarman, 2007).

During and since the ego psychology era, analytically oriented researchers have studied defenses, ego strength, developmental challenges, individual differences, and related topics, creating an extensive empirical literature (e.g., Bellak & Goldsmith, 1984; Cramer, 2006; Fisher & Greenberg, 1985, 1996; Masling, 1986; Vaillant, 1992). Yet the relative isolation of psychoanalytic training institutes from most academic settings during the reign of the ego psychologists, along with the arrogant beliefs of many in the (then) largely medical psychoanalytic community that only physicians could treat psychological problems and that the clinical wisdom of doctors did not need further empirical validation, distanced analysts from researchers. Such provincialism generated a backlash, characterized by inattention to subsequent empirical work that supports analytic concepts and the widespread misperception that their scientific status is dubious (see Eagle, 2010; Leichsenring & Rabung, 2008; Shedler, 2010; Westen, 1998).

Most analysts today have rejected sterile versions of ego-psychological models and techniques. Popular texts on psychoanalysis and psychoanalytic therapies (e.g., Gabbard, 2010) note the pluralism of the field and ground their clinical advice in recent research. In response to developments in science, psychology, and philosophy, post-Freudian analysts have continually modified their theories and practices to address the needs of different client populations, cultural surrounds, and pressures

---

[2]Interestingly, the phrases "blank screen" and "blank slate" do not occur in the writings of Freud. Although it is true that he urged analysts to be disciplined and not to act out with their patients, his own style was warm and personal (Lohser & Newton, 1996). The idea that the analyst should be as "blank" as possible seems to have been a construction of American ego psychologists, who selectively seized on Freud's warnings against therapeutic overinvolvement and elevated them to a preeminent rule. Wallerstein (1998) suggested that the idea of a sterile technique became popular in response to anxieties that psychoanalysis would be seen as "wild" or unscientific.

on practice. Having isolated themselves in free-standing institutes and practitioner communities, however, they have not effectively communicated with their university colleagues, some of whom consequently maintain early 20th-century stereotypes of analytic therapy.

OBJECT RELATIONS THEORY AND INTERPERSONAL PSYCHOANALYSIS

By the 1950s, analysts such as Fairbairn, Klein, and Winnicott were focusing on *internalized relationships* and their affective themes (Guntrip, 1971; Hughes, 1989). In the United Kingdom, in line with Freud's formulation of love and aggression as having a source, aim, and *object* (the object usually being a person), this body of work was called *object relations theory*. In the United States, a parallel movement led by Sullivan and his colleagues (see Mitchell & Black, 1995) called itself *interpersonal psychoanalysis*. This shift reflected, among other influences, therapists' experiences with children, psychotic patients, and people whose mental lives were dominated by dynamics other than those common in neurosis, such as paranoid, psychopathic, narcissistic, addicted, and severely traumatized individuals (Fromm-Reichmann, 1950). As object-relations and interpersonal communities evolved, they stimulated, and were subsequently influenced by, advances in research, especially investigations of attachment and separation such as those by Mahler and Bowlby (see Blatt & Levy, 2003).

To object-relational and interpersonal analysts, the Freudian focus on drive, conflict, and defense seemed less relevant to their clients' problems than core relationship issues (Guntrip, 1971). They found themselves accounting for pathology by reference to individuals' childhood contexts rather than fixation at a particular developmental phase. Stressing basic *security operations* and *sense of self* more than issues of gratification and frustration, they were more apt, for example, to explain obsessive perfectionism in terms of experience with a controlling parent than in terms of fixation at the anal stage. The two explanations are not mutually exclusive, but they have different implications for the focus of comments to patients (e.g., "You want to make a mess, but you're afraid to let yourself go" vs. "You're terrified of your mother's criticism if you're not perfectly neat").

One group of patients whom analysts found easier to understand from an object-relations perspective included those we eventually called *borderline*. This term reflected a clinical consensus that some people seem psychologically to inhabit the border between neurosis and psychosis. They show a "stable instability" (Grinker, Werble, & Drye, 1968), lack a cohesive sense of identity, suffer intense and dysregulated affect, and use primitive defenses such as *splitting* (seeing things as all good or all bad), yet they are grounded in reality and hence lack hallucinations, delusions, and thought disorders (Kernberg, 1975). They have also been seen as stuck at the border between Klein's (1952) *paranoid-schizoid* and *depressive positions* (two hypothesized basic, universal psychological orientations, the former absolutist and self-referential, the latter more nuanced and appreciative of others' separateness).

Clients in this borderline group felt controlled and engulfed in their relationships but abandoned and desperate when alone (Masterson, 1976). They reacted to treatment with intense transferences that they could not see *as* transferences (insisting, for example, "It's my bad luck to get a therapist exactly like my mother!"). Analysts noted powerful reactions (*countertransferences*) to them. Object relations theories helped us to maintain empathy with, and to be a steadying presence for, people who might treat us as a benevolent rescuer one day and an evil persecutor the next.

Eventually, several specific psychoanalytic therapies were developed to address the needs of this group (e.g., the mentalization-based therapy of Peter Fonagy and his colleagues, the transference-focused psychotherapy of Otto Kernberg and his colleagues, and the psychodynamic/interpersonal therapy of Russell Meares), all of which drew on object-relations concepts (see Bateman & Fonagy, 2004). Although differing in their respective emphases, they all involve setting clear boundaries, confronting self-destructive behaviors, tolerating affect storms, fostering the capacity for reflecting on the self, and appreciating the separate subjective states of others.[3]

From an object-relations perspective, issues of basic security, closeness, and sense of agency are more primary than issues of drive satisfaction. Love is the original human condition (Balint, 1968), and it is more important to understand attachment than sexual and aggressive wishes and conflicts. Implications for therapy include noticing what earlier relationships the patient has internalized or "introjected." A therapist influenced by object relations theory would be more likely to ask a self-attacking client, "Whose critical voice is that?" than to comment on superego versus id demands.

THE SELF PSYCHOLOGY MOVEMENT

By the 1970s, as extended families and traditional communities splintered, social and technological change accelerated, and mobility increased, Western analysts were seeing more and more nonpsychotic

---

[3]Notwithstanding its having been derived mostly from cognitive–behavioral sources, it is interesting that Linehan's (1993) dialectical behavior therapy also shares these overall features.

clients who suffered from feelings of emptiness, low self-esteem (often coexisting with grandiose claims or ambitions), and confusion about their identity and direction. Their psychology was hard to represent in terms of either conflict/defense or internalized love objects: What seemed broken or stunted was their basic sense of self. Incapable of valuing themselves reliably, they craved validation from outside. They tended to treat others with either *idealization* (compensating for their self-esteem deficits by feeling attached to putatively superior beings) or *devaluation* (offsetting low self-esteem by feeling superior to others). Their histories suggested that caregivers had used them as *narcissistic extensions,* whose role was to compensate for the parent's failed ambitions and unfulfilled self-esteem needs. Not having felt loved with their realistic strengths and weaknesses, they seemed unable to love others as they are.

Freud (1914/1957) had considered such patients untreatable. They resist making a therapeutic alliance, appear not to have analyzable transferences, and may experience interpretation as judgmental or irrelevant or both. There gradually arose a rich clinical and empirical literature on *narcissism,* the psychoanalytic term for these deficient self-states and compensatory attitudes. Kernberg (e.g., 1975), blending ego psychology and object relations theories, advocated interpreting their defensive devaluation and underlying envy. Kohut (1971, 1978) construed their responses to the therapist as *self-object transferences* that require acceptance, not interpretation, and argued that they need a reparative experience of *empathic attunement.* Most analytic therapists combine these ideas in their work with people with pervasive self-esteem deficits.

Kohut's ideas inspired the *self psychology* movement. His attention to empathy, nonjudgmental acceptance, and authenticity echoes the ideas of Rogers (1951), with the key addition that, given the predictable repetition of childhood shame experiences in the analytic relationship, the therapist will inevitably hurt the client's feelings and must repair such ruptures nondefensively. Progress occurs as the client develops a *transmuting internalization:* The therapist's empathic voice is slowly taken in until it is a reliable part of the patient's inner world. Self psychologists theorized needs to feel valued, and the shame that went with those needs (especially when unmet), more than the guilt dynamics that analysts had previously emphasized. (Freud's focus on guilt and relative neglect of shame is a good example of his universalizing issues that were central to his conscious understanding of himself, while overlooking dynamics that were less in his awareness.)

By the 1970s, analysts were increasingly sensitive to dynamics that characterize more collectivist, shame-oriented cultures with different organizations of self-experience (Roland, 1996, 2003). Self psychology moved analysis away from the Western tendency to see individuals as having isolated minds and purely individual consciences (Atwood & Stolorow, 1993). As analysts became more sensitized to self-esteem issues, we began seeing the applicability of a self-psychological orientation to all clients. Kohut and subsequent self psychologists put empathy in the foreground rather than the background of healing and ushered in an era of greater flexibility in practice. They have urged us to choose clinical interventions not on the basis of whether they conform to a standard technique but according to whether they will be experienced as empathically attuned.

Because their theories privilege developmental deficit over unconscious conflict, therapists from this orientation have framed the therapist's role as addressing unmet maturational needs sensitively rather than bringing conflicts into consciousness (Lichtenberg, Lachmann, & Fosshage, 1992). For example, in the face of a client's provocative behavior, a self psychological therapist would try to tune into the pain behind it, understand its adaptive function, and find a way to express an empathic response to that pain rather than interpreting the client's actions in terms of unconscious aggressive drives and defenses against them.

THE INTERSUBJECTIVE AND RELATIONAL MOVEMENTS

Despite their appreciation of the fact that the analyst as well as the patient has an unconscious mental life, the foregoing theories assume that the well-analyzed therapist can be a relatively objective, dispassionate observer. Contemporary analysts have challenged the concept of neutrality, even as an ideal (Stolorow & Atwood, 1997), arguing that the analyst's subjectivity is constantly affecting, and being affected by, the unconscious dynamics of *both* parties to the therapy (see Wachtel, 2007). In this view, transference is not a distortion, something projected on to a blank-screen therapist, but instead is a *co-construction*, reflecting the analyst's and patient's *intersubjectivity*.

Influenced by infant research, affective neuroscience, postmodern philosophy, systems theories, Eastern spiritual traditions, relationally inclined forebears, and personal frustrations with rigidly "neutral" analysts, relational thinkers have accomplished a significant paradigm shift, generally referred to as the *relational turn* in psychoanalysis (Aron, 1996; Hoffman, 1998; Mitchell, 2000). Partly in response to research and clinical experience with traumatized clients (Bromberg, 1998; Davies & Frawley, 1993; Herman, 1992; Howell, 2005; D. B. Stern, 1997), most relational analysts consider *dissociation* rather than repression to be the process that keeps painful mental contents at bay. They may reject Freud's surface-to-depth images of psychological phenomena (defense covering anxiety, anxiety covering conflict over drives) and imagine instead the simultaneous coexistence of conscious mental life and a range of *self-states,* some of which may be dissociated.

Relational analysts characterize the therapy relationship as mutual despite its asymmetricality (Aron, 1996). Skeptical of claims of clinical or scientific detachment, they assume they will find themselves participating in *enactments* (behavioral repetitions of themes from the client's life that evoke responsive themes in them). The therapist's job is to perceive such enacted patterns, name them, and reflect on their meanings and implications. Instead of "interpreting the transference" ("You're reacting as if I'm your critical father"), relational analysts may note mutual enactments ("You and I seem to be relating to each other like a critical father and a criticized child"). If they believe that such disclosures will deepen the work, they may judiciously share their own emotional reactions. Important relational themes that have been elaborated include reducing unconscious polarities of "doer and done-to" (Benjamin, 1995) that organize much psychological experience and the necessity for both patient and therapist to tolerate "standing in the spaces" (Bromberg, 1998) between different self-states rather than dissociating painful or hated aspects of self.

Many schools of psychoanalytic thought have thus evolved in response to different clinical challenges. I have grouped them along general lines of emphasis (cf. Pine, 1990), but they can also be described in terms of the influence of one or more founding analysts (e.g., Carl Jung, Karen Horney, Melanie Klein, Jacques Lacan, James Masterson, Harold Sampson and Joseph Weiss, Hyman Spotnitz, Harry Stack Sullivan, the Stone Center). As theory and practice have evolved, each orientation has highlighted a significant dimension of human experience and a therapeutic practice directed toward that dimension. Most contemporary analytic therapists draw flexibly from these approaches in response to the distinct psychological needs of each patient.

SHORT-TERM AND FOCUSED PSYCHOANALYTIC THERAPIES

The architects of most psychoanalytic theories have assumed that the therapist is the patient's employee and can be retained for as long as both patient and therapist see fit. Freud saw most people for weeks or months rather than years; it was later analysts who found that to make lasting changes, most of us require more time. Still, there have been many attempts to streamline therapy (see Bellak, Abrams, & Ackermann-Engel, 1991; Messer & Warren, 1995), starting with Karl Abraham's effort to bring brief treatments to working-class patients at the Berlin Polyclinic in the early 1900s—a movement that Freud enthusiastically supported (Danto, 2007). As treatment has lost its stigma and attracted more clients, market forces and other limiting factors have exerted pressures to create short-term and delimited analytic therapies, of which many have been developed.

Psychoanalytic ideas have influenced a range of treatments, from exploratory to supportive, from open-ended to time limited, with highly diverse patients and problems. Analytic therapists treating specific populations (e.g., infants; children; couples; trauma victims; substance abusers; sufferers of psychoses; individuals in sexual, religious, or ethnic minorities) have designed many approaches for their particular clienteles. Such treatments are too numerous to review here, but I mention them to make the point that what makes a therapy psychodynamic is not a specific population or technique. Rather, it is whether there is attention to *unconscious processes, especially as they are manifested and potentially influenced in the relationship with the therapist.*

RESEARCH CONTRIBUTIONS TO, AND SUPPORT FOR, PSYCHOANALYTIC THERAPIES

Psychoanalytic therapies tend to be complex, open-ended, and individualized, making them hard to investigate via randomized controlled trials. Historically, as I have noted, analysts have been uncertain about whether good research on their nuanced art is necessary or even possible. Now beset by demands for evidence of effectiveness, however, most of us have come to value research, including randomized controlled trials of structured analytic treatments. A literature is emerging on evidence-based psychodynamic therapy (e.g., Summers & Barber, 2010; Weiner & Bornstein, 2009).

Four general areas lend empirical support to psychodynamic approaches. First, several meta-analyses have found that *relationship variables* account for more variance in therapy outcome than any other factor, including type of treatment (Ackerman & Hilsenroth, 2003; Norcross, 2002; Shedler, 2010; Wampold, 2001, 2010). The *quality of the therapeutic alliance* seems particularly critical to outcome (Safran & Muran, 2000). Such meta-analyses vindicate the psychoanalytic emphasis on growth within relationship. From Freud's discovery of transference, through the ego psychology emphasis on the therapeutic alliance, to object-relational and self-psychological concerns with attachment, to the current relational focus on intersubjectivity and mutuality, the analytic tradition has consistently emphasized and explicated emotionally meaningful interpersonal connection—it is the bright red thread that runs through all analytic schools of thought.

Second, these meta-analyses demonstrate that individual differences correlate with outcome. Evidence for the impact of personality variables on the results of therapy confirms the wisdom of the traditional analytic emphasis on such factors. Moreover, such findings suggest that the research paradigm of trying to find specific treatments for discrete disorders listed in the *Diagnostic and Statistical Manual of Mental Disorders* (*DSM*) while ignoring personality-based disparities among those who suffer them, is an insufficient approach to psychotherapy research (Blatt & Zuroff, 2005).

Third, outcome research on psychoanalysis and psychoanalytic treatments attests to their helpfulness. Some studies, especially the oldest, have serious methodological flaws (see McWilliams & Weinberger, 2003), but the overall take-away message, especially of recent meta-analyses, is that (a) psychoanalytic therapy is helpful; (b) the longer people continue in it, the more helpful it is; and (c) improvement in overall mental functioning goes on after analytic treatments are terminated (Abbass, Hancock, Henderson, & Kisely, 2006; Blomberg, Lazar, & Sandell, 2001; Doidge, 1997; Fonagy, 2006; Galatzer-Levy, Bachrach, Skolnikoff, & Waldron, 2000; Leichsenring, 2006; Leichsenring & Leibing, 2003; Leichsenring & Rabung, 2008; Sandell et al., 2000; Westen, Novotny, & Thompson-Brenner, 2004). Meticulously designed randomized controlled trials of specific analytic therapies have been conducted in recent years (e.g., Clarkin, Levy, Lenzenweger, & Kernberg, 2007; Levy et al., 2006; Milrod et al., 2007), with positive results, and encouraging follow-up data are beginning to appear.

Finally, there are extensive empirical literatures on attachment, defense, emotion, personality, and other areas relevant to analytic theory and treatment that support the models and inferences of analytic therapists. Contemporary neuroscientists (e.g., Damasio, 1999; Panksepp, 2004; Panksepp & Biven, 2012; Solms & Turnbull, 2002) can now describe in physical and chemical terms many of the unconscious processes for which our predecessors could only formulate hypothetical structures and metaphors. Schore's (2003) research on right-brain-to-right-brain communication has exposed the neural basis of nonverbal transference and countertransference, and considerable research shows that all psychotherapies cause changes in the brain (Karlsson, 2011).

Weiss and Sampson (see Silberschatz, 2005) have provided empirical support for the idiopathic nature of effective therapy. Their data have suggested that each client approaches treatment hoping to disconfirm idiosyncratic, unconscious *pathogenic beliefs*. As the relationship with the therapist does so, the person improves. Such findings are consistent with the ideas of cognitive therapists, but analysts also emphasize the emotional aspects of internal, unconscious schemas. Krause's research on facial affect in therapists and patients (e.g., Merten, Anstadt, Ullrich, Krause, & Buchheim, 1996) has demonstrated similar phenomena at the level of nonverbal affect transmission.

In other examinations of individuality, Blatt (e.g., 2008) has done extensive research on the therapeutic implications of whether one is oriented more toward self-definition or more toward communality. A huge body of empirical work (see Holmes, 2009; Mikulincer & Shaver, 2007; Wallin, 2007) has suggested that individuals with different attachment styles have different therapeutic needs. Because of their experience with how divergently different patients can experience the same externally observable symptoms, analytic practitioners have been more interested in these kinds of research than in randomized controlled trials of specific treatments for discrete *DSM*-defined disorders.

I should add that analysts have followed scientific discoveries that have disproved some psychoanalytic ideas. We now know, for example, that the hippocampus, which manages episodic memory, may be closed down by the glucocorticoids secreted during trauma (Solms & Turnbull, 2002). This explains why some patients with abuse histories cannot remember their abuse: Their episodic memories were not *repressed;* instead, they were never laid down. Victims of childhood trauma may generate what Freud called "screen memories" ("false memories" in the language of later critics) to account for the semantic, procedural, and emotional memories that such clients do retain. But the "I-was-there-and-it-happened-to-me" experience is absent and hence not retrievable. Tentative hypotheses about trauma are often the best we can do; although we often have clear evidence *that* the patient was traumatized, we often cannot know exactly *how* or *by whom.*

In view of the fact that we could not study evolutionary hypotheses without the reports of Darwin that first generated them, or sterilization without Lister's original observations, psychodynamic therapists value naturalistic observation as an essential part of science. Thus, they respect sources of evidence that are less controllable than those used in the currently favored paradigms for empirical research. Despite their limitations, case reports remain valuable to us (Fishman, 1999), as do qualitative studies (Gergen, 2001). We support hypothesis testing, but we worry that the progress of both science and psychodynamic therapy will be limited if the historically fertile body of clinical wisdom as a source for hypothesis generation is summarily rejected (cf. Greenberg, 1991).

Over several generations, analytic therapists have formulated many researchable ideas. Reichenbach (1938) contrasted the "context of discovery" (methods appropriate to generating hypotheses) with the "context of justification" (methods appropriate to testing hypotheses). Historically, psychoanalysis has lacked a credible context of justification, while current calls for "evidence-based" therapies often lack a credible context of discovery. I am hoping that one side effect of the American Psychological Association's (APA's) filming of three seasoned therapists with the same client is to call into question the assumption among many nontherapists that accumulated clinical wisdom, as expressed in the art of the experienced clinician, is inevitably an inferior source of knowledge about how to help a suffering person.

PROFESSIONAL AND CULTURAL CONSEQUENCES OF THE PSYCHOANALYTIC MOVEMENT

Because the relational factors to which analytic practitioners ascribe progress operate in other treatments as well, many concepts from psychoanalysis have been exported to other approaches (e.g., "working through," "secondary gain," "projection," "denial," "insecurity," "attachment problems"). Instruments such as the Myers-Briggs Type Indicator, Minnesota Multiphasic Personality Inventory, and Rorschach Inkblot test are based on psychodynamic concepts. Psychoanalytic themes have infused the arts, social sciences, literature, biography, and other areas of intellectual life. When it was the "latest thing," psychoanalysis was overvalued. Now that it has been around for over a century, it tends to be dismissed as passé. Both attitudes distort a complex reality.

In a post-Freudian world, much of what was once stunning or revelatory has been assimilated into common knowledge. A person reporting an "identity crisis" is quoting Erik Erikson (1959); people who accuse others of "defensiveness" are referencing ego psychology (A. Freud, 1936/1966); those who call their fastidiousness "anal" are invoking early drive theory (Freud, 1908/1959a), as are parents who reassure themselves that their child is "going through a phase." Psychoanalysis has permeated Western cultures, for better and for worse (see Eisold, 2005; Hale, 1995; Safran, 2012; Zaretsky, 2005).

Via their clinical experience, psychoanalytic therapists have slowly come, unlike Freud the generalizer, to appreciate that what is true for themselves, and perhaps for people somewhat like themselves, may not be true for others, who have distinct, unique internal lives. Perhaps the greatest contribution of the psychoanalytic literature has been its in-depth depiction of diversity in individual subjectivities and in the relationships they influence. Psychoanalytic work on differences in personality, development, affect patterns, sexuality, organizing cognitions, sources of anxiety, and other areas of unconscious and subjective life may help therapists of any orientation adapt their expertise to each new clinical challenge. Ironically, the ultimate impact of Freud's generalizing, universalizing opus is to have sensitized us all to the exquisite *specificity* of everyone's internal experience (cf. Bacal & Carlton, 2010).

Principal Therapeutic Techniques

Each generation of intellectuals tends to view the language of its predecessors as antiquated. Because psychoanalysis has been around longer than other therapeutic movements, its arcane terminology can be an obstacle. As I have noted, many current nonpsychodynamic therapy approaches borrow from prior psychoanalytic concepts (e.g., the alliance, resistance, identification) or rename, from their own perspective, core analytic concepts (e.g., "implicit" replaces "unconscious," "schema" replaces "internalized object relations," "cognitive reframing" replaces "interpretation"). In watching my colleagues in the *Three Approaches to Psychotherapy* videos, I was struck as much by our similarities as by our differences. For current purposes, however, I try to sharpen up the differences by emphasizing what is unique, distinctive, or seminal about the analytic tradition per se.

First, there has never been, and continues not to be, one basic "psychodynamic technique." The analytic answer to most questions about what one should do in any specific clinical situation is: "It all depends." It depends, among other things, on the therapy context (e.g., short or long term; inpatient or outpatient; voluntary or involuntary; once weekly or more intensive; individual, couple, or group); age and developmental status of the person seeking treatment; and the client's ethnicity, cultural context, sexuality, religious beliefs, socioeconomic status, and other attributes. It also depends on the personality and preferences of the patient, the personality and theoretical proclivities of the therapist, the goals of the treatment, the stage of the therapy, and the emotional ambiance of the moment. The therapist's attunement to all these factors is vital.

I therefore start with a disclaimer. Among many analysts, the idea of a doctrinaire "technique" is anathema. A recent discussion on the listserv of the International Association for Relational Psychoanalysis and Psychotherapy documented how leery many of us are about even thinking in such terms. Instead, we focus on participating authentically in a relationship in which a therapeutic process evolves in an organic, unforced way. We view therapy not as something one person "does to" or "provides for" another but as something the two parties undertake mutually under uniquely boundaried conditions. Still, there are clearly activities that analytic therapists promote, ways of relating that differ from ordinary social discourse (e.g., Fink, 2007; Maroda, 2010; Stark, 1999). We may give ourselves over to a process, but we are part of that process, and what we do or avoid doing can be, to at least some extent, named. In contrast to those who avoid explicating techniques, there are distinct analytic therapies that emphasize specific procedures, such as attunement and mirroring (Rowe & MacIsaac, 1989) or clarification, confrontation, and interpretation (Clarkin, Yeomans, & Kernberg, 2006). I will represent both sensibilities, the distrust of conveying what we do in terms of technical interventions and the acknowledgment that analysts deliberately foster and engage in certain processes.

THE PSYCHOANALYTIC SENSIBILITY

I want to speak first of a psychoanalytic "attitude" or "sensibility" from which any intervention with a unique patient derives. Some scholars (e.g., Frank & Frank, 1993) have situated our profession in the universal, age-old role of the healer, with all its attendant moral obligations. Contemporary analytic wariness about specifying techniques is not an "anything goes" position. Rather, it appreciates that we do not know in advance what any given patient will need from us and that technical choices arise only in the context of an overall psychoanalytic ethic. Schafer (1983) described that ethic in terms of avoiding either–or thinking, attempting to understand rather than to teach or advise, and trying to be helpful. I have written (McWilliams, 2004) about curiosity and awe, the assumption of complexity, the willingness to identify with the patient, empathic immersion, reliance on a disciplined subjectivity, attunement to affect, appreciation of attachment, and faith. Buechler (2004) emphasized curiosity, hope, kindness, courage, a sense of purpose, emotional balance, the capacity to bear loss, and integrity. Such values may, of course, infuse many approaches to psychotherapy, but because the analytic tradition emphasizes relationship over discrete activities of therapist and patient, they tend to be explicitly front and center in psychodynamic thinking and therapy.

This encompassing sensibility includes a radical effort to be honest about what we know and do not know. There is a self-conscious humility in it (however much individual analysts may lack that quality), a continuity with Freud's ongoing readiness to change his theories when he ran into their limitations, a modesty about how much we can ever understand another person's experience or imagine the best solutions to anyone else's singular dilemma. Although this attitude does not call into question therapists' realistic competence and legitimate authority about psychological issues, it is essentially egalitarian and open to new learning via a process of mutual discovery.

Again, such attitudes may pervade many therapies, but in the analytic tradition (which shares this perspective with the therapies of Carl Rogers and later humanistic or "third force" writers), they are the main event rather than the scenery. They are assumed to be central to a multifactorial healing process, not simply the necessary background conditions that make other interventions more likely to succeed. Early in treatment, they set a tone that increases the probability that a therapeutic alliance will evolve. It is in this assumptional context that analytic therapists may ask questions such as "How do you find yourself feeling with me?" "How are you feeling about our conversation?" "Do you have any questions or misgivings about how we are working together?" and so on.

THE THERAPIST'S SELF-KNOWLEDGE

Most analysts agree that the most vital preparation to be a therapist is one's own treatment (the *training analysis,* as it is termed by postgraduate institutes). If we take seriously the power of unconscious motivation and interaction, then the therapist's unconscious life is as critical to examine as the patient's. Experience as a patient—the more intensive and extensive the better—ideally familiarizes us with our particular dynamics, narcissistic vulnerabilities, blind spots, affect patterns, relational tendencies, and explanatory biases (Fromm Reichmann, 1950; McWilliams, 2004; Yalom, 2002). Self-understanding coming from our own treatment helps us appreciate that a patient's anxiety or depression or eating disorder may be felt quite differently, and have a different meaning, from ostensibly similar phenomena in ourselves. Thus, our own therapy helps us to avoid misunderstanding our clients by over-identifying with them.

It also helps us to avoid underidentifying, in the form of objectifying and distancing from our patients' experience. Our own treatment familiarizes us with the feelings that may attend the role of client (e.g., shame, vulnerability, fear of criticism or exploitation) and the defenses that may handle those feelings (e.g., idealization or devaluation, intellectual distancing, regression, projection), thereby increasing our empathy with our clients. I remember being startled the first time I approached my analyst's office: Despite my conscious conviction that there is nothing shameful in asking for help, and that there is *especially* no stigma in getting treatment "for professional reasons," I found myself worrying that someone might see me going through his door.

When one is in the role of therapist, being constantly aware of one's own feelings and mindful of one's own dynamics may prevent interactions from reaching an intensity that is damaging to the patient or the treatment process. Harmful scenarios may include, for example, rationalizing getting rid of a patient because one cannot bear the feelings of dread that precede the person's sessions, or indulging narcissistic needs for reassurance of one's competence at the expense of the patient's freedom to comment on one's failings, or trying to be seen as sexually attractive in order to increase one's sense of power in the relationship, or enacting a rescue fantasy that undermines the patient's own capacity to solve problems. The smarter a therapist is, the greater the risk that he or she can rationalize interventions that may fail to help or even do emotional harm (Strupp, Hadley, & Gomez-Schwartz, 1977). Perhaps the overall best outcome of a therapist's personal treatment is humility: a deep sense of one's limits, weaknesses, and fallibility (see Orange, 1995)—a good basis for an authentic, egalitarian healing connection.

Long-term tx is one of the few thgs that can bring ⊕ change in one's attachment style.

Psychodynamic Therapy | 89

THE THERAPEUTIC ALLIANCE

A comfortable, reliable working alliance is both a prerequisite for attaining other aims and a healing phenomenon in itself. Some clients are able to feel securely attached early in the first session, taking the therapist's goodwill for granted from that time on, whereas others need constant or recurrent attention to their difficulties in feeling a sense of basic safety, constancy, and freedom to be themselves. Research by Mikulincer and Shaver (2007) has shown that attachment styles can change from insecure to secure in a devoted, long-term relationship, including intensive therapy. For some clients (e.g., those with significant paranoia), the attainment of a deep sense of dependable connection with another person is the main overall goal of therapy, a goal that may take years to achieve.

Both collective clinical experience and disciplined empirical investigations have confirmed the critical relationship of the alliance to therapeutic outcome (Norcross, 2002; Safran & Muran, 2000; Summers & Barber, 2010; Wampold, 2001, 2010). Establishing an alliance is thus a primary treatment goal, and repairing a damaged alliance is the first order of business in a therapy that founders. As Greenson (1967) noted, many treatments have failed because the therapist wrongly assumed an alliance and began to "do therapy" before the client felt safely held and respected as a partner in the process. When a patient seems unable or unwilling to continue to talk sincerely, or expresses skepticism about the value of the therapeutic collaboration, or flirts with quitting, or acts in ways that threaten his or her safety or the integrity of the treatment, the attention of a psychoanalytic therapist goes immediately to restoring the safety and value of the relationship.

This restoration may require sympathetic attention to the patient's experience of the therapist as unreliable or psychologically dangerous, or confrontation of ways that the person's self-destructive actions have jeopardized the treatment, or clarification of the boundary conditions of the therapy, or an apology for a misunderstanding, or any other effort to address the disconnection and renew the earlier feeling of we-ness. Earlier analysts (e.g., Fenichel, 1941) referred to this priority in their admonition to "analyze resistance before content." Contemporary analytic writers (e.g., Josephs, 2000; Safran & Muran, 2000) are more likely to emphasize the "cycle of rupture and repair."

A critical factor in situations of felt impasse is the therapist's capacity to bear the client's frank expression of negative feelings about the therapist and the treatment. Consequently, in analytic training programs great emphasis is put on helping beginning therapists to tolerate being objects of hatred or criticism or scorn—and, for that matter, to bear being objects of desire and idealization. Willingness to accept *negative transferences* has been emphasized as a condition of therapeutic effectiveness since at least Reich's (1933/1972) work on what we now call personality disorders. We have learned that if negative feelings are not addressed quickly and directly, the client may act them out in various harmful ways, not the least of which is to drop out of treatment precipitously.

In an extensive review of the comparative psychotherapy process literature, Blagys and Hilsenroth (2000) found that emphasis on the therapeutic relationship was one of seven factors that distinguish psychodynamic from cognitive–behavioral treatments. The others are (a) focus on affect and the expression of emotion; (b) exploration of the patient's efforts to avoid certain topics or engage in activities that retard therapeutic progress; (c) identification of patterns in the patient's actions, thoughts, feelings, experiences, and relationships; (d) interest in past experiences; (e) focus on interpersonal experiences; and (f) explorations of wishes, dreams, and fantasies. In the analytic clinical literature, these processes may be referred to as emotional engagement, exploration of resistance, attention to internalized object relations or inner working models, developmental (maturational or "genetic") considerations, transference and countertransference processes, and fantasy and dream analysis. These are recognizable parts of every psychoanalytic school of thought, from Freud on, though particular schools may emphasize the components differently.

The necessary *preconditions* for all these activities—conditions that the researchers and the clinicians they studied probably took for granted—are (a) the encouragement of the patient to talk freely; (b) the particular kind of listening with which the therapist responds; and (c) the effort to find meaning in the client's communications, including making a tentative diagnostic and dynamic formulation about his or her personality and problems. Some elaboration on these topics follows.

FREE ASSOCIATION

As I have mentioned, an early patient of Freud's taught him the value of saying everything that comes to mind. Eventually, he would call this process of speaking with scrupulous, unrelenting honesty (Thompson, 2003) the "basic rule" of analysis. A person who contracts for psychoanalysis several times a week (a therapy increasingly limited to those in analytic training and those few who can afford it) may still be asked explicitly to lie down, relax, and "say everything." These days, most psychodynamic therapy occurs on a once-a-week frequency (and face-to-face), however, and the "basic rule" tends to be communicated in less specific ways—for example, by the therapist's inviting the client to try to speak as openly as possible and then looking together at instances when that seems difficult (i.e., when there is resistance to the invitation to expose all aspects of the self).

We now know that by encouraging free expression, we are activating neural associative networks that the process of therapy helps to reorganize (Bucci, 2002). An interesting paradox in this connection is that in urging clients to say everything, we are asking them to do something that we know they will find impossible. Edgar Levenson (2008) defined psychoanalysis, only partly tongue-in-cheek, as "the process by which we ask people to do what we know they can't do and then try to understand together why it's impossible." Mutual exploration of why certain things are hard to say tends to lead to *transference* issues (e.g., "I felt critical of you, but I was reluctant to tell you because whenever I had any criticisms of my father, he would freak out" or "I was ashamed, and I expected you, like my mother, to treat me with contempt").

Given the traditional emphasis on free association, analytic therapists are probably more concerned than other clinicians to keep their eye on whether a client is holding anything back. Having been patients ourselves, we know how hard it is to be ongoingly honest. Having asked many clients about how they see us, we have learned we cannot assume that simply because we are nonshaming and compassionate, they will feel free to tell us everything we need to know to help them. As I stated to Jon Carlson on camera, I have often found out something important years into treatment (e.g., that a client has bulimia or a previously denied substance use disorder or is having an affair). Patients who withheld such data had to log enough time with me to overcome their fear of my reaction, or they had to grow in critical ways before they could tolerate feeling and sharing things they had dissociated. Analytic therapists may thus make periodic tactful inquiries about whether there is anything the client is having trouble bringing up.

RESPECTFUL, OPEN-MINDED, OPENHEARTED LISTENING

With this heading I want to capture Freud's (1912/1958) "evenly hovering attention," Reik's (1948) "listening with the third ear," Ogden's (1997) "reverie," Casement's (1985) "unfocused listening," and Bion's (1970) exhortation to analysts to listen "without memory or desire." Although, depending on the clinical presentation, there are different things that the therapist may selectively tune in on (Hedges, 1992), the overall "feel" of the listening process in analytic therapy involves a trancelike state of deep relaxation and high concentration comparable to light hypnosis or meditation. This receptive mental condition is hard to describe, but it includes a sense of inner serenity or surrender (Ghent, 1990) and is not far from what spiritually oriented people call "reverence."

Psychoanalytic listening is often construed as both active and empathic, but it is also absorbent and respectful. Although *respect* has not been comprehensively theorized in the analytic literature, this attitude is critical to the listening stance of psychodynamic therapists. Blass (2006), who interviewed experienced analysts on the topic of respect for the client, found that his interviewees typically differentiated between respect and empathy, often finding the former a harder attitude to maintain. They mentioned categories of patients (e.g., pedophiles, drug abusers, faithless partners) for whom it is easy to feel empathy once one has heard their painful stories but for whom it is a challenge to feel consistently respectful. That challenge was never far from their minds.

The essence of respect, I think, is a kind of *looking up* rather than looking down—or even across—at the client. It includes empathy but goes beyond it. This looking up is not necessarily with admiration, but with the expectation that we will learn something, that the client has something of value to give us (a new idea, a moving experience, an inspiring metaphor, an example of living life well). Freud (1912/1958) had this openness to learning from patients; his theories derived directly from his listening respectfully to the hysterically disabled women who were disparaged and dismissed by many in his era. Several decades ago, Searles (1975) was writing about "the patient as therapist to his analyst," a concept that has been thoughtfully developed since (e.g., Jacobs, 1996).

Some early analysts followed Freud's lead in emphasizing the effort to stay open to being surprised by the patient's insights (e.g., Reik, 1937), whereas others (e.g., Strachey, 1934) tried to develop a standard technique based on the idea that analysts' knowledge of unconscious processes was sufficient for them to take a more authoritative stance. Recent writing in the relational literature, partly in reaction against the tone of some analysts in the latter group, has dealt in depth with respect (Aron, 1996; D. B. Stern, 1997), usually under the rubrics of *mutuality* and subject-to-subject relationship (Benjamin, 1995).

A primary aim of psychodynamic therapy is the fostering of clients' capacities to solve their own problems. This effort requires an atmosphere of joint exploration rather than the compliance of one party with the expert agenda of the other (Sullivan, 1970). The principle of honoring clients' potential autonomy does not oblige analytic therapists to maintain long silences or to withhold useful information. It does, however, require that when we make interpretations (e.g., "Perhaps you're angrier than you've been aware"), observations ("I'm seeing a look of deep sadness as you say that"), or suggestions ("I'm not sure it's a good idea to act before you understand yourself better"), our tone should generally be tentative—the voicing of a hypothesis that the client is free to question or reject. And when we have been wrong or hurtful, we should apologize and explore the patient's reactions to the disruption of the emotional safety of the relationship.

In the United States, we admire activity, pragmatism, and problem solving and are less valuing of reflection, deliberation, meditative experiencing, and acceptance of limits, paradoxes, and trade-offs. The analytic tradition reflects a more European sensibility (a "tragic" rather than a "comic" orientation, as Messer and Winokur, 1984, observed). It assumes that comfort in the face of painful realities is often what is called for, that the suffering person may need the emotional space to grieve for what cannot be fixed. Westerners often rush to "solve" problems (an active, pragmatic attitude that has increasingly characterized efforts to evaluate psychotherapies). Psychodynamic therapists have learned to view being listened to as *in itself* a therapeutic experience, especially for clients who have little prior familiarity with respectful attention to their inner lives. We also emphasize the importance of learning to address the many difficult situations that life brings and developing a sense of acceptance, serenity, and compassion.

THE SEARCH FOR MEANING

While listening in their oddly intent and yet unfocused way, analytic therapists try to find meaning in their patients' experiences. The sources of this meaning are sought in both left-brained (more rational and experientially objective) and right-brained (more subjective, intuitive, and experientially visceral) processes. To derive a narrative that makes sense of a client's suffering, we draw on knowledge of personality, attachment, conflict, development, sexuality, diversity, and other psychological areas, as well as on our own identifications, emotional responses, bodily sensations, and fleeting impressions. We try to make sense holistically of the interaction of personality, stress, context, cognition, emotion, sensation, and behavior that the client's communications reveal.

Unless there is a forensic or research context to the work, we are unlikely to use assessment instruments at the beginning of a treatment. In the face of a confusing diagnostic picture (e.g., behavior that suggests brain injury, or evidence of dissociation of which the patient is unaware, or hints of a thought disorder), we may refer a prospective patient for psychological testing. But in general, although we value assessment instruments for research, counseling, and forensic purposes, we prefer to attend more holistically to the varieties of data that come our way in an interview. Our knowledge of our own personality (deepened in our own treatment), along with our accumulated clinical knowledge, allows us to use ourselves as the "analytic instrument" (see Lasky, 2002) through which we receive and process most clinical data.

In initial meetings, we typically try to engage our clients' curiosity about the sources and meanings of the painful experiences for which they have come for help, conveying verbally and nonverbally the following message: "If we can understand this together, we can figure out what to do about it." We may ask what the client's theories are about why these problems have emerged, and why now. We may suggest a hypothesis about the appearance of the symptoms and then ask whether that resonates with the client's understanding. Overall, we try to convey the conviction that psychological suffering does not happen randomly, arbitrarily, and meaninglessly, and that suffering psychologically does not equate with weakness or badness or ill-fatedness and is no cause for shame. Again, these articles of faith have come to characterize many therapies, but analysts are probably particularly aware of their continuity with Freud's seminal conviction that sense could be made of the seemingly meaningless symptoms of his first patients.

Diagnostic Formulation

Analytic therapists differ in their attitudes toward psychodiagnosis, some stressing their clients' uniqueness to the point of seeing labels as meaningless, and some finding diagnosis a valuable guide to treatment. They also differ in how consciously and deliberately they engage in a diagnostic process. I suspect that some analysts who eschew diagnostic formulations are nevertheless influenced in their work by certain basic analytic notions about individual differences. Psychodynamic diagnosis attends less to categorical *DSM* or International Classification of Diseases concepts than to inferred levels of personality organization, from the psychotic range through the borderline conditions to neurotic and normal levels (Kernberg, 1984; Steiner, 1993), and to the person's personality patterns and defenses (McWilliams, 1994, 2011; PDM Task Force, 2006).

Dynamic Formulation

Even analysts without much respect for diagnostic labels try to develop hypotheses about each person's constitutional and temperamental givens, maturational challenges, defenses and coping strategies, affective patterns, identifications and counteridentifications, relational patterns, unconscious belief systems, and ways of supporting self-esteem (McWilliams, 1999), all of which, of course, constitute a kind of diagnosis, if diagnosis is understood to be a way of organizing understanding. We try to discern the causes and meanings of the client's presenting problem and recurrent patterns, generating multiple answers to the questions "Why this symptom?" and "Why now?" We have come to believe that most psychological problems are *overdetermined* (Waelder, 1960)—that is, that they have many interacting causes—and as we feel we are coming to understand each determinant, we may share our inferences with the client.

The main analytic criterion for evaluating any intervention is whether the client generates new, meaningful associations and emotional experience in response. Although we hope our clients will consciously resonate to our hypotheses, we appreciate the power of defense and hence do not assume that a person's compliance with our ideas always means that we are right. Similarly, we do not assume that the client's disagreement always means that we are wrong—some people tend to be oppositional because they unconsciously associate negativism with the survival of their separate sense of self. Instead, we look to whether the therapeutic process is moving forward and whether the relationship feels increasingly authentic, emotionally meaningful, creative, and generative of new behavior.

ATTENTION TO THE UNSPOKEN

Investigating the unstated conditions of therapy may be distinctive of the sensibility of analytic clinicians. In line with our commitment to radical honesty, we ask ourselves what is *not* being talked about, what is taken for granted, what is being danced around, what could be named and owned. We orient toward the "unthought known" (Bollas, 1987), looking for what we may be colluding with our clients to ignore. This attentiveness goes beyond openness to possible negative transferences; it also concerns the conditions of the treatment. Thus, we may query clients about their reactions to changes in appointments, to our starting or ending a session late, to our office decor, to our having lost weight or grown a beard, and so on. The reason for this socially atypical interrogation of the ordinary and the obvious is that in clients' reactions to prosaic and unspoken aspects of the therapeutic relationship, numerous important issues may hide. There are many areas in which the clinician and client may be complicit, more or less unconsciously, in ignoring an elephant in the room. Such elephants may include issues of ethnicity, religion, race, gender, sexuality, socioeconomic status, physical appearance, disability, and other topics that most people keep out of ordinary social discourse. As one of my supervisors once remarked, "Psychoanalysis is not a tea party."

ATTENTION TO RESISTANCE

When people come to a therapist, it is often because all the other ways they have tried to solve a problem have failed. They may realize that there is some part of their psychology that is working against the change that they seek, or they may simply feel helpless. The human organism is a bit like a complex bureaucratic organization: Efforts to influence it toward a healthy flexibility create anxiety, resulting in attempts to cling to the old ways, however maladaptive they have been (cf. Schlesinger, 2003). Despite the popular stereotype that analysts "accuse" patients of "resisting," there is nothing condemnatory in appreciating the fact that systems—including our individual systems of acting, thinking, managing emotion, experiencing our bodies, and relating to others—resist change. In fact, if we did not resist change, we would be sitting ducks for all kinds of glib manipulation. Psychodynamic therapists respect the reality of resistance to even benign influence, try to find ways to address it in themselves and the people they treat, and try to reduce their clients' shame about how hard it is to change.

We may note patients' strengths as well as weaknesses. We convey our belief that psychopathology expresses positive efforts to solve a problem, not just the negative outcomes that may preoccupy the patient. In the process of *working through* repeated expressions of the client's problematic cognitive, affective, and behavioral patterns, especially as they emerge and can be named in the present, we hope that our participation in a new, emotionally honest partnership will modify the person's unconscious expectations about relationship. In terms of cognitive neuroscience, we engage in new learning that allows the prefrontal cortex to "talk back" to the automatic and currently maladaptive solutions that were the best available in childhood (Lane & Garfield, 2005).

ATTENTION TO TRANSFERENCE AND COUNTERTRANSFERENCE

Perhaps the greatest difference in practice between analytic approaches and others lies in attention to transference and countertransference. Clients are often willing to talk about their problematic behavior *outside* the therapy office, but they may try to keep painful, shame-ridden self-states out of the therapeutic relationship. In psychodynamic treatment, on the principle that new emotional learning is catalyzed when experienced in the here-and-now, they are generally encouraged to find the negative parts of themselves (along with their more lovable qualities) *in the therapy relationship*. It is this process that most stresses therapists and that requires so much personal experience in the patient role.

It can be difficult to absorb and simply *contain* (Bion, 1967) nondefensively the client's most painful feelings and negative attributions. It can also be hard to take in a person's flattering comments without getting narcissistically inflated and ignoring problematic aspects of the client's need to idealize, or to welcome expressions of sexual desire with equanimity and without seductiveness. Because of these challenges, analytic therapists tend to emphasize lifelong supervision and consultation with colleagues (see Levenson, 1982), especially about how to deal with transference issues. Noticing transference does not necessarily mean that one interprets it, and if one does interpret, tact and timing are critical. This clinical wisdom has been supported by some research on brief psychodynamic therapy: Directly addressing a client's transference may be helpful if done skillfully and respectfully (Hoglend et al., 2007) or counterproductive if pursued in too headlong a fashion (Piper, Azim, Joyce, & McCallum, 1991).

Despite its reputation for endlessly rehashing childhood experiences, analytic therapy orients to feelings, perceptions, and actions that are happening right now, in the office and in the patient's life. When we ask the client to explore them, key memories usually come up. But we emphasize in-the-moment self-understanding in both therapist and client—not necessarily because insight leads to change (although it is often a component or result of the change process; Messer & McWilliams, 2006) but because when something is out of awareness, one tends to dissociate it or enact it or experience it in the body. The process of understanding is in itself therapeutic: The habit of inquiry strengthens overall reflective functioning and has been shown empirically to improve security of attachment (Blatt & Auerbach, 2003; Fonagy, Gergely, Jurist, & Target, 2002).

What may be most difficult when we find ourselves the object of the client's disturbing attributions and affects is not so much the negative feelings per se as the sense of our being almost willfully misunderstood. We have to remind ourselves that clients often need to see us in a certain way so that they will not feel crazy for having the intense negative reactions that their attachment histories have made inevitable in intimate relationships. Early analysts emphasized the distortion in this process. Contemporary practitioners tend to frame it in terms of the client's selective perception of qualities that are present in the therapist but often not in awareness. Some blind spots in the therapist result from the fact that a particular intersubjective relationship can evoke qualities that may not appear in the therapist's relationships with most people.

Sampson and Weiss and their colleagues (see Silberschatz, 2005) found that clients unconsciously know what they need and repeatedly test us to see whether we can provide it. They do this via *transference tests,* in which the implicit question is "Will you react like my parent, or will you give me a new experience?" and by *passive-into-active transformations,* in which they treat us as they were treated and then see whether we can respond more effectively than they could in childhood. In response to the first type of test, our countertransference tends to be *complementary* (we find ourselves feeling like the client's early caregivers); in response to the second, it tends to be *concordant* (we find ourselves feeling like the client at the hands of those caregivers; Racker, 1968).

Awareness of these emotional processes allows us to name them, to avoid extreme enactments of them, and to invite new learning. Relational analysts emphasize that it is impossible to avoid enactments, that given the intersubjective nature of relationship, we will find ourselves participating in the emotional repetition of the client's main schemas. Yet we can be mindful about what is happening, and we can try to be used as a *transformational object* in this process (Bollas, 1987), helping to influence the familiar but problematic narrative in a different and healthier direction.

To clients, one of the most meaningful outcomes of elaborating transference feelings is the realization that one has been accepted despite one's most hateful qualities and difficult behaviors. The fact that the therapist can survive the patient's toxic attributions can be healing. The fact that relationships can be repaired after angry disruptions may surprise those whose histories are full of hostility or estrangement. This process may provide or reinforce the normal maturational achievement of going through a negativistic period and realizing that, despite one's attacks on them, one's parents are still there and devoted (cf. Winnicott, 1971). It allows for a fuller acceptance of self that does not depend on one's dissociating disturbing elements of self-experience.

Overall, we try to help clients as fast as possible to feel better and to change what they came in upset about. I know of no data showing that psychodynamic treatments are any slower than other therapies in mitigating presenting problems. In addition to relief of symptoms, however, we evaluate therapeutic growth by noting progress in identity integration, sense of agency, object constancy, resilience, realistic self-esteem and values, thought and affect tolerance, emotional regulation, self-reflectiveness, appreciation of others' mental states, flexibility and maturity in defenses, intimacy, vitality, balance between self-definition and communion, and capacity to grieve and accept what cannot be changed. We do not see most symptoms as existing in isolation from these other areas of functioning, and we have learned that lasting change most often occurs when the depth and breadth of the client's personality is acknowledged in the therapeutic process.

SUITABILITY FOR PSYCHODYNAMIC THERAPY

Clients who do well in this kind of therapy include those who are curious, at least minimally self-reflective, and not too afraid of attachment. We have developed ways of working with people who lack these attributes, but with such clients there is usually a longer period of socializing them to the process. Psychoanalytic therapy has widely been seen as the treatment of choice for personality disorders and entrenched problems in living. Clients who suffer from conditions such as addiction, extreme anorexia, severe antisocial tendencies, obsessive–compulsive disorders, major depression, and acute borderline and psychotic states may need specific interventions and boundary conditions (medical and otherwise) in addition to psychotherapy; psychodynamic treatment by itself is not usually sufficient. Analysts originally learned this the hard way; for example, by trying to help severe alcoholics via standard treatment alone, which usually failed.

Before analytic therapies had been subject to much empirical research, there was a clinical literature on "analyzability" (see Greenson, 1967; Karon, 2002). The topic eventually faded because opinions about who does well in analysis were so conflicting (Fine, 1990). In addition, some of the answers to the question of who benefits apply to all therapies, not to analytic work in particular. It may be true that the clients dismissively denoted by Schofield's (1964) YAVIS acronym (young, attractive, verbal, intelligent, successful) are good candidates for analytic treatment, but they are also good candidates for cognitive, behavioral, family systems, humanistic, and emotion-focused therapies. It is easier for all clinicians to help competent, cooperative, highly motivated people.

Given the vast analytic literature on psychosis, personality disorders, dissociation, and other challenging problems, the psychodynamic tradition may be a fertile source of help for therapists of any orientation struggling with more difficult clients. It seems commonsensical that people who want a directive clinician may do better in more structured therapies, but I am reluctant to generalize. I know of individuals who seemed to have all the qualities associated with thriving in analytic treatment and yet did not find it helpful, and also individuals with virtually every negative prognostic sign who found a well-matched psychodynamic therapist and made remarkable progress (cf. Bach, 2011).

Case Applications With Chi Chi

In this section, I reflect on ways in which I tried to exemplify with Chi Chi the elements of the psychodynamic approach as I have just described it, emphasizing the psychoanalytic sensibility; the therapist's self-knowledge; the therapeutic alliance; free association; respectful listening; the search for meaning; attention to the unspoken; and attunement to unconscious resistance, transference, and countertransference.

EMBODYING A PSYCHOANALYTIC SENSIBILITY

I hope my behavior in the videos exemplifies a psychoanalytic sensibil-ity. I liked Chi Chi and was genuinely trying to understand her. Because it is a background attitude more than a set of procedures, I leave it to viewers to assess the degree to which I embodied the analytic values I have mentioned.

I was acutely aware during the filming, and later in watching the DVD, that it is impossible to demonstrate a psychoanalytic *process* under the circumstances in which we were filmed. I think I communicated some psychoanalytic *content*, but the general sense of an ongoing safe relationship in which the patient finds *within herself* the sources of healing cannot really come through in a short, videotaped encounter. Although I was very much my professional self in the role of Chi Chi's temporary therapist, I talked more than I ordinarily talk in sessions, made more connections than I would in an ongoing therapy, and found myself in teaching mode more than is typical.

USING THE THERAPIST'S SELF-KNOWLEDGE

In the APA filming, I was trying to stay aware of several potentially interfering dynamics in myself. For example, I am a pretty competitive person, and despite the fact that APA carefully framed the project as a comparison of three good treatments rather than a competition for which approach is best in some overall way—a construction with which I am intellectually in strong agreement—I felt a subtle internal pres-sure to "be the best." Because I was consciously in sync with the official attitude, I was not entirely aware of this drive in myself until I noticed that I was more anxious than I had felt before doing a prior APA video that had involved only me as an individual therapist. When I associ-ated to the anxious feeling, what came to mind was the pep talk "Go out and win one for the [psychoanalytic] team." I hope my being aware of this competitive agenda reduced my tendency to act it out in ways that would undermine what my better self saw as a legitimate effort to compare and contrast, without better-and-worse rankings.

I was also in touch with a sense of tension between attempting to be of maximal help to the client, as I would try to be in any session, and recognizing that this was an inevitably contrived situation, a meeting for demonstration purposes in which both parties were keenly aware of being filmed and also knew they would not be working together after their two scheduled meetings—hardly the usual clinical state of affairs. Although Dr. Carlson's intake conversation was intended to enable us to "do therapy" rather than to spend time on intake and formulation, this was my first day with Chi Chi, and one cannot simply dive into a stranger's mental life as if one already has a therapeutic alliance.

Finally, I was alert to the fact that there was a present and future audience and that the point of the meeting was to demonstrate how analytic ideas translate into a therapeutic process. There were moments when I completely lost the sense of there being onlookers and immersed myself in the interaction with Chi Chi, but there were other moments when I found myself feeling that "I'd better try to make something happen here that I can talk about intelligently later." My own narcissism, hitching a ride with my more acceptable wish to teach something of value, was a constant complicating factor.

ESTABLISHING AND MAINTAINING THE THERAPEUTIC ALLIANCE

Because of the delimited nature of the *Three Approaches* video sessions, I was more self-disclosing than I would ordinarily be in an initial meeting with someone who had come to me for open-ended therapy. When I had asked Chi Chi (in the session not used for the final DVD) why she had volunteered for the project, she mentioned liking to act, and then she looked at me in a way that hinted at a worry that I would be critical of that motive. So I commented that I enjoy acting, too, and that I get how satisfying it can be. Such disclosures devolved from the artificiality of the demonstration situation. I was trying to foster a therapeutic alliance by conveying that I had vivid personal reasons for appreciating her experience. In ordinary practice, I would not have volunteered this; biographical self-revelation, before one knows the client well enough to have a sense of how it will be taken in, can have problematic effects on a psychoanalytic process.

In this situation, however, I saw no reason to preserve my anonymity. I did not have to worry about "contaminating" a transference that would not have any time to be elaborated. If I had been working long term with Chi Chi, I would have inquired about the look on her face, inviting expression of any worries that I was critical, and urging her to explore such perceptions so that she might become aware of the depth of her fear that other people will see her badness and reject her for it. I suspect that when she was expressive as a child and rebellious as a teenager, her rather stoic parents viewed her as overly dramatic. If so, any worries that I saw her as unacceptably exhibitionistic would have eventually arisen in her transference experience of me. If she had been a regular patient, my letting her know that I have an exhibitionistic streak and like to perform could have shut down this important opportunity for increased self-knowledge. But my main goal under the circumstances was to be of some therapeutic value in a single day.

Other ways in which I was trying to establish an alliance are probably obvious. My tone was conversational. I tried to express ideas tentatively, inviting a collaborative conversation. I sometimes explained why I asked about something, as in my letting Chi Chi know that I was throwing something out to see if it would strike a chord in her. I indicated verbally and nonverbally that I did not want to push her too far beyond her comfort zone. I tried to welcome any negative reactions to me or the situation. I think I did not do this last part enough with Chi Chi, but more on that later.

ENCOURAGING FREE ASSOCIATION

Chi Chi was articulate and forthright. I did not feel I had to make the point that she should be as open as possible with me; she was savvy about therapy and knew that it depends on uncensored self-disclosure. But I saw her as having significant resistances to sharing her pain in all its emotional intensity. She was notably reluctant to talk about the lost relationship that had most devastatingly affected her adult life; she seemed to be afraid that she would go into a bottomless abyss of pain or be exposed humiliatingly as a failure in relationships. Because what happened in that love affair seemed so critical to the unhappiness that she was trying to address, I did press her to try to talk about it.

LISTENING RESPECTFULLY, OPEN-MINDEDLY, AND OPENHEARTEDLY

Again, I hope the video speaks for itself in this area. I was interested in Chi Chi, was touched by her story, and looked forward to learning from her. Because of the stresses of the one-shot, filmed situation, I was not able to relax into the state of reverie that would have evolved naturally if I had been working with her under normal clinical circumstances. But I tried to be as receptive to, and as viscerally affected by, her words and their background music as I could in the face of those contingencies.

INFERRING MEANING

Although I saw her as struggling with important, repetitive psychological issues, themes that ran through her history and suffused her personality, I did not see Chi Chi as having a personality "disorder." She seemed to me to operate predominantly in what many analysts construe as the "neurotic range" of personality organization (McWilliams, 2011). This inference was based on her awareness of internal conflicts, ability to reflect on her own psychology and the psychologies of others, and capacity to make a friendly, collaborative alliance.

Diagnostic Formulation

I saw Chi Chi as having a hypomanic defense against a basically depressive psychology (her hypomanic denial, a pattern of turning deadening negative affects into their opposites, is probably why she did not score high on the Beck Depression Inventory when Dr. Beck administered it). Although this personality type is no longer in the *DSM* because of a (scientifically questionable) decision to put all mood problems under Axis I, there is a long-standing clinical literature (e.g., Akiskal, 1984; Kernberg, 1984; Lewin, 1941) on hypomanic and cyclothymic personality patterns. In the interview with Dr. Carlson, Chi Chi had mentioned struggles with anger outbursts, impulsive spending, hypersexuality, and excessive drinking—all characteristic of this kind of personality (Akhtar, 1992)—and I knew from conversations with others who knew her that she was unusually funny and lively. This animation coexisted with her crying uncontrollably with both Dr. Carlson and me when past losses came up. I inferred from her history and interpersonal manner that her attachment style was deeply ambivalent.

Dynamic Formulation

As the daughter of a diplomat, Chi Chi had moved from country to country throughout her childhood, and her father was frequently separated for long periods from his family. She tended to minimize the impact of these painful, involuntary losses, which I saw as intimately connected to her presenting problem of self-sabotage. I had found Chi Chi's description of her first memory striking: At age 4, she was put in day care. She screamed and had tantrums but then made the best of it and had a good time with a new friend. It has been psychoanalytic experience that one's earliest memory contains important data about recurring issues and patterns (a phenomenon that has inspired some interesting empirical work; e.g., Cogan, Stringer, Aldredge-Clanton, & Porcerelli, 2004). Chi Chi's first memory contains both devastation about separation and a solution to the problem that emphasizes cutting off grief and throwing oneself into having fun without the primary attachment figure.

In her interview with Dr. Carlson, I had been struck by the tenderness in Chi Chi's voice when she talked about her love for Dickens's novel *Bleak House*. Even the title is resonant of the emotional poverty of her upbringing. I looked up the plot and characters before I met with her and found that the hero of the story is considered one of the kindest characters in all of English literature. I felt that she was drawn to the compassion she had noted in describing the novel, but I suspected that unconsciously she felt she did not deserve such compassion and could not trust that it would last.

My preliminary understanding of Chi Chi's reported undermining of her own success, both in work and in love, was that it was a compulsive repetition of the pattern of making attachments and traumatically losing them—unconsciously recreating trauma in the effort to master it by *this time* initiating it herself. I found myself thinking of Fairbairn's (1952a) concept of the "internal saboteur." I saw Chi Chi as having a depressive psychology of the introjective type (Blatt & Bers, 1993), in which there is a deep, powerful unconscious pathogenic belief by which she had made sense of her childhood experiences:

> I suffered painful losses because I was wasn't good enough. People who get to know me deeply will see my badness, and I will lose them as I lost places and relationships that I loved as a child. So before this happens, I will precipitate these inevitable losses. In that way, I will at least have some control over when, where, and how they happen.

I say more about this shortly.

There is a vast clinical and research literature on attachment and separation, beginning with the studies by Dorothy Burlingham and Anna Freud (1944) of British children who had been sent away from their parents to the countryside during World War II. In spite of being physically safe, the evacuated children did not fare nearly as well psychologically as those who stayed with their families in London as it was being bombed. Premature, nonvolitional separations from a home or from a parent can damage a child's capacity for secure attachment, both directly and because of depressive reactions in a remaining parent who is coping alone (Massie, Bronstein, & Afterman, 1996). I thought I was seeing the effects on Chi Chi of multiple forced childhood moves and possible maternal depression.

I could identify with her hypomanic defenses. My own psychology includes depressive elements and defenses against them. For example, before my analysis, I was in the habit of saying I had had a "happy childhood" despite multiple serious losses and moves. In developing hypotheses about the meaning of Chi Chi's experience, however, I was not self-consciously diagnosing or applying techniques or looking for similarities between us. Like most analysts, I experience my work as deeply organic, as the complex result of my identifications with my own analyst, my supervisors, my teachers, and the writers and theorists whose metaphors and concepts have illuminated mysterious psychological phenomena for me. I do not operate very intellectually when I am sitting with a client; usually it is only *after* a session that I can articulate relevant diagnostic concepts, dynamic formulations, and theoretical models that the patient's story and personal presence have brought to mind. In the moment, I was simply opening myself to one after another point of identification with Chi Chi's pain and attempting to feel out what it is like to live in her subjective world.

I tried to share my hypothesis about her presenting issue in a tentative, user-friendly way. I was hoping that Chi Chi would respond by feeling understood and would experience the gain in self-esteem that can come from making sense of a problem in the self that otherwise can get attributed to weakness, stupidity, or perversity. If she had felt I was off base, I would have asked her to correct my misperceptions and refine the process of trying to make sense of her suffering. Chi Chi minimized the impact of her childhood losses. Abandonment and impermanence were ego-syntonic to her—invisible, uninvestigated facts of life, like water to the proverbial fish. In the small amount of time she and I had together, I tried to make such experiences more ego-alien to her (and when I did, she had a confirmatory association: her memory of how her British friends who had been sent away to boarding schools had never forgiven their parents).

SPEAKING THE UNSPOKEN

Jonathan Shedler once commented to me that he had not seen any therapist in the APA Psychotherapy Video Series ask the client why he or she had volunteered for the filming. His observation struck me as important, and I pursued the issue with Chi Chi. Like many responses to queries about the less-acknowledged conditions of a relationship, her answers to my question (in the session not shown on the APA DVD) about why she had volunteered surprised me and gave me important clues about her psychology. She said that she had been the patient in several videos in the APA Psychotherapy Video Series; she liked to be on stage, and she felt she got something from the process. This response evoked my hypothesis that she had been trying to get help for her psychological problems in brief, one-shot doses, perhaps to avoid becoming deeply attached to one practitioner and then facing what she unconsciously assumed to be the inevitability of losing that relationship traumatically, as she had lost connection after connection in her childhood.

That is, I understood Chi Chi's therapy-in-bits-and-pieces pattern as related to her having been the daughter of a diplomat whose career had required her to give up her attachments again and again. I saw it as an unconscious effort to protect herself from reexperiencing unbearable pain, an "I'll leave you before you traumatize me by leaving me" solution to an old problem that no longer characterized her life. I thought that her habit of sabotaging relationships and jobs as they got increasingly satisfying was inadvertently recreating this traumatic history. This is a phenomenon that Freud (1909/1959c) termed the "return of the repressed" and Mowrer (1950) called the "neurotic paradox": What we try to do to avoid childhood trauma tends to recreate that trauma. I thought that Chi Chi's affect in the conversation after this inquiry supported that interpretation.

In another instance of my trying to open up the possibility of talking about the unstated, I brought up another incident with Chi Chi, who I think would have been too tactful to mention it on camera without an invitation. Although I raised this in the hour that was not used for the final DVD, there is a reference to it in the session chosen for the final training video as "the makeup incident." I had had my makeup done for the filming by a professional, whose idea of making me "look natural" turned me into a person I did not recognize. When I saw myself in the mirror just before I was to do my first interview with the male patient, I was horrified, and I went back, greatly upset, to the makeup artist, asking her to tone it down.

As I was making this distraught plea to the cosmetician, I realized that the woman now in her makeup chair was the patient I would be interviewing in an hour! (So much for APA's careful efforts to keep us apart until we would "meet" on camera.) Chi Chi, seeing my distress, immediately reached out sympathetically, saying, "Doesn't it feel terrible when your makeup isn't right?!" When we sat down together to be filmed, I had no idea what she had made of seeing me in that unhinged state of mind, or what that experience would have provoked in her, and so I raised it early in our first meeting. I am not sure she told me everything she thought and felt about the incident (if I had been the patient, I think I would have worried that the therapist was either a nutcase or a prima donna or both), but it did allow us to laugh over it, one woman to another, and my hope was that raising this issue would underscore a general tone that I was trying to set that all topics were welcome, even those that embarrass the therapist.

WORKING WITH RESISTANCE

It felt to me as if Chi Chi wanted to relate intimately and not to do so at the same time, as illustrated in the emotional quality of her reluctant account of a significant personal loss. I suspect that she unconsciously views motherly people with a lot of mixed feelings. She had reported childhood attitudes of having idealized her father and found her mother somewhat rigid and out of touch, and although she related to me cordially, I felt a subtle reserve from her. I later learned from the woman who had recruited her to do the video that Chi Chi had come to the filming with negative feelings about intensive, long-term therapy, having had a prior unsatisfactory experience with it. Some of the resistance I felt may have been related to that fact of her background, of which I was ignorant during the filmed sessions.

When I tried to interpret what I took to be Chi Chi's transference fears that deep attachment would lead to inevitable traumatic loss, she was outwardly accepting, but apparently inwardly skeptical, of what I said. I did not sufficiently attend to my own sense that she was not fully on board with my advocating that she get "real" therapy (by which I meant not necessarily analytic treatment but an ongoing, open-ended, devoted therapeutic relationship and not a one-shot exposure). In my eagerness to leave Chi Chi with what I saw as the main therapeutic message I could deliver in one afternoon, I missed a chance for us to look together at her negative reactions to what I was saying. Her comment in the exit interview that she had not felt fully safe with me may reflect my not having given her enough space to express her skepticism and sense of threat when being urged to make a deep therapeutic attachment.

WORKING WITH TRANSFERENCE AND COUNTERTRANSFERENCE

Chi Chi's early attachment experiences seem to have been good enough to have laid the groundwork for her seeing the possibility that other people may be well-intentioned and helpful. From my own warm countertransference, I concluded that she had been loved enough to elicit loving responses from others. There was not sufficient time for other transference–countertransference experiences to emerge clearly in the natural and spontaneous way that they do in ordinary treatment, but there were elements of some other transference reactions that I thought I was seeing in her.

I wondered, for example, how she had processed the makeup incident. I also privately wondered throughout the filmed session if Chi Chi was "yessing" me as she had probably done many times with her mother—being overtly compliant and covertly oppositional. Her posture indicated a kind of casual avoidance of connection. Chi Chi's mixed reviews of her session with me are a good example of how one cannot conclude from the fact that a client is compliant and deferential that what the therapist is saying is helpful. The more accurate indicators of the rightness or wrongness of an intervention include, as I have noted, confirmatory associations, increased openness, changes in behavior, and general improvement in functioning.

Another way of thinking about the down side of what happened between us is that our session involved an unexplored enactment of what had been a familiar pattern for Chi Chi. In trying to persuade her to go into long-term treatment and hang in with one therapist, I was pushing an agenda that she did not experience as freely chosen. This could be seen as emotionally comparable to what happened to her every time her mother tried to get her on board with a family relocation. Our interaction can be seen as a subtle replay of the dynamics that had fueled her enraged adolescent reactions.

FINAL COMMENTS

Chi Chi's possible conflicts about deep attachments and preexisting aversion to exploratory therapy may have made it hard for me to do effective psychoanalytic work with her. Some of my colleagues would say she was not a good candidate for this approach. But I wish I had encouraged her more than I did to talk out loud about negative feelings about the kind of therapy I do. I continue to wonder whether more extensive exploration of that territory would have made her feel both safer and more helped.

Case Applications With Kevin

In the following sections, I review the major elements of the psychodynamic approach as I have previously elaborated on them and as I tried to embody them as Kevin and I worked together to try to understand and improve his psychological situation.

EMBODYING A PSYCHOANALYTIC SENSIBILITY

With Kevin, I felt an easy comfort rather quickly, and I hope I conveyed to him the psychoanalytic sensibility I have described. Because of the problems I have noted in demonstrating a psychoanalytic process in this exercise, I would not consider our filmed session "typical" of my daily work. Although I remained my usual professional self in the role of Kevin's temporary therapist, I talked more than I ordinarily talk in sessions, made more interpretive connections than I would in an ongoing treatment, and found myself in teaching mode more than usual. These deviations from a quieter, more absorbent stance reflect my trying to give him something useful in a brief, artificial encounter. Despite all this, the session on the DVD represents my therapeutic presence and values fairly well.

USING THE THERAPIST'S SELF-KNOWLEDGE

As I mentioned in the section on working with Chi Chi, I was keenly aware of my narcissistic and competitive dynamics in this situation and was trying not to act them out in ways that would have negative consequences for either Kevin or the educational purposes of the project. I was consciously constraining this part of my psychology throughout the session with him.

In addition, throughout the session I was attuned to other internal reactions, especially to my identifications (and possible overidentifications) with Kevin. Like him, I have a highly sensitive temperament; I am drawn to music; I am half Irish; I am the middle child of three siblings of my gender; I lost my same-sex parent at age 9; and after my mother died, I attempted to comfort my beloved surviving parent by trying not to cause trouble in an already stressed family. Beyond those similarities, I had a feel for Kevin's histrionic defenses—the facial dramatization of feelings, for example—because my own dynamics include hysterical themes. In my personal analysis I came to understand and work through an anxiety-based tendency to distance from feelings by slightly exaggerating and play-acting emotional states that feel threatening.

ESTABLISHING AND MAINTAINING THE THERAPEUTIC ALLIANCE

As with Chi Chi, I was more self-disclosing than I would typically be in an initial meeting with someone who had come for help under ordinary circumstances. I did this to create and strengthen the alliance so that a relatively deep connection might be possible in a short time. In my first session with Kevin, the one not used in the DVD, I let him know that I had lost my mother at the age of 9, and that, like him, I had counted the exact number of days beyond my parent's final birthday. (He referred to this disclosure in the filmed meeting, noting, "You did the same thing.") This comparable experience remains vivid to me. I had had a subclinical depression when I reached 44, my mother's age when she died. One day that year, I suddenly felt lighter and no longer vaguely blue. I counted the days since my 44th birthday and realized I had lived one day beyond my mother's life span. Unconscious time keeping can be uncanny.

In regular therapy, premature disclosure to Kevin of my parallel loss could have preempted his exploring his unique experience of bereavement in childhood, especially as it differed from mine. In whatever transference he would have developed with me, he might need to assume that I had no feeling for what he had been through and to allow himself—finally—the therapeutic experience of anger at a caregiver who, like his preoccupied mother after his father's death, did not fully see or acknowledge the suffering behind his helpful demeanor. Under these circumstances, those normal considerations did not apply.

Other ways in which I was attending to our alliance included a conversational tone and an effort to engage Kevin in evaluating whether what I said felt right to him. My particular emphasis on his testing what I observed against his *own* feelings came from my seeing him as habitually deferential to the ideas and needs of others. I picked up rather quickly that he was deeply conflicted about authentic closeness, and I tried to respect both sides of that conflict: his facility to express feelings as well as his intense discomfort, evident in his facial affect, when he tried to speak starkly from the heart.

ENCOURAGING FREE ASSOCIATION

Like Chi Chi, Kevin needed no explicit invitation to be as open as possible with me; he had been in an insight-oriented counseling relationship for some time and was used to an atmosphere of nonjudgmental openness. But I saw him as having significant and subtle defenses against intimate relating. He was good at seeming to be closely attached while subjectively feeling at a great distance from the other person. I have a special fondness for people with this psychology, a feeling that has deepened as they have responded warmly to my writing about schizoid dynamics (e.g., McWilliams, 2006). When I thought I was seeing in Kevin a mild schizoid dissociation, so common in sensitive musicians, I tried to name it (without resorting to diagnostic jargon) so that he could feel known and accepted, even if he could not change such characteristics, which have a strong constitutional component.

LISTENING RESPECTFULLY, OPEN-MINDEDLY, AND OPENHEARTEDLY

I was genuinely interested in Kevin, identified closely with his story, and looked forward to learning from him. Although I found it impossible during the filming to relax into the state of reverie that would have evolved naturally if I had been working with him under normal clinical circumstances, I tried to be as open to both conscious and less conscious aspects of his subjective world as I could be under the circumstances.

INFERRING MEANING

Despite Kevin's schizoid trends, and despite what I construed as his histrionic defenses against feeling too exposed, I did not see him as having a personality "disorder." Unlike someone organized at a borderline or "preoedipal" level of functioning, Kevin could describe internal conflict, reflect on his psychology, tolerate strong affect, and relate to me as a whole person (rather than as an all-good or all-bad object). He did not totally split off painful mental states. His capacity for tolerating mixed feelings was evident, for example, in his statement "I have a grasp on the contradiction now."

Diagnostic Formulation

In addition to his having an anxiety disorder (the morning panic attacks), I saw Kevin as having a schizoid personality—not as the *DSM* depicts it but as described in the psychoanalytic literature (e.g., Guntrip, 1969). His attachment style seemed avoidant and somewhat dismissing (Blatt & Levy, 2003). In the interview with Dr. Carlson, he had described central problems with closeness, a need for boundaries against others' incursions, and a highly visual style of thinking. He critiqued his younger self for "slipping out of reality too much" and noted that with his daughter, "I have to be present and that's been a struggle." In the sessions with me, he repeatedly withdrew behind the invisible shield that he eventually talked about.

As I have commented, I saw him as also having some histrionic defenses. Kevin tended to dramatize emotional reactions slightly, mostly via facial affect. Many highly sensitive individuals defend against painful emotions by play-acting them in a subtle way. This performative quality has the function of simultaneously both acknowledging and distancing feelings (Bromberg, 1996). People with anxieties about being emotionally penetrated and "seen into" tend to do this, and because this behavior may evoke irritated countertransferences, it is important that the therapists of such clients maintain empathy with the fears behind the self-dramatization.

Finally, my formulation about Kevin's overall psychology included attention to his ethnic background. As someone of similar heritage who admires McGoldrick's (2005) writing on therapy-relevant Irish cultural phenomena, I suspected that his predominantly Irish background may have given Kevin little practice in the direct expression of feeling.

Dynamic Formulation

I construed Kevin's chief complaint about waking up with a terrifying feeling of doom as essentially posttraumatic, as what Freud (1926/1959b) termed *signal anxiety*. As I suggested to him, I wondered if he was waking up in a state of dread because the upcoming separation from his daughter felt unconsciously as if it would be a loss as disastrous as the death in his childhood of his father. I remember associating to Winnicott's (1974) trenchant observation that the trauma we fear is the trauma that has already happened. I learned that this affective state was reinforced by an anniversary reaction (Pollock, 1989); on the birthday before his symptoms appeared, Kevin had reached the age at which his father had died.

As I have noted, I found myself readily identifying with Kevin. But in developing my ideas about the meaning of his experience, I was not self-consciously diagnosing or applying techniques or evaluating similarities and differences between us; I was taking in his state of mind more impressionistically. I was grateful for points of identification with Kevin's pain. It has taken me years of immersion in the subjective lives of diverse others to appreciate the kind of suffering that accompanies schizoid solutions to overstimulation and impingement. I hoped that Kevin would respond to my efforts to convey my understanding, however incomplete, by feeling known and would experience the gain in self-esteem that can come from being seen and accepted as one is.

From friends and clients with personalities like Kevin's (those who would score on the Myers-Briggs Type Indicator as the rather rare INFJ type: Introverted-Intuitive-Feeling-Judging), I have come to understand that people with schizoid dynamics are often misunderstood and even disdained by those who do not share their temperament. Just being able to elaborate safely who they are can be powerfully therapeutic to them. If Kevin had conveyed, verbally or nonverbally, that I was *not* "getting" him, I would have tried to make him feel comfortable correcting me. (This would not have been easy, given his transferential tendency to try assiduously to avoid injuring my narcissism.)

SPEAKING THE UNSPOKEN

As with Chi Chi, I asked Kevin why he had volunteered to be filmed in a therapy session. His response, framed in terms of higher versus lower purposes, told me something about the internal split or schizoid tendency that I saw as characterizing his symptoms, his personality, and the patterns of his life. His bluntly stating that money was a key part of his volunteering startled me. I had not known, or thought about, whether the clients were being paid—an interesting piece of obliviousness on my part about the conditions of our meeting that made me wonder what *else* was invisible to me.

I think I missed an opportunity here to explore Kevin's possible shame about doing the sessions for payment. My lapse may reflect gender differences: In general, financial success seems to be more central to male than to female self-esteem, and when treating men I have often missed—until the patient hits me over the head with it—the issue of shame over whether one makes enough money. Kevin's statement did make the extent of his financial anxiety much more vivid to me, however; it increased my empathy with his struggles to support himself and his daughter financially.

As for the therapeutic impact that such an inquiry can allow, my hope was that his having aired this more "base" motivation and having it welcomed as understandable and realistic made Kevin feel more deeply known, and known without being shamed. Given my understanding of him as a highly sensitive person with an avoidant attachment style who did not easily feel safe in intimate relationships, I hoped it would give him an experience of acceptance that he might build on, perhaps encouraging him to look for a deeper level of intimacy with a woman, especially as his daughter's upcoming departure for college could be expected to leave him lonely.

WORKING WITH RESISTANCE

While appreciating that habitual defenses cannot be changed in one session, I tried with Kevin to address the ways in which he automatically dissociated from painful feelings. I privately noted his nervous laugh and his facial expressions—both highly mobile and somewhat exaggerated—and felt I could not push him any harder than I did. Occasionally I commented directly on elements of resistance, such as when I noted, "You're talking *over* some of the feelings."

Several times, I gently confronted Kevin's tendency to tell me what he thought I wanted to hear. When, in the last minutes of our meeting, he compared his regular therapy somewhat unfavorably with his sessions with me, for example, I tried to contextualize his tendency to idealize a one-shot connection. I was not comfortable with his idealization; I experienced it as an enactment of his compulsive need to make the other person feel good, much as he had tried to woo his mother into competent functioning after his father's death. I did not doubt his sincerity, and I appreciated the compliment, but I also saw its defensive side and was concerned that our meeting not be used in the service of his distancing from his counselor.

WORKING WITH TRANSFERENCE AND COUNTERTRANSFERENCE

Kevin seems to have had a "good-enough" (Winnicott, 1960) start in life to lay the groundwork for his seeing others as at least potentially well-intentioned. His initial transference seemed benign; I was surprised to learn from the exit interview that his first impression of me had been negative (maybe it was the pancake makeup?). From my own warm countertransferences, I concluded that he had been loved enough to elicit loving responses from others. Despite insufficient time for other transference–countertransference experiences to emerge as they do in ordinary treatment, there were some elements of other transference reactions that I thought I was seeing in him.

As I worked with Kevin, I became aware, mostly through my countertransference feelings, that he was a virtuoso at making motherly figures feel good about themselves. I felt taken care of by him, and I wondered with him whether he had responded to his father's death and his mother's subsequent devastation by trying to take care of her in a certain way—specifically, by reassuring her that he was doing fine on his own. The psychoanalytic literature on parental loss in children (e.g., Akhtar, 2011; Furman, 1974) contains observations that the bereaved child tends to feel a double loss: of the parent who has died and of the parent who lives, who so often falls apart and fails to be as competent a caregiver as before the death of the spouse. Kevin's associations supported this formulation, which I had offered in my first meeting with him, and he began our second meeting by commenting on how he had not previously appreciated this pattern.

FINAL COMMENTS

I feel good about my work with Kevin. I was fortunate to have been filmed with a person with whom I had a rich basis for empathy. I have previously written about how clinicians seeing schizoid individuals need to keep their eye on whether such clients apply their insights to improving their lives outside the office—sometimes they feel a lot better in treatment but remain withdrawn from other relationships (McWilliams, 2011). In that context, it was particularly encouraging that Kevin e-mailed me the night after our meetings with the news that he had talked with his daughter, telling her he had realized that he had been subtly withdrawing from her over the past months as he anticipated her leaving him for college. She had responded that she had been trying to tell him this for some time. They then had a deeply satisfying talk. This confirmation in real life of a therapeutic effect means a lot more than flattering verbalizations or "aha!" experiences.

Final Reflections

In recent years, the dominant academic paradigm for thinking about therapy has reflected assumptions that propel a particular kind of research: (a) a focus on "disorder" categories as defined by externally observable symptoms and traits, and (b) development of manualized treatments that ameliorate those measurable phenomena. This paradigm fits awkwardly at best with the sensibilities, philosophical predilections, knowledge base, and experience of most analytic therapists. Although we appreciate, and may incorporate into our work, specific interventions (e.g., medication, elements of cognitive–behavioral therapy) that help our patients with specific problems, our practice does not privilege circumscribed techniques applied to carefully circumscribed populations. Instead, it emphasizes dynamic individuality and our immersion in empirically informed subjective experience: our own, our patient's, and the verbal and nonverbal relationship that we mutually create.

We frame what we say on the basis of observed unconscious dynamic themes that appear in the transference, whether we call them internalized object relations (Fairbairn, 1952b), inner working models (Bowlby, 1969), repetitive structures (French, 1958), nuclear conflicts

(Malan, 1976), representations of interactions that have been generalized (D. N. Stern, 1985), core conflictual relationship themes (Luborsky & Crits-Cristoph, 1990), internal relational models (Aron, 1991), emotion schemas (Bucci, 1997), fundamental repetitive and maladaptive emotional structures (Dahl, 1988), implicit relational knowing (Lyons-Ruth, 1999), or personal schemas (Horowitz, 1998). To understand such patterns, we draw heavily from scientific research on attachment, development, neuroscience, personality, defense, and individual and systemic diversity of many kinds. We also rely on a disciplined self-awareness and a deeply personal knowledge of unconscious processes.

Categorical trait and symptom-relief models miss the fact that Chi Chi not only denies and avoids strong emotions but also feels them intensely. She is not only genuinely upbeat (with traits of extroversion and agreeableness), she is also deeply unhappy and self-critical and repeatedly enacts that side of her inner tension. Kevin not only shrinks from intimate attachment, he also craves it. The theme of closeness versus distance organizes his psychological experience in multiple pervasive ways. He does not simply have the measurable trait of introversion; he has a conflict about emotional intimacy, and his behavior expresses both sides of that conflict. I think any effective therapist of any orientation would eventually have to appreciate such inner dynamisms; perhaps this is why we are currently seeing so many ideas that originated in analytic experience being rediscovered and integrated under other names into other approaches.

I have reviewed some central values, assumptions, and empirical foundations of psychodynamic practice and have commented on ways in which my work with Chi Chi and Kevin expressed this sensibility. Because those orienting attitudes guide in-the-moment clinical decisions (e.g., to question or mirror or confront), I have not gone into detail about specific analytic techniques. Such choices follow naturally from an understanding of personality, development, and defense—areas that until relatively recently were given primary emphasis in most clinical training programs. It is probably clear to readers that I would like to see them reemphasized.

In summary, analytic practitioners believe that we are more effectively helped in our work by understanding people in all their complexities than by mastering techniques that are used in isolation from such understanding. Although it will be important for the future of analytic practice for psychodynamic researchers to continue to do randomized controlled trials of manualized psychoanalytic therapies, thus implicitly accepting the assumptions of the currently dominant model (if we do not, we will be increasingly discredited as not "evidence based"), it is also important for the mental health community at large to appreciate the value of process research, qualitative research, case studies, and accumulated clinical wisdom. Discrete elements of practice and progress may be easier to study empirically than more subtle aspects of therapeutic process and relationship, but that does make them definitional of effective psychotherapy.

References

Abbass, A. A., Hancock, J. T., Henderson, J., & Kisely, S. (2006, October). Short-term psychodynamic psychotherapies for common mental disorders. *Cochrane Database of Systematic Reviews, 4,* CD004687.

Ackerman, S. J., & Hilsenroth, M. J. (2003). A review of therapist characteristics and techniques positively impacting the therapeutic alliance. *Clinical Psychology Review, 23,* 1–33. doi:10.1016/S0272-7358(02)00146-0

Akhtar, S. (1992). *Broken structures: Severe personality disorders and their treatment.* Northvale, NJ: Aronson.

Akhtar, S. (2011). *Matters of life and death: Psychoanalytic reflections.* London, England: Karnac.

Akiskal, H. S. (1984). Characterologic manifestations of affective disorders: Toward a new conceptualization. *Integrative Psychiatry, 2,* 83–88.

Aron, L. (1991). Working through the past—Working toward the future. *Contemporary Psychoanalysis, 27,* 81–109.

Aron, L. (1996). *A meeting of minds: Mutuality in psychoanalysis.* Hillsdale, NJ: Analytic Press.

Atwood, G. E., & Stolorow, R. D. (1993). *Faces in a cloud: Intersubjectivity in personality theory.* Northvale, NJ: Aronson.

Bacal, H. A., & Carlton, L. (2010). *The power of specificity in psychotherapy: When therapy works and when it doesn't.* Northvale, NJ: Aronson.

Bach, S. (2011). *The how-to book for students of psychoanalysis and psychotherapy.* London, England: Karnac.

Balint, M. (1968). *The basic fault: Therapeutic aspects of regression.* London, England: Tavistock.

Bateman, A., & Fonagy, P. (2004). *Psychotherapy for borderline personality disorder: Mentalization-based treatment.* New York, NY: Oxford University Press.

Bellak, L., Abrams, D. M., & Ackermann-Engel, R. (1991). *Handbook of brief and emergency psychotherapy* (2nd ed.). New York, NY: CPS.

Bellak, L., & Goldsmith, L. A. (1984). *The broad scope of ego function assessment.* New York, NY: Wiley.

Benjamin, J. (1995). *Like subjects, love objects: Essays on recognition and sexual difference.* New Haven, CT: Yale University Press.

Bion, W. R. (1967). *Second thoughts.* London, England: Karnac.

Bion, W. R. (1970). *Attention and interpretation*. New York, NY: Aronson.

Blagys, M. D., & Hilsenroth, M. J. (2000). Distinctive of short-term psychodynamic-interpersonal psychotherapy: A review of the comparative psychotherapy process literature. *Clinical Psychology: Science and Practice, 7*, 167–188. doi:10.1093/clipsy.7.2.167

Blanck, G., & Blanck, R. (1974). *Ego psychology: Theory and practice*. New York, NY: Columbia University Press.

Blass, O. (2006). *Respect for the patient: A qualitative study*. Unpublished doctoral dissertation, Rutgers, The State University of New Jersey, New Brunswick, NJ.

Blatt, S. J. (2008). *Polarities of experience: Relatedness and self-definition in personality development*. Washington, DC: American Psychological Association. doi:10.1037/11749-000

Blatt, S. J., & Auerbach, J. (2003). Psychodynamic measures of therapeutic change. *Psychoanalytic Inquiry, 23*, 268–307. doi:10.1080/07351692309349034

Blatt, S. J., & Bers, S. (1993). The sense of self in depression: A psychoanalytic perspective. In Z. V. Segal & S. J. Blatt (Eds.), *The self in emotional distress: Cognitive and psychodynamic perspectives* (pp. 171–210). New York, NY: Guilford Press.

Blatt, S. J., & Levy, K. N. (2003). Attachment theory, psychoanalysis, personality development, and psychopathology. *Psychoanalytic Inquiry, 23*, 102–150. doi:10.1080/07351692309349028

Blatt, S. J., & Zuroff, D. C. (2005). Empirical evaluation of the assumptions in identifying evidence based treatments in mental health. *Clinical Psychology Review, 25*, 459–486. doi:10.1016/j.cpr.2005.03.001

Blomberg, J., Lazar, A., & Sandell, R. (2001). Outcome of patients in long-term psychoanalytical treatments: First findings of the Stockholm Outcome of Psychotherapy and Psychoanalysis (STOPP) study. *Psychotherapy Research, 11*, 361–382. doi:10.1093/ptr/11.4.361

Bollas, C. (1987). *The shadow of the object: Psychoanalysis of the unthought known*. New York, NY: Columbia University Press.

Bowlby, J. (1969). *Attachment and loss: Vol. 1. Attachment*. London, England: Hogarth Press.

Brenner, C. (1976). *Psychoanalytic technique and psychic conflict*. New York, NY: International Universities Press.

Breuer, J., & Freud, S. (1955). Studies on hysteria. In J. Strachey (Ed. & Trans.), *The standard edition of the complete psychological works of Sigmund Freud* (Vol. 2, pp. 1–305). London, England: Hogarth Press. (Original work published 1893–1895)

Bromberg, P. M. (1996). Hysteria, dissociation, and cure: Emmy von N revisited. *Psychoanalytic Dialogues, 6*, 55–71.

Bromberg, P. M. (1998). *Standing in the spaces: Essays on clinical process, trauma, and dissociation*. Hillsdale, NJ: Analytic Press.

Bucci, W. (1997). *Psychoanalysis and cognitive science*. New York, NY: Guilford Press.

Bucci, W. (2002). The referential process, consciousness, and the sense of self. *Psychoanalytic Inquiry, 22,* 766–793.

Buechler, S. (2004). *Clinical values: Emotions that guide psychoanalytic treatment*. Hillsdale, NJ: Analytic Press.

Burlingham, D., & Freud, A. (1944). *Infants without families*. London, England: Allen & Unwin.

Casement, P. J. (1985). *Learning from the patient*. New York, NY: Guilford Press.

Clarkin, J. F., Levy, K. N., Lenzenweger, M. F., & Kernberg, O. F. (2007). Evaluating three treatments for borderline personality disorder: A multiwave study. *The American Journal of Psychiatry, 164,* 922–928. doi:10.1176/appi.ajp.164.6.922

Clarkin, J. F., Yeomans, F. E., & Kernberg, O. F. (2006). *Psychotherapy for borderline personality: Focusing on object relations*. Washington, DC: American Psychiatric Association.

Cogan, R., Stringer, A. C., Aldredge-Clanton, J., & Porcerelli, J. H. (2004). Diagnosis of ovarian cancer: Regression to early memories in the face of danger. *Journal of the American Psychoanalytic Association, 52,* 1242–1243.

Cramer, P. (2006). *Protecting the self: Defense mechanisms in action*. New York, NY: Guilford Press.

Dahl, H. (1988). Frames of mind. In H. Dahl, H. Kachele, & H. Thomae (Eds.), *Psychoanalytic process research strategies* (pp. 51–66). New York, NY: Springer-Verlag. doi:10.1007/978-3-642-74265-1_4

Damasio, A. (1999). *The feeling of what happens: Body and emotion in the making of consciousness*. New York, NY: Harcourt Brace.

Danto, E. A. (2007). *Freud's free clinics: Psychoanalysis and social justice*. New York, NY: Columbia University Press.

Davies, J. M., & Frawley, M. G. (1993). *Treating the adult survivor of childhood sexual abuse*. New York, NY: Basic Books.

Doidge, N. (1997). Empirical evidence for the efficacy of psychoanalytic psychotherapies and psychoanalysis: An overview. *Psychoanalytic Inquiry, 17*(Suppl. 001), 102–150. doi:10.1080/07351699709534161

Eagle, M. N. (2010). *From classical to contemporary psychoanalysis: A critique and integration*. New York, NY: Routledge.

Eisold, K. (2005). Psychoanalysis and psychotherapy: A long and troubled relationship. *The International Journal of Psychoanalysis, 86,* 1175–1195. doi:10.1516/8RMN-4EQF-LG1E-JG03

Eissler, K. R. (1953). The effect of the structure of the ego on psychoanalytic technique. *Journal of the American Psychoanalytic Association, 1,* 104–143. doi:10.1177/000306515300100107

Erikson, E. H. (1959). *Identity and the life cycle*. New York, NY: Norton.

Fairbairn, W. R. D. (1952a). Endopsychic structure considered in terms of object relationships. In *Psychoanalytic studies of the personality* (pp. 82–132). London, England: Routledge & Kegan Paul.

Fairbairn, W. R. D. (1952b). *An object relations theory of personality*. New York, NY: Basic Books.

Fenichel, O. (1941). *Problems of psychoanalytic technique*. Albany, NY: Psychoanalytic Quarterly.

Fine, R. (1990). *The history of psychoanalysis*. Northvale, NJ: Aronson.

Fink, B. (2007). *Fundamentals of psychoanalytic technique: A Lacanian approach for practitioners*. New York, NY: Norton.

Fisher, S., & Greenberg, R. P. (1985). *The scientific credibility of Freud's theories and therapy*. New York, NY: Columbia University Press.

Fisher, S., & Greenberg, R. P. (1996). *Freud scientifically reappraised: Testing the theories and therapy*. New York, NY: Wiley.

Fishman, D. (1999). *The case for pragmatic psychology*. New York, NY: New York University Press.

Fonagy, P. (2006). Evidence-based psychodynamic psychotherapies. In PDM Task Force (Ed.), *Psychodynamic diagnostic manual* (pp. 765–818). Silver Spring, MD: Alliance of Psychoanalytic Organizations.

Fonagy, P., Gergely, G., Jurist, E., & Target, M. (2002). *Affect regulation, mentalization, and the development of the self*. New York, NY: Other Press.

Fonagy, P., & Target, M. (1996). Playing with reality: I. Theory of mind and normal development of psychic reality in the child. *The International Journal of Psychoanalysis, 77*, 217–233.

Frank, J. D., & Frank, J. B. (1993). *Persuasion and healing: A comparative study of psychotherapy*. Baltimore, MD: Johns Hopkins University Press.

French, T. (1958). *The integration of behavior: Vol. 3. The reintegrative process in a psychoanalytic treatment*. Chicago, IL: University of Chicago Press.

Freud, A. (1963). The concept of developmental lines. *The Psychoanalytic Study of the Child, 18*, 245–265.

Freud, A. (1966). *The ego and the mechanisms of defense*. New York, NY: International Universities Press. (Original work published 1936)

Freud, S. (1953a). Papers on technique. In J. Strachey (Ed. & Trans.), *The standard edition of the complete psychological works of Sigmund Freud* (Vol. 12, pp. 89–173). London, England: Hogarth Press. (Original work published 1911–1915)

Freud, S. (1953b). Three essays on the theory of sexuality. In J. Strachey (Ed. & Trans.), *The standard edition of the complete psychological works of Sigmund Freud* (Vol. 7, pp. 135–243). London, England: Hogarth Press. (Original work published 1905)

Freud, S. (1955). The psychotherapy of hysteria. In J. Strachey (Ed. & Trans.), *The standard edition of the complete psychological works of Sigmund Freud* (Vol. 2, pp. 255–311). London, England: Hogarth Press. (Original work published 1895)

Freud, S. (1957). On narcissism: An introduction. In J. Strachey (Ed. & Trans.), *The standard edition of the complete psychological works of Sigmund*

Freud (Vol. 14, pp. 67–102). London, England: Hogarth Press. (Original work published 1914)

Freud, S. (1958). Recommendations to physicians practicing psycho-analysis. In J. Strachey (Ed. & Trans.), *The standard edition of the complete psychological works of Sigmund Freud* (Vol. 12, pp. 111–120). London, England: Hogarth Press. (Original work published 1912)

Freud, S. (1959a). Character and anal eroticism. In J. Strachey (Ed. & Trans.), *The standard edition of the complete psychological works of Sigmund Freud* (Vol. 9, pp. 169–175). London, England: Hogarth Press. (Original work published 1908)

Freud, S. (1959b). Inhibitions, symptoms and anxiety. In J. Strachey (Ed. & Trans.), *The standard edition of the complete psychological works of Sigmund Freud* (Vol. 20, pp. 75–176). London, England: Hogarth Press. (Original work published 1926)

Freud, S. (1959c). Some general remarks on hysterical attacks. In J. Strachey (Ed. & Trans.), *The standard edition of the complete psychological works of Sigmund Freud* (Vol. 9, pp. 227–234). London, England: Hogarth Press. (Original work published 1909)

Freud, S. (1961). The ego and the id. In J. Strachey (Ed. & Trans.), *The standard edition of the complete psychological works of Sigmund Freud* (Vol. 19, pp. 3–66). London, England: Hogarth Press. (Original work published 1923)

Freud, S. (1962a). Heredity and the aetiology of the neuroses. In J. Strachey (Ed. & Trans.), *The standard edition of the complete psychological works of Sigmund Freud* (Vol. 3, pp. 141–156). London, England: Hogarth Press. (Original work published 1896)

Freud, S. (1962b). The neuro-psychoses of defence. In J. Strachey (Ed. & Trans.), *The standard edition of the complete psychological works of Sigmund Freud* (Vol. 3, pp. 45–61). London, England: Hogarth Press. (Original work published 1894)

Freud, S. (1962c). Sexuality in the aetiology of the neuroses. In J. Strachey (Ed. & Trans.), *The standard edition of the complete psychological works of Sigmund Freud* (Vol. 3, pp. 261–285). London, England: Hogarth Press. (Original work published 1898)

Fromm-Reichmann, F. (1950). *Principles of intensive psychotherapy.* Chicago, IL: University of Chicago Press.

Furman, E. (Ed.). (1974). *A child's parent dies.* New Haven, CT: Yale University Press.

Gabbard, G. O. (2010). *Long-term psychodynamic therapy: A basic text* (2nd ed.). Washington, DC: American Psychiatric Association.

Galatzer-Levy, R. M., Bachrach, H., Skolnikoff, A., & Waldron, S., Jr. (2000). *Does psychotherapy work?* New Haven, CT: Yale University Press.

Garcia, E. E. (1991). The life and work of Josef Breuer. *The International Review of Psycho-Analysis, 18,* 572–576.

Gay, P. (1988). *Freud: A life for our time.* New York, NY: Norton.

Gergen, K. J. (2001). Psychological science in a postmodern context. *American Psychologist, 56,* 803–813. doi:10.1037/0003-066X.56.10.803

Ghent, E. (1990). Masochism, submission, surrender—Masochism as the perversion of surrender. *Contemporary Psychoanalysis, 26,* 108–136.

Greenberg, L. S. (1991). Research on the process of change. *Psychotherapy Research, 1,* 3–16. doi:10.1080/10503309112331334011

Greenson, R. (1967). *The technique and practice of psychoanalysis* (Vol. 1). New York, NY: International Universities Press.

Grinker, R. R., Werble, B., & Drye, R. C. (1968). *The borderline syndrome: A behavioral study of ego functions.* New York, NY: Basic Books.

Guntrip, H. (1969). *Schizoid phenomena, object relations and the self.* New York, NY: International Universities Press.

Guntrip, H. (1971). *Psychoanalytic theory, therapy, and the self: A basic guide to the human personality in Freud, Erikson, Klein, Sullivan, Fairbairn, Hartmann, Jacobson, and Winnicott.* New York, NY: Basic Books.

Hale, N. G. (1995). *The rise and crisis of psychoanalysis in the United States: Freud and the Americans, 1917–1985.* New York, NY: Oxford University Press.

Hartmann, H. (1958). *Ego psychology and the problem of adaptation* (D. Rapaport, Trans.). New York, NY: International Universities Press. doi:10.1037/13180-000

Hedges, L. E. (1992). *Listening perspectives in psychotherapy.* Northvale, NJ: Aronson.

Herman, J. L. (1992). *Trauma and recovery: The aftermath of violence—from domestic abuse to political terror.* New York, NY: Basic Books.

Hoffman, I. Z. (1998). *Ritual and spontaneity in the psychoanalytic process: A dialectic-constructivist view.* Hillsdale, NJ: Analytic Press.

Hoglend, P., Johansson, P., Marble, A., Bogwald, K.-P., & Amlo, S. (2007). Moderators of the effects of transference interpretations in brief dynamic psychotherapy. *Psychotherapy Research, 17,* 160–171. doi:10.1080/10503300701194206

Holmes, J. (2009). *Exploring in security: Towards an attachment-informed psychoanalytic psychotherapy.* New York, NY: Routledge.

Horowitz, M. J. (1998). *Cognitive psychodynamics.* New York, NY: Wiley.

Howell, E. F. (2005). *The dissociative mind.* Hillsdale, NJ: Analytic Press.

Hughes, J. M. (1989). *Reshaping the psychoanalytic domain: The work of Melanie Klein, W. R. D. Fairbairn, and D. W. Winnicott.* Berkeley, CA: University of California Press.

Jacobs, T. J. (1996). The patient as instrument of change in the analyst. *Psychoanalytic Inquiry, 16,* 314–339. doi:10.1080/07351699609534086

Josephs, L. (2000). Self-criticism and the psychic surface. *Journal of the American Psychoanalytic Association, 48,* 255–280. doi:10.1177/00030651000480011101

Karlsson, H. (2011). How psychotherapy changes the brain: Understanding the mechanisms. *Psychiatric Times, 28*(8), 21–25.

Karon, B. P. (2002). Analyzability or the ability to analyze? *Contemporary Psychoanalysis, 38,* 121–140.

Kernberg, O. F. (1975). *Borderline conditions and pathological narcissism.* New York, NY: Aronson.

Kernberg, O. F. (1984). *Severe personality disorders: Psychotherapeutic strategies.* New Haven, CT: Yale University Press.

Klein, M. (1952). The origins of transference. *The International Journal of Psychoanalysis, 33,* 433–438.

Kohut, H. (1971). *The analysis of the self.* New York, NY: International Universities Press.

Kohut, H. (1978). *The restoration of the self.* New York, NY: International Universities Press.

Lane, R. D., & Garfield, D. A. (2005). Becoming aware of feelings: Integration of cognitive-developmental, neuroscientific, and psychoanalytic perspectives. *Neuropsychoanalysis, 7,* 5–30.

Lasky, R. (2002). Countertransference and the analytic instrument. *Psychoanalytic Psychology, 19,* 65–94. doi:10.1037/0736-9735.19.1.65

Leichsenring, F. (2006). Review of meta-analyses of outcome studies of psychodynamic therapy. In PDM Task Force (Ed.), *Psychodynamic diagnostic manual* (pp. 819–837). Silver Spring, MD: Alliance of Psychoanalytic Organizations.

Leichsenring, F., & Leibing, E. (2003). The effectiveness of psychodynamic therapy and cognitive behavior therapy in the treatment of personality disorders: A meta-analysis. *The American Journal of Psychiatry, 160,* 1223–1232. doi:10.1176/appi.ajp.160.7.1223

Leichsenring, F., & Rabung, S. (2008). Effectiveness of long-term psychodynamic psychotherapy: A meta-analysis. *JAMA, 300,* 1551–1565. doi:10.1001/jama.300.13.1551

Levenson, E. (1982). Follow the fox: An inquiry into the vicissitudes of psychoanalytic supervision. *Contemporary Psychoanalysis, 18,* 1–15.

Levenson, E. (2008, April). *Striking the elusive mutative experience.* Workshop presented at the spring meeting of the Division of Psychoanalysis (39) of the American Psychological Association, New York, NY.

Levy, K. N., Meehan, K. B., Kelly, K. M., Reynoso, J. S., Weber, M., Clarking, J. M., & Kernberg, O. F. (2006). Change in attachment patterns and reflective function in a randomized control trial of transference-focused psychotherapy for borderline personality disorder. *Journal of Consulting and Clinical Psychology, 74,* 1027–1040. doi:10.1037/0022-006X.74.6.1027

Lewin, B. (1941). Comments on hypomania and related states. *Psychoanalytic Review, 28,* 86–91.

Lichtenberg, J. D., Lachmann, F. M., & Fosshage, J. L. (1992). *Self and motivational systems: Toward a theory of psychoanalytic technique*. New York, NY: Routledge.

Linehan, M. M. (1993). *Cognitive-behavioral treatment of borderline personality disorder*. New York, NY: Guilford Press.

Lohser, B., & Newton, P. M. (1996). *Unorthodox Freud: The view from the couch*. New York, NY: Guilford Press.

Luborsky, L., & Crits-Cristoph, P. (1990). *Understanding transference: The CCRT method*. New York, NY: Basic Books.

Lyons-Ruth, K. (1999). The two-person unconscious: Intersubjective dialogue, enactive relational representation, and the emergence of new forms of relational organization. *Psychoanalytic Inquiry, 19,* 576–617. doi:10.1080/07351699909534267

Malan, D. H. (1976). *The frontier of brief psychotherapy*. New York, NY: Plenum Press. doi:10.1007/978-1-4684-2220-7

Maroda, K. J. (2010). *Psychodynamic techniques: Working with emotion in the therapeutic relationship*. New York, NY: Guilford Press.

Masling, J. (Ed.). (1986). *Empirical studies of psychoanalytic theories* (Vol. 2). Hillsdale, NJ: Analytic Press.

Massie, H., Bronstein, A. A., & Afterman, J. (1996). Role of depressive affects in close maternal involvement with children. *Psychoanalytic Psychology, 13,* 53–80. doi:10.1037/h0079638

Masterson, J. F. (1976). *Psychotherapy of the borderline adult: A developmental approach*. New York, NY: Brunner/Mazel.

McGoldrick, M. (2005). Irish families. In M. McGoldrick, J. Giordano, & N. Garcia-Preto (Eds.), *Ethnicity and family therapy* (3rd ed., pp. 595–615). New York, NY: Guilford Press.

McWilliams, N. (1994). *Psychoanalytic diagnosis: Understanding personality structure in the clinical process*. New York, NY: Guilford Press.

McWilliams, N. (1999). *Psychoanalytic case formulation*. New York, NY: Guilford Press.

McWilliams, N. (2004). *Psychoanalytic psychotherapy: A practitioner's guide*. New York, NY: Guilford Press.

McWilliams, N. (2006). Some thoughts about schizoid dynamics. *Psychoanalytic Review, 93,* 1–24. doi:10.1521/prev.2006.93.1.1

McWilliams, N. (2011). *Psychoanalytic diagnosis: Understanding personality structure in the clinical process* (Rev. ed.). New York, NY: Guilford Press.

McWilliams, N., & Weinberger, J. (2003). Psychodynamic psychotherapy. In G. Stricker & T. Widiger (Eds.), *Comprehensive handbook of psychology: Vol. 8. Clinical psychology* (pp. 253–277). New York, NY: Wiley.

Merten, J., Anstadt, Th., Ullrich, B., Krause, R., & Buchheim, P. (1996). Emotional experience and facial expression during a therapeutic process and its relation to treatment outcome. *Psychotherapy Research, 6,* 198–212. doi:10.1080/10503309612331331708

Messer, S., & McWilliams, N. (2006). Insight in psychodynamic therapy. In L. Castonguay & C. Hill (Eds.), *Insight in psychotherapy* (pp. 9–29). New York, NY: Springer.

Messer, S. B., & Warren, C. S. (1995). *Models of brief psychodynamic therapy: A comparative approach.* New York, NY: Guilford Press.

Messer, S. B., & Winokur, M. (1984). Ways of knowing and visions of reality in psychoanalytic theory and behavior therapy. In H. Arkowitz & S. B. Messer (Eds.), *Psychoanalytic therapy and behavior therapy: Is integration possible?* (pp. 63–100). New York, NY: Plenum Press. doi:10.1007/978-1-4613-2733-2_5

Mikulincer, M., & Shaver, P. R. (2007). *Attachment in adulthood: Structure, dynamics, and change.* New York, NY: Guilford Press.

Milrod, B., Leon, A. C., Busch, F., Rudden, M., Schwalberg, M., Clarkin, J., . . . Shear, M. K. (2007). A randomized controlled clinical trial of psychoanalytic psychotherapy for panic disorder. *The American Journal of Psychiatry, 164,* 265–272. doi:10.1176/appi.ajp.164.2.265

Mitchell, S. A. (2000). *Relationality: From attachment to intersubjectivity.* Hillsdale, NJ: Analytic Press.

Mitchell, S. A., & Black, M. J. (1995). *Freud and beyond: A history of modern psychoanalytic thought.* New York, NY: Basic Books.

Mowrer, O. H. (1950). *Learning theory and personality dynamics.* New York, NY: Ronald Press.

Norcross, J. C. (Ed.). (2002). *Psychotherapy relationships that work: Therapist contributions and responsiveness to patients.* New York, NY: Oxford University Press.

Ogden, T. H. (1997). *Reverie and interpretation: Sensing something human.* Northvale, NJ: Aronson.

Orange, D. (1995). *Emotional understanding: Studies in psychoanalytic epistemology.* New York, NY: Guilford Press.

Panksepp, J. (2004). *Affective neuroscience: The foundations of human and animal emotions.* New York, NY: Oxford University Press.

Panksepp, J., & Biven, L. (2012). *The archeology of mind: Neuroevolutionary origins of human emotions.* New York, NY: Norton.

PDM Task Force. (2006). *Psychodynamic diagnostic manual.* Silver Spring, MD: Alliance of Psychoanalytic Organizations.

Pincus, D. (2006). Who is Freud and what does the new century behold? *Psychoanalytic Psychology, 23,* 367–372. doi:10.1037/0736-9735.23.2.367

Pine, F. (1990). *Drive, ego, object, and self: A synthesis for clinical work.* New York, NY: Basic Books.

Pinsker, H. (1997). *A primer of supportive psychotherapy.* Hillsdale, NJ: Analytic Press.

Piper, W. E., Azim, H. F., Joyce, A. S., & McCallum, M. (1991). Transference interpretations, therapeutic alliance, and outcome in short-term individual psychotherapy. *Archives of General Psychiatry, 48,* 946–953. doi:10.1001/archpsyc.1991.01810340078010

Pollock, G. H. (1989). *The mourning-liberation process* (Vols. 1 and 2). Madison, CT: International Universities Press.

Racker, H. (1968). *Transference and countertransference*. New York, NY: International Universities Press.

Reich, W. (1972). *Character analysis* (V. Carfagno, Trans.). New York, NY: Farrar, Straus, and Giroux. (Original work published 1933)

Reichenbach, H. (1938). *Experience and prediction*. Chicago, IL: University of Chicago Press.

Reik, T. (1937). *Surprise and the psychoanalyst* (M. R. Green, Trans.). New York, NY: E. P. Dutton.

Reik, T. (1948). *Listening with the third ear: The inner experience of a psychoanalyst*. New York, NY: Farrar, Straus.

Rockland, L. H. (1992). *Supportive therapy: A psychodynamic approach*. New York, NY: Basic Books.

Rogers, C. R. (1951). *Client-centered therapy: Its current practice, implications, and theory*. Boston, MA: Houghton Mifflin.

Roland, A. (1996). How universal is the psychoanalytic self? In A. Roland (Ed.), *Cultural pluralism and psychoanalysis: The Asian and North American experience* (pp. 3–21). New York, NY: Routledge.

Roland, A. (2003). Psychoanalysis across civilizations. *The Journal of the American Academy of Psychoanalysis and Dynamic Psychiatry, 31,* 275–295. doi:10.1521/jaap.31.2.275.22118

Rowe, C. E., & MacIsaac, D. W. (1989). *Empathic attunement: The "technique" of psychoanalytic self psychology*. Northvale, NJ: Aronson.

Safran, J. D. (2012). *Psychoanalysis and psychoanalytic therapies*. Washington, DC: American Psychological Association.

Safran, J. D., & Muran, J. C. (2000). *Negotiating the therapeutic alliance: A relational treatment guide*. New York, NY: Guilford Press.

Sandell, R., Bloomberg, J., Lazar, A., Carlsson, J., Broberg, J., & Schubert, J. (2000). Varieties of long-term outcome among patients in psychoanalysis and long-term psychotherapy: A review of findings in the Stockholm outcome of psychoanalysis and psychotherapy project (STOPP). *The International Journal of Psychoanalysis, 81,* 921–942. doi:10.1516/0020757001600291

Schafer, R. (1983). *The analytic attitude*. New York, NY: Basic Books.

Schlesinger, H. J. (2003). *The texture of treatment: On the matter of psychoanalytic technique*. Hillsdale, NJ: Analytic Press.

Schofield, W. (1964). *Psychotherapy: The purchase of friendship*. Englewood Cliffs, NJ: Prentice Hall.

Schore, A. N. (2003). *Affect regulation and the repair of the self*. New York, NY: Norton.

Searles, H. (1975). The patient as therapist to his analyst. In P. Giovacchini (Ed.), *Tactics and techniques of psychoanalytic therapy* (Vol. 2, pp. 95–151). New York, NY: Aronson.

Shedler, J. (2010). The efficacy of psychodynamic therapy. *American Psychologist, 65,* 98–109. doi:10.1037/a0018378

Silberschatz, G. (2005). *Transformative relationships: The control mastery theory of psychotherapy.* New York, NY: Routledge.

Solms, M., & Turnbull, O. (2002). *The brain and the inner world: An introduction to the neuroscience of subjective experience.* New York, NY: Other Press.

Stark, M. (1999). *Modes of therapeutic action: Enhancement of knowledge, provision of experience, and engagement in relationship.* Northvale, NJ: Aronson.

Steiner, J. (1993). *Psychic retreats: Pathological organizations in psychotic, neurotic and borderline patients.* London, England: Routledge. doi:10.4324/9780203359839

Stern, D. B. (1997). *Unformulated experience: From dissociation to negotiation in psychoanalysis.* Hillsdale, NJ: Analytic Press.

Stern, D. N. (1985). *The interpersonal world of the infant: A view from psychoanalysis and developmental psychology.* New York, NY: Basic Books.

Stolorow, R. D., & Atwood, G. E. (1997). Deconstructing the myth of the neutral analyst: An alternative from intersubjective systems theory. *The Psychoanalytic Quarterly, 66,* 431–449.

Strachey, J. (1934). The nature of the therapeutic action of psychoanalysis. *The International Journal of Psychoanalysis, 15,* 127–159.

Strupp, H., Hadley, S., & Gomez-Schwartz, B. (1977). *Psychotherapy for better or worse: An analysis of the problem of negative effects.* New York, NY: Aronson.

Sugarman, A. (2007). Whatever happened to neurosis? Who are we analyzing? And how? The importance of mental organization. *Psychoanalytic Psychology, 24,* 409–428. doi:10.1037/0736-9735.24.3.409

Sullivan, H. S. (1970). *The psychiatric interview.* New York, NY: Norton.

Sulloway, F. J. (1992). *Freud, biologist of the mind: Beyond the psychoanalytic legend.* Cambridge, MA: Harvard University Press.

Summers, R. G., & Barber, J. P. (2010). *Psychodynamic therapy: A guide to evidence-based practice.* New York, NY: Guilford Press.

Thompson, M. G. (2003). *The ethic of honesty: The fundamental rule of psychoanalysis.* New York, NY: Rodopi.

Vaillant, G. E. (1992). *Ego mechanisms of defense: A guide for clinicians and researchers.* Washington, DC: American Psychiatric Association.

Wachtel, P. L. (2007). *Relational theory and the practice of psychotherapy.* New York, NY: Guilford Press.

Waelder, R. (1960). *Basic theory of psychoanalysis.* New York, NY: International Universities Press.

Wallerstein, R. S. (1998). *Lay analysis: Life inside the controversy.* Hillsdale, NJ: Analytic Press.

Wallin, D. J. (2007). *Attachment in psychotherapy.* New York, NY: Guilford Press.

Wampold, B. E. (2001). *The great psychotherapy debate: Models, methods, and findings*. Mahwah, NJ: Erlbaum.

Wampold, B. E. (2010). *The basis of psychotherapy: An introduction to theory and practice*. Washington, DC: American Psychological Association.

Weiner, I. B., & Bornstein, R. F. (2009). *Principles of psychotherapy: Promoting evidence-based psychodynamic practice*. New York, NY: Wiley.

Westen, D. (1998). The scientific legacy of Sigmund Freud: Toward a psychodynamically informed psychological science. *Psychological Bulletin, 124,* 333–371. doi:10.1037/0033-2909.124.3.333

Westen, D., Novotny, C. M., & Thompson-Brenner, H. (2004). The empirical status of empirically supported psychotherapies: Assumptions, findings, and reporting in controlled clinical trials. *Psychological Bulletin, 130,* 631–663. doi:10.1037/0033-2909.130.4.631

Winnicott, D. W. (1965). Ego integration in child development. In *The maturational processes and the facilitating environment*. London, England: Hogarth Press.

Winnicott, D. W. (1971). The use of an object and relating through identification. In *Playing and reality* (pp. 86–94). New York, NY: Basic Books.

Winnicott, D. W. (1974). Fear of breakdown. *The International Review of Psychoanalysis, 1,* 103–107.

Yalom, I. D. (2002). *The gift of therapy: An open letter to a new generation of therapists and their patients*. New York, NY: HarperCollins.

Zaretsky, E. (2005). *Secrets of the soul: A social and cultural history of psychoanalysis*. New York, NY: Vintage.

Amy Wenzel

Cognitive Therapy 4

C ognitive therapy is an active, collaborative, present-focused approach to psychotherapy that aims to help clients understand the manner in which their thinking and behavior contribute to their distress, develop strategies to overcome unhelpful cognitive and behavioral patterns, solve their current life problems, and apply the strategies they have learned to manage life's challenges well after therapy has ended. Many courses of cognitive therapy are relatively short term and time limited; a typical course of cognitive therapy is 12 or 16 sessions (Wenzel, Brown, & Karlin, 2011), and some clients even see substantial change in as few as four sessions (Hirsch, Jolley, & Williams, 2000). However, cognitive therapy can run a lengthier course for challenging clients (J. S. Beck, 2005), such as those with multiple life problems, comorbid Axis I disorders, and/or Axis II disorders.

Cognitive therapy was originally developed as a treatment for depression (A. T. Beck, 1976; A. T. Beck, Rush, Shaw, & Emery, 1979), and it has since been adapted for the

http://dx.doi.org/10.1037/14253-004
Exploring Three Approaches to Psychotherapy, by L. S. Greenberg, N. McWilliams, and A. Wenzel

treatment of anxiety disorders (A. T. Beck & Emery, 1985), substance abuse (A. T. Beck, Wright, Newman, & Liese, 1993), eating disorders (Fairburn, 2008), personality disorders (A. T. Beck, Freeman, Davis, & Associates, 2004), and suicidal behavior (Wenzel, Brown, & Beck, 2009). More recently, it has been developed as an adjunctive treatment for serious psychiatric conditions, such as bipolar disorder (Basco & Rush, 2005) and schizophrenia (A. T. Beck, Rector, Stolar, & Grant, 2009). Cognitive therapy's versatility is also evidenced by the fact that it can be delivered in formats other than individual psychotherapy, such as in groups (Bieling, McCabe, & Antony, 2006) and with couples and families (Dattilio, 2010). These are but only a handful of the adaptions of cognitive therapy, and there are many more for additional psychiatric disorders, psychological problems, and medical conditions with psychological components, all of which have been demonstrated to be efficacious by empirical research.

Mental health practitioners learning cognitive therapy often wonder how cognitive therapy is similar to and different from cognitive–behavioral therapy (CBT). In fact, many scholars and clinicians use the terms *cognitive therapy* and *CBT* interchangeably (e.g., J. S. Beck, 2011; Epp & Dobson, 2010; Wenzel, Liese, Beck, & Friedman-Wheeler, 2012). One way to view this issue is that CBT can be regarded as a broad field that encompasses a family of psychotherapies, with cognitive therapy being one of the founding members within this family (K. S. Dobson, 2012). Cognitive therapy was developed and tested during a time in which a number of psychotherapies with a cognitive and/or behavioral focus were simultaneously being developed and tested. Examples of these other therapies include (but are not limited to) rational emotive behavior therapy (Ellis & Harper, 1975), stress inoculation training (Meichenbaum, 1985), and systematic desensitization (Wolpe, 1969). Complicating matters further is that these treatments did not remain isolated from one another, so as the field progressed, researchers and clinicians were influenced by these myriad protocols and incorporated elements from many of them as they refined their treatments. As a result, many specific CBT protocols overlap significantly, and aspects of cognitive therapy, in particular, can be found in many, if not all, of the members of the cognitive–behavioral family. Today, the field of CBT encompasses an array of treatment approaches, including (but not limited to) cognitive therapy, behavioral activation (Addis & Martell, 2004), panic control treatment (Barlow & Craske, 2006), problem-solving therapy (D'Zurilla, & Nezu, 2007), and dialectical behavior therapy (Linehan, 1993). One can argue, however, that cognitive therapy holds special importance within the broader CBT field, as it has the greatest depth and breadth of empirical support for its efficacy and effectiveness

(K. S. Dobson, 2012; Epp & Dobson, 2010), and it has significantly influenced newer CBT protocols.

Because of the overlap among CBT protocols, it is important to understand what makes cognitive therapy unique, innovative, and influential. Some mental health professionals mistakenly view cognitive therapy as a set of techniques that treat a client's symptoms but that are not woven into a coherent theory and that do not resolve underlying issues. In actuality, cognitive therapy is a highly intricate system of psychotherapy (K. S. Dobson, 2012) in which clients' clinical presentations are understood according to the cognitive and behavioral factors that precipitated, maintain, and exacerbate their distress. This way of understanding is called *cognitive case conceptualization* (J. S. Beck, 2011; Kuyken, Padesky, & Dudley, 2009), and it serves as the foundation for cognitive therapy with any one client, as it provides a coherent template to organize a client's disparate presenting problems, and it guides the strategic implementation of clinical interventions. A second feature of cognitive therapy that makes it unique is its session structure, which allows therapists to systematically monitor their clients' progress in treatment, model an organized approach to solving life's problems, and ensure that strategies to reduce distress are being practiced in and out of session. A final feature of cognitive therapy that makes it unique is, indeed, the set of therapeutic techniques that it offers to therapists in order to achieve meaningful cognitive and behavioral change. However, effective cognitive therapy is much less dependent on the use of a specific technique than it is on the understanding of the client's clinical presentation according to the cognitive case conceptualization and the strategic and skilled application of techniques to address the conceptualization's many layers.

All of these unique features of cognitive therapy are discussed in more detail in the sections that follow in this chapter. The first section describes cognitive therapy's theoretical underpinnings and the manner in which understanding of these theoretical underpinnings can facilitate cognitive case conceptualization. The second section of this chapter describes the principle techniques of cognitive therapy, with a focus on their strategic application in light of the cognitive case conceptualization. The third section identifies the manner in which these techniques were delivered by a cognitive therapy expert, Dr. Judith Beck, to the clients who served as case demonstrations on the DVDs, *Three Approaches to Psychotherapy With a Male Client* and *Three Approaches to Psychotherapy With a Female Client*. This section describes the rationale for the strategic application of these techniques and considers the overall effectiveness of Dr. Beck's work with the clients in the case demonstrations. The chapter concludes with a brief consideration of cognitive therapy's empirical base and directions for future research and development.

Theoretical Underpinnings

The premise that inspired Dr. Aaron T. Beck, often regarded as the "father" of cognitive therapy, to develop this therapeutic approach was a simple one: He observed in his clinical practice that the manner in which his clients were perceiving or interpreting events in their lives seemed to have a profound effect on their mood, as well as on their subsequent behavioral and physiological responses. He concluded that it was not as much situations in his clients' lives that contributed to their distress as it was the meaning that these situations held for his clients (A. T. Beck, 1976; J. S. Beck, 2011). Thus, cognition plays a central role in the theory that underlies cognitive therapy. *Cognition* is defined as internal activity, such as thoughts, images, interpretations, judgments, attitudes, and so on, that help us make sense of information that we encounter in our daily lives. Cognition encompasses both processes (i.e., *how* people think) as well as the *products* of this processing (i.e., *what* people think; Ingram & Kendall, 1986). Figure 4.1 displays the basic premises of this theory.

Consider, for example, a mother who learns that her son was suspended from school after getting into a fight with another child. If she

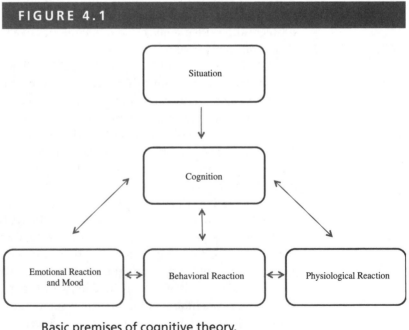

FIGURE 4.1

Basic premises of cognitive theory.

thinks something like, "He is so disrespectful! He did this just to spite me," it is logical that her emotional response would be one of anger. Behaviorally, she might yell excessively at her child, and physiologically, she might experience rapid heart rate and shallow breathing. If she thinks something like, "Oh no, now the parents of the other child will be mad at me," it is logical that her emotional response would be one of nervousness. Behaviorally, she might avoid telephone calls for fear that the other child's parents might be calling to confront her, and physiologically, she might experience a sense of restlessness and of being keyed up. If she thinks something like, "This just confirms that I'm a horrible parent," then her emotional response would be one of sadness. Behaviorally, she might give up on disciplining her child, with the attitude of "why bother?", and physiologically, she might experience a sense of dread in the pit of her stomach. When people repeatedly respond to life events in such a way, such that their responses are exaggerated relative to what is called for by the situation, take into account only part of the picture, and/or are otherwise unhelpful, they are vulnerable to emotional distress such as anger, anxiety, and depression. Cognitive therapists call these types of thoughts *automatic thoughts,* with the idea that these thoughts arise so quickly that many people do not realize that they are exerting a noticeable effect on their mood, behavior, and physiology (J. S. Beck, 2011).

The most common way to identify automatic thoughts that are associated with unhelpful emotional, behavioral, and physiological reactions is to ask a person what was running through his or her mind just then. Indeed, much of our cognition is experienced as verbal thoughts that run through our minds or as verbal statements that we make to ourselves. However, notice that the definition of cognition provided earlier in this section also refers to images. At times, cognition occurs in pictorial form, rather than in verbal form. For example, the mother who has a nervous emotional response to her son being suspended from school might have a catastrophic mental image of the other child's parents arriving at her front door, screaming and threatening her. The mother who has a sad emotional response to her son being suspended from school might have a memory of getting in trouble when she was a child and of being told that she cannot do anything right. Thus, it is important to conceptualize automatic thoughts broadly as mental activity that carries significant meaning, regardless of the format in which it is experienced.

Although the central premise of cognitive theory is often stated, simplistically and mistakenly, as "cognition *causes* emotion, behavior, and physiological responses," seasoned cognitive therapists recognize that the relations among these constructs are much more complex than this. It is true that, according to cognitive theory, unhelpful cognition indeed influences uncomfortable and/or maladaptive emotional, behavioral, and physiological responses. However, this does not mean that cognition is viewed as the sole cause of emotional, behavioral, and physiological responses—cognitive therapists recognize that these reactions are multidetermined and arise through many pathways, such as those that are biological, environmental, and psychological in nature. Moreover, notice the bidirectional arrows in Figure 4.1. These bidirectional arrows represent instances in which emotion, behavior, and physiology can, in turn, have just as significant an effect on cognition. For example, the mother who has a sad emotional response to her son being suspended from school might use effective parenting strategies despite the fact that she views herself as a horrible parent. If these parenting strategies succeed in ensuring that her son learns a lesson and is not suspended again, she might reevaluate her view that she is a horrible parent and draw a more balanced conclusion. Thus, cognition, emotions, behaviors, and physiological responses affect one another, and it has been proposed that intervening at the level of one of these constructs has the potential to facilitate change in the others (Borkovec, Newman, Pincus, & Lytle, 2002).

The theory described in this chapter to this point captures the psychological processes that are proposed to explain the manner in which clients respond to situational stressors. However, cognitive theory also provides a rich conceptualization of people's underlying belief systems that can, in part, explain the specific automatic thoughts, emotions, behaviors, and physiological responses that arise in any one situation. Figure 4.2 displays the expanded cognitive model, which captures these additional layers of psychological processes.

According to cognitive theory, people develop fundamental beliefs about themselves, others, the way the world works, and the future (i.e., *core beliefs;* J. S. Beck, 2011) through formative experiences. Often these formative experiences occur during childhood, but significant events experienced during adulthood (e.g., being in combat) can also influence beliefs. A particular formative experience does not necessarily guarantee the type of belief that develops; rather, these experiences interact with a person's biology (e.g., genetic vulnerability to a mood disorder) and psychological characteristics (e.g., difficulty tolerating uncertainty) in shaping a person's belief system. In most instances, people are characterized by both helpful (e.g., "I'm a good person") and unhelpful (e.g., "I'm a failure") beliefs. When times are relatively calm, the helpful beliefs are most likely to be activated. However, in times of stress, the unhelpful beliefs are more likely to be activated. In Figure 4.2, there is a circle around the icons representing unhelpful beliefs and stress because, according to theory, when unhelpful beliefs are activated in times of stress, there is an increased likelihood that people will experi-

FIGURE 4.2

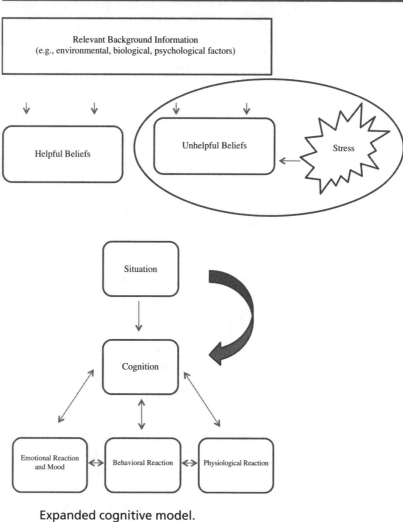

Expanded cognitive model.

ence thoughts and images consistent with those beliefs when they are faced with a challenging situation. Thus, cognitive theory is an example of a *diathesis-stress* approach to understanding psychopathology (cf. Ingram, Miranda, & Segal, 1998; Wenzel & Beck, 2008), such that the unhelpful beliefs are viewed as a diathesis, or vulnerability, that exerts influence only in times of stress or difficulty.

Another important feature of cognitive theory is that it proposes an association between specific types of cognition and specific emotional responses (i.e., *cognitive content specificity*; A. T. Beck, Brown,

Steer, Eidelson, & Riskind, 1987). If a person has recurrent cognitions that reflect a theme of hopelessness, then the most likely emotion that he would experience is depression. In contrast, if a person has recurrent cognitions about threat or an inability to cope, then the most likely emotion that she would experience is anxiety. This aspect of cognitive theory means that the cognitions that a person experiences in any one situation are not random; rather, their underlying meaning is related to beliefs that are activated. For example, the mother who has a nervous emotional response to her son being suspended from school might be operating according to the belief "I'm weak and vulnerable." In contrast, the mother who has a sad emotional reaction to her son being suspended from school might be operating according to the belief "I'm worthless."

The activation of unhelpful core beliefs does more than just affect the thoughts and images that a person has in any one situation. Core beliefs also provide a context for people to develop rules, assumptions, and attitudes that guide the manner in which they live their lives and respond to life's challenges, which J. S. Beck (2011) termed *intermediate beliefs*. These intermediate beliefs often give rise to stress, disappointment, and difficulty adapting to the demands of life's challenges because they can be quite rigid and inflexible. Consider the mother whose core belief "I'm worthless" has been activated. She might live by the rule "If my son gets into trouble at school, then it means I am a horrible parent." She might make the assumption that her parenting is the only determinant of her son's behavior, failing to acknowledge other, equally powerful influences that contribute to her son's behavior. She might take on the attitude "The worst thing in the world would be for my son to get in trouble at school." Intermediate beliefs usually set unreasonably high standards for one's own and others' behavior, failing to take into account the ebb and flow of life events and the challenges that people invariably experience. As a result, they prime the person to experience unhelpful automatic thoughts when the person's personal experience does not match with the rules, assumptions, and attitudes by which he or she lives.

Unhelpful core beliefs are also associated with strategic behavioral patterns that are designed to protect a person from the pain and distress that typically accompany these beliefs, called *compensatory strategies* (J. S. Beck, 2011). At times, these behavioral patterns serve to maintain the core belief. This type of strategy is exemplified by the mother who has a sad emotional reaction when her son gets in a fight at school when she gives up on disciplining him altogether. Other behavioral patterns are engaged in an attempt to prove the core belief wrong. This type of strategy would be exemplified by the same mother who, instead of giving up on disciplining her son, becomes overly involved in all aspects of his life to monitor him, such as by volunteering in his classroom, becoming the den mother of his Cub Scout troop, and hosting play dates at her home rather than allowing him to attend play dates at other people's homes. Still other behavioral patterns reflect an attempt to avoid confrontation of the core belief altogether. Compensatory strategies, then, usually serve to engrain the unhelpful core belief even further. This association between compensatory strategies and core beliefs is yet another illustration of the dynamic interplay between cognition and behavior.

In summary, cognitive theory specifies that the manner in which people view and make meaning of situations they experience in their lives has a substantial influence on their mood, their behavior, and their physiological sensations. Mood, behaviors, and physiological sensations can also amplify a person's thoughts and beliefs. Cognitive reactions to situational stressors do not occur at random; rather, they are predictable in light of the person's beliefs about himself or herself, others, the world, and the future. Under stress, there is an increased likelihood that unhelpful beliefs are activated. These beliefs develop through a person's formative experiences, his or her biological makeup, and psychological tendencies, and they give rise to rigid and inflexible rules, assumptions, and behavioral patterns that have the potential to exacerbate emotional distress. This theoretical foundation provides a rich tapestry of varying layers of cognition, emotion, and behavior that can account for a client's current functioning in light of his or her background and experiences.

The manner in which this theoretical foundation translates to clinical care is through the cognitive case conceptualization. As was stated previously, cognitive case conceptualization is the manner in which a therapist applies cognitive theory to describe and explain a client's clinical presentation and current distress (J. S. Beck, 2011; Kuyken et al., 2009). It allows therapists to systematically organize information that they have learned about their client according to the constructs described thus far in this chapter (e.g., core beliefs, rules and assumptions). It guides therapists in selecting the most relevant therapeutic techniques, as therapists use the conceptualization to identify strategies that will help their client address current problematic situations and that have the potential to, in turn, begin to modify or deactivate an unhelpful belief system or counteract unhelpful behavioral patterns. The cognitive case conceptualization allows for cognitive therapy to be much more than the application of various techniques; instead, it provides a cogent framework for therapists to characterize the psychological processes that contribute to, maintain, and exacerbate emotional distress and to strategically intervene on the basis of this understanding. It ensures that therapeutic techniques are not selected and implemented willy-nilly, but instead so that they are applied strategically with the aim of modifying a fundamental cognitive or behavioral process that is theorized to account for significant variance in the client's clinical presentation.

Principle Techniques

Despite the name *cognitive therapy,* behavioral strategies are seen by cognitive therapists as just as important as cognitive ones. Thus, both cognitive and behavioral techniques are regarded as principle in cognitive therapy. In addition, cognitive therapists also use techniques to organize the session and orient clients to their symptoms and the therapeutic approach itself, such as an organized session structure and psychoeducation. Moreover, they also use techniques to promote relapse prevention and ensure that clients can apply the strategies they have learned after therapy has completed. This section describes the following cognitive therapy techniques: (a) session structure, (b) psychoeducation, (c) cognitive restructuring, (d) behavioral strategies, (e) problem solving, and (f) relapse prevention.

SESSION STRUCTURE

Cognitive therapists follow a session structure in order to model a systematic approach to solving life's problems and to ensure that clients leave the session with something tangible to address their distress. Each component of the session structure is administered strategically to move therapy forward. Cognitive therapy session structure can be viewed as a technique because it can help clients acquire an organized framework to respond to life's challenges. Typical cognitive therapy session structure components include (a) brief mood check, (b) bridge from the previous session, (c) setting of the agenda, (d) discussion of agenda items, (e) periodic summaries, (f) homework, and (g) final summary and feedback (J. S. Beck, 2011).

The brief mood check is a means to obtain information about clients' current mood state, compare it with their mood state in other sessions in order to monitor progress, and check in regarding other issues relevant to clients' individual clinical presentations (e.g., suicidal ideation, alcohol or drug use). In addition, it is a way that cognitive therapists show care and concern for their clients' well-being in order to foster the therapeutic relationship (J. S. Beck, 2011; Wenzel et al., 2011). Many cognitive therapists find it helpful for information about clients' current mood state to be obtained using a quantitative scale. A quantitative scale allows the therapist and client, together, to evaluate the client's progress and treatment and ensure that the techniques that have been applied thus far are associated with noticeable improvements in mood. Some cognitive therapists use established self-report inventories to facilitate the brief mood check, such as the Beck Depression Inventory–II (A. T. Beck, Steer, & Brown, 1996). Other cognitive therapists use Likert-type scales, such as 0 = *no depression;* 10 = *worst depression.*

The bridge from the previous session allows clients to articulate what they took away from the previous session and the manner in which those conclusions and skills applied to events in their lives in the time in between session. Not only does this aspect of cognitive therapy session structure orient the client to his or her therapeutic work, it also ensures that a thread is woven across sessions so that consistent progress is being made toward treatment goals. In addition, the bridge from the previous session provides an opportunity for the therapist to assess whether clients had a negative reaction to anything that was said or done in the previous session. Moreover, for clients who have a difficult time with concentration and memory, the bridge from the previous session allows for the therapist to remind them of the events of the previous session and identify issues that require continued discussion in the current session.

A central technique that emerges from cognitive therapy session structure is the setting of an agenda, or items to be covered in the current session. Because cognitive therapists want their clients to leave the session with something that will help to reduce distress or solve a problem, they use the agenda as a way to ensure that discussion is targeted and focused. In many instances, clients will have a number of issues that are bothering them that they wish to discuss, and therapists help them to identify these issues up front and decide the amount of time to allocate to each one of them. Approaching the session in this manner often provides hope to clients that their life problems can indeed be organized and addressed using a systematic framework. There are times when, as the session progresses, it becomes clear that there will not be enough time to discuss all of the issues that were identified by the client, or that new issues have arisen that were not anticipated when the agenda was set. In these instances, cognitive therapists revisit the agenda collaboratively with their client and, together, they make a reasoned decision about how best to use the remaining time. The agenda is not meant to limit the type of discussion that ensures during the course of the session, but it helps to ensure that client and therapist are not swept away by tangential discussion that leaves little promise for cognitive and behavioral change.

Discussion of agenda items is at the heart of every cognitive therapy session, as the majority of the session is devoted to addressing the issues that are concerning to the client. In keeping with cognitive therapy's systematic approach, cognitive therapists are mindful to limit discussion that is overly detailed and descriptive. Rather, the cognitive therapist takes care to apply a cognitive therapy framework to understanding clients' current problems and to set up a strategic intervention that will provide some relief from these problems. In other words, clients usually bring the *content* to each session, and therapists usually bring the *structure* and *strategy* to each session. Cognitive therapists provide an environment that helps clients to understand their problems in a different and presumably more helpful light, and they select from their wide range of techniques to help clients acquire a skill or a strategy for addressing their problems. As each agenda item is discussed, cognitive therapists make periodic summaries to ensure that they understand the nature of their clients' concerns and that their clients have, indeed, gained a new understanding and/or have acquired a skill for addressing them.

Another central component of cognitive therapy session structure is the expectation that clients will continue their therapeutic work outside of session, which is often referred to as *homework*. The rationale for homework is that it allows an opportunity for clients to generalize the gains made in session to their daily lives outside of session. There is evidence that the more clients comply with homework, and the more competent cognitive therapists are in working collaboratively with clients to develop homework, then the more likely it is that clients will respond to treatment (Addis & Jacobson, 2000; Ryum, Stiles, Svartberg, & McCullough, 2010). Homework is usually most effective when it flows logically from the discussion of agenda items, is written down, and is started and practiced in session. Because homework plays such an important role in cognitive therapy, it is critical for cognitive therapists to thoroughly review clients' homework at the time of the subsequent session.

At the end of each session, cognitive therapists ask for a final summary and feedback. The summary allows the therapist and client to review the main take-home points of the session, which allows clients to consolidate their learning and ensure that they do not overlook an important conclusion that was drawn earlier in the session. Devoting time for feedback ensures that therapists (a) know whether clients understand the cognitive model and ways to apply cognitive and behavioral strategies to their lives, (b) have a sense of the degree to which their clients view this approach as helpful and applicable, and (c) are made aware of anything that bothered their clients about the session. Asking for feedback in this manner facilitates a collaborative therapeutic relationship because it communicates to clients that their input is valuable and that they play an active role in treatment.

PSYCHOEDUCATION

One important aspect of cognitive therapy is that it is a transparent process, meaning that therapists aim to provide their clients with enough information and rationale so that their clients, eventually, no longer need therapy. The adage used by cognitive therapists is that they want their clients to put them out of business, so that clients can become their own therapists and no longer need to attend sessions. Thus, cognitive therapists continually provide education to their clients, with the goal of empowering them to use this information in a manner that will address their emotional distress and life problems. *Psychoeducation* is defined as the provision of information to clients so that they can better understand their clinical presentation and the therapeutic approach to treating it.

Cognitive therapists provide many different types of psychoeducation at many different times during the course of treatment. In the early phase of treatment, cognitive therapists often provide psychoeducation about the nature of the psychiatric disorder with which the client is diagnosed. Many clients are relieved to know that there is a name for the symptoms that they are experiencing and that the symptoms can be understood, logically, as being a part of a larger syndrome. Also in the early phase of treatment, cognitive therapists provide psychoeducation about cognitive therapy. Typical pieces of information to include in this discussion are (a) the nature of cognitive therapy (e.g., short term, time limited, active, collaborative); (b) the manner in which cognitive therapy can be applied to understand and address their specific clinical presentation (i.e., cognitive model); and (c) evidence for the efficacy and effectiveness of cognitive therapy, in language that is understandable and meaningful to clients. Many cognitive therapists find that psychoeducation about the nature of and expected results from cognitive therapy instills hope in their clients.

Although psychoeducation usually plays a less prominent role as treatment progresses, it continues to be critical in helping clients to understand the rationale behind the intervention strategies that are being suggested and practiced. Thus, when therapists identify a particular intervention strategy on the basis of the cognitive case conceptualization, they provide clients a detailed and understandable rationale for the purpose underlying the intervention. In addition, cognitive therapists link the rationale back to the cognitive model that was presented to clients in the early phase of treatment in order to reinforce the applicability of the model to their specific life circumstances. The provision of this type of psychoeducation often motivates clients to use the interventions, as they can see a clear path from the application of their intervention to relief from their emotional distress and life problems. It also allows clients to absorb the cognitive and behavioral principles that underlie treatment so that they can remember these principles when they are not in session.

COGNITIVE RESTRUCTURING

Cognitive restructuring is the process by which therapists work collaboratively with their clients to identify, to evaluate, and if necessary to modify cognitions that were experienced in situations in which the client experienced emotional distress (K. S. Dobson, 2012). The goals of this process are to help clients (a) recognize the manner in which their cognition affects their mood and (b) modify inaccurate and/or unhelpful cognition that is exacerbating emotional distress. Therapists use cognitive restructuring with their clients during sessions in order to coach clients in acquiring these skills and allowing them to practice, and they encourage clients to systematically apply these skills in their daily lives in between sessions. This technique is used when therapists learn that clients indeed experience inaccurate and/or unhelpful automatic thoughts in situations that are associated with distress and when there is evidence that clients are operating under the activation of an unhelpful core belief.

A typical first step in cognitive restructuring is to educate clients about the basic model, perhaps even sharing a diagram like that displayed in Figure 4.1. When providing this education to clients, cognitive therapists take care to describe the model in compelling and understandable language, such as by illustrating the model with a vivid example (e.g., the mother who has three different reactions when her son gets in a fight at school) and applying it to a situation in their clients' own lives. In addition, they help their clients to begin to recognize their own automatic thoughts. A standard question that cognitive therapists ask their clients is, "What was running through your mind when that occurred?"

It is not uncommon for clients to have difficulty identifying cognition when they are first being socialized into this strategic process. At first glance, their experience is one in which they perceive that something "bad" happens, and they have an emotional reaction without having anything that runs through their minds. Thus, cognitive therapists are prepared to assess for inaccurate and/or unhelpful cognition in a number of different ways. For example, the cognitive therapist might give an example of two different thoughts—one being close to what the therapist hypothesizes that the client experienced and the other being very different from what the therapist hypothesizes that the client experienced—and then ask the client to choose the one that was more likely. Recalling the fact that cognition can encompass more than verbal thoughts, the cognitive therapist might ask the client if he sees a distressing mental image or if she is remembering a painful memory. The cognitive therapist might ask, "What did that situation mean to you or about you?" in order to get at the fundamental idea that is associated with the client's emotional distress.

Once clients have mastered the ability to recognize automatic thoughts that are associated with emotional distress, they work with their therapist to evaluate the degree to which these automatic thoughts are accurate and helpful. Cognitive therapists take care not to directly "challenge" their client's cognition for a number of reasons. First, in many instances there is a "grain of truth" in the manner in which clients are viewing problems in their lives, and adopting a challenging stance has the potential to invalidate the emotional pain that clients are experiencing. Second, it is more meaningful for clients to conclude on their own that their thinking is inaccurate or unhelpful, rather than being told so by a therapist who challenges them, so that they learn to recognize inaccurate and unhelpful thinking on their own, in their own environment outside of the session. Thus, therapists create an environment of *guided discovery* (cf. J. S. Beck, 2011), such that therapists ask questions that stimulate clients to think critically about the manner in which they are viewing their problems so that they can, on their own, draw an alternative, more balanced conclusion. Cognitive therapists often regard this process as one in which they function, collaboratively, with their clients as detectives or scientists, examining objectively all of the "evidence" or "data" and then drawing a conclusion. After drawing a more balanced conclusion, cognitive therapists and the clients consider the impact of believing this new cognition, such as whether clients' emotional distress has diminished and/or whether clients will do something differently now that they are viewing their problem in a more objective or helpful manner. This new cognition is often referenced by several different names, such as an *alternative response,* an *adaptive response,* a *balanced response,* and/or a *rationale response* (J. S. Beck, 2011; D. Dobson & Dobson, 2009; Greenberger & Padesky, 1995; Wright, Basco, & Thase, 2006).

To facilitate this process of guided discovery, cognitive therapists use strategic *Socratic questions* to encourage clients to evaluate their thinking (e.g., J. S. Beck, 2011). Socrates was a Greek philosopher who had a major influence on the development of Western philosophy. He was known for his teaching style, in which he would ask his students questions that would allow them to formulate a thoughtful answer. As described previously, cognitive therapists adopt this same approach with their clients when using cognitive restructuring techniques. One straightforward line of Socratic questioning is to ask clients to consider the evidence that both supports and does not support the automatic thought under consideration. When using this specific technique, cognitive therapists are careful to focus the discussion as much as possible on evidence that is factual. Many clients believe they can easily identify a great deal of evidence that supports an inaccurate or unhelpful automatic thought, only to later realize that the evidence in support of the cognition was overstated or their own interpretation of the facts.

Another group of Socratic questions targets automatic thoughts that are predictions of a worst-case scenario (i.e., *decatastrophizing questions;* J. S. Beck, 2011). It is common for clients in cognitive therapy to make negative predictions of events that will occur in the future, which is often associated with a great deal of anxiety and dread as well as self-defeating behavior (e.g., avoidance of solving a problem). To address this type of unhelpful automatic thought, cognitive therapists often ask their clients to consider the worst, best, and most realistic outcomes of the problem or situation. Examining automatic thoughts in this manner often helps clients to see that there is a very low probability, and sometimes no probability, of the worst-case scenario occurring. Even when there is a realistic probability of a worst-case scenario occurring, cognitive therapists can work with clients to evaluate how they would cope if the worst-case scenario were to occur. On the basis of this questioning, clients often conclude that although the worst-case scenario might not be pleasant, they will be able to survive it and obtain some valuable wisdom from it.

A third group of Socratic questions targets automatic thoughts that are largely accurate but nevertheless seem to be contributing to clients' emotional distress and/or ineffective problem solving. Cognitive therapists ask their clients to consider the degree to which fixating on a particular cognition is helpful or hurtful to them, or the advantages and disadvantages that are associated with the particular automatic thought. These questions often help clients to come to some acceptance about a problem or circumstance in their lives that they cannot change so that they can cope as effectively as possible.

A useful tool for organizing the information used in the cognitive restructuring process is the *Thought Record.* The Thought Record allows clients to systematically record information about a problematic situation, the automatic thoughts and emotional reactions that they experienced, adaptive responses, and outcomes of adopting the adaptive response. Various cognitive therapy texts and therapist manuals present the Thought Record in slightly different formats (e.g., J. S. Beck, 2011; D. Dobson & Dobson, 2009; Greenberger & Padesky, 1995; Wright et al., 2006). In general, many cognitive therapists first use a Three-Column Thought Record (i.e., consideration of situations, automatic thoughts, and emotions) to provide an opportunity for their clients to gain practice in recognizing inaccurate and/or unhelpful automatic thoughts and to see that there is an association between cognition and emotion in their own lives. When clients gain proficiency in recognizing inaccurate and unhelpful cognitions, cognitive therapists then will introduce a Five-Column Thought Record, which adds two additional columns for the adaptive response and the outcome of adopting the adaptive response. Regardless of their specific format, Thought Records are often important supplements to the cognitive restructuring work that is done in session because they allow clients to see these psychological processes at work in written form and to gain structured practice in using the cognitive restructuring skills that they are acquiring in session.

The Thought Record is but one of many specific tools that cognitive therapists use as an aid in the process of cognitive restructuring. In reality, cognitive therapists use an array of tools to facilitate cognitive restructuring, and the selection of any one tool is made on the basis of the client's unique learning style as well as on the client's preferences that are expressed in context of the collaborative therapeutic relationship. For example, a *coping card* is a tool that allows clients to record on an index card an inaccurate or unhelpful automatic thought along with a compelling adaptive response, using an adaptive response that is arrived at through cognitive restructuring work done in session (J. S. Beck, 2011). Coping cards allow clients to have "easy access" to the fruits of their cognitive restructuring work in their daily lives when they experience similar types of automatic thoughts and associated emotional distress. A *behavioral experiment* is a tool that allows clients to test negative predictions experientially in their own environments, in order to gather "real-life" data that will support or refute an inaccurate or unhelpful automatic thought (J. S. Beck, 2011). Many clients find behavioral experiments to be especially powerful in helping them to reframe problematic automatic thoughts, as they see firsthand that their negative predictions are inaccurate. In general, cognitive therapists can be as creative as possible in developing tools collaboratively with clients to evaluate inaccurate and unhelpful automatic thoughts. The key in developing and implementing these tools is to use cognitive theory as a foundation and to be sure that the specific aims of the tool match the client's needs, which are identified through cognitive case conceptualization.

The reevaluation of situation-specific thoughts is perhaps the most central technique used by cognitive therapists. Many clients find that acquisition of the tools to gain perspective on inaccurate and unhelpful automatic thoughts is sufficient to achieve relief from emotional distress; in these cases, therapy is considered to be short term, and treatment is completed after there is evidence that clients have achieved a reduction in symptoms and can apply these strategies in their daily lives. However, other clients, particularly those with chronic Axis I disorders or Axis II pathology, require extended practice with cognitive restructuring and the restructuring of underlying beliefs that perpetually prompt inaccurate and unhelpful automatic thoughts that occur in specific situations. Cognitive therapists can use many of the same cognitive restructuring techniques for belief modification as those used for modification of situation-specific automatic thoughts. There also exist many other techniques that are specific to belief modification (J. S. Beck, 2011; Wenzel, 2012), all of which require clients to articulate the underlying belief; develop a new, healthier belief; and strategically shift the client from the old, unhelpful belief to the new, healthier belief. Cognitive therapists generally find that shifting to a healthier belief takes more time than shifting to a more helpful situational automatic thought, but that doing so is associated with sustained improvement in many areas of their clients' lives.

BEHAVIORAL STRATEGIES

As can be surmised by their name, behavioral strategies are those that target the behavioral manifestation of clients' emotional distress. Whereas the general cognitive restructuring approach can be applied in a similar manner to clients with many types of presenting problems, behavioral strategies are highly tailored to the client's specific clinical presentation. Thus, a sound cognitive case conceptualization plays a key role in pointing to strategic behavioral interventions that might have promise with any one client.

To take but one example, it has long been observed that depressed clients are often characterized by prominent symptoms of anhedonia and fatigue, which prevent them from actively engaging in their environment and which in turn further entrenches their mood disturbance (e.g., Lewinsohn, Sullivan, & Grosscup, 1980). A strategy often used by cognitive therapists in this situation is to first reengage clients in their environment by having them engage in activities that provide them with a sense of pleasure and/or mastery (A. T. Beck et al., 1979; J. S. Beck, 2011; Wenzel et al., 2011). Such an approach has been integrated and expanded into a contemporary therapeutic approach called *behavioral activation* (Addis & Martell, 2004), which is a member of the larger family of CBTs. It is thought that once clients begin to feel some relief from their painful depressive symptoms by approaching pleasurable and meaningful activities rather than by avoiding them, they have started to build momentum toward recovery and can make better use of the wide array of strategic interventions that cognitive therapy has to offer.

Cognitive therapists use two specific techniques to achieve this aim. *Activity monitoring* is an activity in which clients record the activities in which they engage in the time between sessions and provide three ratings: (a) the degree of mastery (or sense of accomplishment) they get out of the activity, (b) the degree of pleasure they get out of the activity, and (c) an overall depression rating for the day. In the subsequent session, cognitive therapists review this form in detail with their clients, paying close attention to the association between the mastery and pleasure ratings and the overall depression rating for each day. Using guided discovery, cognitive therapists ask their clients to draw conclusions about the manner in which the current way they are spending their time might be exacerbating their mood disturbance. If it is concluded that the activities in which clients are engaging are giving them little mastery or pleasure, then cognitive therapists and their clients undertake *activity scheduling.* Activity scheduling allows clients to commit to engaging in activities that are associated with high levels of mastery and pleasure in the time between sessions, with the idea that they will reevaluate their depression at the subsequent session and determine whether engaging in these new activities is effective in improving their mood. Many clients in cognitive therapy experience a noticeable reduction in depression when they begin to engage more actively in their environments.

Anxiety, in contrast, is often treated using different behavioral strategies. The cornerstone of the behavioral treatment of anxiety is *exposure,* such that cognitive therapists work with their anxious clients to develop and execute a systematic plan for making contact with a feared stimulus or situation (Abramowitz, Deacon, & Whiteside, 2011). The rationale for this treatment is that anxiety is typically accompanied by avoidance behavior, and avoidance maintains anxiety through negative reinforcement. That is, an anxious person experiences a sense of relief when she is able to avoid a feared stimulus. Because that sense of relief is reinforcing, it increases the likelihood that she will avoid the stimulus again in the future. Thus, cognitive therapists use exposure strategies to break the cycle of avoidance, which allows their anxious clients to fully experience anxious arousal so that they can develop a new cognitive and behavioral repertoire when they have contact with the feared stimulus or situation (Abramowitz et al., 2011). Although exposure is, in itself, a behavior in which cognitive therapists encourage their clients to engage, it is important to acknowledge that there are important cognitive effects from engaging in it. Specifically, clients begin to collect additional data about the likelihood of worst-case scenarios occurring and an inability to cope, which ultimately reduces their expectancy of harm (Hofmann, 2008). In other words, exposure can function as a behavioral experiment, and the data from the behavioral experiment can be used to reframe clients' views of the feared stimulus or situation. This is another example of the dynamic interplay between cognition and behavior.

Other behavioral strategies are aimed at reducing clients' high arousal in order to achieve a calm physiological and emotional state, engage in reasoned problem solving, and refrain from acting impulsively or aggressively. Examples of these strategies include progressive muscle relaxation (Bernstein & Borkovec, 1973) and diaphragmatic breathing (Barlow & Craske, 2007). These strategies can be applied in a versatile manner, depending on the needs of the individual client. For example, some clients are overwhelmed and agitated when they arrive for session, making it difficult for them to focus systematically on their problems. Practicing a relaxation or breathing technique at the beginning of each session will allow them to achieve a state of calm, so that they can be more centered when they approach the remainder of their therapeutic work. Other clients believe that they overreact when they perceive that they are being threatened in their daily lives outside of session. These clients can be taught a relaxation or breathing exercise in session; they can then practice the exercise systematically at times when they are not experiencing emotional distress, in order to develop the skills; once they have mastered the skills, they can apply them when they notice an increase in emotional distress. As clients learn to use relaxation and breathing techniques, cognitive therapists encourage them to pay close attention to their emotional state before and after using the strategy in order to gather evidence for the strategy's usefulness. Cognitive therapists are also mindful of instances in which clients use these skills as safety signals, such that they are relying on these strategies to help them avoid intense affect, thereby interfering with learning that intense affect is not dangerous. Thus, these behavioral coping strategies are best used when they facilitate clients to approach their problems and situations they view as threatening, rather than to avoid them.

Finally, some clients lack effective communication skills, which has the potential to reinforce negative beliefs about the self, as well as to interfere with the attainment of pleasure and mastery from their environments. In these instances, cognitive therapists work with their clients on communication skills training, such as developing skills to be assertive, to be responsive to others, and/or to enhance connection in their close relationships. Cognitive therapists and their clients can work on both verbal and nonverbal skills, as well as the application of these skills to particular situations and contexts (e.g., making small talk; Herbert et al., 2005). Psychoeducation is often used to educate clients about the importance of the skill, as well as the finer points of implementing the skill. Cognitive therapists also make creative use of role-playing as they target the acquisition of effective communication skills with their patients. For example, they might first demonstrate the appropriate use of the skill in a role-play (e.g., the therapist models making a request of others to their client), and then the client might be asked to assume the same role and practice it, with the therapist on the receiving end. At times, cognitive therapists find that there is a need to incorporate cognitive restructuring into their work on effective communication skills, as some clients experience unhelpful cognitions that interfere with the effective execution of these skills. A logical homework exercise is for clients to practice the skills they have learned in between sessions.

PROBLEM SOLVING

Because of its focus on the present, much of cognitive therapy is devoted to problem solving. In fact, some cognitive therapy experts view some types of pathological behavior, such as a suicide attempt, as essentially stemming from maladaptive problem solving (Reinecke, 2006; Wenzel et al., 2009). As with the other strategies described in the chapter to this point, cognitive therapists use a guided discovery approach to problem solving with their clients. That is, they create an environment for clients to acquire skills that will help them to solve problems in their lives and for clients to draw their own conclusions on the basis of problem solving. In other words, cognitive therapists neither tell their clients how to solve their problems nor give their clients direct advice. Instead, they help their clients gain skills and confidence in solving their problems so that clients can address other problems in their lives that arise when they are no longer in therapy.

Many cognitive therapists base their problem-solving approach on the noteworthy work of D'Zurilla and Nezu (2007), who developed an entire cognitive–behavioral treatment approach to problem solving. Using this framework, cognitive therapists recognize that there are (at least) four distinct steps to problem solving. First, cognitive therapists work with their clients to identify and describe the problem using objective language. Oftentimes clients present for therapy in significant distress because they are overwhelmed by many life problems, some of which overlap with one another. Taking the time to identify and describe the problem helps clients to select one targeted problem to address and ensures that the problem is manageable. Second, cognitive therapists encourage their clients to brainstorm all possible solutions to their targeted problem. This step requires adequate attention, as many clients, when they are in distress, are quick to dismiss possible solutions without thoroughly considering their merits and drawbacks. It is often the case that, as a result of problem solving, clients select a solution (or a combination of solutions) that would initially have been dismissed had they not removed their initial judgment of the solution. Third, cognitive therapists provide a forum for clients to evaluate the advantages and disadvantages of each possible solution, which allows them to decide on a solution. A logical homework exercise is for clients to implement the selected solution for homework. When clients return to the subsequent session, cognitive therapists take care to thoroughly evaluate the degree to which the solution achieved its desired aims. If it indeed achieved its desired aims, cognitive therapists use the experience as positive reinforcement for the development of clients' self-efficacy. If it did not achieve its desired aims, cognitive therapists identify the obstacles that interfered and use other cognitive therapy techniques to address them.

Cognitive therapists often find it important to integrate other techniques with problem solving. For example, some clients report unhelpful cognitions about the problem or their ability to solve it, which could interfere with their motivation or ability to implement a solution as effectively as possible (i.e., a negative problem orientation; D'Zurilla & Nezu, 2007). Cognitive restructuring techniques could be used to address these negative cognitions. Other clients have problems that require interpersonal interaction, and it is clear that they lack the skills to communicate effectively. Communication skills training could be used to address these behavioral deficits.

RELAPSE PREVENTION

Cognitive therapists approach treatment with their clients with an end in sight, such that it is clear that treatment will eventually be completed, and clients will be able to implement cognitive and behavioral strategies in their own lives, without needing the support of a therapist. Clients know from the onset of treatment that it will eventually end. Cognitive therapists recognize that they have reached the later phase of treatment through many means, such as (a) a sustained decrease in mood scores obtained during the brief mood check, (b) the fact that clients have met the treatment goals that they established at the onset of treatment, and (c) clients' demonstration of the ability to effectively use the cognitive and behavioral strategies in their own lives. When it is recognized that clients have made significant progress in one or more of these areas, cognitive therapists develop a plan collaboratively with their clients to end treatment. Thus, treatment does not end suddenly on the same session in which it is acknowledged that clients have made these gains. Rather, cognitive therapists and their clients, together, review progress in treatment and decide on an individualized approach to ending treatment. In many instances, that individualized approach involves the tapering of sessions to a lower frequency and/or scheduling a "booster" session several months following the end of treatment.

An important order of business to complete with all clients before ending therapy is to engage in *relapse prevention*, which is defined as a set of techniques for clients to learn to recognize when they need to use the strategies taught in therapy and to plan for setbacks (J. S. Beck, 2011;

D. Dobson & Dobson, 2009; Wenzel et al., 2011). One relapse prevention technique involves reviewing the signs and symptoms of the clinical issue that first brought clients into treatment. The intent of this technique is to ensure that clients recognize subtle indicators of emotional distress so that they can take skillful action before there is a recurrence or relapse of the psychiatric disorder that brought them into treatment. A second relapse prevention technique is the consolidation of learning. Although most cognitive therapists take intentional steps to consolidate learning during each session, during the later sessions of cognitive therapy, they review the intervention strategies used across sessions and the manner in which they applied to the client's life. Cognitive therapists will often ask their clients to describe, in detail, the rationale for various strategies and the manner in which they actually implemented them in their own unique life circumstances. Some cognitive therapists ask clients to imagine a future stressor or crisis and to walk them through the application of the cognitive and behavioral strategies (Wenzel et al., 2009). A third relapse prevention technique is to encourage clients to write down the specific contact information for their care providers (e.g., their therapist, their psychiatrist) so that they can easily locate this information in times of need. Finally, cognitive therapists use cognitive restructuring techniques to ensure that clients have accurate expectations for the course of their clinical presentation posttreatment. For example, clients are encouraged to recognize that some degree of variability in mood is to be expected, depending on the stressors that they are experiencing in their lives. Cognitive restructuring is also used to address any unhelpful automatic thoughts that clients have about the end of treatment (e.g., that the therapist is abandoning them).

A CAVEAT

Although this section describes some basic cognitive therapy techniques, it is important to know that, in reality, seasoned cognitive therapists have a deep arsenal of strategic techniques from which they can choose and that many of those techniques, particularly those that address underlying beliefs and compensatory strategies, are quite rich and complex. In fact, entire books have been written that describe cognitive therapy techniques in detail (e.g., Leahy, 2003). Moreover, cognitive therapists do not limit themselves only to techniques that are described in books on this therapeutic approach; cognitive therapists borrow techniques from other therapeutic schools in order to help their clients achieve lasting cognitive and behavioral change. They keys in implementing any technique in cognitive therapy, whether it is a standard cognitive therapy technique or one that is borrowed from another therapeutic school, is that it (a) is logical to administer in light of the individual client's cognitive case conceptualization, (b) has a clear rationale that is communicated to the client and that underlies its strategic application, and (c) is seen through by the therapist in its entirety in order for it to make its greatest impact.

Case Applications

In this section, many of the techniques described in the previous section are illustrated with the clients Kevin and Chi Chi, who were portrayed on the DVDs *Three Approaches to Psychotherapy With a Male Client* and *Three Approaches to Psychotherapy With a Female Client*.

KEVIN

Dr. Beck had access to a transcript of Kevin's intake interview, so she knew a bit about his background, current life stressors, and symptoms. On the basis of this information, she hypothesized that he did not meet the criteria for an Axis I psychiatric disorder, although she speculated that he likely met the criteria for a major depressive episode in the past and that it was quite possible that he continued to experience residual symptoms of depression. She also noted that he reported anxiety that was bothersome to him. She used this information to begin to conceptualize the factors that contribute to his current emotional distress. The following section describes and provides a rationale for the many strategic therapeutic interventions that Dr. Beck used with Kevin. When applicable, decision points are illustrated, and potential consequences of those decision points are considered.

Assessing Automatic Thoughts

Toward the beginning of the session, Kevin referenced apprehension that he believed "comes up automatically." Dr. Beck responded with, "What's it saying?" and then asked him to go a step further after he responded with, "It's saying 'stop, you don't want to do this.'" The rationale for asking "What's it saying" is to identify a cognition that is paired with the emotional experience of apprehension. Thus, Dr. Beck was subtly socializing Kevin into the process of recognizing what he is thinking when he experiences an uncomfortable emotion. She asked him to follow up on the thought "Stop, you don't want to do this," because she recognized that there was likely an underlying meaning to the situation that was far more powerful—and more directly associated with apprehension—then a reactionary type of statement such as that one. Many clients, when they first start cognitive therapy, identify automatic thoughts that are not particularly useful for cognitive restructuring. Such automatic thoughts can be reactionary statements like the one Kevin made, or they can be descriptive statements that give more detail about the situation without referring to its meaning. With careful listening and experience, cognitive therapists have a sense of the degree to which identified automatic thoughts will be useful or not useful to work with in session, and if they are not useful, they ask additional questions to identify the fundamental, more central automatic thought that is most closely associated with distress.

After identifying meaningful automatic thoughts, many cognitive therapists will use guided discovery to help clients see that they are associated with emotional distress and gain perspective on them by evaluating the degree to which they are accurate and helpful. Dr. Beck could have taken this approach with Kevin in order to model, early on in the session, the power of cognitive restructuring in helping clients to reduce their emotional distress. However, Dr. Beck instead made a statement suggesting that they should talk about this idea further, and she asked Kevin whether there was anything else that he would like to discuss. These statements reflect an attempt at agenda setting, such that she aimed to clarify the topics they should cover in the session before getting into more detail. This therapeutic choice is useful for clients like Kevin, who are very verbal and who tend to jump from topic to topic. Thus, although Dr. Beck began to model the beginnings of cognitive restructuring to socialize him into the approach, she believed it was more important to model a systematic approach to addressing his life problems before moving on. Failing to clarify the agenda would have the potential to mirror what, quite possibly, is the typical haphazard way he has approached problems in his life in the past, which has not always been effective. Moreover, Dr. Beck did not lose the opportunity to model the cognitive restructuring process, as she revisited it later in the session to build on the foundation that she had established in these early moments of the session.

Focusing on the Present

After Kevin's apprehension was initially identified as an agenda item, he began to provide details about the origins of his apprehension, which he believed were rooted in childhood. A typical course of cognitive therapy is to first begin with a focus on the present and clients' current emotional distress and life problems. The goal of this present focus is to ensure that clients notice meaningful changes in their lives in as timely a manner as possible. For many clients, this present focus is sufficient. Clients who have chronic Axis I disorders or Axis II disorders might benefit from a focus on formative experiences that contributed to their problems. However, even in these instances, the focus is on understanding how these experiences influenced the development of underlying beliefs and compensatory strategies that affect their current life circumstances, rather than a lengthy exploration of the details of these formative experiences. Moreover, such discussion of formative experiences from one's past usually only occurs after clients have acquired cognitive and behavioral strategies that have the potential to address these patterns.

Thus, Dr. Beck was faced with a choice about whether to intervene or whether to give Kevin space to expound on the details. On the one hand, she chose to allow him to provide some details, with the sense that he needed to talk about them. This decision had the potential to enhance the therapeutic relationship, as it subtly demonstrated to Kevin that Dr. Beck was being responsive to his needs. In fact, cognitive therapists are generally encouraged to balance attention to the therapeutic relationship and cognitive and behavioral change in any one moment in treatment (Wenzel et al., 2011). On the other hand, Dr. Beck indeed intervened when Kevin made a statement suggesting that he realized he was becoming tangential (i.e., "And so I'm not sure that's relevant to this, but . . ."). Specifically, she made a statement that tied the discussion back to the main point—apprehension (i.e., "Well, I think the one thing it has in common is apprehension"), and she followed up with a series of statements about staying in the present in order to continue to socialize Kevin into the cognitive therapy approach. All the while, she checked in with him for his feedback (e.g., "Does that sound right to you?") to ensure that he was on board with the rationale she suggested, that he believed she understood his issues, and that their collaborative therapeutic relationship was maintained.

Thus, the choices in this situation were to allow Kevin to provide great detail about his childhood or to intervene and refocus him on the present. Dr. Beck recognized that there was a rationale for both, and she successfully allowed him to speak some about childhood issues that he believed were important without getting so far off track that valuable session time was spent on description, rather than on intervention. An additional technique that Dr. Beck could have integrated at this point in the session is to ask Kevin directly about his assumptions about the activities in which clients typically engage in therapy. Kevin was currently seeing a therapist; it was quite possible that his therapist operated according to a different theoretical approach, such as one that focused more heavily on childhood experiences. When cognitive therapists sense that clients would like to use their time differently than what had been agreed on when they were educated about cognitive therapy's present focus, they can inquire directly about these attitudes and assumptions and examine their relevance using cognitive therapy strategies. Doing this allows cognitive therapists to model a cognitive approach to addressing issues that arise in "real time" during the course of treatment and come to some sort of mutual understanding of the focus that treatment will take, reducing the likelihood that those attitudes and assumptions will emerge and possibly interfere with therapeutic work later in the course of treatment.

Problem Solving

After Dr. Beck refocused Kevin into the present-focused nature of cognitive therapy, they regrouped and focused on a specific problem that was associated with apprehension, which was Kevin's desire to develop a support system. Dr. Beck asked Kevin, "What steps could you take to develop a better support system?" Kevin readily gave her a list of steps he would take, and from this information, Dr. Beck concluded that Kevin does not demonstrate impairment in problem solving. Thus, there was no need to coach him in systematically acquiring all of problem-solving skills described earlier in this chapter. Rather, it became evident that Dr. Beck's main role was to help Kevin clarify, more precisely, the type of support that he was hoping to develop because he was describing support in a vague manner. It is possible that Kevin's characteristic style of jumping from topic to topic had been preventing him from fully clarifying the problem and settling on concrete steps to solve it.

Kevin's focus was on obtaining support in his role as a self-employed businessman. Dr. Beck inquired about another type of support—emotional support from friends and family—stating that this had been her first impression of what he meant when he first introduced the issue of developing a support system. Because Kevin admitted that both types of support would be helpful, Dr. Beck chose to continue clarifying problems he is encountering in his emotional support system. Although she began discussion about the emotional support he receives and could receive from his mother, it became clear that Kevin was not particularly interested in obtaining more emotional support from his mother than he was currently getting.

An alternative approach for addressing this issue of support would have been to continue to focus on his desire to develop a professional support system, with the reasoning that it was the issue of greatest importance to Kevin, and it is important to solve one problem as completely as possible before moving onto another problem. Dr. Beck hypothesized that Kevin has a core belief of helplessness, such that he believes he cannot get a handle on his problems. Thus, she might have asked him how, precisely, having a professional support system would be helpful to him in order to identify any automatic thoughts about his ability to succeed professionally. Then, they could have addressed the larger problem (i.e., apprehension about his career) using two approaches: (a) clarifying a specific source of professional support that he would pursue (i.e., solving a concrete problem) and (b) restructuring automatic thoughts about his ability to succeed that might, possibly, have been undermining his performance.

Both of these approaches (i.e., adding a focus of emotional support, staying only on the topic of professional support) had the potential to yield fruitful results. Although the discussion of emotional support from his mother did not solve Kevin's problem, it led to discussion of emotional support from a romantic interest and the apprehension that he experiences, more generally, in romantic relationships. Dr. Beck checked in with Kevin to identify the direction in which he thought it would be best to go, and he chose to focus on apprehension in romantic relationships. Dr. Beck readily integrated cognitive restructuring techniques to address some automatic thoughts about relationships that were likely to interfere with relationship initiation and maintenance, so Kevin was, indeed, able to learn the same techniques that he would have learned if they had solely focused on automatic thoughts about his career. Moreover, in actuality, Dr. Beck revisited apprehension about Kevin's career toward the end of the session, after they had applied the cognitive skills to concerns about romantic relationships. In contrast, had Dr. Beck chosen the alternative route described previously (i.e., keeping the focus on professional support only), she might have helped Kevin to solve his apprehension about his career more thoroughly. However, she might not have gotten to another important piece of his apprehension that was clearly associated with emotional distress.

This example demonstrates that there are many decisions cognitive therapists can make, and that in many instances there is no one "right" choice. The keys are that (a) the chosen intervention has a basis in the cognitive case conceptualization, (b) the focus of discussion is decided on collaboratively by the therapist and client, (c) the therapist sees the intervention through before moving onto an unrelated topic, and (d) a clear take-home point emerges from the discussion that will help the client deal with the problem outside of session. Dr. Beck accomplished all of these points in her demonstration.

Educating About the Cognitive Model

As Kevin discussed the apprehension that he experiences in romantic relationships, Dr. Beck took care to clarify his automatic thoughts (e.g., "Oh, no, there's no way that this is gonna turn out well. In one way or another, it will be a calamity"). In order to begin to educate Kevin about the cognitive model, she contrasted his thought with an automatic thought that was very different: "Oh, great! I'll meet a wonderful woman. We'll have a good life together." With each automatic thought, she pointed out the likely emotional reaction (i.e., happiness and optimism vs. apprehension). This type of psychoeducation is essential in cognitive therapy so that clients can understand the rationale for the strategic interventions that cognitive therapists make.

Dr. Beck took psychoeducation a step further by asking for feedback from Kevin, such that she asked him to articulate, in his own words, what he heard her say about the relation between cognition and emotion. Solicitation of this type of feedback is critical, as many clients agree that the model makes sense, but they have a difficult time understanding it beyond mere agreement with their therapist. Such clients usually have difficulty applying these principles in their daily lives, outside of session. Kevin, in contrast, clearly understood the cognitive model and began to entertain the possibility that his apprehension was more about his perception of the situation than the situation itself.

Evaluating Automatic Thoughts

Because Kevin readily grasped the cognitive model and the manner in which it applied to his life, Dr. Beck began to orient him to strategies he could use to evaluate his negative predictions. Specifically, she educated him about examining the evidence that supports and refutes the negative prediction, as well as about decatastrophizing questions. They then applied these techniques to the evaluation of his prediction that if he gets into a relationship, it will become impossible and end. Dr. Beck also could have chosen to educate Kevin about other sets of questions, such as questions that stimulate clients to (a) consider alternative explanations, (b) consider the consequences of responding to or not responding to the automatic thought, (c) evaluate the usefulness of the thought, and (d) get some distance from their thought by considering what they would tell a friend or family member in a similar situation (J. S. Beck, 2011). Had Dr. Beck been continuing to see Kevin, it is likely that she would have educated him about these additional sets of questions across the course of several sessions.

During this part of the discussion, several new, albeit related, issues arose, and Dr. Beck was mindful of balancing attention to the original prediction (i.e., that the relationship would be impossible and end) with acknowledging the manner in which these other issues complicate the problem. For example, Kevin stated that one of his strengths is interpersonal problem solving, but that this quality might make it difficult to have relationships because he is prone to recognizing problems. Dr. Beck chose to make a small intervention to address this concern (i.e., helping him to see that if this trait begins to interfere with a new relationship, that there is hope that he can work it out with his therapist). However, she quickly asked questions to refocus discussion on the evidence that supports and does not support the idea that he cannot have a long-term romantic relationship. In addition, Kevin expressed concern that he is not a good judge of relationship partners and that he has difficulty coping with rejection. Dr. Beck noted that these are both important issues, but she chose not to pursue them because she was mindful of the time remaining in the session, and she wanted to ensure that she achieved some closure on the original topic of discussion.

Because Kevin demonstrated the ability to understand and apply the cognitive restructuring techniques to his apprehension about romantic relationships, Dr. Beck asked him if he would like to apply these skills to his apprehension about his career. This intervention demonstrated respect for his role in the therapeutic relationship, as he had initially indicated that he wanted to work on apprehension about his career. It also consolidated his learning because he had the opportunity to apply the skills to a very different area of his life, thus promoting their generalizability.

This case demonstration was one in which the cognitive restructuring process went smoothly, as Kevin was readily able to understand cognitive theory, acquire the skills, and apply them in a thoughtful way to his life. As clients go, Kevin was characterized by a number of strengths, such as the fact that he was not experiencing significant enough symptoms of emotional distress to interfere with his concentration and memory, his openness to the cognitive interventions, and his psychological-mindedness. This is not always the case with other clients. Thus, cognitive therapists expect that they might have to educate clients about the cognitive model in many different ways, such as by having some compelling examples pre-prepared that vividly demonstrate the relation between cognition and emotion and by recognizing and working with automatic thoughts as they arise during the course of session. It also is common for cognitive therapists to spend more time working with clients to identify key automatic thoughts (e.g., across more than one session) before beginning to evaluate them, as many clients require sustained practice with the identification process.

Writing Down Key Points

Toward the end of the session, Dr. Beck wrote down the two sets of questions that they had considered in evaluating Kevin's negative predictions: (a) questions that will allow Kevin to examine the evidence that supports and does not support his thoughts, and (b) decatastrophizing questions. Cognitive therapists believe that therapeutic techniques make the greatest impact if clients have reminders of the fruits of their work that they can consult in their lives outside of session. Thus, after most cognitive therapy sessions, clients will leave with a written reminder of the main conclusions that were drawn as a result of the work done in therapy, with the idea that this will serve as a memory aid in times of need.

Two points deserve note here. First, Dr. Beck decided to write down the sets of questions for Kevin, which often occurs in cognitive therapy. However, in other instances, cognitive therapists have clients write down these take-home points for themselves. Cognitive therapists often find that having clients write down the main points of the session in their own words helps to increase their ownership over the therapeutic work and consolidates their learning. In Kevin's case, this strategy was not needed because he readily expressed enthusiasm for and commitment to the new knowledge that he acquired.

Second, Dr. Beck did not work with Kevin to develop a homework exercise, beyond the implicit expectation that he would consult the questions when he notices himself making negative predictions. Dr. Beck made this choice because they are not continuing their therapeutic work together. However, had they been in an ongoing therapeutic relationship, Dr. Beck would have spent more time with Kevin collaboratively developing a homework exercise to solidify these skills. For example, she could have introduced him to the Five-Column Thought Record so that he could practice, in between sessions, the ability to generate compelling alternative or adaptive responses.

Obtaining Feedback

At the end of the session, Dr. Beck obtained feedback from Kevin regarding his views of the session and whether he had the sense that she got something wrong or did not understand. Solicitation of feedback in this manner is another way to enhance the collaborative therapeutic relationship, as it communicates to clients that their views and opinions are important. In this case, Kevin was quite positive about the experience and provided feedback about an aspect of the session that he found helpful—the structure. In instances in which cognitive therapists are in ongoing relationships with clients, and those clients provide feedback suggesting that they are unhappy with the session, cognitive therapists take these concerns seriously and either attend to them at that moment or invite them to address their concerns in the next session as a high priority agenda item.

In addition to soliciting feedback about his satisfaction with the session, Dr. Beck could have asked for a summary of the main points of the session and an indication of the most important take-home points. This strategy allows clients to remind themselves of the important points that emerged from discussion of all agenda items, as frequently more than one main topic is discussed in session, and clients often have a "recency effect" for discussion of the final agenda item. Moreover, it allows clients another opportunity to articulate their understanding of the cognitive model and the rationale for the strategies that they plan to use in their daily lives.

Discussion

Overall, Dr. Beck's session with Kevin appeared to be quite effective. She socialized him into several core features of cognitive therapy, such as its present focus and targeted approach to addressing a specific life problem. She invited collaboration at many steps along the way, inviting him to make choices on the specific topic on which they would focus and checking in to ensure that he agreed with the rationale for her interventions. She educated him about the cognitive model and specific strategies for evaluating automatic thoughts that are associated with emotional distress (i.e., examining the evidence, decatastrophizing). She provided a forum for Kevin to put his own words on the cognitive model and realize the manner in which the strategies can apply to his specific life circumstances. Kevin left the session with a written record of these strategies that he can consult in times of distress in his everyday life. Thus, Dr. Beck achieved an important aim shared by all cognitive therapists—that the client leaves with something more than he had at the beginning of the session that has the potential to make a difference in his current level of emotional distress and life problems.

As was described earlier in this chapter, cognitive therapists use a session structure to maximize the likelihood that clients have tangible take-home points that they can use in between sessions to address current problems that are contributing to their emotional distress. This structure was evident in Dr. Beck's work with Kevin. Kevin introduced a number of issues in the session, including a desire to find a professional support group, a general feeling of apprehension, childhood roots of his apprehension, and negative predictions about romantic relationships. Using cognitive therapy session structure, Dr. Beck helped Kevin to focus on the issue he viewed as most relevant, while at the same time weaving a coherent thread across the issues (i.e., apprehension). In this way, Kevin was able to make progress in addressing two issues—apprehension about work and apprehension about romantic relationships—and to practice strategies that he can use to evaluate negative cognitions that emerge in specific situations representative of both domains.

Thus, a major advantage of beginning the session as Dr. Beck did was that it oriented Kevin to the type of active, structured work that is done in cognitive therapy, and it began to focus him on a specific issue that he had hoped to address in the session. Cognitive therapists would likely not see any disadvantages to this approach to beginning the session. At times, therapists who practice from different theoretical orientations wonder whether session structure, particularly setting an agenda near the beginning of the session, inhibits clients from speaking what is on their mind later in the session if it is different from what had been included on the agenda. The concern here is that the agenda is perceived as inflexible, and that material that is especially central to clients' core issues would not be pursued in session simply because it had not been identified as relevant at the onset of the session. However, notice that Dr. Beck revisited the agenda on several occasions throughout the session, as Kevin introduced different issues. At each juncture, rather than being swept away into discussion that may or may not be productive, Dr. Beck acknowledged that Kevin had shifted to a different subject and worked collaboratively with him to decide the most important issue to address. This deliberate choice acknowledges that an issue arose that might not have been considered when the agenda was first set, but it also models a systematic approach to addressing clients' problems so that the short time in session can be used as productively as possible.

If Dr. Beck were to continue working with Kevin, in the subsequent session she would check in with him on two issues. First, she would assess the degree to which he was making progress in pursuing a professional support group, as he stated that this was his goal in the previous session. Second, she would assess the degree to which he was able to use the evidence and decatastrophizing questions to reduce emotional distress in between sessions. If Kevin was making progress in these areas, she would ask him how he was able to use the skills learned in therapy to achieve his aims and how he can generalize this learning to other issues that arise in his life. If Kevin was not making progress in one or both of these areas, she would invite him to put this problem on the agenda for further discussion. During this further discussion, Dr. Beck would work with Kevin to determine the obstacles that interfered with making progress in these areas and brainstorm ways to overcome those obstacles. She might look specifically for unhelpful automatic thoughts that interfere with the generalization of the work done in treatment to his daily life (e.g., "What's the point? I don't have the ability to do this"), with the idea of using cognitive restructuring tools to reframe those thoughts. Dr. Beck also might invite Kevin to engage in further practice with the evidence and decatastrophizing questions so that he can become more skilled in applying them.

Dr. Beck could also choose to incorporate other cognitive therapy strategies in her work with Kevin. For example, she could pursue the two issues that Kevin introduced toward the end of the session but for which there was little time remaining to address: (a) his perception that he is a poor judge of potential relationship partners, and (b) his fear of rejection. She could use many of the same cognitive restructuring techniques as she did in the demonstration to evaluate and modify automatic thoughts associated with these issues. Doing this would not only allow Kevin more practice with these tools, but it would also demonstrate the versatility of the tools so that Kevin can see how they would apply to many of his issues surrounding relationships. If it becomes clear that he is passing on potential relationship opportunities because he believes he will be rejected, Dr. Beck could use a behavioral experiment to test out this prediction systematically before Kevin draws a conclusion. In contrast, if it becomes clear that he is passing on potential relationship opportunities because he approaches them in an awkward, potentially ineffective manner, then Dr. Beck could harness communication skills training, perhaps using role-playing or modeling in order to hone his interpersonal effectiveness. Yet another avenue Dr. Beck could take would be to gather data to test a hypothesis that she was beginning to form with Kevin during her work with him, namely, that he views problems as bad. Cognitive restructuring techniques could be used to evaluate this idea, rather than taking it as a guaranteed fact, and to implement behavioral experiments that would allow Kevin to see that, in some cases, problems can result in new opportunities rather than negative consequences.

Dr. Beck's work with Kevin might be short-term if he demonstrates the ability to apply cognitive therapy strategies in his life, reduce his emotional distress, and solve his problems. However, therapy might extend beyond the typical 12 to 16 sessions if he readily acquires these skills, but he continues to experience emotional distress and perceives that he has been unable to solve his problems. In the latter scenario, Dr. Beck could very well discuss experiences from earlier in his life that Kevin viewed as contributing to his sense of apprehension, with the aim of putting words to one or more core beliefs that resulted from these experiences. To achieve this aim, as Kevin describes relevant formative experiences, Dr. Beck would ask him about messages that he received from these experiences, such as messages about his worth as a person, messages about his responsibility to his family, and messages about his ability to cope. On the basis of the session recorded for the DVD demonstration, it is possible that Kevin has an unhelpful core belief that accompanies a sense of helplessness, such as "I am incompetent."

After establishing the existence of one or more unhelpful core beliefs, Dr. Beck would guide Kevin back to the present in order to identify, specifically, when these core beliefs are activated in his current life and the cognitive, emotional, and behavioral consequences of their activation. Subsequently, they would work toward defining a new, more helpful core belief (e.g., "I am competent"), and Dr. Beck could apply specific techniques in order to reinforce this new, more helpful core belief. One of many techniques that she could apply would be a historical test of the unhelpful core belief (J. S. Beck, 2011), such that she would work with Kevin to evaluate systematically distinct periods of his life (e.g., elementary school, high school, early adulthood before his daughter was born, early adulthood after his daughter was born) and identify instances that are inconsistent with this unhelpful core belief. Using this technique, most, if not all, clients find that their unhelpful core belief is a vast overgeneralization, failing to account for specific instances that contradict it.

There were many elements of this session that were typical of cognitive therapy. Dr. Beck implemented many session structure techniques, including reference to a brief mood check, a bridge from the previous session, setting of the agenda, discussion of agenda items, periodic summaries, and a final summary and feedback at the end of the session. She socialized Kevin into the cognitive therapy approach and model overtly by providing psychoeducation and subtly by assessing for cognition when he discussed his apprehension. She maintained a strong therapeutic relationship by inviting collaboration and by asking for frequent feedback, all the while ensuring that there was a specific focus of their discussion so that their time could be used as productively as possible. Moreover, she introduced specific cognitive therapy techniques, with the hope that they will be useful for Kevin to apply in his life outside of the session.

As was stated previously, the most atypical aspect of this session was the fact that homework played a less central role than it does in most cognitive therapy sessions. Kevin and Dr. Beck only had a brief period of time in between sessions; thus, there was not enough time for him to implement or practice a homework exercise that would have been developed in the previous session. Had a homework exercise been developed, however, Dr. Beck would have been sure to review it systematically during the second session. In addition, if they were to continue their work together, they would have developed a more concrete homework exercise for Kevin to implement or practice after the second session.

CHI CHI

Dr. Beck's initial conceptualization of Chi Chi incorporated the fact that Chi Chi does not meet diagnostic criteria for an Axis I disorder. As such, Dr. Beck viewed Chi Chi as functional in many areas of her life and that adopting a problem-solving focus on current issues that are stressful for Chi Chi might be sufficient to reduce her emotional distress. The following section describes and provides a rationale for many strategic therapeutic interventions that Dr. Beck used with Chi Chi. When applicable, decision points are illustrated, and potential consequences of those decision points are considered.

Facilitating Collaboration

As is standard practice in cognitive therapy, Dr. Beck and Chi Chi set an agenda for the manner in which they would use their time together in session. Although Chi Chi indicated that she had hoped to talk about anxiety at work, Dr. Beck suggested that they also focus on the degree to which the break-up of a relationship that ended 15 years ago was still causing Chi Chi distress. Dr. Beck made this suggestion on the basis of the transcript of Chi Chi's intake interview that she read before meeting with Chi Chi. During that intake interview, Chi Chi became visibly upset when she referred to that previous relationship. Dr. Beck hypothesized that the dissolution of this relationship held great meaning for Chi Chi and that this topic might yield powerful cognitions that could be addressed using cognitive restructuring.

It is important to note that Dr. Beck did not dictate the agenda for the session. She communicated, up front, to Chi Chi that she could opt not to broach that topic if she did not want to do so. This strategy facilitated collaboration in the therapeutic relationship, in that both Dr. Beck and Chi Chi contributed to the agenda, and Chi Chi's wishes were respected when she indicated that she did not want to talk in detail about the breakup. Dr. Beck could have made a stronger recommendation about the importance of talking about this relationship, with the idea that the session would be most productive if they addressed a topic that she had been avoiding dealing with for several years. When cognitive therapists make a recommendation like this one, they provide a clear rationale to the client, obtain their client's understanding of the rationale, obtain the client's consent, and monitor closely the therapeutic alliance. If clients continue to express clearly that they do not want to discuss a topic, cognitive therapists will respect that wish; note this avoidance as important information for the cognitive case conceptualization; and remain cognizant to catch signs that the topic is exerting unwanted effects on clients' cognition, emotion, and behavior. In the few instances in which clients refuse to talk about a particular topic, it is often the case that they become more comfortable in doing so later in the course of cognitive therapy, when they are more mindful of the manner in which cognition is associated with emotional distress and self-defeating behavior, when the therapeutic relationship has developed further, and when they have demonstrated skill in applying cognitive and behavioral tools to address their life problems.

Clarifying Meaning

While respecting Chi Chi's wishes not to discuss the details of the dissolution of the previous relationship, Dr. Beck simultaneously continued
to view another aspect of this issue as having the potential for great
importance in understanding Chi Chi's clinical presentation: Chi Chi's
fears about talking about emotionally laden subjects. Dr. Beck used two
strategies to maintain the collaborative relationship: (a) she asked for
Chi Chi's permission to talk about those fears, and (b) she posed the
plan of talking about these fears for a couple of minutes and then deciding whether continued discussion would be worthwhile.

To initiate consideration of this issue, Dr. Beck asked, "So if you were
to talk about it, what's the worst thing you'd be afraid of happening?"
Chi Chi replied that she would be overwhelmed and stuck. Dr. Beck followed up and asked, "And what does being stuck there mean?" This question represents an attempt to get at the underlying meaning of Chi Chi's
automatic thought and reflects the strategic application of the downward
arrow (A. T. Beck et al., 1979; Burns, 1980). Therapists who use this tool
ask repeatedly about the meaning of situational automatic thoughts until
they arrive at a belief whose meaning is so fundamental that there is no
additional meaning associated with it. Using this technique, Dr. Beck was
able to identify an important meaning associated with Chi Chi's view that
she would be overwhelmed and stuck, such that she would be mired in
the idea that she has not moved on from her past and has not forgiven
herself. Although Chi Chi's latter observation that she has not forgiven
herself is important material to address in psychotherapy conducted from
any theoretical approach, Dr. Beck did not follow up on that because she
had assured Chi Chi that she would respect her wishes not to discuss the
details of that topic. Instead, Dr. Beck clarified the two parts of Chi Chi's
belief—that she will get emotional if she talks about a difficult topic and
that this emotion would substantially burden her. Alternatively, Dr. Beck
could have continued to apply the downward arrow technique to elicit
even more fundamental meaning associated with Chi Chi's beliefs that she
would become stuck in her emotional state. Specifically, she could have
asked, "What does it mean about you if you were stuck in that emotional
state?" It is possible that Chi Chi would have identified a core belief such
as "I'm emotionally vulnerable," which would assume a central focus
in treatment.

Because Chi Chi began to talk more about the manner in which
her emotional reactions interfere with effective communication, particularly with her current boyfriend, Dr. Beck clarified the focus of their
work together. They decided to address this issue in light of an important conversation that Chi Chi believes that she needs to have with her
boyfriend, but that she also believes will cause her great emotional distress. Dr. Beck proceeded to work with Chi Chi on the specific problem

of having a conversation with her boyfriend about her lack of desire to have children, all the while keeping in mind the manner in which this problem relates to Chi Chi's belief that she will become stuck in her emotional state if she talks about difficult issues.

Communication Skills Training

Dr. Beck began to collect data about the typical manner in which Chi Chi's conversations with her boyfriend proceed, as well as the specific manner in which Chi Chi would communicate her main points. Putting herself in the shoes of Chi Chi's boyfriend, Dr. Beck hypothesized that some aspects of Chi Chi's approach had the potential to put her boyfriend on the defensive, which ultimately would steer her away from the desired outcome of the conversation. Dr. Beck then modeled an alternative approach for Chi Chi to communicate her message, and Chi Chi evaluated the degree to which this approach would achieve its desired outcome. By using techniques to address Chi Chi's communication style for discussing an important issue with her boyfriend, Dr. Beck ensured that progress would be made toward addressing a tangible issue that was of concern to Chi Chi.

Mindful of ensuring that Chi Chi leave the session with a concrete plan for having the conversation with her boyfriend, Dr. Beck made a number of direct suggestions during this portion of the session. Alternatively, Dr. Beck could have incorporated a greater emphasis on guided discovery. For example, she made the direct observation that having sensitive conversations via telephone is often difficult. Instead, she could have asked Chi Chi, "Have you thought about the particular modality in which you would have this conversation? What are the advantages about having this conversation in person, rather than on the phone?" Later, Dr. Beck suggested that "there might be another way to approach" her boyfriend. Dr. Beck could have first asked Chi Chi to consider the merits and drawbacks of the approach that she had just described, and if Chi Chi identified some drawbacks, she could ask, "What might be a different way to phrase this, given the drawbacks you just identified?" These questions would have allowed Chi Chi to draw her own conclusions about her communication style, rather than relying on Dr. Beck's direct suggestions. When there is sufficient time, cognitive therapists usually rely on the guided discovery approach so that clients are able to consolidate their learning, which increases the likelihood that they can use these skills and knowledge in situations that occur in their lives outside of session.

Evaluating the Worst-Case Scenario

As they were discussing the new approach for having the conversation with Chi Chi's boyfriend about having children, Dr. Beck sensed that there may be another piece of the problem, unspoken to that point in the session, that could contribute to Chi Chi's fear that she would become emotional during the conversation. She checked out this hunch by asking Chi Chi, "Now, are you fearful that he may want to break up with you?" Dr. Beck proposed that they consider how she would handle a break-up, keeping in mind that the dissolution of Chi Chi's relationship from 15 years ago holds profound meaning for her. Dr. Beck asked the question, "Are you in the same position in life as you were 15 years ago?" in order to give Chi Chi space to consider the manner in which she has achieved personal growth on which she can rely in times of adversity, such as the break-up of a long-term relationship. In addition, recalling that Chi Chi has the belief that experiencing negative emotion would keep her stuck, Dr. Beck asked, "Are you afraid of that negative emotion you'll feel if it happens?" and followed up by asking Chi Chi to describe an image of what it would be like if her boyfriend ended the relationship and she experienced the negative emotional consequences. Chi Chi did not describe the image in great detail, instead drawing the conclusion that "it wouldn't kill" her. Seeing that Chi Chi was readily able to draw a balanced response in light of this worst-case scenario, Dr. Beck began to work with Chi Chi to acknowledge the coping skills and resources that she has to manage the emotional distress associated with the ending of her relationship and the apprehension about the possibility of starting a new relationship.

Thus, this line of discussion resulted in Chi Chi concluding that she could cope if the unlikely worst-case scenario were to occur as a result of a heart-to-heart conversation with her boyfriend about not wanting to have children. This example illustrates the fact that cognitive restructuring does not always require the therapist to present information in a didactic manner (e.g., education about evidence and decatastrophizing questions). Rather, the therapist can pose Socratic questions that are tailored to clients' individual life circumstances in order to stimulate critical thinking and to facilitate the construction of a balanced, adaptive way of viewing the problem under consideration.

Putting Conclusions in Clients' Own Words

As she was working with Chi Chi to identify and evaluate automatic thoughts about her current boyfriend, the degree to which she could cope with the ending of that relationship, and her judgment about future relationship partners, Dr. Beck recognized that several tangible take-home points had come out of that discussion. As such, she proposed that they begin to write down some of these points so that Chi Chi would have access to them after the session. Dr. Beck took care to work with Chi Chi to ensure that the main points were worded according to Chi Chi's understanding, not her own understanding.

Writing clients' main take-home points and conclusions in their own words is essential to (a) ensure that they understood the work that had been completed in the session, and (b) allow them to take ownership over their therapeutic work so that it has maximum usefulness in their lives.

Shifting the Next Agenda Item

Dr. Beck reserved some time in the session to address the agenda item that Chi Chi had initially identified at the beginning of the session, and she suggested that they apply some of the tools that they had developed earlier in the session to address that specific problem. Dr. Beck took the opportunity to reinforce the relation between cognition and emotion by demonstrating that a balanced, adaptive response (i.e., "I've always gotten my projects done in the past") is associated with less anxiety than Chi Chi's original thoughts. She educated Chi Chi about evidence and decatastrophizing questions, and using guided discovery, she allowed Chi Chi space to examine her responses to these questions and the implication of those responses for the manner in which she was viewing her work situation. Dr. Beck worked specifically with Chi Chi's automatic thought that she would get fired from work if she made a major mistake by asking her whether other people have made mistakes but were not fired.

During this discussion, Dr. Beck directly pointed out to Chi Chi that she is a "known quantity" to her boss, with the rationale that this is another piece of evidence that is inconsistent with Chi Chi's prediction that she would get fired. Alternatively, Dr. Beck could have incorporated a greater emphasis on guided discovery by asking questions such as "Can you think of any other pieces of evidence that might counteract the idea that you will get fired if you make a mistake?" and "How, in particular, would the fact that you're a known quantity affect the likelihood that you would be fired if you made a mistake?" Guided discovery questions along these lines stimulate clients to see alternative viewpoints on their own, rather than relying on their therapist to point them out for them.

Discussion

When Dr. Beck asked Chi Chi for feedback at the end of the session, she indicated that she viewed her problems as "enormous" when she first started to work with Dr. Beck but that after two sessions, these problems seemed much more manageable because they were broken down into smaller pieces. Chi Chi is describing an important outcome for which cognitive therapists strive: that the systematic examination and modification of various aspects of life problems, such as the cognitive components and the behavioral components, solve current problems in clients' lives, even problems that had been viewed as chronic or daunting before clients began therapy. Thus, this session was quite effective because Chi Chi gained tangible tools to address two life problems (i.e., communication skills to address a conversation that she believes she needs to have with her boyfriend; cognitive restructuring skills to evaluate thoughts about her relationship and her job that are associated with emotional distress). The session also was effective because it was identified that Chi Chi carries the beliefs that she will become emotional when talking about difficult topics and that she will become stuck in that emotional reactivity, and because Chi Chi saw that she has more resources at her disposal than she had realized for coping with this emotional distress.

Dr. Beck began the session using typical cognitive therapy session structure, including addressing the brief mood check and the bridge from the previous session and setting an agenda. As was stated previously, cognitive therapists view this approach to beginning sessions as advantageous because it models a systematic approach to solving life's problems, it ensures that there is a thread that runs across sessions, and it ensures that time is used productively so that clients can leave with tangible conclusions and tools to address their life problems. In this particular case, Dr. Beck proposed an agenda item that was unrelated to the agenda item that Chi Chi had identified. Dr. Beck made this choice because she viewed the dissolution of Chi Chi's previous relationship as a topic that would yield fruitful discussion for which cognitive restructuring would be valuable, and that viewing that issue in a different light would have a particularly meaningful impact on Chi Chi's level of emotional distress.

Because cognitive therapy is a collaborative venture between therapists and their clients, there are many instances in which cognitive therapists propose items for the agenda that are not necessarily identified by clients. An advantage of doing this is that it ensures that topics most relevant to clients' emotional distress and case conceptualization, which might otherwise be avoided, are addressed. Avoidance is a central part of many types of psychiatric disorders (e.g., depression [Addis & Martell, 2004]; anxiety [Abramowitz et al., 2011]), and it is possible that reinforcing avoidance by not talking about issues that clearly are associated with significant emotional distress would ultimately exacerbate aspects of clients' clinical presentations. A disadvantage of doing this is that it could have a negative effect on the therapeutic relationship, with clients perceiving that they are being asked to face an issue before they believe that they are ready to do so. Dr. Beck successfully resolved any potential tension associated with this suggestion by respecting Chi Chi's wishes not to talk about the details, but to instead address the meaning associated with talking about such emotionally laden topics. Discussion of this issue demonstrates that cognitive therapy need not only focus on concrete, external problems in clients' lives; it is also a rich framework to address clients' beliefs about internal experiences, such as emotional processing.

If Dr. Beck were to continue working with Chi Chi, she would likely check in with her at the next session to determine (a) how the conversation went with her boyfriend if he had, indeed, been in town since the previous session, and (b) the degree to which Chi Chi has been applying the cognitive restructuring tools in her life. The conversation with Chi Chi's boyfriend, if it occurred, would likely be the main agenda item for the subsequent session because it was associated with a number of unhelpful beliefs that had been the focus of the previous session. Dr. Beck would look for evidence that refutes those beliefs in order to continue to have Chi Chi reevaluate them and develop a more balanced, adaptive perspective. If Chi Chi's boyfriend was in town, but she did not have the conversation with him, then this would also likely be the main agenda item, as it would give Dr. Beck additional evidence for Chi Chi's avoidant style of dealing with strong emotions that arise in the context of close relationships. If this were the case, Dr. Beck would rely on cognitive techniques to identify, evaluate, and modify additional automatic thoughts that fuel avoidance and that were not identified in the previous session. She would also use behavioral techniques to overcome avoidance (e.g., additional communication skills training, scheduling conversations about topics of increasingly greater depth so that Chi Chi gains practice in having these conversations).

Dr. Beck could pursue a number of additional avenues in her continued work with Chi Chi. Although not captured in the session on the DVD, Dr. Beck and Chi Chi had also worked on techniques to overcome her procrastination. Dr. Beck would also check in with Chi Chi to assess the degree to which she was successfully in applying those techniques in her daily life. If she was having difficulty doing so, and in light of Chi Chi's avoidance of talking about emotional topics, Dr. Beck would likely conceptualize procrastination as a larger compensatory strategy of avoidance and use many cognitive and behavioral strategies to overcome avoidance. For example, using a guided discovery framework, she might encourage Chi Chi to engage in an honest analysis of the advantages and disadvantages of her avoidance behavior. She also might work with her to develop behavioral experiments to evaluate the degree to which approaching, rather than avoiding, difficult situations actually results in positive outcomes (e.g., closure to a problem, relief). She might even implement a unique behavioral experiment strategy by having Chi Chi, in between sessions, "act as if" her tendency was to be proactive rather than to procrastinate and to evaluate what happens (cf. J. S. Beck, 2011).

Cognitive therapy with Chi Chi would be short term if she reported a significant reduction in emotional distress, met the goals she set at the beginning of treatment, and demonstrated the ability to apply the strategies in her daily life. Therapy might continue if Chi Chi persisted in demonstrating avoidance of taking the steps necessary to meet her longer term goals (e.g., writing, having honest conversations with her boyfriend). In this case, Dr. Beck would work with Chi Chi to identify a core belief that might be fueling her avoidance behavior. For example, Dr. Beck might work with Chi Chi to identify formative experiences that provided important messages about herself and contributed to the manner in which she views herself today.

One possibility is that Chi Chi views herself as unworthy. Although she is currently in a stable job and romantic relationship, there is the sense that Chi Chi has made some self-defeating decisions in the past (e.g., she is ashamed of the manner in which she acted in her previous long-term relationship; she has been fired from jobs in the past). It is possible that these are behavioral manifestations of a larger compensatory strategy to protect herself from her belief that she is unworthy. Stated differently, it is possible that Chi Chi thwarts important relationships and life goals because she does not believe that she is worthy enough to have them. Rather than proposing this hypothesis directly to Chi Chi, Dr. Beck would work with Chi Chi from a guided discovery framework to examine relevant formative experiences (e.g., excessive criticism from her mother), to have Chi Chi put her own words on her core belief, and to be vigilant for automatic thoughts that represent this core belief when she is faced with a task that she is procrastinating but that could be an important step to reaching a long-term goal. Then, Dr. Beck would work with Chi Chi to apply cognitive restructuring to reframe those automatic thoughts in the moment as well as to develop a new, healthier core belief and to use core belief modification strategies to adopt that new belief.

There were many aspects of this session that were typical of cognitive therapy. Dr. Beck incorporated many aspects of cognitive therapy session structure, including clarifying the focus of the session by setting an agenda and obtaining feedback at the end of the session. Dr. Beck adopted a present-focused problem-solving orientation to move from a general discussion about Chi Chi's concerns about becoming emotional during discussion of important topics to a targeted consideration of a conversation that she needs to have with her boyfriend about not having children. Dr. Beck incorporated subtle cognitive restructuring into the session, which allowed Chi Chi to conclude that she would be able to cope with the dissolution of her current relationship if it were to occur, as well as formal cognitive restructuring, when she educated Chi Chi about evidence and decatastrophizing questions and applied them to her concern that she would be fired from her job. Throughout the session, Dr. Beck maintained a collaborative therapeutic relationship with Chi Chi and obtained feedback at multiple points to ensure that Chi Chi agreed with the focus of discussion.

The one aspect of the session that was less typical of cognitive therapy sessions occurred when Dr. Beck was working with Chi Chi to determine a time and place to have a conversation with her boyfriend, as well as the specific points that Chi Chi would communicate. Because Dr. Beck had limited time with Chi Chi, she made directive suggestions about having the conversation in person rather than on the phone, for specific words to use when introducing the discussion with her boyfriend, and for the timing at which to have the conversation (i.e., earlier in the visit rather than later in the visit). When cognitive therapists have more time to work with their clients, they would integrate a guided discovery approach into their communication skills training.

For example, cognitive therapists might also spend more time with Chi Chi's initial attempt at communication with her boyfriend, such that they would encourage Chi Chi to take her boyfriend's perspective and consider the manner in which it would feel to experience the conversation on his end. This exercise would allow Chi Chi to draw her own conclusion that her communication style might not be as effective as it could be to meet her aims. Cognitive therapists might also first ask Chi Chi to supply an alternative way to approach the conversation and if it still appeared that her communication would have the potential to be ineffective, at that point take the lead in proposing an alternative. When cognitive therapists propose a specific way for clients to communicate something to others, they often provide psychoeducation about the specific communication skill they are modeling so that clients understand its rationale and intended effects. Like Dr. Beck, they would conduct a role-play in which they modeled the new approach to communication, and they would seek feedback from Chi Chi about how the new approach felt and the degree to which she anticipates it would be effective. Cognitive therapists might also reverse the role-play so that Chi Chi could gain practice in using the new communication approach and refine it according to her own style. Should cognitive therapists choose to implement communication skills training in this systematic manner, it would likely take an entire session, and the equally important cognitive restructuring work that Dr. Beck demonstrated in this session would likely be pursued in subsequent sessions.

Conclusion and Future Directions

This chapter and the DVD demonstration have modeled cognitive therapy's active, collaborative, present-focused approach. They have shown that clients not only acquire tools for managing the cognitive and behavioral aspects of their current distress but also develop a sophisticated understanding of the components of their life problems. They also emphasize that cognitive therapy is flexible in that it provides a rich framework for understanding the development of underlying unhelpful beliefs and behavioral patterns, as well as for shifting these patterns, in clients who need to do so.

A final important aspect of cognitive therapy deserves mention— the extensive empirical basis for its efficacy and effectiveness. *Efficacy* is demonstrated when cognitive therapy is associated with more significant and meaningful treatment gains than control conditions in tightly controlled settings, such as in the laboratory of a researcher who aims to systematically examine aspects of cognitive therapy while keeping many other variables constant. In contrast, *effectiveness* is demonstrated when cognitive therapy is associated with more significant and meaningful treatment gains than control conditions in real-life settings, such as a community mental health center, where there is wide variability in many factors (e.g., therapists' training, clients' diagnoses). Since the late 1970s, countless studies have been published that speak to cognitive therapy's efficacy (e.g., Kovacs, Rush, Beck, & Hollon, 1981; Rush, Beck, Kovacs, & Hollon, 1977), and more recently there has been a movement to disseminate cognitive therapy to the community and to evaluate its effectiveness (e.g., Gibbons et al., 2010). A meta-analysis that examined 78 randomized controlled clinical trials evaluating the efficacy of cognitive therapy found that clients who receive cognitive therapy achieve a 29% benefit, relative to clients who do not receive therapy; a 15% benefit, relative to clients who receive antidepressant medications; and a 10% benefit, relative to clients who receive other types of psychotherapy, such as supportive psychotherapy and interpersonal therapy. Moreover, cognitive therapy was associated with significantly less relapse across follow-up periods than antidepressant medication (Gloaguen, Cottraux, Cucherat, & Blackburn, 1998).

Results from older research have suggested that cognitive therapy is appropriate for mild clinical presentations, but not necessarily for moderate to severe clinical presentations (Elkin et al., 1989). However, results from newer research studies refute this notion. For example, DeRubeis et al. (2005) determined that cognitive therapy was as efficacious as antidepressant medications (i.e., paroxetine, with adjunctive medication added as needed) for moderate to severe depression. After a 12-month follow-up period, clients in this trial who received cognitive therapy relapsed less frequently than those who had received antidepressant medications and had comparable relapse rates to clients who continued on antidepressant medications (Hollon et al., 2005). Moreover, recent research has demonstrated that cognitive therapy is a useful adjunct to treatment as usual for serious conditions, such as a recent suicide attempt (Brown et al., 2005) and low-functioning schizophrenia (Grant, Huh, Perivoliotis, Stolar, & Beck, 2012).

What is in store for the future of cognitive therapy? Four exciting trends are gaining an increasing amount of momentum from scholars and practitioners alike. First, researchers are beginning to move beyond evaluation of the question "Does cognitive therapy work?" to consideration of the question "*How* does cognitive therapy work?" This line of research examines the mechanisms of change in cognitive therapy, or the specific variables that can account for cognitive therapy's efficacy through mediation analyses. Although research conducted to date has generally suggested that cognitive therapy is associated with a change in unhelpful cognition and that change in unhelpful cognition predicts response to treatment (e.g., Hofmann, 2004; Hofmann et al., 2007), the majority of studies that compare cognitive change across different treatment modalities have found that all treatments, even pharmacotherapy, produce cognitive change (see Garratt, Ingram, Rand, & Sawalani, 2007, for a review). One particularly innovative set of studies found that both cognitive therapy and pharmacotherapy produced equivalent changes in dysfunctional attitudes, but that when clients were subjected to a sad mood induction, only those who had received pharmacotherapy reported an increase in dysfunctional attitudes (Segal, Gemar, & Williams, 1999; Segal et al., 2006). These results raise the possibility that (a) cognitive change may be a causal agent in cognitive therapy but a consequence in other treatment approaches, and (b) cognitive therapy may be especially adept in preventing cognitive reactivity toward stress and life's changes, which would, in turn, be associated with low rates of relapse (Garratt et al., 2007; Segal et al., 2006). Research in this area would benefit from more studies that include rigorous designs to test mediation with adequate sample sizes, to test the conclusions drawn from the work by Segal and his colleagues, and to consider other specific mediators that are relevant to cognitive therapy strategy (e.g., cognitive processing; cognitive products that are specific to each client; acquisition of problem-solving skills; Wenzel, 2007).

A second contemporary trend for cognitive therapy practice and research is the integration of mindfulness and acceptance-based frameworks and strategies. Although there is much debate about whether mindfulness and acceptance-based approaches are fundamentally different from cognitive therapy or new packages for similar frameworks and strategies, like cognitive therapy, they have undergone significant theoretical development and have been subjected to scientific scrutiny, and many cognitive therapists have eagerly adopted these new approaches into their practices (Herbert & Forman, 2011). The specific framework that is, perhaps, the most congruent with cognitive therapy is mindfulness-based cognitive therapy (MBCT), which is a relapse-prevention protocol designed to be administered to clients who are currently in remission but who have a history of multiple depressive episodes (Segal, Williams, & Teasdale, 2002). The rationale for this treatment is that negative thinking patterns in remitted but chronically depressed clients are easily activated and that these clients would benefit from strategies to increase their awareness of these thinking patterns and take skillful action before they experience a full relapse. Results from empirical studies suggest that clients in remission who have had three or more previous depressive episodes and who participate in MBCT have a smaller rate of relapse/recurrence than those who receive only usual care (Ma & Teasdale, 2004; Teasdale et al., 2000) and that MBCT's benefit is extending to clients with other clinical presentations, such as anxiety, stress, and insomnia (e.g., Ree & Craigie, 2007). Thus, mindfulness and acceptance-based protocols have the potential to supplement cognitive therapy for acute psychiatric disorders in clients with chronic psychopathology, and the field is witnessing an explosion of research designed to evaluate the efficacy of these approaches and the manner in which they can be reconciled with or integrated into traditional cognitive therapy (Herbert & Forman, 2011).

A third contemporary trend for cognitive therapy practice and research is the development of treatment packages that pertain to emotional disorders, in general (i.e., a transdiagnostic approach), rather than to only one psychiatric disorder (e.g., Barlow et al., 2011). The idea behind these treatment protocols is that many psychiatric disorders are similar in their causes, biology, and behavioral consequences, and that, more often than not, clients meet criteria for more than one of these psychiatric disorders (Wilamowska et al., 2010). Thus, these treatment protocols incorporate cognitive and behavioral principles and strategies (e.g., psychoeducation, cognitive restructuring) that cut across several similar but distinct psychiatric disorders, allowing for therapists to become proficient in one protocol (rather than learning many disorder-specific protocols) and ensuring that clients receive treatment for basic psychological processes that contribute to emotional distress. Preliminary data suggest that the majority of clients with heterogeneous mood and anxiety disorders are classified as responders and achieve high end-state functioning after completing treatment and at follow-up (Wilamowska et al., 2010). Thus, the development of transdiagnostic treatment protocols has the potential to be particularly relevant to real-life clients seen in clinical practices with symptom overlap and comorbidity.

Finally, a fourth contemporary trend for cognitive therapy practice and research is the focus on dissemination of cognitive therapy to community agencies. The idea behind this movement is to address the discrepancy between the large body of research supporting cognitive therapy's efficacy and the paucity of available cognitive therapists in the community. Preliminary research suggest that community therapists under ongoing supervision can be trained to competence in cognitive therapy and that they retain their skills during follow-up. Moreover, this research has demonstrated that clients being treated in community settings with trained cognitive therapists achieve greater decreases in depression and anxiety than clients who receive treatment as usual (Simons et al., 2010). Scholarly inquiry into dissemination also examines barriers and obstacles to dissemination, such as institutional support and negative therapist attitudes (Taylor & Chang, 2008), as well as the administration of cognitive therapy in alternative, easily accessible formats, such as computerized protocols (Green & Iverson, 2009). Cognitive therapy manuals for specific community settings, such as Veterans Affairs Medical Centers (Wenzel et al., 2011), have recently been developed. It is hoped that research on the dissemination of cognitive therapy will provide further data that speak to cognitive therapy's effectiveness and that, ultimately, will allow for more people in the community to have the option to be treated with cognitive therapy.

There are many avenues for interested readers to learn more about cognitive therapy. Professional societies dedicated to the advancement and dissemination of cognitive therapy include the Academy of Cognitive Therapy (http://www.academyofct.org), the International Association for Cognitive Therapy (http://www.the-iacp.com), and the Association for Behavioral and Cognitive Therapies (http://www.abct.org). These organizations provide mental health professionals and students with training in cognitive therapy, exposure to the latest research on cognitive therapy, and opportunities for dialogue with other professionals about cognitive therapy. In addition, readers may wish to consult books that describe the cognitive therapy approach and its strategies in more detail. References indicated by an asterisk (*) indicate those that would allow readers to attain this information. Interested readers are encouraged to investigate these sources and receive supervision in attaining competence in cognitive therapy.

References

*Abramowitz, J. S., Deacon, B. J., & Whiteside, S. P. H. (2011). *Exposure therapy for anxiety: Principles and practice.* New York, NY: Guilford Press.

Addis, M. E., & Jacobson, N. S. (2000). A closer look at the treatment rationale and homework compliance in cognitive-behavioral therapy for depression. *Cognitive Therapy and Research, 24,* 313–326. doi:10.1023/A:1005563304265

Addis, M. E., & Martell, C. R. (2004). *Overcoming depression one step at a time: The new behavioral activation approach to getting your life back.* Oakland, CA: New Harbinger.

Barlow, D. H., & Craske, M. G. (2007). *Mastery of your anxiety and panic* (4th ed.). New York, NY: Oxford University Press.

Barlow, D. H., Ellard, K. K., Fairholme, C. P., Farchione, T. J., Boisseau, C. L., Allen, L. B., & Ehrenreich-May, J. T. (2011). *Unified protocol for transdiagnostic treatment of emotional disorders.* New York, NY: Oxford University Press.

*Basco, M. R., & Rush, A. J. (2005). *Cognitive-behavioral therapy for bipolar disorder* (2nd ed.). New York, NY: Guilford Press.

*Beck, A. T. (1976). *Cognitive therapy and the emotional disorders.* New York, NY: International Universities Press.

Beck, A. T., Brown, G., Steer, R. A., Eidelson, J. I., & Riskind, J. H. (1987). Differentiating anxiety and depression: A test of the cognitive content-specificity hypothesis. *Journal of Abnormal Psychology, 96,* 179–183. doi:10.1037/0021-843X.96.3.179

*Beck, A. T., & Emery, G. (1985). *Anxiety disorders and phobias: A cognitive perspective.* New York, NY: Basic Books.

*Beck, A. T., Freeman, A., Davis, D. D., & Associates. (2004). *Cognitive therapy for personality disorders* (2nd ed.). New York, NY: Guilford Press.

*Beck, A. T., Rector, N. A., Stolar, N., & Grant, P. (2009). *Schizophrenia: Cognitive theory, research, and therapy.* New York, NY: Guilford Press.

*Beck, A. T., Rush, A. J., Shaw, B. F., & Emery, G. (1979). *Cognitive therapy of depression.* New York, NY: Guilford Press.

Beck, A. T., Steer, R. A., & Brown, G. K. (1996). *Manual for the Beck Depression Inventory–II.* Dallas, TX: The Psychological Corporation.

*Beck, A. T., Wright, F. D., Newman, C. F., & Liese, B. S. (1993). *Cognitive therapy of substance abuse.* New York, NY: Guilford Press.

*Beck, J. S. (2005). *Cognitive therapy for challenging problems.* New York, NY: Guilford Press.

*Beck, J. S. (2011). *Cognitive behavior therapy: Basics and beyond* (2nd ed.). New York, NY: Guilford Press.

Bernstein, D. A., & Borkovec, T. D. (1973). *Progressive relaxation training: A manual for the helping profession.* Champaign, IL: Research Press.

*Bieling, P. J., McCabe, M. E., & Antony, M. M. (2006). *Cognitive-behavioral therapy in groups*. New York, NY: Guilford Press.

Borkovec, T. D., Newman, M. G., Pincus, A. L., & Lytle, R. (2002). A component analysis of cognitive-behavioral therapy for generalized anxiety disorder and the role of interpersonal problems. *Journal of Consulting and Clinical Psychology, 70,* 288–298. doi:10.1037/0022-006X.70.2.288

Brown, G. K., Ten Have, T., Henriques, G. R., Xie, S. X., Hollander, J. E., & Beck, A. T. (2005). Cognitive therapy for the prevention of suicide attempts: A randomized controlled trial. *JAMA, 294,* 563–570. doi:10.1001/jama.294.5.563

*Burns, D. D. (1980). *Feeling good: The new mood therapy*. New York, NY: Signet.

*Dattilio, F. M. (2010). *Cognitive-behavioral therapy with couples and families: A comprehensive guide to clinicians*. New York, NY: Guilford Press.

DeRubeis, R. J., Hollon, S. D., Amsterdam, J. D., Shelton, R. C., Young, P. R., Salomon, R. N., . . . Gallop, R. (2005). Cognitive therapy vs. medications in the treatment of moderate to severe depression. *Archives of General Psychiatry, 62,* 409–416. doi:10.1001/archpsyc.62.4.409

*Dobson, D., & Dobson, K. S. (2009). *Evidence-based practice of cognitive-behavioral therapy*. New York, NY: Guilford Press.

*Dobson, K. S. (2012). *Cognitive therapy*. Washington, DC: American Psychological Association.

*D'Zurilla, T. J., & Nezu, A. M. (2007). *Problem-solving therapy: A positive approach to clinical intervention* (3rd ed.). New York, NY: Springer.

Elkin, I., Shea, M. T., Watkins, J. T., Imber, S. D., Sotsky, S. M., Collins, J. F., . . . Parloff, M. B. (1989). NIMH Treatment of Depression Collaborative Research Program: General effectiveness of treatments. *Archives of General Psychiatry, 46,* 971–982. doi:10.1001/archpsyc.1989.01810110013002

Ellis, A., & Harper, R. A. (1975). *A new guide to rational living*. Oxford, England: Prentice-Hall.

Epp, A. M., & Dobson, K. S. (2010). The evidence base for cognitive-behavioral therapy. In K. S. Dobson (Ed.), *Handbook of cognitive-behavioral therapies* (3rd ed., pp. 39–73). New York, NY: Guilford Press.

*Fairburn, C. G. (2008). *Cognitive behavior therapy and eating disorders*. New York, NY: Guilford Press.

Garratt, G., Ingram, R. E., Rand, K. L., & Sawalani, G. (2007). Cognitive processes in cognitive therapy: Evaluation of the mechanisms of change in the treatment of depression. *Clinical Psychology: Science and Practice, 14,* 224–239. doi:10.1111/j.1468-2850.2007.00081.x

Gibbons, C. J., Fournier, J. C., Stirman, S. W., DeRubeis, R. J., Crits-Cristoph, P., & Beck, A. T. (2010). The clinical effectiveness of cognitive therapy for depression in an outpatient clinic. *Journal of Affective Disorders, 125,* 169–176. doi:10.1016/j.jad.2009.12.030

Gloaguen, V., Cottraux, J., Cucherat, M., & Blackburn, I.-M. (1998). A meta-analysis of the effects of cognitive therapy in depressed patients. *Journal of Affective Disorders, 49,* 59–72. doi:10.1016/S0165-0327 (97)00199-7

Grant, P. M., Huh, G. A., Perivoliotis, D., Stolar, N. M., & Beck, A. T. (2012). Randomized trial to evaluate the efficacy of cognitive therapy for low-functioning patients with schizophrenia. *Archives of General Psychiatry, 69,* 121–127. doi:10.1001/archgenpsychiatry.2011.129

Green, K. E., & Iverson, K. M. (2009). Computerized cognitive-behavioral therapy in a stepped care model of treatment. *Professional Psychology: Research and Practice, 40,* 96–103. doi:10.1037/a0012847

*Greenberger, D., & Padesky, C. A. (1995). *Mind over mood: Change how you feel by changing the way you think.* New York, NY: Guilford Press.

Herbert, J. D., & Forman, E. M. (2011). The evolution of cognitive-behavior therapy: The rise of psychological acceptance and mindfulness. In J. D. Herbert & E. M. Forman (Eds.), *Acceptance and mindfulness in cognitive behavior therapy: Understanding and applying the new therapies* (pp. 3–25). Hoboken, NJ: Wiley. doi:10.1002/9781118001851

Herbert, J. D., Gaudiano, B. A., Rheingold, A. A., Myers, V. H., Dalrymple, K., & Nolan, E. M. (2005). Social skills training augments the effectiveness of cognitive behavioral group therapy for social anxiety disorder. *Behavior Therapy, 36,* 125–138. doi:10.1016/S0005-7894(05)80061-9

Hirsch, C., Jolley, S., & Williams, R. (2000). A study of outcome in a clinical psychology service and preliminary evaluation of cognitive-behavioral therapy in real practice. *Journal of Mental Health, 9,* 537–549. doi:10.1080/09638230020005264

Hofmann, S. G. (2004). Cognitive mediation of treatment change in social phobia. *Journal of Consulting and Clinical Psychology, 72,* 392–399. doi:10.1037/0022-006X.72.3.392

Hofmann, S. G. (2008). Cognitive processes during fear acquisition and extinction in animals and humans: Implications for exposure therapy for anxiety disorders. *Clinical Psychology Review, 28,* 199–210. doi:10.1016/j.cpr.2007.04.009

Hofmann, S. G., Meuret, A. E., Rosenfield, D., Suvak, M. K., Barlow, D. H., Gorman, J. M., . . . Woods, S. R. (2007). Preliminary evidence for cognitive mediation during cognitive-behavioral therapy of panic disorder. *Journal of Consulting and Clinical Psychology, 75,* 374–379. doi:10.1037/0022-006X.75.3.374

Hollon, S. D., DeRubeis, R. J., Shelton, R. C., Amsterdam, J. D., Salomon, R. M., O'Reardon, J. P. . . . Gallop, R. (2005). Prevention of relapse following cognitive therapy vs. medications in moderate to severe depression. *Archives of General Psychiatry, 62,* 417–422. doi:10.1001/archpsyc.62.4.417

Ingram, R., & Kendall, P. C. (1986). Cognitive clinical psychology: Implications for an information processing perspective. In R. Ingram (Ed.), *Information processing approaches to clinical psychology* (pp. 3–22). New York, NY: Academic Press.

Ingram, R. E., Miranda, J., & Segal, Z. V. (1998). *Cognitive vulnerability to depression.* New York, NY: Guilford Press.

Kovacs, M., Rush, A. J., Beck, A. T., & Hollon, S. D. (1981). Depressed outpatients treated with cognitive therapy or pharmacotherapy: A one-year follow-up. *Archives of General Psychiatry, 38,* 33–39. doi:10.1001/archpsyc.1981.01780260035003

*Kuyken, W., Padesky, C. A., & Dudley, R. (2009). *Collaborative case conceptualization: Working effectively with clients in cognitive-behavioral therapy.* New York, NY: Guilford Press.

*Leahy, R. L. (2003). *Cognitive therapy techniques: A practitioner's guide.* New York, NY: Guilford Press.

Lewinsohn, P. M., Sullivan, J. M., & Grosscup, S. J. (1980). Changing reinforcing events: An approach to the treatment of depression. *Psychotherapy: Theory, Research & Practice, 17,* 322–334. doi:10.1037/h0085929

Linehan, M. M. (1993). *Cognitive-behavioral treatment of borderline personality disorder.* New York, NY: Guilford Press.

Ma, S. H., & Teasdale, J. D. (2004). Mindfulness-based cognitive therapy for depression: Replication and exploration of differential relapse prevention effects. *Journal of Consulting and Clinical Psychology, 72,* 31–40. doi:10.1037/0022-006X.72.1.31

Meichenbaum, D. (1985). *Stress inoculation training.* New York, NY: Pergamon Press.

Ree, M. J., & Craigie, M. A. (2007). Outcomes following mindfulness-based cognitive therapy in a heterogeneous sample of adult outpatients. *Behaviour Change, 24,* 70–86. doi:10.1375/bech.24.2.70

Reinecke, M. A. (2006). Problem solving: A conceptual approach to suicidality and psychotherapy. In T. E. Ellis (Ed.), *Cognition and suicide: Theory, research, and therapy* (pp. 237–260). Washington, DC: American Psychological Association.

Rush, A. J., Beck, A. T., Kovacs, M., & Hollon, S. D. (1977). Comparative efficacy of cognitive therapy and pharmacotherapy in the treatment of depressed outpatients. *Cognitive Therapy and Research, 1,* 17–37.

Ryum, T., Stiles, T. C., Svartberg, M., & McCullough, L. (2010). The effects of therapist competence in assigning homework in cognitive therapy with cluster C personality disorders: Results from a randomized controlled trial. *Cognitive and Behavioral Practice, 17,* 283–289. doi:10.1016/j.cbpra.2009.10.005

Segal, Z. V., Gemar, M., & Williams, S. (1999). Differential cognitive response to a mood challenge following successful cognitive therapy or pharmacotherapy for unipolar depression. *Journal of Abnormal Psychology, 108,* 3–10. doi:10.1037/0021-843X.108.1.3

Segal, Z. V., Kennedy, M. D., Gemar, M., Hood, K., Pederson, R., & Buis, T. (2006). Cognitive reactivity to sad mood provocation and the prediction of depressive relapse. *Archives of General Psychiatry, 63,* 749–755. doi:10.1001/archpsyc.63.7.749

Segal, Z. V., Williams, J. M. G., & Teasdale, J. D. (2002). *Mindfulness-based cognitive therapy for depression: A new approach to preventing relapse.* New York, NY: Guilford Press.

Simons, A. D., Padesky, C. A., Montemarano, J., Lewis, C. C., Murakami, J., Lamb, K., . . . Beck, A. T. (2010). Training and dissemination in cognitive behavior therapy for depression in adults: A preliminary examination of therapist competence and client outcomes. *Journal of Consulting and Clinical Psychology, 78,* 751–756. doi:10.1037/a0020569

Taylor, C. B., & Chang, V. Y. (2008). Issues in the dissemination of cognitive behavior therapy. *Nordic Journal of Psychiatry, 62,* 37–44. doi:10.1080/08039480802315673

Teasdale, J. D., Segal, Z. V., Williamson, J. M. G., Ridgeway, V. A., Soulsby, J. M., & Lau, M. A. (2000). Prevention of relapse/recurrence in major depression by mindfulness-based cognitive therapy. *Journal of Consulting and Clinical Psychology, 68,* 615–623. doi:10.1037/0022-006X.68.4.615

Wenzel, A. (2007, November). Cognitive therapy: Models and processes of change. In J. L. Boulanger (Chair), *Models and processes of change in psychotherapy: An overview.* Symposium presented at the 40th annual meeting of the Association for Behavioral and Cognitive Therapies, Philadelphia, PA.

Wenzel, A. (2012). Modification of core beliefs. In I. R. de Oliveira (Ed.), *Cognitive behavioral therapy.* Rijeka, Croatia: Intech (available online at http://www.intechopen.com). doi:10.5772/30119

Wenzel, A., & Beck, A. T. (2008). A cognitive model of suicidal behavior: Theory and treatment. *Applied & Preventive Psychology, 12,* 189–201. doi:10.1016/j.appsy.2008.05.001

*Wenzel, A., Brown, G. K., & Beck, A. T. (2009). *Cognitive therapy for suicidal patients: Scientific and clinical applications.* Washington, DC: American Psychological Association. doi:10.1037/11862-000

*Wenzel, A., Brown, G. K., & Karlin, B. E. (2011). *Cognitive behavioral therapy for depressed Veterans and Military service members: Therapist manual.* Washington, DC: U.S. Department of Veterans Affairs.

*Wenzel, A., Liese, B. S., Beck, A. T., & Friedman-Wheeler, D. G. (2012). *Group cognitive therapy for addictions.* New York, NY: Guilford Press.

Wilamowska, Z. A., Thompson-Hollands, J., Fairholme, C. P., Ellard, K. K., Farchione, T. J., & Barlow, D. H. (2010). Conceptual background, development, and preliminary data from the Unified Protocol for Transdiagnostic Treatment of Emotional Disorders. *Depression and Anxiety, 27,* 882–890. doi:10.1002/da.20735

Wolpe, J. (1969). *The practice of behavior therapy.* Oxford, England: Pergamon Press.

*Wright, J. H., Basco, M. R., & Thase, M. E. (2006). *Learning cognitive-behavior therapy: An illustrated guide.* Arlington, VA: American Psychiatric Association Press.

Appendix A
Client Intake Transcript: Kevin

Jon Carlson:	Well, Kevin, thank you for being willing to do this. I wanna start with some questions. Kevin, it sounds like an Irish name, is that an Irish name?
Kevin:	Yes, it is. My last name is pretty Irish as well.
Jon Carlson:	I see. It's a 100% Irish?
Kevin:	No, probably 25% but it was my father's father so I got the name, you know, the name just came back.
Jon Carlson:	And then the other ethnicity that stands out in your upbringing?
Kevin:	My mom is Lithuanian. I heard she grew up in household where they spoke Lithuanian so that's really the other dominant ethnicity.
Jon Carlson:	And what's your current age right now?
Kevin:	Forty-three.
Jon Carlson:	Forty-three, okay. When you grew up did you just speak English in the home or was that—
Kevin:	Oh, yeah, my mom never really learned Lithuanian. Apparently the story was she could understand what they were saying but she didn't speak it, so.
Jon Carlson:	I see, yeah, okay.
Kevin:	I heard a little bit of it but, yeah, spoke other languages.
Jon Carlson:	And what was your presenting concern in terms of—what is it that bothers you these days, something that you'd like to see worked on?
Kevin:	I've struggled quite a bit with anxiety. That's really the main thing.
Jon Carlson:	And anxiety to you means—if you had one word to describe anxiety, what would it be?
Kevin:	One word?
Jon Carlson:	Yeah.
Kevin:	It's fear.

Jon Carlson:	Fear?
Kevin:	Yeah, absolutely.
Jon Carlson:	And can you talk about maybe an example of when this anxiety or fear occurred?
Kevin:	I notice it particularly when I first wake up and it's mainly a daytime issue. It seems to—I generally worked from 3 to 8 and that—and it seems to fade away throughout the day.
Jon Carlson:	So like 3 on—3 during in the day?
Kevin:	So like when I wake up till I go to work there's a time period and usually that's where the anxiety is the greatest. When I go to work—
	[Simultaneous talking]
Kevin:	Yeah, it seems—it generally goes away, the feeling itself. But right now I'm raising my daughter on my own. She's 17 and it's—for the past 4 years I've been doing it on my own. And although I had a lot of struggles when mom was around as well they have definitely intensified.
Jon Carlson:	And mom being? When mom—
Kevin:	She's moved—She's moved away. She's still alive.
Jon Carlson:	Okay.
Kevin:	She didn't pass away or anything.
Jon Carlson:	But she's not in the area and you were like coparenting before and now you're a sole parent?
Kevin:	Yes.
Jon Carlson:	Okay, yeah. We will find out some more about that. So, that's the time it did, you know, occurs. And what would the symptoms be of this fear?
Kevin:	There's definitely some physical symptoms, just sort of an intensity in this area right here but there's also a lot of—there's some dialogue, internal dialogue that goes along with it. But really it's—it's more of—almost this visual picture of the world as a place to fear. That there's problems that I'm not gonna be able to overcome. I'm gonna lose my apartment [laughter], whatever it means, you know, financial devastation, things like that.
Jon Carlson:	And if those symptoms were gone, how do you think your life might be different?
Kevin:	[Laughter] Well, I guess I could think back to when they weren't there before.
Jon Carlson:	So there was a period of time when this weren't there?
Kevin:	Yeah. Like being a parent has definitely intensified those feelings for me. Before that I—you know, I was much more carefree but that was—You know, there are problems with that as well. That could come—that could be brought to a point of negligence where—after having a child what I learned is that before that I was sort of in denial of a lot of emotions, not just in myself but in other people as well. Grief was one of them. And so if I did something to cause somebody else grief I would really downplay quite a bit. And so there were some revelations I had after being a parent for a while that's—wow, I've been hurting people [laughter], so.
Jon Carlson:	And so if you were symptom free?
Kevin:	I'm not saying I would go back to hurting people. I think I've learned quite a bit in the meantime. I would have to be careful of, you know, slipping out of reality too much and, you know, parenting has grounded me quite a bit. But with that I had to touch base with a lot of—I can't run from my feelings anymore. I have to be present and that's been a struggle. [Laughter]
Jon Carlson:	Well, often in therapy we talked about what's wrong and I've already started with what's wrong. But what would you say that you do well?
Kevin:	Well, I'm a great musician, very creative, and I might actually be very organized as well which, that's actually a really good combination for a musician. A lot

of musicians I worked with are amazed how I've got repertoire lists for every occasion. So I'm pretty—pretty intense with those things. I got a pretty sharp mind. And I'm actually—I'm a great parent as well. I'm there for my daughter. I worked with her through intense issues that she goes through.

Jon Carlson: So what have you learned from all of the things that you've gone through? Kind of any life lessons you have?

Kevin: What have I learned? That's a really big question. Well, let me start here. One of the things that I'm dealing with now or working with now is being able to draw boundaries with people. And being able to identify when I've got a close friendship with somebody but it's—they're doing things that are making me very uncomfortable, maybe putting me in danger somehow. Or if they're being dishonest with me and I'm learning how to draw boundaries with that and confront those issues.

Jon Carlson: So you've learned that that's an important thing to do?

Kevin: Yes. I think I just stumbled on it when I said the word confront, confronting problems is I think one of the biggest things that I've learned from parenting and from other things as well, so.

Jon Carlson: Where do you get your source of strength?

Kevin: Well, that's interesting [laughter]. Well, you've had some great questions here. You know the first thing that comes to my mind is my father. He actually died when I was 9, but I had an enough time with him to remember quite a bit about him.

Jon Carlson: Your Irish father?

Kevin: Yes. Yes, yes. And I, you know, saw him as a very strong, honest, sort of dedicated person. He was a good man. I heard a lot of that after he died as well, how good of a man he was. And I really think that [laughter] he's been a big role model for me.

Jon Carlson: That's the source of your strength then?

Kevin: Yes.

Jon Carlson: So who do you use or where does any support come from for the present difficulties that you have?

Kevin: My family has definitely been a big support for us. My mom and stepdad were—well actually they were great. They lived locally till about 6 months ago and they moved down to Florida and it's nice for them. They've got a nice place down there. And they helped us out quite—I mean me and daughter lived in their house for about 10 years or so and then even after that they were—there was a place for her to go, for us to get some time [laughter] away from each other. But they moved to Florida, so that support has kinda gone away.

Jon Carlson: Yeah, 4 years ago the mother moved away?

Kevin: Well, it was actually 6 years ago and then my daughter moved away with her for about a year and then she came back.

Jon Carlson: Any other sources of support right now for the present difficulties?

Kevin: There's not really anything on a daily basis. I've got a couple of brothers and they are—they're both single guys. No kids. If things got really bad, I could probably go to them.

Kevin: But the family that you're referring to was your mom and your stepdad.

Kevin: Yeah, they were the ones who really provided.

Jon Carlson: Now, in terms of any previous counseling that you've had?

Kevin: I've been seeing a counselor for 2 years.

Jon Carlson: Okay.

Kevin:	Almost to the day.
Jon Carlson:	Alright, and has that been helpful?
Kevin:	Absolutely. Yes.
Jon Carlson:	And what was—what's been the outcome of those meetings with the counselor for the last 2 years?
Kevin:	There were few meetings early on that I went in there, I'm having really bad days, just very dark—dark feelings. You know, not like suicidal or anything like that, just heavy grief.
Jon Carlson:	And grief from?
Kevin:	Sorry, I don't know where this is coming from.
Jon Carlson:	No, it's okay. Yeah.
	[Crying]
Jon Carlson:	Tissues—let's see if we can get some, yeah. Yeah.
Kevin:	I'll get through this, I just need to release it, but it's good.
Jon Carlson:	That's fine.
	[Crying]
	[Inaudible remark]
Kevin:	Okay, you know, one of the things about that is that I don't really know where it comes from.
	[Laughter]
Jon Carlson:	Yeah.
Kevin:	It just kinda builds up and then I as—you know, once I release it, I'll be fine. It just—I need to get, pass through it.
	[Crying]
Kevin:	Sure, yeah, yeah, that's fine. Yeah, uh-huh. Yeah.
	[Pause]
Jon Carlson:	We've all developed our strategies for handling our emotions, yeah. And have you always been so good at expressing them?
Kevin:	No, like I said, you know, there was a long period of time where I was pretty good at just avoiding them, you know, and whatever other—whatever way. I think music was actually a big way for me to that. I would get lost in music and it's a great way to avoid.
Jon Carlson:	And so when you begin counseling a couple of years ago there was some real grief and sadness at that time?
Kevin:	Yes, and I would go in there and have the session and walk out feeling healed you know. That was the initial.
Jon Carlson:	And then the question I had was the grief and sadness, was it over, what? Were you able to identify?
Kevin:	Well, yeah. A lot of it was just things that have built up. At that point my daughter was 15, and ages 14 to 15 were really intense for us. Yeah, she—she had some traumatic incidents when she lived—when she moved away with her mom for a year. And so when we came back she was starting to recover from those. So she was going through counseling as well. And couldn't get up for school, truancy issues, you know, financial issues, and we had just moved out of the place with my parents so I was getting back on my feet as far as that. I took on the second job and it just got overwhelming, you know, so.
Jon Carlson:	Yeah, sounds like it.
Kevin:	Yeah, it was pretty intense, so.
Jon Carlson:	Did they ever prescribe like medication?
Kevin:	No, no.

Jon Carlson:	Have you ever seen a psychiatrist or—
Kevin:	I haven't—My daughter does. She's on medication and I've been, you know, in on some appointments. But that's one of the things I'm glad that the—I think it's called talk therapy what I do with my therapist. In a way I can consider that an achievement that's been successful and I haven't had to do any meds.
Jon Carlson:	Okay, well, sure.
Kevin:	That's my personal opinion, but—
Jon Carlson:	Yeah, okay. And in terms of the diagnoses—that was the only time you've been in counseling was like for the last 2 years?
Kevin:	Yes.
Jon Carlson:	And do you know if there was a diagnosis or—that you were given at that time?
Kevin:	Not—I don't remember her ever giving me a definite diagnosis but I do know when I, you know, called to make the appointment I said, "Depression and anxiety," which were the terms that I was familiar with mainly through what my daughter was going through. And it's entirely possible that that might have just been validated.
Jon Carlson:	Yeah. Okay.
Kevin:	You know, so.
Jon Carlson:	And have you ever have like thoughts to want to take your life or to end your life?
Kevin:	No, no I haven't.
Jon Carlson:	Have you known people who have?
Kevin:	Yes. Yes, I have.
Jon Carlson:	Alright. And do you understand what that might be like? You said before though that you haven't—at sometimes been a danger to other people?
Kevin:	Well, I think there was a time where I just was inconsiderate to the people's feeling if I was doing things that were [laughter] making them angry or, you know, grief. It could just mean, you know, breaking up with the girl and not telling her about it maybe, and not even caring if it hurt 'cause all I needed—all I knew is that this was a situation I couldn't—be in anymore.
Jon Carlson:	So it was more emotional harm?
Kevin:	Yeah.
Jon Carlson:	Yeah. Now—And when you think of your counseling over the last 2 years or any other kind of help that you've received, what worked and what didn't worked? And you said talk counseling, talking seemed to help.
Kevin:	Sure, definitely. That's—and one of the things that I noticed. I don't know if this is getting off, let me know, is that's—in the early days of the counseling and previous to that is when I was alone that things would get really dark for me. And I'd notice when I go out in public that feeling would go away, when I was interacting with the people.
Jon Carlson:	So that's something you've found that helps is to interact with others?
Kevin:	So that's why I think the talk therapy is an important part of that—
Jon Carlson:	Anything that didn't help?
Kevin:	There's been a few. Actually every now and then she'll recommend a book to me and generally the books that I've gotten I haven't really gotten much except there is one that has. In general a lot of books, noticing that maybe they're the female authors, the different approach although my counselor is a female but that might be a part of it. That seems kind of flowery.
Jon Carlson:	Oh, the book that helped?
Kevin:	The Four Agreements.
Jon Carlson:	Okay.

Kevin:	And now the interesting thing about that book, it's not really—are you familiar with that book? It's not really—
Jon Carlson:	Yeah, it's Ruiz, Miguel Ruiz.
Kevin:	Yes. It's not a very—It's not a real emotion-based book. It's not flowery and worksheets and stuff. It's kinda like, hey, these are four things that if you do this you're gonna be messing things up for yourself, so get with it, you know. [Laughter]
Jon Carlson:	So it's kinda—you like to hear it straight?
Kevin:	Yes, when it comes to emotional struggles, that's how it—yes.
Jon Carlson:	How about your physical health?
Kevin:	Quite good actually.
Jon Carlson:	Have you seen a doctor recently?
Kevin:	Yeah, I have regular checkups and things like that.
Jon Carlson:	And you're medically uninteresting?
Kevin:	Absolutely. [Inaudible remark]
Kevin:	As a matter of fact I just started a life insurance policy for my daughter so they drew blood and every, you know, possible [laughter]—they may you take and—apparently I'm disease free.
Jon Carlson:	Have you ever had any health concerns?
Kevin:	Never, any—anything like medical. I did have a hernia operation about 15 years ago. Apparently that's back but as long as I don't do any heavy lifting it's fine. And some, you know, spinal stress tension, aching, things like that.
Jon Carlson:	No chronic problems that you are aware? Ones that just continue all the time?
Kevin:	Not really. I mean the—you know, my spine is pretty stiff most of the time like it's not painful, it's just when I move it around I feel that there's tension in there.
Jon Carlson:	Have you ever been in an accident or—?
Kevin:	Yeah, I was in—Well I was in several fender benders like in the '80s, early '90s.
Jon Carlson:	Any times that your head was injured?
Kevin:	Well, I was in a bus once when we got rear-ended and I did have some chiropractic work done after that. Not had an injury like some really minor spinal things—adjustments.
Jon Carlson:	And your head wasn't hit?
Kevin:	No.
Jon Carlson:	Okay. How about legal history? Did you ever have any trouble with the law?
Kevin:	Well, when I was 19, I did get taken in a couple of times. Me and a couple of friends were out being rowdy and, you know, they took us in and mom had to come pick us up.
Jon Carlson:	And rowdy means?
Kevin:	We were drunk and loud [laughter] in a mall one—the first time. Second time was in a car and so— [Simultaneous talking]
Kevin:	It was 24 years ago.
Jon Carlson:	Anything since then?
Kevin:	Well, we—I had a custody battle with my daughter's mom when she was 2. I'm glad it happened before she could remember it. I think that saved her a lot of trauma. There's been enough trauma anyway [laughter] without her having to go through that. But that's something that, you know, things need to be cleared up and we use the legal system to clear things up.
Jon Carlson:	So no other arrest?

Kevin:	No.
Jon Carlson:	No DWIs or any other challenges that you can remember?
Kevin:	No.
Jon Carlson:	Okay. Now, in terms of a job what do you do?
Kevin:	I teach guitar and I perform. And I also do—I do a lot of recording on my own but I'm starting to include that in my, you know, career and my income.
Jon Carlson:	And so you're the sole source of income for the home?
Kevin:	Yes.
Jon Carlson:	And is that like—did you get like a paycheck or you kind of an independent contractor?
Kevin:	Officially, I'm self-employed. I teach at a music store but I collect from the students.
Jon Carlson:	Okay, yeah, so, alright, and the same thing on your musical when you perform?
Kevin:	Yes. Mainly I have a partner who—he books most of the gigs, that's his strong point. And he collects, you know, from the bar owner or whoever and he just gives me my cut.
Jon Carlson:	No other benefits, child support, veteran support, anything, other things coming your way?
Kevin:	Well, we—As far as child support, in general we've got nothing from mom except about 2 years ago or so I think she sends $150, $200 possibly. And last month she sent $80 because—I mean she should contribute but I—you know, I don't mind struggling, doing it on my own if I'm making it but things started getting really rough last month. So I send her a text and said you need to send our daughter some money 'cause things are about to slip here. [Laughter]
Jon Carlson:	And if they were tough last month, they're probably tough this month too?
Kevin:	Yeah, we just squeaked by last month and this month isn't looking much better. I mean we're not gonna starve to death. We're just—
Jon Carlson:	You may starve but you'll still live.
Kevin:	Yeah, we do—getting food on the table is a struggle, yeah. We don't have all that we need.
Jon Carlson:	Is there anything that looks optimistic in the future?
Kevin:	Well, one of the things that's—that I've noticed is in summertime things get rough and a lot of my guitar students go on vacation during summer or they'll take 2 weeks off of month and my income drops quite a bit.
Jon Carlson:	So this is August and so this is the summer. So maybe come in the fall?
Kevin:	Yeah, I got three or four students that I'm expecting to come back in September. And we generally get a lot of new signups in September too. So I might get maybe six more students, hopefully.
Jon Carlson:	Okay. Alright, so there's some hope out there?
Kevin:	Yes.
Jon Carlson:	In terms of your education, how far in school did you go?
Kevin:	I have a bachelor's degree in music, music education actually.
Jon Carlson:	And let's see if I can—And did you do that—Did you go away to school or how did you?
Kevin:	No, I didn't—right—I went Rich South back in the class of '84 and I went to Prairie State for one year and then I got tired of that. I went to DePaul School of Music for a year and didn't go back after that. I like—needed a break from school. There was pressure that I needed to get out from under. And then I moved out to California, lived there for 8 years. And every—I remember every September I'd be like, "Man,

it would be nice to go back to school." I get like school fever. But it wasn't till I was 33 and my daughter started first grade, so she was actually in school all day that I was like, "Wow. I actually have, you know, time, what am I gonna do with my life?" And I ended up going back to school and finishing my degree, so.

Jon Carlson: So what did you find easy about school?

Kevin: Well, I was studying music and I loved it. And I actually, my first—very first class that I went back for was an English class and on the first day the professor said, "The first thing you need to do is you need to understand what the assignment is." And for some reason that clicked with me and all through my college career I made sure I needed—I knew exactly what the professor was expecting with everything and I was very successful in my classes I think because of that. Plus I—you know, I—things took a dive when I went to college when I was 18 or 19, I was very restless and now I knew that I needed to focus and stick with it and not quit. So those are the things that—

Jon Carlson: And was there something you found difficult about school or sounds like focusing until you found new insight?

Kevin: Well, I don't think so because I was able to—well, we could say that my social life was difficult because my—I took a train downtown from Richton every day. And I didn't see my friends around here for, you know, 3 months at a time. I didn't see that coming but by the second, third semester my friends knew to expect that I wouldn't be around [laughter] until break came around anymore. So I guess it's—put some social struggles.

Jon Carlson: Do you have any—have any special programming when you were in the school? When you were in high school, grade school?

Kevin: Not really. No.

Jon Carlson: Now if we were to look at your current social situation, you told us you were married.

Kevin: I've never been married.

Jon Carlson: Okay. You told me that you have a child?

Kevin: Yes.

Jon Carlson: Okay. And can you kind of give me idea of your relationship history? How it's gone?

Kevin: Yes. That's a long story, we—how much time do we have left?

Jon Carlson: Yeah, how about the short part—

Kevin: Yeah, the short story?

Jon Carlson: —of the long story.

Kevin: I was a Catholic boy and I was kind of a late bloomer around town but I think that really meant that I had started at a healthy age. I was 16—I was 16 when I really had my first serious relationship and it seemed like the public school kids around me were already doing things around 13, 14, [laughter] so, which I think that made me uncomfortable then, but that's a long time ago. No problems there. And I was pretty restless when I was younger between age 16 and, you know, 27. It was hard for me to settle down and be faithful.

Jon Carlson: So there are long-term relationships during that time?

Kevin: Well there was one, when I went to California it was to be with a girl that I met out here and we did live together for 4 years. In retrospect, we weren't exactly faithful with each other. We talked about that afterwards. We're actually still really good friends. So that's kind of how things were back then. And then I—my daughter came around and her and her mom, me and—her mother and I, sorry, never got married and she had two other kids so she had just gotten out of a divorce and we kind of talked about marriage and sort of laughed about it, shrugged it off. And we lived together for a year in California while she was pregnant and a little bit after my daughter was born. In retrospect that's really the last long-term relationship that I had.

Jon Carlson: So that, what, 17 years ago?

Kevin: Yeah.

Jon Carlson: Okay.

Kevin: And there was—there are quite a few short-term relationships in the '90s, but really in the past—in the past 10 years I've had an 8-month relationship, a couple 1-months.

Jon Carlson: And where you at now in terms of relationship?

Kevin: Well, I'm sort of kind of seeing somebody but they're in a relationship so it's not anything I can take seriously.

Jon Carlson: So you sort of kind of seeing somebody and—

Kevin: And they live an hour away and so—

Jon Carlson: And they're married or with somebody?

Kevin: In a relationship.

Jon Carlson: Yeah.

Kevin: So we e-mail a lot. And really what—we're support for each other in a lot of ways. We definitely—we're kinda there for each other on the bad days. [Laughter]

Jon Carlson: So she's kind of an electronic friend? Someone that you can e-mail, talk to on the phone.

Kevin: That's what it is right now, yeah, for the most part.

Jon Carlson: Would she'd be someone—you said that your brothers too are nearby, would she be a source of support?

Kevin: Well, on an emotional level, spiritual level.

Jon Carlson: Is there anybody else that you're dating these days?

Kevin: No.

Jon Carlson: Okay. So if you were to kind of put this on a scale from 0, I'm not doing, I'm doing poorly with relationships these days, and 10, things are going really well, would you give it a number?

Kevin: Yeah, my first instinct was 0 but I have to take probably a 1.

Jon Carlson: A 1. Okay.

Kevin: Yeah.

Jon Carlson: Now, how would you describe yourself like in social relationships, like when you're with other people? And I can give you words like affection and avoidant, a leader, a follower.

Kevin: Actually I've given a lot of thoughts to all of those words before [laughter]. I thought about my role as a leader and a follower. I kinda had to confront that after I got my music ed. degree and thought about myself as running a music program in a school.

Kevin: And I realized that it's not for me. I'm much better with one-on-one because I'm really not comfortable as a leader. Not really comfortable as a follower either. What I found is that I'm more of a helper. I'm kind of a great support guy, helping to fix up the things. I'm very—socially, I'm not affectionate. I used to be and deep inside of me I am but I've become—at one point I kinda can trace it back to—there's a point where my daughter started being—stopped being affectionate with me, which I think is natural. And I started being less affectionate in general with people around the same time.

Jon Carlson:	Pulled back. Okay.
Kevin:	Yeah.
Jon Carlson:	And you mentioned your daughter and that she's 17. How would you describe your relationship with her in let's say from 1 to 10. From 1 isn't very good, 10 is incredible, you know, these days.
Kevin:	Yeah, it's pretty high, 8 or 9.
Jon Carlson:	And what would make it a 9 or a 10?
Kevin:	Her turning 18 six months from now, will kick it up I think.
Jon Carlson:	Okay. And how is the—?
	[Laughter]
Kevin:	Well, I think that's gonna take a lot of pressure off of me because—
Jon Carlson:	Does something happen at 18?
Kevin:	There will no longer be any legal obligations for me. Well, I shouldn't say that. A lot of legal obligations are gonna be relieved. And first response I get from people, especially people who have adult telling her, "Your job is not over," and I say, "That's not what I'm saying." You have to understand the way that I work is that when the pressure is off, that's when I shine. But when there's pressure on me I freak out.
Jon Carlson:	So you think at 18 the pressure will be off somewhat—
Kevin:	A lot of pressure will be off, yes.
Jon Carlson:	If we look at hobbies that you have these days, hobbies or interests, what would they be?
Kevin:	Well, one thing I love to go for walks. I actually like going for bike rides in the summertime too, but our bike was stolen last winter, so I go for more walks than I used to and I really enjoy doing that. It's very therapeutic for me.
Jon Carlson:	And walks, what do you mean?
Kevin:	Well, I live in a little old town area so I just walk out my door and I'm kind of in a really nice little old historic area. And I just walk around town for, you know, an hour.
Jon Carlson:	So around town around with there's people?
Kevin:	Yeah, yeah. I also like, you know, walks out in nature as well. I think having a little bit of both is really what I like to do. I need some walks around town.
Jon Carlson:	Any other hobbies? Music is a job but is that a hobby too?
Kevin:	Yes, it really is. I spend most of my free time on musical things. Really I spend most of my free time working on my original music, recording, fixing up old recordings, and also making videos which I'm not real savvy with, you know, videotaping things but I'm getting good with photos and putting lyrics up and so I'm building a YouTube library of my original music. And so that's—that could be considered a hobby for now 'cause it's not bringing in income.
Jon Carlson:	And if you had a night to go out and do something and you had free time. Your daughter was out and you have a few jingles in your pocket, what would you do? [Laughter]
Kevin:	I'd probably go see a movie, have dinner, take a walk. Maybe do that in the city. Go to a nice theater somewhere, nice restaurant.
Jon Carlson:	Now, if we look at in terms of spirituality, how important are spiritual matters to you?
Kevin:	Extremely important, yeah.
Jon Carlson:	Can you expand a little bit on that?
Kevin:	Sure. I've said quite a few times that the state of mind that I'm in all day long is spiritual based. I'm always aware of what I'm doing and how it relates to

spirituality. That sounds really generic. Everything that I do I'm weighing it. And how important it is if it's, you know, gonna cause problems for me down the line or anybody else if it's—you know, if I'm contributing to society in a positive way.

Jon Carlson: So you ask a lot of questions.

Kevin: Yes, yes.

Jon Carlson: Are you a member of any formal religious group? I mean you talked about being raised a good—a Catholic boy.

Kevin: Yes. No, I'm not.

Jon Carlson: Are you okay with that or is that—?

Kevin: Well, for the most part, yes, yes. We—I went to Catholic school till eighth grade and then my younger brother was there for 3 more years and after that we really didn't have much to do with the church anymore. I think a large part of that was my father was really the strong Catholic of the family and he died. My mother grew up Catholic as well but she was a little disenchanted with the church and so we just moved down from that and became a very secular family. And then through my adult life I did a lot of searching with, you know, various religions and really the one that—that hit home with me the most about 4 years ago or so was the Unitarian Church. And what I liked was how they—they're sort of a religion that sort of it doesn't mind making fun of religion but they also at the same time when you go to their services each week you're gonna get information from different religions from all around the world, so I really liked that approach.

Jon Carlson: Do you go to that church?

Kevin: No, it's been—it's been—

Jon Carlson: It's been a while.

Kevin: Yeah, about 3 or 4 years.

Jon Carlson: Okay. Let's switch focus a little bit to your family, and you described your dad and, you know, how he was kind of the source of strength for you and he died when you were 9 that—what was his occupation?

Kevin: He was a salesman for a food broker.

Jon Carlson: And did he have any history of mental illness that you know of or any substance abuse?

Kevin: Well, the typical things that men did back in the '70s, he was a heavy smoker for one, heavy chain smoker. I think he was constantly smoking and he did die of arterial sclerosis, heart—that's heart disease, I believe, the same thing which is probably because of the smoking. But he also lived a pretty, you know, stressful life raising four kids back in the '70s, commuting to the city, and you know he—apparently the big drinking night was Friday night. He'd go out with the office guys and so—but I don't remember him drinking during the week, but I do remember him getting drunk and my mom getting angry about it. As far as any narcotics, I don't think there was anything like that growing up.

Jon Carlson: And how about your mom? How about with her, did she have any history or problems that you're aware of?

Kevin: No, neither one of them like had any severe issues or diagnosis. My father did go through some depression. I found some old writings of his and he was—there was some pretty heavy depression there. As far as my mom, she was—you know, she probably could have been diagnosed as sort of a bipolar. She could be, you know, very mom-ish and she's sweet and affectionate, but she could also be ferocious to use somebody else's term that I talked to her about. It might have been my current therapist. But you know she was raising three boys. I had an older sister as well but—so you know I'm sure we pushed her to her limits and so.

Jon Carlson:	And how old were you when your stepdad came into your life?
Kevin:	I was—I would have been 10, almost 11.
Jon Carlson:	So pretty quickly?
Kevin:	[Inaudible] a year and a half later.
Jon Carlson:	And your parents were married when your dad died?
Kevin:	Yes.
Jon Carlson:	Yeah. And what was your relationship like with your stepdad?
Kevin:	At first he was really fun and he was just kind of a goofy guy. He had a lot of cool interests, he had these—well, he was a projectionist and he had a movie projector so we'd watch movies and things like that. You know, he was sort of childish in a way. What happened was I saw this happen with my older brother and it happened with me right around age 13 or 14, started to clash with the stepdad. And there were some moods that happened during those clashes that really never went away. I mean they were there kinda underlying every family gathering that we had years later. And I noticed the same thing started happening with my daughter around age 13 or 14, she's started clashing, so.
Jon Carlson:	Okay. And your relationship with him now seemed to be pretty good though?
Kevin:	Yeah, I mean he—I guess he mellowed out. As he got older, it got less confrontational or plus they moved away to Florida so I really don't see him anymore.
Jon Carlson:	Okay. And then there were four kids you said. Who was the oldest?
Kevin:	My sister was the oldest.
Jon Carlson:	And how much older was she than you?
Kevin:	Eight years older than me.
Jon Carlson:	Okay, and then who was next?
Kevin:	Next was my older brother John. He was 3 years older than me.
Jon Carlson:	Okay. And then who's next?
Kevin:	And then it was me.
Jon Carlson:	Okay, and 43 and then your younger brother?
Kevin:	He's 3 years younger than me.
Jon Carlson:	Three years younger. So what's your sister like?
Kevin:	She's fun. Yeah. I hope she never sees this but she irritates me quite a bit [laughter]. I signed a form that said anything I say out here could be, you know, publicly shown. But she's—I think we've got some different—actually it's not just me, my brothers as well. We've got different interests or different views politically, religiously. She lives down in Florida. My parents are with her now. And as long as we don't talk about those things. I love her a lot.
Jon Carlson:	So you know what—
Kevin:	I don't say that about many people but I do love her a lot.
Jon Carlson:	But you're different.
Kevin:	Yeah, yeah.
Jon Carlson:	Okay. And how about—is your sister married?
Kevin:	Yes, she's married.
Jon Carlson:	One time?
Kevin:	This is—she's on her third husband.
Jon Carlson:	On her third husband, okay. And how about your brother John? What's it about him?
Kevin:	John is the—well, it's interesting you asked this because I've often said me and my brothers, there're three of us and we each got a different part of my father. We each got a very different part of him. My older brother is the smoker, drinker, you know, works steady, 9 to 5 job. You know, he's functional but on

his weekends he goes out and lets off the steam. But he—he's not married and he doesn't have kids so little different situation than my father. So that's him.

Jon Carlson: So what part did you get?

Kevin: I got the creative side, the eccentric side, the emotional side.

Jon Carlson: And how would you—

Kevin: The good father side.

[Laughter]

Jon Carlson: How were you known in high school if you were to go back to a high school class reunion? Let's say hey, here's comes Kevin—

Kevin: Misunderstood. I was pretty quiet in general. I was always—I was very studious so I was—got really good grades. I did my work. Not freshman year. Freshman year, my brother—older brother was a senior and I used to get rides to school from him and there were some shaky influences there—that first year and—but sophomore year I recovered and from that point on. I got back to where I was in grade school as very studious. But I had you know long hair as a musician and I—people probably saw me as sort of mysterious actually.

Jon Carlson: And how about your baby brother?

Kevin: He was the jock. He was—he's the biggest—

Jon Carlson: That's the part of your dad he got?

Kevin: Yes. He's the biggest one. He's kind of macho. Not like, you know, beat you up macho, although at one point maybe he was—he was the wrestler. Very reserved, great sense of humor, so he's kind of like—

Jon Carlson: And what's his relationship history. Is he married? Is he—

Kevin: Well—by the way, my older brother was married for about a year.

Jon Carlson: Okay.

Kevin: And since then no marriage. Younger brother, never been married before, so right now we're all in a way bachelors. My older brother's marriage barely even counts.

Jon Carlson: And your sister kind of has—

Kevin: She's had enough marriages for all of us.

Jon Carlson: For all of you, yeah, okay.

Kevin: She's on her third. She seems to be really happy with the guy she's married to.

Jon Carlson: Any hypothesis or guesses that you might have, as a studious guy, about why that would be that he'd have four kids and no long-term successful marriages—

Kevin: Right.

Jon Carlson: yet. Just any guesses you might have.

Kevin: Oh, sure, well, no—these are the things I've thought about quite a bit. Well, for one thing my mom was married to my father for 19 years. I guaranteed she was faithful to him 100%. And then she got remarried a year and a half later, and she's been married to him for 33 years, I think, totally faithful. Nothing that she's done. She's been a great role model as far as marriage. And my father, there were no issues there. However, my mother's family and my father's family were a mess. They were a complete mess. My mother's mother had six kids by four different men I think.

Jon Carlson: Well, yeah.

Kevin: And my father's father left when he was a baby, left a family of 5, just bailed in the depression so they were a mess [laughter]. And I don't know, maybe it skipped a generation or I think—I think, you know, I think it is there's two different reasons with my sister then with my brother. And my sister is hard to figure out. It's easier for me to figure out with my brothers is that we are very protected. We've got these massive veils of protection around us. I think that's definitely related to our relationship with our mom. I think—do you want me to go into this? Is this—

Jon Carlson: No, I don't think it's necessary.

Kevin: Stop me when I elaborate 'cause I can go on and on.

Jon Carlson: Yeah. But it sounds interesting that you see yourself as protected and yet you and I are talking like this. You seemed pretty open to me. That's kind of a puzzle for me.

Kevin: Oh, sure, I can express myself all day long. But if you—you know, you know, wanna give me a hug on the way out I'll give you a hug but I'm like hugging a vampire probably.

Jon Carlson: Yeah. Okay, so there's being close is not an easy thing, yeah.

Kevin: These days.

Jon Carlson: And were you aware of any complications your mom had during her pregnancy with you?

Kevin: Oh, massive, she was bedridden.

Jon Carlson: Oh.

Kevin: Yeah. They—I think they were worried if I was even gonna make it or if she was gonna make it.

Jon Carlson: Oh, wow. And do you remember when you grew up and you mentioned your mom was kind of up and down. Were all of your needs met—food, shelter, clothing?

Kevin: Sure. Absolutely.

Jon Carlson: There weren't any problems along those lines. Were you ever abused, you know, physically and verbally, sexually, emotionally or—?

Kevin: Well, we—you know, we—spanking was the mode of, you know, punishment up until my father died. I don't remember it happening after that. And I don't remember any intense beatings. As a matter of fact I think I probably like freaked out so much that you know just—'cause I freaked out about a lot of things when I was young. That's a whole new thing to go. Yeah, I think I freaked out so much that they probably didn't you know, even hit me that hard. I was like, yeah.

Jon Carlson: But yet you were quiet in school?

Kevin: Yes. Yes.

Jon Carlson: Okay. Now did you have a history of using alcohol or drugs?

Kevin: Yeah, yeah. By the way, I've been completely substance free for a year now, including caffeine.

Jon Carlson: Okay.

Kevin: Actually 13 months, which I'm really proud of that. That's something that's great. But yeah, I you know had—did my share of drinking when I was young and even, you know, up to a few years ago.

Jon Carlson: And how would you say your usage was, daily, weekly, hourly?

Kevin: We could probably say 5 days a week.

Jon Carlson: Five days a week.

Kevin: Yeah, and generally in the evenings. Never was like a daytime drinker with a few exceptions.

Jon Carlson: And the kinds of things that you would drink?

Kevin: Generally I just like—I like beer. I, you know, the older I got it was really more of an aesthetic thing. Just drinking good beers and, you know, enjoying the taste.

Jon Carlson: But yet you decided for some reason at least to stop that at some point in time?

Kevin:	Yeah, what happened was—a couple of years ago, I started gigging a lot in bars and we usually get free drinks when you're gigging in a bar. It's not always but they're usually covered. And I found myself drinking a lot more.
Jon Carlson:	Oh, I see.
Kevin:	And it really wasn't an issue with intoxication necessarily but it was more of my stomach not feeling good.
Jon Carlson:	Have you ever taken any other drugs?
Kevin:	I used to smoke marijuana pretty regularly as well. Those were really the only two that I did on a regular basis.
Jon Carlson:	And over what period of time would you say you smoked pot?
Kevin:	Well, the first time I did was when I was 12 which that was completely a result of peer pressure and actually the first time I did smoke or I think I—it was pretty intense that night I smoked again and I went into a state of mind that was really—that really freaked me out [laughter]. I was terrified. And the interesting thing was later on like in my 20s I was trying to get back to that state which was kind of bizarre to think about that.
Jon Carlson:	Practicing pretty hard at that time?
Kevin:	What do you mean by that?
Jon Carlson:	You're smoking a lot at that time trying to—to find that state?
Kevin:	That's kind of what I would do when I would smoke. I never really like smoked large quantities like—I had friends who used to wake up, you know, smoking joints all through the day. To me it would be just like a puff or two to, you know, take the edge off.
Jon Carlson:	Any pills you ever did, needles?
Kevin:	No, never shot anything up.
Jon Carlson:	Anything in your nose?
Kevin:	When I was—I lived in California back in the 20's and like two or three times tried, you know, coke and meth. You know, maybe I don't know three times but those things never really did anything for me.
Jon Carlson:	Any other compulsive kind of behaviors. Are you a gambler, are you a—
Kevin:	No, never gambled.
Jon Carlson:	Okay.
Kevin:	Well, done a couple of football pools here and there and that's like—that's even scary to me. It's like, "Oh, man, you know, I gotta lay down two dollars here."
Jon Carlson:	Okay. Okay, so—it sounds like the heaviest period of use was—from what period of time for you?
Kevin:	Well, I would point to two, two periods. Once when I was—or one period was around age 25, 26, and then things started getting pretty regular again a couple of years ago.
Jon Carlson:	A couple of years ago means from you were when?
Kevin:	2008 and '09, so that would put me around age 41, 42.
Jon Carlson:	And then you stopped.
Kevin:	Yeah.
Jon Carlson:	And you remember how you did that? I mean what led you to that point?
Kevin:	Sure. What happened was I got a cold and usually when I get a cold I'd stop, you know, smoking the weed because otherwise my throat would be completely trashed. And—but I—not to go in the details but I lost my voice and my throat swelled up. And so I went on some antibiotics to take care of that and so I stopped drinking because of that so I was like, wow, I just quit smoking weed

and drinking and I kinda—I really wanted to do that for a long time but—so I found an opportunity to do it and so I was like I'm just not gonna start anymore and I decided to quit caffeine as well. I didn't drink coffee much before 'cause coffee to me is like a narcotic. The long-term effects of me being a coffee drinker are really bad, so I was usually just a tea drinker so I quit that as well. So that's—I had an opportunity to stop it.

Jon Carlson: I asked you a lot of questions. Anything that I didn't ask you that I should know?

Kevin: Not that I can think of, no.

[Laughter]

Jon Carlson: Okay.

Kevin: We talked in a lot of areas.

Jon Carlson: You and your daughter now, she's doing okay? You mentioned there was a period.

Kevin: Yeah, things have gotten a lot better, 14 or 15 more rough years.

Jon Carlson: Okay. But they're okay now?

Kevin: Yes, in general. She is on a medication right now and that's helped her to stabilize quite a bit. We've had a lot of family counseling, which has helped as well. I am a little, you know, we had an argument last night. We haven't really been able to talk about it yet, so that's kind of resonating in me a little bit. We'll work it out. I just feel a little bad because I yelled at her and, you know, just need to talk through that a bit.

Jon Carlson: Well, thank you.

Kevin: You're welcome.

Jon Carlson: And I appreciate your frankness in sharing all that.

Kevin: Sure.

[Laughter]

Appendix B
Client Intake Transcript: Chi Chi

Jon Carlson:	So I'm gonna ask you a few questions, Chi Chi, and I wanna start with is Chi Chi your name? Is that—?
Chi Chi:	It's a nickname.
Jon Carlson:	And what's your real official?
Chi Chi:	Carmel.
Jon Carlson:	Carmel, okay. Is Carmel an ethnic name?
Chi Chi:	Italian, I was named after one of my grandmothers, Carmela.
Jon Carlson:	Okay, Italian, wow, okay. And your age and date of birth?
Chi Chi:	I'm 47, October.
Jon Carlson:	October.
Chi Chi:	'62.
Jon Carlson:	'62, okay. Now do you speak Italian?
Chi Chi:	I do.
Jon Carlson:	Yeah.
Chi Chi:	We lived there when I was younger. When I was a teenager we lived there so I've probably forgotten a lot now but at one time I did speak it fluently, so.
Jon Carlson:	Now by coming in and talking to our three therapists, what presenting concern do you have? What would you like to see—what do you want to work on?
Chi Chi:	The main thing that I think is a constant that affects many areas of my life is I'm trying to think of a best way to describe it. I guess it comes down to an inability to keep focused and keep direct, self-directed to do things. I'm always coming up with big plans, things that I wanna do, things that I would enjoy doing, things that I feel would improve my life in a lot of ways and I never follow through with them. And it's not that I don't have the ability or that they're

just crazy pipe dreams or anything like that. It's just that for some reason, I sabotage myself. It's just I never follow through with anything.

Jon Carlson: So you have a lot of ideas and they're realistic ideas.

Chi Chi: They're realistic.

Jon Carlson: Yet somehow you can't put the plans into action.

Chi Chi: Yeah, I never get anything and it affects like I said it affects every part of my life from minor to major things. My job, my—just my overall sense of having some control of my life that not having a life that just drifts along, just filling up time. I think that's the main thing, the—where I've had problems, that's the real.

Jon Carlson: And if you can achieve this in counseling, how would things be different?

Chi Chi: I think that I would—I think that I would really feel like I was using my time for the things that I really wanna do, the things that really make me happy rather than just drifting along.

Jon Carlson: So if you could do this you'd be happy?

Chi Chi: I'd be happier.

Jon Carlson: Happier, okay. So what are some things that you do well?

Chi Chi: I'm a very good writer, I'm a good actress, I'm a good talker to people and a listener of people, probably there's—

Jon Carlson: So what kinds of applications do you have for your strength, like what have you gone through and what have you learned from things in your life?

Chi Chi: You mean—

Jon Carlson: Well, are there any obstacles that you had to face?

Chi Chi: Yeah, I mean, I think that the things that most people have to go through, I've had—I've had family loss, my father died about 10 years ago. That was probably the hardest thing I had to go through. I've had job losses. I've had—for a while I—I had a lot of things happen at the same time where I ended up in just a bad life situation and I had to—I felt like I had to crawl my way back up from the bottom.

Jon Carlson: What are sources of strength that you draw on when you find yourself in that?

Chi Chi: What did I do? I was fortunate to have a very supportive relationship with my boyfriend who I'm still with. We've been together 10 years. And that was a big help. Just—I wouldn't say I've had—unfortunately, I wouldn't say my family—my family is supportive in some ways but that's a particular area that they're not very supportive in. So I can't say that I turn to them very much. My friends.

Jon Carlson: With present difficulties who helps you?

Chi Chi: I don't really have—I don't think I really have any big difficulties right now, I would say my friends—my friends and again I do get emotional support from my family in areas of my life that are not connected to my work, my career, personal issues. So—

Jon Carlson: Okay. Let me switch gears a little bit and ask you, have you ever had any previous counseling?

Chi Chi: Years ago, yes, yes. And—

Jon Carlson: What time in your life?

Chi Chi: Oh, let's see. I wanna say about 15 years ago.

Jon Carlson: So early 30s?

Chi Chi: Yes. I had just ended a relationship that was very important to me and so I wanted help with coping with that. And I also at the time had anger-management problems. So I wanted help with that. I feel like it did help me with that.

Jon Carlson: And did it involve any psychiatric treatment, any medications?

Chi Chi: No medication, no.

Jon Carlson: And did they give you a diagnosis at the time?

Chi Chi:	No [laughs]. I didn't know, I didn't get an actual diagnosis. And we did, my therapist did suggest that group therapy would be helpful for me because a lot of the issues I was having at the time had to do with interpersonal relations. So I did that as well.
Jon Carlson:	Now you described an anger-management problem and does that anger ever come towards yourself, have you ever hurt yourself?
Chi Chi:	I've never tried to kill myself or cut myself or anything like that. In fact, my therapist said I was a person least likely to commit suicide that he had ever met, so [laughs] cause I always—he said I always had good resources for coping with feelings of depression or anything like that. I think I hurt myself in more subtle ways.
Jon Carlson:	Now is your anger directed towards others?
Chi Chi:	Yes. But—yes [laughs]. Yeah.
Jon Carlson:	And what exactly—how did you direct it? Is it—physical? Is it—?
Chi Chi:	No, it's not physical, it's always verbal, it's always verbal. But it can be very devastating for the other person and for me. Although for me, obviously it's not as devastating or I wouldn't do it. But I think that's something that I've dealt with pretty well. I don't think that that's so much of a problem anymore. I really think the therapy helped me a lot with that, you know.
Jon Carlson:	So in the therapy relationship, in the process you went through, what helped and what didn't help?
Chi Chi:	I think what helped the most was having directed things to, you know, actual things to do being given direction, that helped a lot.
Jon Carlson:	What didn't help?
Chi Chi:	I'm trying to think.
	[Pause]
Chi Chi:	I don't think it helped too much to talk about things that were really deeply personally emotional because I would get too upset and then I couldn't go on. So—
Jon Carlson:	Now in terms of your physical health, are there any health issues that you have?
Chi Chi:	No, I've always been really lucky that way.
Jon Carlson:	When was your last physical exam?
Chi Chi:	It was a year ago and no problems. Unfortunately, I keep quitting smoking and starting again—currently I'm not smoking but that could change. So I would say that, I mean, that is a big health—a problem but everything else is fine.
Jon Carlson:	And it's kinda self-imposed.
Chi Chi:	Yeah [laughs], yeah.
Jon Carlson:	Are there any illnesses or serious illnesses or surgeries that you've had in the past?
Chi Chi:	No, I've never been in a hospital, I've never had any serious illness or I've been really lucky.
Jon Carlson:	No car accidents, no head injuries?
Chi Chi:	I was in a car accident about 3 years ago, a pretty bad one. I wasn't hurt badly, I had a broken rib, that was all. But the car was completely totaled, it was really frightening. It was extremely frightening. But—
Jon Carlson:	No head injuries?
Chi Chi:	No.
Jon Carlson:	Okay. Now are you currently taking any medication?
Chi Chi:	No.
Jon Carlson:	And have you ever taken medicines that you can remember?
Chi Chi:	No, I really haven't been—

Jon Carlson: How about legal history? Have you ever had any trouble with the law?

Chi Chi: With the law?

Jon Carlson: The law? Yeah.

[Laughter]

Chi Chi: I was arrested one time for driving on a suspended license. But I—that's—

Jon Carlson: It was handled out of jail, it was—

Chi Chi: Pardon me?

Jon Carlson: It was handled out of jail?

Chi Chi: I did go to jail but only for a couple of hours.

Jon Carlson: Did you ever have an operating while intoxicated ticket?

Chi Chi: No.

Jon Carlson: And no other arrests other than this one?

Chi Chi: No.

Jon Carlson: So it's nothing that your temper has not caused problems?

Chi Chi: No, no.

Jon Carlson: Okay. In terms of finances, on a scale like from 1 to 10, with 1 totally uncomfortable with my finances to 10 I'm totally secure, where would you put yourself?

Chi Chi: Probably about a 6.

Jon Carlson: Okay.

Chi Chi: I guess. Yeah.

Jon Carlson: So more good than bad?

Chi Chi: Yeah but yeah, I think there's room for improvement there too. I think that gets back to the same presenting issue of planning better how to spend my money rather than just impulsively spending it. So I think that's another area where it could be better.

Jon Carlson: And you're currently employed.

Chi Chi: Yes.

Jon Carlson: And you've been employed at this particular organization for how long?

Chi Chi: About 8—wait a minute, 7, 8 years almost.

Jon Carlson: And that's the primary source of your income, are there any other sources?

Chi Chi: I work part time as a bartender on weekends, so.

Jon Carlson: Okay. Let me continue to ask other kinds of questions I'm interested in. How about education, can you talk about school?

Chi Chi: College?

Jon Carlson: Well, how far did you go in school?

Chi Chi: I went to college but I didn't graduate.

Jon Carlson: What was your highest grade level?

Chi Chi: I went to—I did 3 years and a bit, I was almost there. I was almost there.

Jon Carlson: And what kind of student were you in, in school?

Chi Chi: Not a good one at all, I'm a terrible student, terrible student.

Jon Carlson: In grade school or high school?

Chi Chi: I think I was okay in grade school as I remember. I remember getting good grades and doing well. High school, no.

Jon Carlson: And what does a terrible student mean for you?

Chi Chi: I never studied, I never, you know I skipped classes, I—you know—I was—certain things I was good at, I was smart enough to get good grades even without doing too much work.

Jon Carlson: So what did you find easy in school?

Chi Chi: Any of the writing, art, history, those kinds of classes.

Jon Carlson: And how about the difficult?

Chi Chi:	Math. Forget it [laughs]. Math, science any of those.
Jon Carlson:	Do they ever—did you ever qualify for any special education programs, anything?
Chi Chi:	No.
Jon Carlson:	Because of your noncooperation.
Chi Chi:	No, no.
Jon Carlson:	Okay.
Chi Chi:	I don't think that was ever brought up as far as I know.
Jon Carlson:	Now your current social support, do you have a network of friends?
Chi Chi:	I do. I have a few friends I consider my really close friends and then other people that I'm friendly with. I wouldn't say they were friends because I think that implies something really—somebody that's really close to you. But acquaintances that I'm friendly with I guess is the right way to put it, and yeah.
Jon Carlson:	And you mentioned that you have a boyfriend and that's been for 10 years. And how is that relationship going?
Chi Chi:	That's going good except for the fact that he is—he is not a military but he works for the navy, he's a contractor. And he's currently posted overseas. So we don't get to see each other very often. And he's been there for a year and a half and possibly will be another year. So that's been a little bit difficult but—
Jon Carlson:	And how often do you get to see him?
Chi Chi:	Maybe three times a year.
Jon Carlson:	His first name is?
Chi Chi:	Mike.
Jon Carlson:	Mike.
Chi Chi:	He hates Michael.
Jon Carlson:	Are you dating anyone else?
Chi Chi:	No.
Chi Chi:	Is he? I don't know [laughs]. Not that I know of.
Jon Carlson:	And what would your sexual orientation be?
Chi Chi:	Straight.
Jon Carlson:	Straight, heterosexual.
Chi Chi:	Heterosexual.
Jon Carlson:	And when you go out in your—you know, if you had to describe yourself in a social relationship, what kind of a person would you see yourself as? Would you be somebody who is more outgoing or introverted or—
Chi Chi:	More outgoing, more outgoing.
Jon Carlson:	Would you see yourself as more involved with people?
Chi Chi:	Yeah.
Jon Carlson:	More affectionate, more of a leader, more of a follower—
Chi Chi:	I don't really see myself as a leader. More of—I want my friends to be happy. I'm more of the person that wants to talk to them if they're having a bad day or help them if they're having a problem with something. I'm more of that type of person. I think—yeah.
Jon Carlson:	And your current living relationship, you live with who?
Chi Chi:	Myself and my cat. I'm not the crazy cat lady.
Jon Carlson:	What exactly does that mean?
	[Laughter]
Chi Chi:	No, it's—you know, the stereotype woman living alone with all her cats, no social life. No—it's not like that. I do have cats but—
Jon Carlson:	Like how many?
Chi Chi:	I have—currently I have five.

Jon Carlson:	Is that like a high number for you?
Chi Chi:	That is a high number, that is a high number. I didn't plan to have that many. I had three and the other two are strays, I took it. So it's—
Jon Carlson:	Okay, could you kind of—you said you're with Mike now and that's been for 10 years and then you described another relationship that ended up in counseling. Can you kind of give a relationship history, you know, if you give kind of an overview of a few of the relationships you've been in. I mean, you began dating at what age?
Chi Chi:	Oh, high school. I guess—
Jon Carlson:	What was the age of your first—
Chi Chi:	Sexual experience?
Jon Carlson:	Yeah, if you would answer that, yeah.
Chi Chi:	First boyfriend, 17.
Jon Carlson:	Seventeen.
Chi Chi:	Seventeen and that was in high school, I guess you'd say that was my first boyfriend.
Jon Carlson:	And how long did that relationship last?
Chi Chi:	Two years. And then we—this was one—my family is living overseas so we just ended up going in our separate ways to different parts of the world. Then, college I had a boyfriend that I lived with and we were together again a couple of years, that relationship ended actually because I met someone else. And so that—that's how that ended. And just—you know—
Jon Carlson:	In the one that you met someone else, did that go over it for very long?
Chi Chi:	It did but he lived in another state, he lived in California and—so we ended up just not you know—we stayed friends but we ended up not—
Jon Carlson:	Geographically undesirable relationship?
Chi Chi:	Yeah, yeah. And I think I was too young to I think if I were older if it was—if that was the situation now I think I would have handled it differently in retrospect, but in any case and then. [Pause] [Laughter]
Chi Chi:	I had a lot of relationships. And I had a lot of—what's the term? In between my long-term relationships I had a high number of short-term ones. So—
Jon Carlson:	Would you describe yourself at those times as promiscuous?
Chi Chi:	Yes.
Jon Carlson:	And the relationship, like the longest relationship that you were in during that period of time?
Chi Chi:	That would have been—oh you mean prior to this one or—?
Jon Carlson:	Well, I suppose it might—it could be the longest.
Chi Chi:	Right.
Jon Carlson:	Were there any?
Chi Chi:	Well yes, the relationship that ended, when I went to therapy—I'm sorry I can't talk about it. That would have been [clears throat] the longest one in that period of time.
Jon Carlson:	And how long was that?
Chi Chi:	Six years.
Jon Carlson:	That's quite a—
Chi Chi:	I'm sorry, I can't.
Jon Carlson:	Looking for some tissues and I'd imagine there are some somewhere—here.
Chi Chi:	That will work, I guess, thank you.

Jon Carlson:	We have to improvise here.
Chi Chi:	Thank you.
	[Pause]
Chi Chi:	I still can't even talk about that one.
Jon Carlson:	That's still pretty fresh.
Chi Chi:	It shouldn't be after all these years but—
Jon Carlson:	And—okay, now have you had children?
Chi Chi:	No.
Jon Carlson:	No?
Chi Chi:	No.
Jon Carlson:	And how does that set with you?
Chi Chi:	Oh, that's fine, I don't actually want any.
Jon Carlson:	Yeah, so that's okay?
Chi Chi:	That's fine. And that's actually never been an issue in any of my relationships.
Jon Carlson:	And in terms of—if I were to ask you things about your hobbies and interests, what would you—what would you put in that category?
Chi Chi:	Gardening, I love to garden. Gosh [laughs]. I do a lot of board games, puzzles that kind of thing—I play on a Team Trivia team every week, yes [laughs]. Probably my biggest hobby right now and it's—
Jon Carlson:	So board games, Team Trivia, gardening—
Chi Chi:	What else, reading—probably the biggest one.
Jon Carlson:	So a lot of your hobbies and interests have more to do with using your mind? Any physical exercise that you—
Chi Chi:	That's another area where I need to—where I go in spurts, I'll go for a long spurt of doing a lot of exercise. And then I'll just stop. And I don't know why because I enjoy it.
Jon Carlson:	Sure.
Chi Chi:	But that's something that I—that's really frustrating to me.
Jon Carlson:	Yeah.
Chi Chi:	That I do that. But generally I get some kind of exercise everyday usually just walking but something.
Jon Carlson:	And how about for entertainment?
Chi Chi:	I would say reading, movies, going out with my friends, those are probably the main things.
Jon Carlson:	How important are spiritual matters to you?
Chi Chi:	I think that I'm spiritual but I'm not religious.
Jon Carlson:	And so how spiritual; would you say a little or a lot, somewhat?
Chi Chi:	I think somewhat.
Jon Carlson:	Are you or were you ever affiliated with a religious group?
Chi Chi:	I was raised Catholic and that's probably the church I feel the closest to, and when I do go to church and that's where I go. So, yeah.
Jon Carlson:	And are there any spiritual issues or matters that are causing you difficulties these days?
Chi Chi:	I don't think that's—I sometimes wish that I could be more connected that way. I think that you know—
Jon Carlson:	Now your family grew up in what part of the country?
Chi Chi:	Well, we—
Jon Carlson:	Where were you were raised and what part of the country?
Chi Chi:	Really Virginia, Maryland, locally this area but we traveled a lot. My father worked for the state department so we were—we lived overseas a lot and—

Jon Carlson: What does that mean exactly, a lot, can you kind of give a chronology?

Chi Chi: Yeah, okay. I was born in the Dominican Republic, we lived there until I was 2. Then we left for the Philippines and I think we came back to the states for a while, then we went to Hong Kong which is where I had most of my grade school. Then back to the states, then Europe.

Jon Carlson: Was that like in your teenage years at that point in time?

Chi Chi: Yes. And then even after that they then were in Japan, South America, Turkey, they were like between the two of them I think they were everywhere.

Jon Carlson: While you remained in the East Coast?

Chi Chi: Yes, I went to school here and—

Jon Carlson: Now you mentioned your father passed away 10 years ago and did your parents remain married?

Chi Chi: Yes, they're married 35 years.

Jon Carlson: Okay. And was their relationship, did you say was a good one—

Chi Chi: I think it was a good one, they stayed together and of course there were problems. But there was no violence, there was no infidelity, there was no you know, none of that. So I think they had a good relationship.

Jon Carlson: Yeah, did your dad ever have any mental health issues, any substance-abuse issues that you're aware of?

Chi Chi: Not that I'm aware of.

Jon Carlson: Any health concerns?

Chi Chi: He had a stroke and that was what led to actually his death 2 years later. He had a heart attack.

Jon Carlson: And what age was that?

Chi Chi: He was 60, 65.

Jon Carlson: 65. And how about your mom? What's her name?

Chi Chi: Dora, she's—

Jon Carlson: Dora, okay.

Chi Chi: She has health problems also. Hers are she is type 2 diabetic and that's because she has a weight problem. And which I've inherited from her but—so she has that as a health problem and I worry about her constantly because of it.

Jon Carlson: And how often do you talk to your mom?

Chi Chi: I probably talk to her once or twice a week. And I see her, I go visit her a couple of times a year.

Jon Carlson: Does she live nearby?

Chi Chi: She lives in Colorado.

Jon Carlson: And how—were there other people significantly involved in raising you?

Chi Chi: One of my aunts when—when we were little my mom's sister came—oh yeah, I forgot we were living in Spain. And she asked her sister to come and live with her and my dad to help her with the kids. And also so her sister could get a chance to do some travel. So she lived with us in Spain for a year and then we came back to the states, she stayed with us—I would say another year maybe two, something like that.

Jon Carlson: Which one of your parents were you closer to?

Chi Chi: Growing up, my mom. We're more alike.

Jon Carlson: In what ways would you and your mom be alike?

Chi Chi: We like the same things and we both have these kind of dramatic personalities, my dad is like more of the calm type.

Jon Carlson: Now in the family you grew up in, you have brothers and sisters?

Chi Chi: I have one older sister and a younger brother.

Jon Carlson:	And how much older is your sister?
Chi Chi:	She's less than a year older. My mom was nursing—my sister when she got pregnant with me, this—my brother is 2 years younger.
Jon Carlson:	So pretty close in age and can you describe your sister for us?
Chi Chi:	She's—my sister is developmentally disabled. It's mild, it doesn't impair her in major ways but it's definitely something that, you know, it's—it's a problem for her. And she lives with my mom. And she's personality wise, she's—she's really just like my dad she even looks like him, much calmer, quieter, and there's my brother.
Jon Carlson:	Can you talk about your brother?
Chi Chi:	Yeah, my brother's a—I don't know he's had some—he's had some issues as we all have. But he's a very sweet guy. He lives in Colorado. So, they're all—they all live up there.
Jon Carlson:	With your mother and sister?
Chi Chi:	No, he—well he was married. He just got divorced.
Jon Carlson:	This is the first divorce?
Chi Chi:	Yes.
Jon Carlson:	And what—and you say he has issues.
Chi Chi:	Yeah. He—he had a lot of problems in his marriage, they should have gotten divorced long before they did. And emotionally it was just—it was—
Jon Carlson:	How long did they stay together?
Chi Chi:	They were together a pretty long time about 10 years, 11 years. They have 2 kids together so now he has joint custody of the kids, so—
Jon Carlson:	And how often do you see him?
Chi Chi:	When I go to Colorado. I don't talk to him that often in between. But I think we're you know we have a close emotional connection.
Jon Carlson:	And is he a successful man?
Chi Chi:	He is, again he had some difficult times. He—after he went to college he went, after he graduated from college he went to law school. He didn't like it. It really wasn't his idea to go so he dropped out after a year. I don't personally see that as a failure but the rest of the family did. But then he moved out to Colorado and he's done well since he's been out there.
Jon Carlson:	You mentioned your sister was developmentally disabled, any complications during—with your mom and your pregnancy coming so close after her?
Chi Chi:	Not that I know of, not that she's ever told me.
Jon Carlson:	I mean when you were a child, do you remember like your needs being met, were there people there to take care of the three kids in a short period of time?
Chi Chi:	Yeah, well see my mom always had someone to help her like I said she had her sister there for few years. I know when we were little and we lived overseas she had help. So I think it was easier for her than it would have been. I think the only time it was really difficult was when we were in Hong Kong. We were in Hong Kong because my dad was in Vietnam. And the war was—it was still going on so they didn't let families go there, so they moved us to Hong Kong so we could get closer to him. And that—I know that was really hard for her being alone in a strange country with 3 kids. I know that was really hard on her, so.
Jon Carlson:	Do you recall were their incidences of physical abuse or emotional abuse or sexual abuse growing up?
Chi Chi:	My mother was—had a—she could be extremely abusive both emotionally and physically when she got angry.
Jon Carlson:	And that was directed towards you?

Chi Chi:	Yes.
Jon Carlson:	Just you?
Chi Chi:	Well I think I was the worse case. I got the most of it. No, at all of us, at all of us.
Jon Carlson:	Any other abuse that you recall?
Chi Chi:	No, I mean, no sexual abuse, nothing like that.
Jon Carlson:	And they just—it sounds like there were special care situations when you grow up because of the people who were there helping her.
Chi Chi:	Uh-hmm.
Jon Carlson:	Yeah. Now your—do you have any history of any illegal drug use—substance use? Marijuana, cocaine—
Chi Chi:	I tried them all but I never got into them. I would say if there is anything that I probably have done to excess in the past it would be alcohol but not any illegal drugs.
Jon Carlson:	And might have done that to excess or you did that to excess.
Chi Chi:	Okay, I did do that to excess.
Jon Carlson:	Do that to excess?
Chi Chi:	I don't think I'm doing more—I certainly have at periods in my life. I certainly have.
Jon Carlson:	And what does that mean exactly? Are there blackouts, are there binges are there—?
Chi Chi:	No.
Jon Carlson:	Daily use?
Chi Chi:	Just—drinking to the point where you just—where you're sick the next day, I think that's excessive, not being able to go work the next day, not being able to do anything the next day.
Jon Carlson:	And how frequent is that in your life these days?
Chi Chi:	These days never. But it has been in the past.
Jon Carlson:	Okay. You mentioned being of an Italian descent and you describe a family, is there a larger family?
Chi Chi:	My relatives are all in Connecticut on dad's side of the family. My mother's side are in Mexico. So—
Jon Carlson:	Is that her history is she—
Chi Chi:	She's Mexican.
Jon Carlson:	And which family did you identify with when you grew up?
Chi Chi:	I guess more, my father side, the Italian side just because they're also here on the east coast so geographically they were closer and we saw them more often than we saw my mother's relatives. But it's you know—so.
Jon Carlson:	And what—was there Spanish spoken in the home?
Chi Chi:	There was. When we were little, we spoke both languages. But at the time I guess my mother said at the time educators thought that it wasn't good for kids grow up bilingual, that they should only have one language. So they told her to only speak English. I think that thinking has changed now but I think at the time apparently it was—that's what they thought, so.
Jon Carlson:	Any feelings you have about growing and of being of Italian or being Mexican descent?
Chi Chi:	When we were little, the—when we were younger kids you know we got a lot of teasing about our mother being Mexican. But not anything—
Jon Carlson:	And teasing being?
Chi Chi:	The usual kind of ethnic slurs, they are making fun of her because she didn't speak English, that kind of thing. So—

Jon Carlson:	Okay, now are there—we've covered a lot of ground here in a short period of time.
Chi Chi:	I know. I feel like I've written my autobiography here.
Jon Carlson:	Are there are things that I might have skipped over and jumped over that you think that would been important for people to know when they think about you?
Chi Chi:	I can't think of anything.
Jon Carlson:	So it would be, I mean, fair to say that you grew up in many places. You've been settled here in the Washington, DC area for how many years.
Chi Chi:	Oh gosh—oh gosh, it must be about 20 years.
Jon Carlson:	And living approximately in the same area, same community?
Chi Chi:	No, no. I used to live in the city. Then I moved to Baltimore, I lived in the city there. And now I live in a small town that's basically between Baltimore and Annapolis.
Jon Carlson:	And so still in this general area—
Chi Chi:	Still in the general area.
Jon Carlson:	In several different communities, yeah. And then you live—your boyfriend to somebody who's sort of in your life.
Chi Chi:	The current time he's sort of physically in my life, yeah.
Jon Carlson:	Do you talk daily?
Chi Chi:	We talk daily, yeah.
Jon Carlson:	So you're connected on that level.
Chi Chi:	Yeah.
Jon Carlson:	Is there any promise that this might come to an end or any thoughts, not necessarily the relationship, but you might be in the same place at the same time for a longer period of time?
Chi Chi:	Yes, yes, the situation is definitely temporary. So—
Jon Carlson:	And it has been a year and a half, so temporary would be?
Chi Chi:	At this point we don't know. It could be another 6 months or it could be another year. Probably a year would be the max. So yeah, so at some point we'll be in the same—we'll be in the same place physically. It really doesn't—I think we were together long enough before this happened and had a good enough relationship before this happened that I don't think it's a major disruption at this point.
Jon Carlson:	Okay. Now one other kind of type of question I wanted to ask, you said you were a reader, what would you say your favorite book is?
Chi Chi:	Just one?
Jon Carlson:	I think to pick one that really stands out or one that—
Chi Chi:	Oh boy that's a—to just pick one. Bleak House.
Jon Carlson:	And what is it about Bleak House that stands out?
Chi Chi:	I think [pause] what is it? [Pause]
Chi Chi:	You know I can't—I would need a minute to think about it. Whenever I'm asked what my favorite book is that I always come—that's always the one that pops into my mind.
Jon Carlson:	I'm not familiar with the book so—
Chi Chi:	I think it's because [pause] well, I could go on a great length about it [laughs]. It depends on how much you want to know. I think Dickens is such a great writer. And he is one of my—definitely one of my favorite writers. That particular book is probably the greatest of his work. It's probably the one that has everything that he is known for, famous for, is in that book.

Jon Carlson:	What do you think that stands out?
	[Pause]
Chi Chi:	His compassion.
Jon Carlson:	Let me ask you what other kind of awkward strange question that you could think back to early in your life for whatever reason we have memories here, you know, there or maybe there are recollections, something under the age of 8, something that might still stand out for you.
Chi Chi:	Under the age of 8?
Jon Carlson:	Uh-huh.
Chi Chi:	Like something that happened or—?
Jon Carlson:	Something you still remember, something that—still remember the details of—still picture it in your mind.
	[Pause]
Chi Chi:	Gosh—
Jon Carlson:	Maybe going to school for the first time, maybe a birthday party.
Chi Chi:	Oh I know—
Jon Carlson:	How old were you?
Chi Chi:	Oh gosh, I must be about 4, I guess, 4 or 5, I guess. It was before kindergarten because my mother had for some reason she had something to do one day and so she was gonna put me in daycare. And I guess I have never been. And so I must have been about 3 or 4 I guess. And—I remember that I didn't wanna go and I screamed and threw a tantrum and just made her life a living hell all morning about going to this daycare. And then when I got there I had the best day of my life. I had so much fun. Then when she came to pick me up I didn't wanna go. So that I think that's one of my—
Jon Carlson:	And what's the most vivid part about that, the part you can clearly see?
Chi Chi:	One of the girls, one of the little girls there made friends with me and started playing with me. And that was what made it fun.
Jon Carlson:	And how did you feel at that time?
Chi Chi:	I had such a great time, I was so happy.
Jon Carlson:	Yeah, okay.
Chi Chi:	I don't know why I'm still crying—
Jon Carlson:	I don't have any other questions, I don't know if you do. Any other comments you might have.
Chi Chi:	No, no.
Jon Carlson:	We really appreciate your honesty in addressing all of these—
Chi Chi:	Thank you.
Jon Carlson:	Many questions.
Chi Chi:	Thank you.
Jon Carlson:	Thank you Chi Chi.
Chi Chi:	Thank you.

Index

About the Authors

Leslie S. Greenberg, PhD, is Distinguished Research Professor of Psychology at York University in Toronto, Ontario. He is a leading authority on working with emotions in psychotherapy and the developer of emotion-focused therapy. He has, with colleagues, authored the major texts on emotion-focused approaches to treatment of individuals and couples, from the original work on emotion in psychotherapy and emotionally focused couples therapy in the 1980s to his more recent books, *Emotion-Focused Therapy for Depression* (2005); *Emotion-Focused Couple Therapy: The Dynamics of Emotion, Love, and Power* (2008); and *Emotion-Focused Therapy* (2011). Dr. Greenberg has published extensively on research on the process of change. He is a founding member of the Society of the Exploration of Psychotherapy Integration and a past president of the Society for Psychotherapy Research. He received the 2004 Distinguished Research Career Award of the Society for Psychotherapy Research. He has been awarded the Canadian Council of Professional Psychology Program Award for Excellence in Professional Training and the Canadian Psychological Association Professional Award for Distinguished Contributions to Psychology as a Profession, as well as the Carl Rogers Award of the American Psychological Association's (APA's) Society for Humanistic Psychology. He is also the recipient of the APA Award for Distinguished

Professional Contribution to Applied Research. Dr. Greenberg serves on the editorial boards of many psychotherapy journals, including the *Journal of Consulting and Clinical Psychology* and the *Journal of Marital and Family Therapy*. He conducts a private practice for individuals and couples and trains therapists in experiential and emotion-focused approaches.

Nancy McWilliams, PhD, is the author of *Psychoanalytic Diagnosis: Understanding Personality Structure in the Clinical Process* (1994, rev. ed. 2011), *Psychoanalytic Case Formulation* (1999), and *Psychoanalytic Psychotherapy: A Practitioner's Guide* (2004), and is associate editor of the *Psychodynamic Diagnostic Manual* (2006). She teaches at the Graduate School of Applied and Professional Psychology at Rutgers, The State University of New Jersey. She is a former president of the Division of Psychoanalysis (39) of the American Psychological Association (APA), is on the editorial board of *Psychoanalytic Psychology* and is a consulting editor for the *Psychoanalytic Review*. Dr. McWilliams has written on personality structure and personality disorders, psychodiagnosis, sex and gender, trauma, intensive psychotherapy, and contemporary challenges to the humanistic tradition in psychotherapy. Her books have been translated into 15 languages, and she has lectured widely, both nationally and internationally. Dr. McWilliams's book on case formulation was given the Gradiva Award for best psychoanalytic clinical book of 1999, and in 2004 she received the Rosalee Weiss Award for contributions to practice by APA's Division of Independent Practitioners. She has received both the Leadership and Scholarship awards from APA's Division of Psychoanalysis, and she is an Honorary Member of the American Psychoanalytic Association. A graduate of the National Psychological Association for Psychoanalysis, she is also affiliated with the Center for Psychotherapy and Psychoanalysis of New Jersey and the National Training Program of the National Institute for the Psychotherapies in New York City. Dr. McWilliams has a private practice in Flemington, New Jersey.

Amy Wenzel, PhD, is owner of Wenzel Consulting, LLC, clinical assistant professor at the University of Pennsylvania School of Medicine, adjunct faculty at the Beck Institute for Cognitive Behavior Therapy, speakers bureau member for Cross Country Education, and an Affiliate of the Postpartum Stress Center. She is an internationally recognized expert on cognitive therapy and regularly provides in-person workshops, webinars, and intensive supervision. Dr. Wenzel has authored or edited 12 books, including *Strategic Decision Making in Cognitive Behavioral Therapy* (2013), *Group Cognitive Therapy for Addictions* (2012), *Anxiety in Childbearing Women: Diagnosis and Treatment* (2011), and *Cognitive Therapy for Suicidal Patients: Scientific and Clinical Applications* (2009). She has published over 100 journal articles and book chapters on diverse topics such as cognitive processes in psychopathology, perinatal distress, suicide prevention, and interpersonal relationships. Her research has been funded by the American Foundation for Suicide Prevention, the National Alliance for Research on Schizophrenia and Depression (now the Brain and Behavior Research Foundation), and the National Institute of Mental Health. She is certified by the American Board of Professional Psychology in the area of cognitive behavioral psychology. Dr. Wenzel is on the scientific advisory board of the American Foundation for Suicide Prevention, and she has held leadership positions in the Association for Behavioral and Cognitive Therapies. Dr. Wenzel currently divides her time between a cognitive therapy-based clinical practice, training and supervision, and scholarly research and writing.

SILHOUETTES
OF
CHARLES S. THOMAS

Charles H. Thomas.

Plate I

SILHOUETTES

of

Charles S. Thomas

COLORADO GOVERNOR and
UNITED STATES SENATOR

By

SEWELL THOMAS

ILLUSTRATED WITH PHOTOGRAPHS

THE CAXTON PRINTERS, LTD.
CALDWELL, IDAHO
1959

The first printing of SILHOUETTES OF CHARLES S. THOMAS is a limited edition of 2,000 copies. One thousand of these are numbered and signed by the author. No. _____ 644 _____

Sewell Thomas

Library of Congress Catalog Card No. 59-7608

For the Library of Ottawa University Gift of the author

April 1962

Printed, lithographed, and bound in the United States of America by
The CAXTON PRINTERS, Ltd.
Caldwell, Idaho
87755

To my wife
—for forty-seven years a delightful companion
and always a great inspiration.

FOREWORD

THIS IS a brief story of the life and times of Charles S. Thomas, with a few silhouettes, or vignettes, of episodes in his career, taken from notes among his personal papers. To these notes are added a few of my own covering events and stories accumulated concurrently with his career in more or less joint association. It is written principally for his family and a few of the old friends and associates of his that are still living.

SEWELL THOMAS

20 August 1958

TABLE OF CONTENTS

LIST OF ILLUSTRATIONS

SILHOUETTES
OF
CHARLES S. THOMAS

CHARLES S. THOMAS
Ardent "Johnny Reb"

CHARLES S. THOMAS, my father, was born December 6, 1849, at a plantation near Darien, Georgia. His father, a cabinetmaker by trade, went to Georgia in 1846 from New England to take over this plantation, with a few negroes, which had come into his hands by inheritance. My father used to say he did not know the circumstances surrounding the inheritance, but he was sure it was left to his father by some man who had a grudge to pay off. The land was about as poor as any arable land could be. His mother's maiden name was Caroline Baldwin Wheeler, and she was the third wife of his father. Charles was the younger of two sons by this marriage; the older boy was named William B. Thomas.

In 1853 his father sold the plantation and bought another one near Macon. He was no great shakes as a farmer and always was in financial straits due to this inexperience in farm management and Southern business practice. He died in 1855, leaving his widow to manage the estate as best she could. She was able to hold things from falling apart until the Civil War broke out.

There was no public school system so Charles and William were placed with a private school conducted by one William Ryder. Under him they got about five years of good schooling. Ryder was an Englishman, an excellent teacher, a strict disciplinarian. He enforced his rules and order with an unsparing rod. He taught declamation and made Charles learn and declaim standard extracts of the orations of Cicero, Demosthenes, Burke, Chatham, and others. This all paid off later in life when politics and the law required facility in public expression of facts and ideas.

At that time schooltime was long—it "took in" at 7:30 A.M. and "took out" at 5:00 P.M. The terms ran from April to November, with a two-weeks-off period during the summer for "cotton chopping."

Politics was a live topic, engaging even the children in its discussion. The slavery ferment, States' rights, and other issues were forever boiling over in the political pot. Young Charles was a fervent Democrat, due to the sentiment of all the people of his environment except a few adhering to the American (Know-Nothing) party. The bugaboo of the region was the Black Republican, a creature to be obliterated if the country was to survive.

In the spring of 1860, Stephen A. Douglas, as the Democratic nominee for the Presidency, decided to campaign in the South, and Macon was designated as a place for a major speech. Charles pleaded with his mother to be allowed to go to Macon to hear his address. After many refusals she broke down and he was permitted to go, in company with an uncle. They went to Macon the night before the big day so as to miss nothing. Charles was rewarded with a view of his paragon, Douglas, at the Lanier House and an opportunity to shake him by the hand. The meeting was scheduled for one o'clock, under the train shed of the new railroad station. Charles decided to go early and was able to do so as his uncle had gone to a meeting of the local Democrats with the visitor. He slipped in from the outer end of the station, went to the speaker's platform, and took a seat on the steps leading up to it. He sat there for two hours, watching the huge crowd assemble.

At one o'clock, Douglas, accompanied by Alexander H. Stephens, shouldered through the crowd to the platform. Stephens spoke first—for three long hours—urging a perpetual Union, which he said was threatened by the candidacy of Abraham Lincoln. Douglas then spoke for two hours, devoting himself to a defense of his position on Kansas and on squatter sovereignty. Charles was enthralled, even though he had had no lunch. At the end he was suddenly tired, weak, and very hungry. He fell asleep eating his supper.

He became a rabid partisan of Douglas. He was against all of his opponents, hating them cordially. He waited impatiently for the election returns, a tardy affair at that time. Sunday afternoon, after election day, his uncle, returning from Macon, said gloomily to his mother, "Lincoln is elected," whereat he burst into tears and his mother said, "God help the country!"

Secession then became the issue to tear apart the state of Georgia. Charles got to Macon again to hear the debate between William L. Yancey, of Alabama, a great partisan for secession, and Benjamin H. Hill, of Georgia, equally partisan against secession. Yancey spoke first. His spell was so potent that the crowd did not want to allow Hill to speak at all. He stood before them, a bitterly hostile audience whose turbulence was too great to be overcome. So Hill abandoned his theme for the moment, coolly informed the crowd it dared not learn the truth; that Yancey's sophistries had paralyzed their reason and sense of justice. He mocked their traditions of courage; told them they were kin to the Abolitionists they claimed to hate. He said, "You are about to leave the Union because your rights to property are assailed. How long will you preserve those rights, even by secession, if you trample on the right of free discussion?" He went on to tell them that he intended to ask the other people of Georgia if, by their votes, they would approve a policy which dared not submit to public criticism.

The crowd quieted and he then was heard on the subject of secession, grudgingly at first, then passively, and finally with tense and absorbing attention. Having secured his audience, Hill not only assailed Yancey's theme, but the man himself. At the end the crowd cheered him and carried him, bodily, to his hotel. His campaign was masterly but he failed. Georgia seceded, but it made Hill one of its senators.

Hill's tongue-lashings made Yancey his mortal enemy. Yancey was sent to the Confederate Senate by Alabama. In an executive session in 1862, another debate between these two men resulted in a personal encounter, fatal to Yancey. The news of it was suppressed, the press being told only that Senator Yancey was stricken suddenly and taken home unconscious.

This secret was kept for ten years. Alexander H. Stephens was Vice-President of the Confederacy and President of the Senate, so he was a witness to the tragedy. Ten years later, Stephens, as editor of the *Atlanta Sun*, became involved in a violent political quarrel with Senator Hill, which culminated in a challenge of Hill by Stephens. Hill declined the challenge. He said in an open letter, "I have a family to support and an immortal soul to save. You have neither." Stephens retaliated by denouncing Hill as a murderer. Hill then revealed the tragic encounter with Yancey, calmly asserting that Stephens alone had betrayed an episode which, for the honor of the Confederacy should not be revealed, closing with the statement, "Perhaps I am a murderer. I may be so judged by the verdict of my countrymen, who already have passed judgment on you. For you, albeit serene, stand self-convicted and infamous."

Young Charles heard his uncle read the Lincoln inaugural address to his mother by the light of the chimney fire. He had heard Lincoln abused as an uneducated, uncouth boor. But here was his uncle rolling off period after period of clear and liquid English, replete with wisdom such that a boy of eleven could readily comprehend.

At the end his mother said, "Surely no man can be a

monster, or even bad, who can speak like this. I believe he means to do right to all of the people."

"He didn't write that speech," said the uncle. "Seward wrote it for him."

Charles worked on the farm during four bitter years which were characterized by the privations imposed on the South. Near the end, when Sherman applied the torch to Atlanta and began his march to the sea, he was drafted, at age fifteen, into the Georgia troops. Having a horse, he was attached to a cavalry regiment, but with no preliminary military training at all. He put in his few months of military service accompanying his regiment in the evasion of General Sherman's forces. Attrition reduced his regiment to a handful of troopers and, near the end, this handful demobilized by unanimous consent, and he returned to the farm.

His memories of his service lay mostly in tiresome withdrawals, lashed by rain, slogging down muddy roads. He recalled one such instance. His command had come off second best with a Federal foraging party. They were walking their horses along a muddy country road, rain beating down; all of them were thoroughly miserable.

An officer trotted forward to join the captain of his troop. "Wesley," he said, "I don't believe it ever will stop raining! I'm so wet now that a new generation of tadpoles are sporting around in my boots. Next Yank foraging party I see, I'm going to surrender to 'em and get a square meal."

"Don't blame you, Joe! This war sure ought to be over now. I'll tell you one thing—when I get to go home again it'll be a Goddam long time before I love another country!"

Federal troops, under General Wilson, occupied Macon. Charles and his mother grew garden produce and managed to exist by selling fresh vegetables to the troops' messes. His mother, a strict and uncompromising Methodist, was outraged by the loose morals of the soldiers in

Macon—drinking and carousing, and playing with loose women—and she never would permit Charles to deliver the produce alone for fear he would get in bad company. She always went along with him in the rickety old farm wagon.

One cold, rainy morning in April, they drove to Macon and stopped, as usual, to get checked in by the provost marshal guard. By way of conversation she asked the guard if there was any news.

"No, ma'am," he said, "nuthin' special. There was a rumor come over the wire that President Lincoln was shot at a theater last night. That's about all."

She drew herself up. "Do you mean to tell me that the President of the United States goes to the theater?"

"I don't know nuthin' 'bout that, ma'am. But that's the way the rumor come on the wire."

"Then, young man, it is a judgment of God!"

"What's the matter with a theater?" asked young Charley.

"It is one of the most sinister devices of the Devil to lure innocent people to sin and destruction. You take warning, Charles, and always remember what has happened to Mr. Lincoln."

Charles and his mother had many trials and tribulations and, often, great danger, from the "bummers" on the flanks and in the rear of Sherman's army. These roving pirates disguised their acts as foraging for the army, but actually they were engaged in the plunder and murder of helpless people and in wanton arson. The Thomas plantation was partly shut in by forested swamps. This was fortunate as they were able to save most of their livestock by sending them deep into the swampland, where it could be tended by the plantation negroes.

Charles, in later years, spoke often of the devotion of his mother's negroes. During the anxious days of the Sherman campaign and the accompanying "bummers," her four negro men came over to the "big house," with their blankets and old Austrian muskets, and slept on the threshold of her bedroom door. They left their families that they might protect "ole Missus" from "de bummers" —with their lives, if need be. His mother told him that they deserved freedom and that they would have attained it if the South had won out. Now they had it, but they could live and have homes on her plantation for as long as she owned it. They looked at her, wide-eyed, and said they didn't "want none of dishyere freedom" if they had to leave the place.

Early in May, 1865, the countryside was littered with President Johnson's proclamation offering $100,000 for the apprehension of Jefferson Davis and all members of his Cabinet, declared responsible for the assassination of President Lincoln and therefore fugitives from justice. Davis was captured shortly thereafter by a cavalry detachment under command of Colonel Pritchard, of Michigan, some thirty miles south of the Thomas plantation. To bring him in to Macon the detachment would have to take the main turnpike to the east. So Charles and his brother started at once for the house of a neighbor, Mr. Perdew, located on the turnpike, to try to get a glimpse of the prisoner. Fronting this house was a well with a long sweep, located under a huge mulberry tree. There the two boys sat for a couple of hours, at the end of which time they saw a column of cavalry approaching down the road. It was made up of some eight hundred men. Midway in the column was an army ambulance. Just when the ambulance was opposite the mulberry tree the column halted. A trooper, riding beside it, dismounted, drew a bucket of water from the well, and, with a small tin pail, offered water to a woman sitting at the rear of the ambulance and holding a baby in her arms. She took it and offered it to a man seated between her and the driver. He rejected it without speaking. Charles recognized him as Jefferson Davis, lately President of the Confederate States of America. He was dressed in a stained gray uniform, wore a slouch hat, was unshaven, and looked the embodiment of despair.

With him were his wife, two daughters, and his son, then about five years old. The elder girl, Charles was to know, many years later, as Mrs. J. A. Hayes, of Colorado Springs. The baby was Winnie, "daughter of the Confederacy." The boy, Jefferson Davis, Jr., was perched on a trooper's horse and seemed to be enjoying the experience no end.

Ten years later, Charles met Mr. Davis in Denver and recalled to him this episode. Jefferson Davis [Hayes], of Colorado Springs, resident there now, is the son of Mrs. Hayes and the grandson of Mr. Davis.

A JOHNNY REB IN THE NORTH

SOON AFTER Appomattox, the Wheeler relatives in Connecticut supplied Charles's mother with sorely needed funds for the necessities of life. She bought two pounds of green coffee for fifty cents—the first coffee for over four years. She parched it and ground it in an old-fashioned hand mill that had been hung up out of the way for all the years. Charley Thomas remembered it to the end of his days as the supreme treat of his life.

Much to Charles's disgust, his mother decided to go north with him and William, to put them in school. Charles protested vigorously—still a very partisan and unreconstructed "Johnny Reb." He detested the North and everybody there; he stormed and begged, sulked and wept, to no purpose.

In July, 1865, the railroads were operable again from Macon to Cincinnati, via Nashville and Louisville. They left the plantation July 12, 1865. Trains ran at about twelve miles per hour during the daytime only. The little party slept their nights in Atlanta, Chattanooga, Nashville, and Louisville. Progress east was faster and they reached New York on July 19. The early part of the trip presented only scenes of desolation; chimneys stood stark and lonely over heaps of cinders and ashes; unfenced fields stretched interminably with nothing in them but rank weeds; Sherman's "hairpins" and "pretzels" —the bent rails of the destroyed railroads—were everywhere.

Charles and William were clothed in made-over Confederate uniforms. They had new shoes, but from a long time of barefoot life, their feet needed grotesquely large ones. The boys and their mother were embarrassed greatly by the stares and snickerings of those taking note of their dress.

In 1865 there was no railroad station at Forty-second Street in New York; it was located at Madison Square. Trains entering New York stopped at Forty-fourth Street. There they were broken up and the separated cars were hauled by mules to Madison Square through the tunnel from Fortieth Street to Thirty-fourth Street, and on the surface from there along Fourth Avenue. As this slow procedure was going on, Charles's mother asked the conductor if he could advise her about a hotel suitable for her.

He replied, "Lady, we are not allowed to recommend hotels to passengers."

"But, sir, I am a complete stranger to New York and do not know where to turn. It is evening now—too late for me to do any looking about."

"Well, lady, all I can say is to tell you there is a new hotel, just opened, across the square from the station. It is named the Fifth Avenue Hotel. I know nothing about it but you will find it respectable."

So Charles, William, and their mother trudged over to the Fifth Avenue Hotel. They did not know that it was the swankiest hotel in the city but they could see that it was most luxurious. They were too tired to look elsewhere so they were registered and assigned a room on the fifth floor for four dollars without meals—an outrageous price. There were no elevators. A husky porter went to the station, shouldered their trunk, and carried it up to the room while they climbed wearily after him. The next day they checked out and sought more modest quarters.

Lodged once again, Mrs. Thomas took the two boys to a neighborhood store for more suitable and less conspicuous clothing. It happened to be Brooks Brothers. They had to run the gamut of supercilious and snickering clerks who, without attempting to disguise their sneers at the country hicks, whispered and pointed at the trio. Citified clothes were obtained, however, and they all felt better.

Charles always remembered the humiliation of this episode. When my own mother took me East to school, he told her that in getting an outfit for me she was to shun Brooks Brothers like a plague, and she did. Some years later I bought some shirts at Brooks Brothers. They were sent to me by express to Denver and father Charles saw the package. He was ready to disown me then and there.

After a few days in New York, the trio entrained again for Westport, Connecticut, where the Wheeler relatives lived. Charles and William were put in school at Bridgeport. The two boys, as Southern rebels, were ostracized at once, a situation obtaining for about three weeks. This interval was punctuated several times by personal encounters, with varying fortunes for the two boys. However, contact at school led to better acquaintance, and this, in turn, to friendship, so the animosities diminished and were finally succeeded by the relations normal to healthy and vigorous youngsters.

The boys remained at school until the fall of 1866. Their mother sold the plantation and then took a trip to Barry County, Michigan, to see a sister living there. She was stricken very shortly after arrival with what was called then "inflammation of the brain." The boys were summoned and they arrived two days before she died. They thus became strangers in a strange land. William left soon after, but Charles remained with his aunt and uncle for nearly a year.

Charles then returned to Bridgeport, seeking a job. He got one after a bit, as a sort of handy man and roustabout in the factory of a hoop-skirt manufacturer. His four-dollar weekly pay was a big help—good wages then.

But the factory folded and left him stranded with a couple of weeks' pay due him with no reasonable prospect that it ever would be collected. He went then to New York and succeeded in getting a job clerking in the store of Arnold, Constable & Co. All went well there until the late spring of 1868. The National Democratic Convention was held then in New York, and Charles, from childhood, was an ardent politician. One morning, on his way to work, he was held up by a parade of a Western delegation on Broadway. They were all costumed alike, in light tan-color dusters, and they carried banners and signs with pictures of their favored candidates. Charles, the ardent Southern Democrat, was carried away and he followed the delegation to the convention hall. En route he talked one of the delegates into taking him with them and, once there, he forgot he had a job. He remained throughout the day, fascinated by the proceedings.

The next day, with some trepidation, he went to the store to go to work. When he checked in with the timekeeper he was told the head of the firm wanted to see him. The head demanded an explanation for his unauthorized absence of the day before. Now Charles's mother had imbued him with a love of truth by means of an unsparing rod, so, instead of pleading illness, he told the exact truth and asked indulgence.

A vain request! The head lectured him severely and at length for his dalliance, and told him that any young man who held his duties to society in such frivolous contempt would be a failure in life and come to no good end. He was then fired and told to take himself off the premises.

Arnold, Constable was his sole background job. He applied for work here and there, and had to give that name as his most recent employer. Invariably a checkup exposed him as completely untrustworthy and he got no new jobs in New York.

In the fall of 1868 he returned to Michigan, spent

a year on his uncle's farm, and then entered the law school of the University of Michigan. He was somewhat better educated than most young men of the day and of his age, so he was able to secure employment for tutoring and thus pay for his college courses. He graduated with the class of 1871.

The University of Michigan in 1868 was, as it now is, the greatest of all state educational institutions. It then had 1,200 students in the three departments of Law, Literature and Medicine, an enrollment unprecedented in that period. The Dean of Law was Thomas M. Cooley, who was also a justice of the State Supreme Court. Associated with him on the faculty were Chief Justice James V. Campbell, Judge Charles L. Walker, and Hon. Charles A. Kent. In Charles's later, and more mature opinion, no greater instructors of young men ever collaborated together. It was his good fortune, while at the university, to hear many of the distinguished speakers of that time and generation—Emerson, Sumner, Phillips, Anna Dickinson, Fred Douglas, Beecher, Gough, Punchon, Theodore Tilton, and George Francis Train. The latter was described later by him as "eccentric, brilliant and, in a sense, incoherent as a speaker, since his theme had about as much relation to his words as can be discovered in a modern Senator's remarks to any subject under discussion."

Upon leaving Ann Arbor he went back to Georgia. He felt that his heart lay in the South and that he should make his home there. But he had been unable to imagine the blight of discouragement and despair which possessed the South, paralyzing its energies and dissipating its substance. The reality showed him very quickly the futility of starting life there again. One of his classmates—Charles Swallow—wrote him from Danville, Illinois. Swallow was much taken with the prospects there and urged him to join with him. So, in August, 1871, to Danville he went. He remained there until November. During this period he made excursions to Missouri and Iowa, surveying other places of seeming promise.

At Danville he met Joseph (Uncle Joe) G. Cannon. He was introduced to him by Judge Oliver N. Davis, with the assurance that "Joe can tell you more about central Illinois than any man at the Bar."

Cannon, he relates later, then was about thirty-two, alert, vigorous, nervous, and tireless. Even then he carried a cigar at the angle that later was to be the delight of cartoonists. He knew everybody by the first name, had an office in the courthouse, and he urged the young Thomas to make it his headquarters in Danville. He reciprocated by briefing his cases for him and listing authorities for his presentation of cases at trial. They became lifelong friends.

Leaving Danville, he returned to Kalamazoo, via Chicago. The Great Fire there had occurred two weeks before this, so he stayed for a day to view the ruin and devastation. He recalled vividly, in comparison, the ruin of Atlanta when Sherman got through with it. Though Chicago was a much larger city and the destruction was therefore the more widespread, it was not more thorough. Thirty-five years later he was to stand on Nob Hill and view the still greater calamity of the San Francisco fire and earthquake.

In Kalamazoo, Charles Thomas had a sweetheart, Emma Fletcher, a gentle, smallish, and very pretty little girl who had been born at St. Catherines, Ontario, Canada. Her parents, with three sisters and two brothers of Emma's, had moved to Kalamazoo to take up residence in the United States. She and Charles had a sort of "understanding." He was too poor then to think of matrimony, but he wanted to see her before taking off again for some permanent location.

He had heard of a place called Denver, capital of Colorado Territory which had been carved out of the prewar Kansas Territory. He was recalling the counsel of

Alexander Stephens to impoverished young men of the South, "Go to the undeveloped territories of the West where people are too few and too busy to discuss the war, or entertain sectional bitterness." So he decided to go to Colorado, try it out, and, if Denver should prove disappointing, to continue on to California.

Two friends of his loaned him funds for the trip West, with an extra bit to keep him going for a short time. He bought a ticket to San Francisco and left Michigan about the middle of December, 1871. Train schedules then were twenty-seven hours to Kansas City, and thirty-six hours from Kansas City to Denver, over the new Kansas Pacific Railroad. When the train left Salina, Kansas, the conductor announced they soon would be in buffalo country. And so it proved. Buffalo began to show up, first in bunches of three or four, and then increasing in numbers until they were sighted by the thousands, with numerous bunches of antelope appearing as well.

He occasionally went buffalo hunting but could perceive no sport in it. It was as exciting as shooting a steer in a crowded stockyard. In 1874, Beverly R. Keim, passenger agent for the Kansas Pacific Railroad, advertised for 100,000 buffalo heads to be mounted and used in the East and in Europe to advertise the railroad. These heads were supplied by contract hunters in three months. By 1882 the buffalo was only an occasional feature of the landscape; by 1884, a curiosity.

DENVER

Johnny Reb Puts Out His Shingle

CHARLES THOMAS reached Denver* very early on
the morning of December 18, 1871. The railroad
station was located where the Union Pacific freight house
now stands. The American Hotel was the chief hostelry;
Larimer Street the main retail thoroughfare. The population was about six thousand people. The *Rocky Mountain News* New Year's edition declared that Denver, before the new century rolled in, would succeed Chicago
as the Great Western Metropolis, since Chicago, after its
big fire, was geographically disqualified to aspire again to
that distinction.

The streets of Denver were lettered instead of numbered. Tenth Street was A, Eleventh was B, and so on.
The best residences were mostly on Champa and E (Fourteenth). Welton Street was the great highway eastward
to the Missouri River, and Broadway was a country road
out on the Great Plains. The Rio Grande Southern Railroad was completed to Pueblo and the Colorado Central
to Golden. Pueblo was a town of 750 people and Boulder
a flourishing mining camp. Central City was the population center of the territory, with Georgetown as a
vigorous and promising contender. The total white population was about forty thousand.

Governor Edward M. McCook was Territorial Executive and Frank Hall Territorial Secretary. Three judicial
districts had as judges Moses Hallett, E. T. Wells, and
James B. Belford. Sitting in banc once a year, the three

---

* See Plate II.

judges constituted the Supreme Court. Delegate to the Congress was Jerome B. Chaffee.

Charles Thomas' train was the last to arrive for more than three weeks. Snowstorms and wind-blown sand so blocked the tracks that operation was impossible. A large celebration was held by the town, en masse, when finally another train arrived.

The Grand Duke, Alexis, of Russia, visited Denver during this winter of 1871-72. He was escorted on a buffalo hunt by Generals Sheridan and Custer, and by Buffalo Bill. The party then went to Denver where they stayed for two days. While the Grand Duke was there the volunteer fire department gave an exhibition of its prowess with some quite unforeseen events accompanying the show. The Ute chief, Colorow, with a considerable number of Indians, was in town. He was most unpopular and his presence at this time was an affront to many old-timers. On this occasion, he and a number of his band rode across the Cherry Creek bridge and came down Larimer Street, reaching the intersection with F (Fifteenth) Street, where two lines of hose were in full action. A policeman, by shout and gesture, warned Colorow to halt but he gave no heed. Evidently he intended to ride, roughshod, through the crowd without regard to the proprieties. This was too much for the fire chief, who ordered the hoses turned on him. A stream of water hit Colorow full in the chest and unhorsed him. The entire band of Indians were thoroughly drenched before they wheeled and fled. The old chief struck an attitude, yelled "Help! Goddam!" and drew his knife. The bystanders promptly disarmed him, and guns began to appear. One Scobey, who knew the Utes well and spoke their language, caught Colorow by the shoulder and urged him to go to the governor's office. Governor McCook explained to him the presence of Big Chief Alexis, Big Chief Sheridan, and Big Chief Custer and told him he must not interrupt their entertainment. He then gave Colorow an old high hat, a pair of used gauntlet gloves and a generous glass of wine. An *entente cordiale* was thus established. Colorow donned the high hat and the gloves, mounted his cayuse, and departed, happy.

Charles Thomas' professional services were not in great demand for a distressingly long time. He had established himself in a small office that was almost eclipsed by a large "shingle" announcing his name and profession. In May, 1872, he took a clerkship in the office of Sayre & Wright, then attorneys for the First National Bank and all the railroads except the Rio Grande. He stayed in this capacity for ten months and, through it, got a fine acquaintance with all of the prominent men of the territory.

During this period he met a nervous young man from Indiana who said he was a visitor looking for a good Western location for himself and an invalid wife. He bought a one-acre lot on the north side, and contracted for a house on it. He employed Charley Thomas to examine and report on the title to his property, and then returned home. From there he sent his business card, which read: "Thomas M. Patterson of White & Patterson, Crawfordsville, Indiana." Patterson returned to Denver with his wife in December of 1872. In the spring of 1873, he and Charles Thomas formed a partnership under the style of "Patterson & Thomas." This association continued for sixteen years, at the end of which time he (Patterson) bought the control of the *Rocky Mountain News*, abandoned the practice of law, and devoted his time to journalism and politics.

President U. S. Grant paid a visit to Denver and Central City, accompanied by his wife and daughter, Nellie. He stayed in Denver at the home of John Evans, at the corner of Fourteenth and Arapahoe streets. Charley Thomas was then a private in a volunteer company of the National Guard, Captain Andrew S. Hughes commanding. His company was mobilized to aid in policing the streets for a reception at Guards Hall, at Curtis and Fifteenth streets. He was very fortunately placed near the President in the hall and had an excellent, close-range view of him and all the proceedings.

The failure of Jay Cooke in November was very disastrous to the West. Money disappeared from circulation and all prospects were most dismal. A plague of locusts overwhelmed the land the following spring and summer. They covered everything, ate every green thing; an open window meant overpowering invasion; they stalled railroad trains. It threatened to drive the white man back to the Missouri River. Many people left the area, if able to get away. Many more stayed because they were too "strapped" to leave. Charley Thomas was among the latter. He had married Emma Fletcher on December 29, 1873, and thus had given his hostage to fortune. Of his marriage, in later years, he said, "Our union has been a long and mutually happy one. Our days of poverty and of prosperity have been shared gladly in common and, to her beautiful character, constant co-operation and unfailing encouragement, I owe whatever of success I may have achieved."

Mining, as a local industry, was becoming increasingly important. He decided that specializing in mining law should pay off best in the new West. He got a copy of the Mining Act of 1872 and learned it almost by heart; he delved into mineral geology and made himself familiar with all the judicial decisions handed down in mine litigation. He took deep interest in the controversies at Central City, though, as yet, he was not personally identified with them. These disputes brought into play such men as Henry M. Teller, Hugh Butler, Pope & Wolcott, and many lawyers from California and Nevada.

In 1875 he was appointed city attorney, a post he held for two years. The pay was fifteen hundred dollars per year, which meant a good living then, with house rent at fifteen dollars per month and other costs in proportion.

The city had a population of about fourteen thousand people, divided into six wards. The government was by mayor and council, the latter was made up of two aldermen from each ward.

The territorial government was from Washington and, during the Grant administration, there arose many aggravating situations due largely to the Grant appointments made to satisfy his friends. Practice, up to this time, had been the distribution of patronage in the territories to Eastern "lame duck" politicians, a species of "carpetbagging" not at all palatable to Western people. In 1873 Jerome B. Chaffee was delegate to Congress and he was on good terms with Grant. At his insistence, S. M. Elbert was appointed territorial governor to succeed Governor McCook. The latter wished reappointment, but he was not popular, while Elbert, an old resident, was a popular choice. It seemed like things were going to change.

Suddenly, very early in 1874, Grant summarily removed all Federal officials in the territory except Judge Moses Hallett. Further to show his displeasure with Chaffee, he appointed McCook as governor again, replaced the other judges with A. W. Brazee and A. W. Stone, and appointed a Philadelphia lawyer, named Alleman, as United States Attorney.

The public, without regard to party, was indignant. Telegrams burned the wires to Chaffee and others in Washington. At Chaffee's suggestion, leading Republicans called a mass meeting at Guards Hall to try to resolve matters. Henry M. Teller was a cousin of Chaffee and was his personal and political enemy. This hatred was cordially returned. Teller saw an opportunity to turn the tables on Chaffee if he could capture this mass meeting and resolve it to one approving the Grant appointments. He arranged a neat combination of anti-Chaffee Republicans and Democrats, cleverly cloaking his purpose until the meeting was organized. He then secured recognition by the Chair, spoke in eulogy of the President, blamed

Chaffee for everything bad, and offered a set of resolutions approving the recent appointments. He moved their adoption and declared them carried. All attempts to secure the floor, or to be heard were unavailing, and the meeting dissolved amid wild disorder.

At the polls in the fall the Chaffee faction made no attempt to control the action of the Republican party. They gave Teller full play, then quietly voted the Democratic ticket which carried the territory with a majority of twenty-five hundred in a total vote of less than twenty thousand. Thomas M. Patterson was the winning candidate for delegate to Congress in this election.

During his incumbency, Patterson and Chaffee, working together, secured the enactment of the bill enabling the people of Colorado to form a constitution and apply for admission as a state. This document was largely framed in the office of Patterson & Thomas. A convention was elected late in 1875, and this constitution was adopted with a few changes. It was approved promptly by the Congress. The constitution was carried at a state election by an overwhelming majority, the greater part of which was spurious. Two weeks before election, rumors of opposition to statehood, based on its expense, began to vex the optimism of Denverites. As some of the rumors received confirmation it was tacitly agreed to "take the lid off" and let the voters vote as they pleased. So men voted early and often. Hack loads of voters visited every polling place, some of them making a second round trip. When returns came in from the country it was shown there had been no serious opposition there. This was fortunate since a contest of the election could have had serious results.

CENTENNIAL STATE
Rugged Politics

THE FIRST state election was held in October, 1876. It was a hotly contested affair. Notable speakers from other states, sent by the National Committees, came to add fuel and sparks to those supplied by the local spellbinders.

Republican candidates for the Senate were Jerome Chaffee and Henry M. Teller. Democrats counted on the Chaffee-Teller feud for their own success but, unfortunately for them, it had been adjusted for the time being and without their knowledge. The feud had been intensified the previous year by a controversy involving control of the Colorado Central Railroad. Teller was chief counsel for the road; Chaffee was heavily interested in the Kansas Pacific Railroad, which controlled the shares in Colorado Central. Judge Stone had appointed David H. Moffatt to be receiver of the Colorado Central and he was proceeding to Boulder to approve the receiver's bond when he was kidnapped, en route, by the men in possession of the railroad. They hoped thus to defeat the receivership. The episode postponed further legal action to the next fall because of the serious political implications, charged with dynamite for the two Republican factions. Meanwhile Chaffee had recovered control of the party machinery and had made his peace with President Grant. The Republican ticket for the state was headed by John L. Routt for governor and J. B. Belford for congressman.

At the time of the party convention Teller was informed that President Grant, at Chaffee's request, would appoint Judge Stone as United States Attorney if the election went Republican. This was a mortal affront to Teller, who notified Moffatt that, if this were true, he would back the Democratic ticket. A secret conference in Chicago, between Teller, Moffatt, and Chaffee, was held and, during it, the differences between Teller and Chaffee were composed. Stone was thrown on the trash heap, Moses Hallett was agreed on for United States District Judge, and the two precious, erstwhile feudists, Teller and Chaffee, were to take the Senate seats.

Hon. Bela Hughes was one of the Democratic candidates for the Senate. Charley Thomas accompanied him as an aide on his campaign tours. A major speech was scheduled for Trinidad. Bela Hughes, that day, ate well but not wisely and, in the evening, was unable to appear as speaker. Charley Thomas had to "pinch-hit" for him. It was to be his debut as speaker at a major rally and he approached it with some trepidation. He had no preparation for it, but decided he would play on the probity of the large Spanish-American citizenry of the area. So, after due apologies for the absence of Bela Hughes, he launched into a statement that Chaffee had said, contemptuously, that he didn't need to campaign in southern Colorado because he could buy every Mexican's vote there for a sack of flour. He went on to say that was a calumny on the integrity of the Spanish-Americans and, as such, he knew they would most properly resent it and vote for his candidate. His speech was well received, but Chaffee won just the same.

A week or two after election, as Charley Thomas was walking on Larimer Street, he saw Chaffee approaching. A little shy about facing him after the Trinidad speech, he crossed to the other side of the street. So did Chaffee. An encounter seemed to be inevitable, so he faced up to it.

Chaffee stopped him and said, "You are the young man

who made that speech in Trinidad for Bela Hughes, aren't you?"

"Yes, I am a modest man, but I can't deny it."

"Well, Thomas, it was a most effective job, but in reverse. I want to give you some well-meant advice as you seem up and coming, even though still wet behind the ears. You shouldn't make such extravagant charges as you did there in Trinidad. Why—I was there right after election day and every damned Mexican in the county was at the railroad station, wanting to know where he might pick up his sack of flour!"

A unique feature of this election was that it operated to clinch the election of Hayes as President. The Republican National ticket carried Colorado by a small majority, but the majority in the state assembly was very large, thus insuring three votes in the Electoral College. These three votes, cast for Hayes, determined the Presidency, as Hayes received, in the Electoral College, a majority of only one vote.

Moses Hallett, as United States District Judge, held over in that capacity until he died. He was sarcastic and dictatorial with the lawyers who had to practice in his court, and, generally, was disliked cordially. He hated lawyers who presented a lot of citations and could be depended upon to make them as uncomfortable as possible with his comments. One day a lawyer appeared for argument, well fortified with citations. He brought in an armful of law books and his assistant came along with another armful. Judge Hallett glared balefully as they piled the books on the floor at a handy distance from counsel's table.

Somebody let a dog get in the courtroom as the argument was about to get under way. The Judge turned his glare to the dog, rapped with his gavel, and said, "Mr. Bailiff! Remove the canine at once!"

The obedient bailiff tried to lay hands on the dog, but

the animal eluded him, jumped the railing, and, while the bailiff detoured for the gate in the railing, the dog paused appreciatively at the stack of law books and raised his leg and let go.

Judge Hallett observed this with great satisfaction, and said, "On second thought, Mr. Bailiff, the canine may remain. He has a better and more mature valuation of citations than that of the members of the Bar!"

LEADVILLE
The Greatest of Them All

IN 1877 LEADVILLE* came into the picture in a big way. The boom there was based solidly on large, widespread deposits of lead-silver ores, with some gold. It was to have a great impact on the growth and economic importance of the state, and of Denver especially.

In the spring of 1860 a couple of groups of prospectors, following the old Ute trails in the mountains, encountered each other in a small meadow along the Arkansas River, in the shadows of the two highest peaks of the state, Mount Elbert and Mount Massive. One group was made up of Georgians, the other of Iowans. A pair of gulches, each running a spring stream of fast water, entered the river near where they met. Gulches meant gravel and all gravel was potential gold-bearing placer. They decided to join forces, one group prospecting one gulch, the second group to take the other gulch. They agreed to fire pistols if either group should make a good "strike," and then join up to work the ground.

With the Georgians was one Abe Lee, a gold miner who had been to California. He picked a likely-looking place a day or so later, dug up a pan of gravel, and washed it expertly. As the sands were carried away, leaving a heavy concentrate of fine black sand, he swirled his pan and disclosed a "string" of bright yellow flakes—unmistakably gold. He whooped for joy, and his companions shouted, "What you got, Abe?"

---

* See Plate III.

"By God! I got Californy here in the bottom of this here pan!"

The Georgians fired a salvo of pistol shots and were soon joined by the Iowa group. The discovery gulch was named California Gulch; the other one Iowa Gulch.

Prospectors flocked there and for some six months there was great excitement. However, the placers were relatively small and only moderately rich; the winters were severe and the work season short. The find was made just after the discoveries at Central City, so the boom at the latter place soon overshadowed this placer discovery. By 1877 activities at Central City had been dwindling greatly, due to the "petering out" of the high values in the mineral veins there.

A town, Oro City, was built near the placer diggings. It never was much of a town. Once the excitement died down, it never got bigger and it never shrank up much, either, as somebody always was working the placers in the summer and fall. There were a store or two, dance halls, several gambling places and saloons, and perhaps one hundred cabins of a more or less permanent character.

History repeated itself in California Gulch. There were heavy, dark-colored sands, pebbles, and rocks in the gravels which clogged the riffles of the long toms and sluices of the placer miners. These materials accumulated in the apparatus and had to be removed and discarded by hand at frequent intervals—most calamitous and aggravating. This same phenomenon occurred in the placers of Gold Canyon, Nevada. There, a pair of smart *hombres*, the Grosch brothers, investigated the material and they found that it was a rich silver sulphide mixed with gold. This discovery led to the revelation of the rich silver veins of the Comstock Lode. It is strange that no wandering miner from Virginia City, Nevada, made his way to California Gulch with this interesting information which was revealed in 1856. However, a Michigan miner, named Alvinus B. Wood, suspected the truth, collected samples of the heavy material, and sent them to St. Louis for identification and assay. Instead of rich silver sulphides, they were rich silver-lead carbonates and ran over five thousand ounces of silver per ton.

Wood, and a friend, W. H. (Uncle Billy) Stevens, traced the source of the heavy rock, finally finding an outcrop in the side of a hill called Iron Hill. They located a group of claims which they called the Iron-Silver Mine. Prospect development of this find disclosed a very rich ore body in place—ore rich enough to ship to St. Louis for smelting.

In the summer of 1876, Charley Thomas had to go to Granite, Colorado, riding circuit with the District Court. The stage from Denver ran only as far as Fairplay, at which point the whole party took horses and rode the rest of the route over Mosquito Pass. They got a hot lunch at Oro City after riding across the unoccupied area that was to be teeming with people as Leadville only a year later. At Granite, a young man riding a white mule approached him, asking for an introduction to James Y. Marshall, saying he wanted an injunction against claim "jumpers" who were digging ores from a claim of his in Stray Horse Gulch. This man was August R. Meyer, an ore buyer for the St. Louis Smelting & Refining Company. He made a fortune in Leadville; built smelters there, in Kansas City, El Paso, and Mexico, and later sold them to American Smelting & Refining Company.

In the winter of 1877 the "boom" started at Leadville. The South Park Railroad was built only to Morrison. From that railhead, men, women, children, household goods and freight, trekked the roads and trails in every conceivable sort of conveyance. Horse-drawn stages made the trip in two days, with an overnight stop at Fairplay. Accommodations there and at Leadville were worse than primitive. To make bad matters worse, the winter was more than usually severe. But the lure of mineral riches was stronger than all obstacles.

Soon the more direct route from Denver, via South Park, was so choked with traffic that new streams of would-be miners began to go by way of Colorado Springs, Canon City, and by way of Georgetown and Argentine Pass. Prices for everything rose sky high. Ranchmen along the routes sold hay for twenty cents per pound, and human rations cost accordingly. By the beginning of 1878 the contagion of Leadville was nationwide, traffic was so heavy that the two stage lines from the South Park railhead each ran twenty stages per day, each way, and the line from Canon City ran twenty-five. Stage routes grew progressively shorter, of course, as railheads advanced—the South Park to Grants, then Jefferson and Como, and finally Leadville; the Rio Grande to Salida, Buena Vista, and finally to Malta, near Leadville.

Overland haulage and local ore haulage by teams gave great impetus to such industries as blacksmithing, harness making, feed stores and corrals, wagon works, and others. Real-estate dealers found opportunity to profit to almost as great an extent as the miner with a shaft in ore. Barrooms, gambling and dance halls, variety shows and the like—all the collateral callings of the wide-open Western town—thrived, with everybody too busy to take heed or even interfere. Lake County was established, with Leadville as the county seat, and it became very quickly the state's center of population, wealth, and commercial activity. No less than fifty thousand people were to be counted in the county. At the height of the "boom," seven smelters were furiously active, extracting metal by pyro-metallurgy from the rich ores of the district and other areas near by. The hills for miles around were stripped bare of trees for mine timbers and for the making of charcoal for the smelter furnaces.

Charley Thomas' first visit to the city of Leadville was in July, 1878. There were twelve thousand people there by that time, with as many more scattered about in the hills. Claims were located all over the ground surface for ten miles around the town; digging in them was fast and furious; claim jumpers daily caused private battles, many of them with fatal results.

The ore deposits were flat-lying "ore-shoots" along a contact line between porphyry and limestones, with many faults displacing them up or down, stratigraphically. So the place was called a "poor man's camp" since a shaft sunk almost anywhere in the mineralized area had a nearly even chance to find "pay" at depths ranging from forty feet on Fryer Hill, to two hundred feet on Breece, Carbonate, and Iron hills. Most mining law up to that time had been based on ownership rights pertaining to the outcrops of fissure veins, cutting across basic rocks, and those attaching to placer gravels lying in stream beds. The new type of deposit in Leadville was at variance and the attempt to apply existing laws to ownership of the ores was a complete failure because of anomalies theretofore unknown. Controversies rose at once and much expensive and savage litigation resulted and had to be resolved by decisions of the courts, all too many of whose judges were too ignorant of the geology of ore deposits to interpret the evidence presented in trials at law with any great degree of justice.

Charley Thomas was well prepared for this upsurge of litigation because of his study of the law and of economic geology. So, also, were some other lawyers of the state to some varying extent. The most notable of the others was Charles J. Hughes, a most distinguished lawyer from Missouri. He and Charles Thomas found themselves speedily engaged in the courts at the intricate business of presenting evidence to support clients' claims at law to contested bodies of ore in the mines. Both men, as leaders at the bar in this field, almost always found themselves opposed to each other in the courts. If one litigant had Charley Thomas as chief counsel, the other one moved

heaven and earth to retain Charley Hughes, and vice
versa. Both men were active in politics, again as opponents, for Hughes was a Democratic contender for candidates often opposed to the following of Thomas. With
all this as background, however, they were warm personal
friends, each man having the highest regard for the character and intellectual attainments of the other.

By February, 1879, the clientele of Patterson & Thomas
in Leadville became so large that, with Patterson in Congress, something had to be done. Charley Thomas decided to locate for a time in Leadville, where the courts
were jammed with mine controversies. So he made an
arrangement with Judge V. D. Markham, adding later
Mr. E. L. Campbell to help in Leadville. Soon the Leadville branch "tail" was wagging the Denver office "dog,"
doing four times as much business. Campbell later (1881)
left the firm to take the presidency of the Bank of Leadville. During the existence of the firm, its Leadville
business yielded an average of over ten thousand dollars
monthly in cash receipts, besides the many cases billed
and never collected. Such fees were huge for those days.
Like everyone else, however, the mining fever raged in
the hearts of the partners and much of the profit was
put into holes in the ground and most of it remains
there to this day.

County officials were then paid under a fee system.
The positions of Clerk & Recorder, Sheriff, Clerk of the
Court, and Police Magistrate were as good as gold mines.
The least of them cleared thirty thousand dollars per
year, and the biennial struggle to get, or retain, the jobs
was always a fierce one. In 1880, a John R. Curley was
Police Magistrate by appointment of the city council.
The validity of the appointment was challenged and denied in the court. Appealed, the Supreme Court sustained
the denial. Curley deposited all fines, costs, and fees in
the bank pending appeal. The deposit was made in his
own name, as he alleged, for his own protection. When

he was ousted the council demanded an accounting. "No," said Curley. "The Court says I am a usurper, so I'll usurp!" And usurp he did.

Among the clients of the Thomas firm was an Irishman named Pat Mulrooney. Pat was a gold mine of fees because of his stubborn Irish disposition. He had located a claim in the district and named it the "Ragged Ass Miner." It developed into a good mine, and Pat wished to get a patent on it from the United States Land Office. This official agency decided the name was too lewd for the public records and they refused the patent unless the name should be changed. Pat was superstitious, feeling that if he didn't stick to his original name the ores might pinch out on him. So he fought the ruling—in the Interior Department and in all courts of jurisdiction. The battle went on for years. Pat finally died and his heirs compromised by accepting the initials of the original name—R.A.M., and so it was patented.

Not all the clients of Charley Thomas belonged to the prosperous circles. He had occasion to act for many poor prospectors and small operators, and he did so with pleasure and with the same expert competence with which he handled the big cases. Many times such work developed into episodes full of humor—sometimes of tragedy. Among his more humble clients was a prospector called Broken Nose Scotty, who went into Leadville from a tour of work in the mountains near by.

People were then locating claims on Carbonate Hill and Scotty decided he might as well emulate them and do likewise. He dug a hole and found ore about forty feet from the surface—it was good ore but not too high grade. He decided to celebrate, and he did so, with no holds barred and the devil take all. He was noisy and belligerent and so disorderly that the town marshal hauled him in. In the morning he was given the choice of paying a fifty-dollar fine or taking thirty days in the cooler. His money was all spent, or had been "lifted" during his spree, so he had to take the cooler.

"What the hell!" said Scotty. "The mine can easy wait for a few days."

The head of a mining company called on him in jail and offered him thirty thousand dollars for his claim. Says Scotty, "It's a deal, but I want a lawyer to pass on it before we close it, and the stiff that let you in here to see me thinks too much of me to let me leave for a while."

"What's the fine?" asked the buyer.

"Fifty cart wheels," says Scotty.

The fine was paid and Scotty accompanied his man to the mine office. "Who do you want for a lawyer?" said the prospective buyer.

"Well, I heard a real talking bastard trying a case in court a couple months back, an' ef I can git him, I want him. Name's Charley Thomas."

Charley Thomas was available; he came to the office and drew up the contract of sale and deed to the property; the buyer and Scotty signed up and they all three then went to the bank where Scotty got thirty thousand dollars in currency. He paid the fee for the legal service, then went straight back to the jail and asked the jailer how many of his inmates he could buy out.

"You can buy all of them and welcome, except horse thieves, burglars, rape hounds, and murderers," said the jailer.

"Fine!" said Scotty. "Send for the judge and I'll buy 'em up."

Scotty took his purchases, some thirty men, to Dave May's department store, bought new outfits for them, then took them to the Saddle Rock Cafe and fed them up with appropriate food and drink. As he dismissed them he gave them each ten dollars. Before morning about half of them were back in jail. Scotty heard about it, appeared at the Police Magistrate's, and said, "Judge, I shouldn'ta given 'em money. I got 'em in again, I guess.

How much you want for the whole gang. Be a sport, Judge, and make it a wholesale deal."

The judge was agreeable, being on a fee system, and again Scotty picked up the tab. This time he warned them that if they got in the cooler again they would just stay there.

Scotty sent enough money, via Charley Thomas, to his old mother in the "hielands" of Scotland to keep her for the rest of her days; then he had himself a wonderful time, blowing in the rest of his stake, and he ended his days out in the hills with a burro and prospecting kit.

Another client of Charley Thomas, and a good one, was a man named Horace A. W. Tabor. He was a native of Vermont and he had been living in Lake Country since the early sixties.

H. A. W. TABOR
Monumental Sucker

CHARLEY THOMAS first met Tabor in the law offices of Sayre & Wright in the summer of 1872. He then was running a general store at Oro City. He had overextended his credit to a firm of contractors, furnishing crossties to the Santa Fe Railway then building up the Arkansas River Valley. The ties were cut near Oro City and were to be floated down the Arkansas River to points below, where needed. One August morning the contractors pulled stakes and departed "silently, in the stilly night," leaving Tabor out on a limb. Through Sayre's efforts the railroad company transferred the contract to Tabor and he performed it and saved himself. Thomas remembered seeing him that fall, up to his neck in the river at Pueblo, breaking up a jam of floating ties.

In 1876 Charley Thomas met him again at Granite. He was county treasurer, and he told Charley his store was prospering, with his wife Augusta Tabor in full charge, and he was also doing very well as a trader in county warrants—an activity in which a county treasurer had a sort of inside track.

When the Iron-Silver Mine started the "boom" at Leadville, Tabor moved his store there and secured the postmastership. Soon after his establishment at that place he was importuned by August Rische and George Hook, shoemakers from Fairplay, for a grubstake. Tabor knew them but, even so, what induced him to grubstake shoemakers as prospectors is a mystery. Besides this, the two men were known to have an avocation of trying to dry up the local supply of liquor by personal consumption. But he grubstaked them with an outfit of hand tools, blasting powder, "grub," a burro, and some small change. The change was invested in a jug of whisky and the two shoemaker-prospectors headed out of town for Fryer Hill. They picked out a large juniper tree, sat down in its shade, and sampled the whisky. As the contents of the jug gurgled away they decided the spot where they were resting looked to be as good a place as any to locate a claim, so there it was located; name, "Little Pittsburg"; a notice, "To whom it may concern," tacked on a post. This done, the two entrepreneurs curled up under the juniper and went to sleep. Another wandering prospector came on the scene, observed the blissfully unconscious figures and the location notice, newly posted. This man, conceiving that they must have a good reason to locate this ground, removed the notice and replaced it with one of his own. He had a pipe and tobacco, and a shotgun. He filled his pipe, made himself comfortable, and waited for the two men to come to. This happened in due course; August Rische observed what had happened, became indignant, and accused the man of claim jumping. Not so, the stranger told him; he showed his shotgun, said his gun was a witness to the deed and would speak up when and as needed. Rische accepted the situation philosophically, moved north a couple of hundred feet, and reposted his notice there.

Rische and Hook spat on their hands and started digging "by guess and by God." The jug of whisky was gone and they had no more money, so they continued to dig for a couple of weeks. At a depth of thirty-three feet the little shaft broke into the top of a bed of rich silver-bearing lead carbonate, and the famous Little Pittsburg Mine was born. Tabor bought Hook's interest in the mine for $150,000. Rische hung onto his share for a time and then sold it to Senator Chaffee for $350,000.

Tabor and Chaffee then incorporated the Little Pittsburg Mining Company, transferred the property to it, and sold a few shares to friends. The company paid dividends of a hundred thousand dollars per month for some three years.

Rische retired from prospecting and went in for politics, getting himself elected to the Leadville city council. The council chamber was a drab sort of place, badly lighted. One of the councilmen thought it should be spruced up with a nice, large, crystal chandelier and offered a motion to effect it. Rische thought it a good idea but said he was worried about where the hell they would find somebody who could play on it. That stumped everybody and the project was tabled.

Next thing, Rische wanted to be mayor of Leadville. A convention was held to pick candidates for the city and county tickets, and Rische asked Charley Thomas to put him in nomination as candidate for mayor. Thomas tried to duck out of it, stating that he already was committed to nominate two other men for county offices; that if he took on Rische the party might think he was trying to hog the show.

"To hell mit that!" said Rische. "You do it anyway und I will take care of de hog business!"

"No, August. I'll tell what I'll do. I'll get another good Democrat to put you in nomination."

"No, no, no! I tell you, Sharley, I don't vant nobody but you! I vant to get nominated by a sonofabitch vat can talk!"

A character in the region, known as "Chicken Bill," a teamster on a freight haul, got a notion he wanted to be a miner. Bill got his nickname from an episode having to do with a freighting job to Gunnison that had, as part of its load, fifty dressed chickens. En route, a blizzard blew up and Bill was snowbound for two weeks. At the end of that time he was found by a search party.

His mules were dead, one wagon was broken up for fuel, Bill was bedded down in the other wagon, and there were no chickens. Bill had been eating chicken for two weeks. He found some open ground out on Fryer Hill and located a claim, named it Chrysolite and started a shaft. After three weeks' hard work digging, with a buddy to handle the windlass, he was down some fifty feet and no ore in sight. Bill was getting awfully tired and his enthusiasm for mining had dwindled considerably. The Little Pittsburg Mine was not too far away, so one night Bill slipped over there and stole several hundred pounds of ore. Some of it he dumped down his shaft, the rest he spread out on his dump to look like it had been spilled from his hoisting bucket. Then he went to town and bought himself a wonderful jag and bragged about the wonderful "strike" of ore at his claim. Tabor heard about it and slipped out to the shaft and looked it over. He confirmed the presence of the ore—just like his Pittsburg ore. He hurried back to town, found Chicken Bill, patted him on the back and bought him a couple of drinks and then bought the mine from him for forty thousand dollars.

It didn't take Tabor long to discover the fraud. "Chicken Bill" was not to be found anywhere and there seemed but little chance to locate him before the money would be gone. Marshall Field was in town, looking for a chance to be a "miner." He had called on Tabor for advice, so Tabor looked him up and sold him a half-interest in the Chrysolite for forty thousand dollars. He put men to work there and, after digging eight feet more, he broke into the rich carbonate ores. The Chrysolite developed into an even richer mine than the Little Pittsburg and Marshall Field made a great deal of money out of it. His partner, Levi Z. Leiter, was not to be outdone this way. He went to Leadville and bought an interest in the Iron-Silver Mine through negotiations instituted for the purpose by Charley Thomas. He also did very well and, soon thereafter, he sold his holdings in the Chicago store to Marshall Field and took himself off to Washington.

Soon after this episode, Tabor obtained, by purchase, a promising-looking property called the Matchless Mine. It was located where the carbonates had been faulted to a lower level; its owners were discouraged, and he was able to buy it at a bargain. This became the best of all his mines as it was developed and opened up.

Tabor became very rich. His mines for some time paid him an income of over two hundred thousand dollars per month, in the days when there was no income tax and a big, round, silver dollar really would buy something. He moved to Denver where he could cut more of a swath and there he set himself up in a style befitting a prince of fortune. He probably was the best citizen that Denver ever had, economically; he built a fine home, the Tabor Grand Opera House, and many other buildings. He was bitten by the political bug and, loving flattery, and getting in a frame of mind to believe it, he soon attracted the attention of a swarm of adventurers who easily induced him to invest his money in numerous enterprises freighted, all too surely, with disaster. The Tabor this and the Tabor that were born, had brief periods of phosphorescent life, then flickered out, each taking with it some of the Tabor millions.

The only rewards he ever obtained were two terms as lieutenant governor and a thirty-day term in the United States Senate, where, all unconsciously, he was the butt for funny-man cracks, grounded on his poor education and pomposity. Eugene Field led in this particular. Field was then editor of the old *Denver Tribune* and he established a column, "grapevine telegraph" connection with Washington, and every morning he presented his avid readers with a "special" which apprised them of all that the Senator did, or refrained from doing. The Tabor lace-trimmed nightshirt was a favored topic and Field made it the subject of some of his verses. A typical Field item was an invitation Tabor purportedly sent to Senator Hoar, of Massachusetts, asking "him and Mrs. W—— to attend the theatre with him and Mrs. T——."

At the height of his prosperity, with Lady Luck making all manner of passes at him, Tabor found his domestic life a bit drab. His Augusta was a plain and rather severe woman; a "good gal" but one without glamor. She was Victorian to the nth degree; she favored the restrained, formal life, unruffled by any bachanalian rites of impromptu entertainment. Tabor felt that his importance required bread and circuses, and many, many cozy corners. A beautiful young lady of Central City went to Leadville in search of the finer things of life; that is, those finer things that had glitter. Baby Doe was the name. She had ideas of a very definite nature, unconnected with the formality of Victorian restraints, and she offered Tabor just what he wanted—a come-hither look and glamor plus.

Tabor went very modern and divorced his first wife. At this time he got the appointment to the Senate for the short, thirty-day term, created by Teller's appointment to the Cabinet of President Arthur. He took Baby Doe to Washington with him, along with his lace nightshirts, and the wedding was pulled off there. President Arthur attended the ceremony and this gave no end of a boost to Tabor's pride and social standing. The day of the wedding, Mrs. Charles Thomas, accompanied by Mrs. Joseph Thatcher, Mrs. Charles Kountze, Mrs. James B. Grant, and others, made formal calls on Mrs. Augusta Tabor, and extended to her their moral support.

The summer after his short honeymoon in Washington as bridegroom and United States Senator, Tabor's political hunger began to gnaw at his vitals. He called on Charley Thomas and told him he wanted to run for governor. He said he thought all the prominent people

should give him an endorsement in view of what he had
done for Denver and Colorado.

He was told, "I can't do that, Horace. You are a
Republican and I am a Democrat. Much as I would like
to accommodate you, it would violate the proprieties."

"This is above partisanship, Charley. It's— it's— well,
it's sort of something that I think is due me."

"Perhaps so, Horace. But there is another reason. I
don't like to bring up the subject, but if I should en-
dorse you I just wouldn't dare to go home!"

"Now, now, Charley, you can be perfectly easy on
that score. You can just tell your sweet little woman
that since Baby Doe and me has been married we both
of us has been behavin' ourselves."

Tabor built another large house in Denver (Augusta
was living in the first one) at Thirteenth and Grant
streets. A low stone wall, topped with an iron fence,
surrounded a large house built of stone. Baby Doe bought
classic statues, mostly nudes, and set them up about the
grounds, in company with iron deer striking startled attitudes. It is said that someone gave her the idea that the
ladies of Denver did not call on her because of the shock-
ing statuary they must see as they went to her front door.
One morning, early, pedestrians passing the house were
startled to see statues draped in modest clothing. It was
futile. The ladies of Denver continued to call on Augusta
Tabor at her house and passed the new Tabor house without a glance.

Tabor had it hard during his declining years—a truly
pathetic figure, not able to realize what had happened
to his once great fortune. Friends, including Charley
Thomas, got him an appointment as postmaster in Denver,
and this job enabled him to live the rest of his life.

Always he enjoined on Baby Doe that never, under
any circumstances, should she give up the Matchless Mine
at Leadville; he told her it was just as good as ever, and
inexhaustible. The poor man simply didn't know what

he was talking about. He had gouged out all the good ore; what was left was of low grade, incapable of paying operating expenses. But Baby Doe took his injunctions literally; she was not burdened of any great intelligence; in fact, in her later years, she was what might be termed, "balmy." She returned to Leadville, after Tabor's death and set up housekeeping in the Matchless Mine shaft house, a crude structure of rough boards with very little protection against the weather. The hardships she endured living thus did damage to a mental equipment never very good. She got a persecution complex; she felt that people were trying to steal the mine from her. If anyone came near the shaft house she would appear, dirty, ragged, burlap sacking wrapped around her feet, hair untidy, and carrying a shotgun. Compassionate friends, strangers; all alike were ordered to go.

The mine was always delinquent in payment of taxes; she almost lost it several times. A kindly old gentleman —John K. Mullen, of Denver—saved it from tax sale, time after time, buying up the tax certificates, but never, so long as she lived, did he use them to acquire title to the mine. She, on her part, was suspicious of his motives; once or twice she went to Denver, dirty and disheveled and smelling not too sweet, to try to get lawyers to sue Mr. Mullen and make him give up his tax certificates. She was often hungry; the ladies of Leadville, repulsed by and threatened with the shotgun, used quietly to slip up to the shaft house and leave baskets of groceries at the door. Nobody ever got any thanks. She was found dead one cold, winter morning by men who noticed no smoke coming from her stove chimney.

There has been much maudlin sympathy and romantic nonsense built up about the life of Tabor and his quite silly Baby Doe. Her faithful guardianship of the mine almost has been canonized; actually it was a self-imposed hardship, since common humanity would have seen to it that she had care during her old age that would have

been free of hardship. Tabor was a quite stupid, though
kindly man, who blundered into great wealth and didn't
know what to do with it. His vanity—a colossal thing
—caused him to dissipate it all, to the end that not only
Baby Doe but two daughters were left penniless. He
fell for a quite stupid, silly woman, with a pretty face,
giving up the woman who had shared the hard times of
his early life. It is difficult to understand the thinking
that can make of Tabor a heroic figure of romance, or
that can glorify Baby Doe for guarding a property that
cannot get away if taxes are paid.

LEADVILLE
More Characters

WILLIAM H. STEPHENS was a character quite as picturesque as Tabor, yet in no wise resembling him. He had spent much time in the copper-producing region of Michigan, and was in his fifties when he went to Colorado. He was florid, redheaded; a one-eyed man of dour visage, short and pugnacious, repellent and suspicious, and easily offended. He was a hard trader, and not too mindful of his agreements if he could evade them. He was a man of means before he joined up with Alvinus Wood in the Iron-Silver deal. After Wood sold his interest to Levi Leiter, Stephens claimed to be the real discoverer of the rich carbonate ores of Leadville.

Stephens located the townsite of Leadville as a placer claim. While patent proceedings dragged along, many squatters settled on the land and they contested his application for patent. He compromised with them by agreeing to convey to each one his lot for twenty-five dollars in cash as soon as the patent was issued. When it was granted he tried to evade the commitment on the grounds of "no consideration." Next day a squatters' committee waited on him and announced that deeds must be forthcoming within forty-eight hours or he would find himself swinging by a necktie from a tree limb.

The man was unperturbed. He told the committee that while they might think him a mean and exasperating old man, his son was twice as mean, and to kill him off would serve only to aggravate their difficulties. But his lawyers, Charley Thomas among them, convinced him he should honor his promise, so grudgingly he executed the deeds.

A particular object of Stephens' animosity was A. W. Gill. Gill was a man of great courage and ability; also he was generous and companionable, good-natured and cheerful. He took delight in goading Stephens at all times, finding willing collaborators everywhere because of Stephens' unpopularity, so Stephens hated him with a ferocity almost inhuman. Gill located some land which Stephens regarded as his, and maintained possession of it successfully until, in two years' time, the courts confirmed his title. Gill then, most fulsomely, thanked Stephens for his chivalrous and generous conduct in the litigation. This almost gave Stephens apoplexy.

Gill's generosity was great; his concern about his debts and other liabilities far from great. When he could pay up he did it; when he couldn't he didn't worry about it. Thomas was Gill's attorney, and one day a man came to his office looking for Gill. He was from New York; he said his name was Keeler. He held two long-past-due notes of Gill's for a quite considerable sum of money. He recited a story of trouble and privation caused by Gill's indifference to his obligation. He waited for Gill to show up; when he did not come, Keeler left word that he would be at, and remain at, the Clarendon Hotel until he heard from Gill. The latter entered the office soon after Keeler left. He was informed that a man was looking for him and wanted him to meet him at the Clarendon Hotel. Gill said he would go right over there, but when informed that the man held two past-due notes of his, he said, "Oh, hell! I thought maybe he wanted to see me about business!"

Gill was a good client—always involved in litigation. He would go to Thomas' office, pull three or four summonses from his pocket, hand them in separately, and say, "Demur to that. Move for a cost bond on that one.

Answer this, denying everything. This one may have a good case; nurse it along until I can get a breather." Once, in London, he cabled about an important matter, adding to his message, "London is a big town but no good. Been here a week and nobody sues me."

In 1879, a young Irishman, a carpenter by trade, became proprietor of the Grand Hotel in Leadville. He dallied in mining and acted as an ore buyer for one of the smelters. His name was Thomas F. Walsh, renowned as the discoverer of the great Camp Bird Mine, at Ouray, Colorado, and for his almost unlimited hospitality. He retained Charley Thomas for all his life and, selling the Camp Bird Mine to the Ventures Corporation, of London, paid him a hundred-thousand-dollar fee for handling the transaction. Walsh then made his home in Washington, was United States Commissioner at the Paris World's Fair, and consorted with King Leopold, of Belgium. His daughter, Evalyn, married Ned McLean, bought the Hope diamond, and put some Camp Bird money in the hands of Gaston Means in connection with the Lindbergh kidnapping case.

Among outsiders attracted to Leadville were Senators John P. Jones, William Stewart, and the latter's son-in-law, Newlands, all of Nevada; Preston B. Plumb, of Kansas; Hon. Stephen B. Elkins, then of New Mexico, and later Secretary of War under President Harrison. These men invested in the Leadville mines and they were not only valued clients but warm, lifelong friends of Charley Thomas.

Other colorful Leadville residents, many of whom put their legal affairs in the hands of Charley Thomas, were David May, whose May Department Stores got started there in 1877; Meyer Guggenheim (and his seven sons) built a smelter in Leadville, foundation of the American Smelting & Refining Company and Guggenheim Exploration Company; James B. Grant, who also had a Leadville smelter; George Pullman, of sleeping car fame; the group who prospered from the Little Johnny Mine—John Campion, A. V. Hunter, Byrd Page, Brown, husband of the "unsinkable Mrs. Brown"; David Moffatt and Eben Smith with the Maid of Erin Mine; Seeley Mudd and John Hays Hammond, and many, many more.

None of these men made the spectacular fortune that came to Tabor, but they all knew and appreciated the risks of business, and what to do with the money. They spread out over the country, most of them to Denver, taking substantial stakes with them, which they used not only to enlarge their own fortunes, but to contribute to the development of America.

LEADVILLE
Labor Troubles

THE FIRST great labor strike of the West developed in the spring of 1880. The miners organized under the leadership of Mike Mooney and demanded a flat rate of pay of $4.50 per day, underground, and $4.00 per day for surface workers. Mine operators turned down the demand as made; a walkout occurred and all mines shut down. Two days later the miners organized a street parade and marched through the main streets, fifteen thousand strong. They were orderly and carried signs, notifying dealers to join them or face an idle, no-business summer. The following Saturday, operators and non-strikers paraded, with an equally potent show of numerical strength. This provoked bitter feeling, and the night was fraught with all the alarums which precede civil conflict. There was aimless shooting in the dark at mine shaft houses. Roughly concerted gangs attacked some of the mines, but shooting was largely sporadic and aimless. Nobody got hurt.

Next morning, a Major A. V. Bohn approached the mayor, demanding that he act to suppress the disorder. But the mayor sat tight; said it would all blow over. Bohn, not satisfied and wanting to do the blowing over himself, recruited a law-and-order group, with him at the head. He formed a "regiment" of six short companies and proceeded to make a demonstration. Charley Boettcher's hardware store was raided for arms and ammunition and the demonstration started. The striking miners, ranged along the streets, jeered at him; they crowded out into his marchers and broke them up into scattered groups. Near the Clarendon Hotel, some one took a pot shot at the major as he rode at the head of a pitifully broken-up "company." The major, who was wearing his fancy Knight Templar sword, drew it and slashed at the man; the sword broke into pieces and he remained impotent, waving the hilt about and cursing roundly. A policeman, standing near by, grabbed the major and yanked him from his horse, and arrested him for disorderly conduct.

Next day the governor proclaimed martial law in Lake County and sent a battalion of militia, commanded by General D. J. Cook, to take charge. He prohibited all meetings likely to disturb the public peace. The strike fell to pieces, the mines started up again, and normal, peaceful conditions succeeded. The principal losers in the affair were Major Bohn, whose sword was broken, and Charley Boettcher who never received compensation for the arms seized at his store.

The governor's conduct was made a political issue by the Democrats, but in vain. The Republicans won out, despite all the fuss and fury. Charley Thomas related that, in that campaign, a colored man who had eight sons of voting age, probably had as much to do with the Republican victory as anyone else. Customarily he hung around until it was clear just what value might be put on his nine votes, then acted. This time he voted them for the Republicans who were paying two dollars in cash for votes and, though the Democrats were paying three dollars, the payment was deferred until after the polls closed. Charley Thomas saw him later and asked him why he voted for only two dollars when he could have had three dollars, only to have him reply, "Well, suh, ah figgered ah'd vote foh de pahty that was de least corrupt!"

The organization of Mike Mooney went on to become

the Western Federation of Miners. Leadville, however, enjoyed industrial peace until 1896, a year when the camp was crippled by the demonetization of silver. In that year a more serious and prolonged strike took place.

MORE POLITICS

IN 1880 CHARLES THOMAS was chosen a delegate to the National Democratic Convention at Cincinnati in July. He served on the Committee on Resolutions where he met and became intimate with many of the party notables—Colonel Henry Watterson, Melville W. Fuller, Rufus H. Peckham, Daniel H. Voorhees, and others. The "bloody shirt" was waved by Daniel Dougherty, of Pennsylvania, in a consummate effort to secure the nomination of General Hancock as a great captain of the Civil War. His effort was successful and Hancock was nominated on the second ballot—remarkable speed for a Democratic convention.

In the election, Grant's activities were disastrous to Hancock. An effort was made by Roscoe Conkling to nominate Grant for a third term and he almost succeeded. Grant was making a tour of the world, where his good reception by foreign courts and rulers had restored him to popular favor at home. His landing at San Francisco was followed by popular ovations during his progress across the country—Napoleon returning from Elba. He was induced to enter the campaign against his old comrade in arms, Hancock, and Garfield won out in the Electoral College, though Hancock polled the majority of the popular vote.

The assassination of Garfield and the succession of Arthur had great influence on Colorado politics, always rife with unexpected turns. In 1878 Senator Chaffee's health became precarious; he announced publicly that he would not be a candidate to succeed himself. Because of this Professor N. P. Hill, Gilpin County, became the candidate for the office and he backed, and got elected, a majority of the Legislature favoring his election. Before the Assembly met, however, Chaffee's health improved so far that he repented his announcement and re-entered the lists. Hill protested violently, quoting a letter from Chaffee endorsing him. Chaffee rejoined spiritedly, but unilluminatingly, and this served to intensify a canvass for a caucus choice. Hill won the fight. Teller, in this episode, though always at war with Chaffee, took the part of the latter. Hill, an able and sound man, made a good though not outstanding senator. He also was a man given to implacable resentments, and Chaffee from then on was his enemy.

When Garfield became President it was evident that Hill was in his good books strong, and that Senator Teller would pay for his partisanship with Chaffee. Soon, however, came the death of Garfield and the accession of Arthur, who made Teller his Secretary of the Interior. The tables were turned and the quarrel became a feud, with Hill in control of the State machine and Teller of all the Federal patronage. The feud carried into the state convention and there, Chaffee, now recovered, won over Hill by an eyebrow.

Senator Hill's candidate for governor was Henry R. Wolcott. He put Henry's brother, Edward Wolcott, later United States Senator, at the head of the organization. He was bold and brilliant, but no match for Chaffee, whose candidate was E. L. Campbell, brother-in-law of Thomas Patterson. Campbell was nominated for governor over Wolcott.

Senator Hill repudiated the ticket. He owned the *Denver Republican*, leaving Chaffee with the *Evening Times* as the party organ. Campbell, unfortunately, denounced the leaders of the Hill revolt bitterly, in a speech made at a time when Chaffee was secretly negotiating for a peace all around. After this speech, reconciliation was impossible.

The Democrats nominated James B. Grant for governor, with Patterson as chairman of the State Committee. Grant was elected — the first Democratic governor of Colorado. He made one of the best executives ever to serve the state, then or since.

The Chaffee-Hill feud boiled and boiled, culminating in the campaign of 1884. Ed Wolcott deserted the Hill faction and went over to the enemy, Chaffee. The State Convention was anti-Hill, nominating B. H. Eaton for governor. Hill, while not submitting, failed to take action. Had he stood out firmly, in this Presidential year, he could have dictated terms and saved his Senate seat. But he entertained the delusion that he could get the support of the Democratic minority which, added to his own faction in the General Assembly, would insure his election. The Republican caucus selected Teller as senatorial candidate, and Hill was badly and permanently beaten. Senator Hill, when the Republicans decided against him, rushed to Patterson's office and asked him to name the terms under which he might negotiate for the Democratic vote. Patterson quietly informed him that the time had passed for bargains. He ended the interview by saying, "As matters now stand, I could not help you if I would and, I may say, I would not help you if I could." For this Hill never forgave him and he instructed the editor of the *Denver Republican* to oppose and assail Patterson whenever possible, personally, professionally, and socially. Thus started a merry and entertaining journalistic war.

Charley Thomas, in 1884, was nominated for congressman, with Alva Adams the nominee for governor. The Republicans nominated Judge George G. Symes to oppose him for Congress. The Democratic ticket was defeated by some four thousand majority, and Charley Thomas did not then go to Congress.

Grover Cleveland was the Democratic President-elect in the fall of 1884. It was thought by Colorado Democrats that a representative of the state party should go to Albany before the General Assembly met and find out, if possible, from him and from Daniel Manning, chairman of the National Committee, who, in view of the lively contests going on, would be thought most desirable for Senator. Charley Thomas was chosen to make the trip. Early in January he went to Albany and met with Manning and to him posed the question. Since Cleveland was staying in Albany until March 4, he sent him direct to Cleveland. He had with him a pleasant, but rather arid interview, Cleveland refusing to be drawn out in any way on the subject.

In commenting later on the President-elect, Thomas has noted:

"As I walked back to my hotel, I entertained a distinct feeling of disappointment, due entirely to the personality of the President-elect. I was familiar with his general appearance through the many pictures and cartoons of the campaign, but I was not prepared for the outward manifestation of grossness which he, all unconsciously, exhibited. His features are large and heavy, his face seemed to bear the permanent traces of an attack of smallpox, although I do not know whether or not he was ever so afflicted. His complexion was rather dark than light, and of a greasy cast, while his breathing was very audible as he listened to me. These characteristics seemed wholly inconsistent with my ideal of what a President of the United States should be."

In February of 1884, I was born, the first son of Charley Thomas. I was preceded by a sister born in 1877 and by another sister born in 1881. Both sisters had the same birthday, November 18.

It was in 1885 that Charley Thomas argued his first case in the United States Supreme Court. The case was *Ehrhardt* v. *Boaro,* a mine dispute originating at Silverton, Colorado. Ehrhardt was a United States Marshal in New York, Boaro, an Italian miner who located a mining claim which was "jumped" by Ehrhardt. Boaro had won in the lower courts and Ehrhardt had carried an appeal to the Supreme Court, under the notion that the property was especially valuable. Ehrhardt's attorney was a young man of about the same age as Thomas. His name was Elihu Root. Root had prepared his case thoroughly and well; he greatly surprised Thomas by his familiarity with mining law and—he secured a reversal of the judgment. The two men became lifelong friends from that contact. Later they were colleagues in the United States Senate.

In the year 1885 Charley Thomas closed the branch office in Leadville and removed permanently to Denver to his old main office with Patterson. In 1887 he took his first vacation—a trip to Alaska, where he gained more acquaintance with primitive, frontier country and encountered the famous Alaska mosquitos.

In 1889 his association with Patterson, as partners in the practice of law, ended. Patterson's son had been admitted to the bar and he quite naturally wanted him to join up with him in his own law office. A year later, Patterson bought the *Rocky Mountain News,* leaving the profession of law. Perhaps he wanted more time to carry on his feud with Hill, a feud that still continued and at which Patterson, journalistically, was infinitely superior. The *Republican* had dubbed him "Old Perplexity," but he never was perplexed when it was meet to fire a broadside. His leaving of the partnership in law served to increase greatly the clientele of Thomas—and to add to his burdens.

From 1884 to 1896 Charley Thomas served as National

Democratic Committeeman from Colorado. This position enabled him to meet and become familiar with all the eminent members of the party the country over. It also seriously depleted both his pocketbook and his nest eggs. During this period the silver issue developed and grew to be a question dividing the party—largely between the East and the West. It had all the staying quality of Banquo's ghost and, in 1896, it became the sole issue of a mighty campaign.

CREEDE

Always Daytime

IN THE late summer of 1889, Eben Smith, mine expert and associate of David Moffatt, went to the office of Thomas & Patterson and asked for Charley Thomas. His wants were simple—he wanted Thomas to go with him to a place known only as Willow Creek, a tributary of the Rio Grande, some forty miles, more or less, from Del Norte, in the San Luis Valley of Colorado. He was going to look over a prospect, named the Holy Moses, for Mr. Moffatt. From the information they had it was likely they would negotiate for it and come to some sort of terms. He wanted Thomas along to draw the papers and look up the title.

Charley Thomas was free and agreed to go. They went as far as Del Norte by train and took a buckboard and team from there.

Eben Smith approved of the mine, terms were agreed upon, and the necessary papers were drawn up; Moffatt bought the mine from Nicholas Creede, the locator, for seventy-five thousand dollars, with a one-third interest in it carried for Creede. The claims had a nice vein, with a good showing of rich horn silver ore, some of which had been shipped by Creede. The mine was located at the top of a rugged mountain with a stream called Willow Creek running swiftly down a rather precipitous canyon.

This sale soon reached the newspapers and a rush of people started for Creede.* Claims were staked all over Campbell Mountain, where the Holy Moses Mine was

---
* See Plate IV.

located. The claim staking spread out to the west across the west branch of Willow Creek, reaching the heights of Bachelor Mountain. Among the claims on Bachelor Mountain was the Amethyst Group, which also was acquired by Moffatt and Charles J. Hughes. An adjoining group, the Commodore, was acquired by A. E. Reynolds and some associates. These two latter groups developed rapidly into very large and rich mines, but the Holy Moses failed to keep the promises the rich outcrop showed up. By the end of 1892 the Amethyst had produced over two million dollars in silver.

Excitement at Creede, as the new town was named, grew great. From 1890 to the latter part of 1891, Creede the town, and Jimtown, a neighbor to the south, grew but slowly up to about one thousand people; by the end of 1892 there were over ten thousand people there and the town, squeezed into a narrow canyon, burst its bounds and spread all over the meadows below the canyon mouth.

The Denver & Rio Grande Railway reached Creede from Wagon Wheel Gap in December, 1891. Trains ran, crowded to the platforms, with newcomers, visitors, and others. Many, at times, rode on top of the cars. Pullman cars were brought in to serve as de luxe hotels, parked at the Creede station.

Rapidly Creede grew into a rough town—some thirty saloons, all with gambling layouts and many with dance floors and music. Many of the dance halls had rooms in connection for strictly temporary use. Streets were thronged with bunco men, promoters, mining sharks, pickpockets and strong-arm holdup men.

In 1893 Bat Masterson came to Creede as manager of a saloon-gambling house. He had a long record as a frontier peace officer—most notoriously as town marshal of Dodge City, Kansas, in its rough, tough days of the cattle drives from Texas to railhead. He had served also at Tombstone, Arizona. Many rough boys had challenged his authority in vain—Bat could really shoot straight. There always was quiet and decorum in his saloon, and if any riotous fighting broke out in any of the neighborhood places, just the appearance of Bat, looking in to see what was cooking, was enough to calm things down.

Girls on the make, like army camp followers, flocked in and frequented the dance halls. They were a bad lot according to the moral code of the day, but the great majority of them were well behaved. One of them, called Creede Lily, was a great and constant faro bank player. She "worked" like the rest of them, but did little drinking and was looked on as "snooty" by most of the other girls because she didn't mix much. She died of pneumonia one day—it was the day Bob Ford was killed—but even with that front-page news she was not forgotten. A collection was made to bury her in style, and even Soapy Smith chipped in. An occasional girl would blow her top and get into a cutting brawl, usually because of some tightwad man refusing to buy drinks when dancing with her.

Soapy Smith was a leading citizen of Creede. His name was Jefferson Randolph Smith, and he hailed from Charley Thomas' state—Georgia. His nickname, "Soapy," was acquired because of his adeptness in a very successful swindle. He would take station at street corners where reasonable crowds of people could be expected to pass, or gather, set up a grip on a tripod, and lay out some bars of soap. As curious people gathered, he would get out a bundle of currency in bills from $10 to $100, riffle them awhile through his fingers and make a "spiel." Then he would wrap up a bill with a cake of soap, or if the crowd was large, he would thus "spike" three or four bars, and then start selling soap at a dollar per bar. A stooge would step up, buy a bar of soap, unwrap it, and find one of the bills. Sales would boom, but no one but a stooge ever got a bill with his bar of soap.

Soapy also was very nimble at the shell game. He ran

gambling saloons, with the usual paraphernalia. He always had with him an experienced gang, well trained in his ways of fleecing the public not only at gambling but in mixing in with local politics. He never stood for any "rough stuff"; law and order was his dish. But he wanted a finger of his own in the business of law and order, so placed that he never had to pay for protection. At times he succeeded in taking over the management of the policing of a town and when he did this he ran it well. Strong-arm men were hazed out of town, burglars were prosecuted vigorously, decent gamblers were protected—at a price. He was smart enough to see that the common citizen, going about his business, was protected against any crooks other than himself. He had a theory that God gave man cupidity in order to make him easy to cheat, so he acted the part of God's agent and saw that the man was cheated. For quite some time Soapy ran the city of Creede, and ran it well.

He opened a saloon called the Orleans Club and put it in charge of an old pal of his, Joe Simmons. He quietly "helped" organize the city government; arranged an election for city officials, picking some of them from his own gang at caucuses, and then saw to it that his men won the voters. For the police chief he brought in a certain John Light from Texas, a good man with a gun. Things then ran smoothly; tramps and panhandlers were run out of town, thugs were run into jail, framed, and sent to the "pen"; good businessmen and investors were welcomed, entertained, and protected.

Soapy did well in Creede until he had played out all his "string" of swindling dodges and the town got wise to him. About that time his old pal, Joe Simmons, took pneumonia and died. Soapy felt this loss very keenly, but he saw to it that Joe had a real funeral, proper and well attended—except for a preacher of the Gospel. Soapy was not one who failed to support the churches—that was part of his "line"—but his friend Joe asked him for one deathbed boon—"he didn't want no preachin' at the buryin'."

A blizzard was at its height when Joe was buried. The casket was perched on a wagon hauled by mules, the mourners followed it in a couple of deep-seagoing hacks, with a string of wagons, carrying other friends, straggling in the rear. Part way up the hill to the cemetery the cortege was stalled; ice underfoot. The mules and horses were unable to get footing and pull the vehicles. Ropes were brought up, attached to the wagons, and friends and mourners had to help haul the whole string of vehicles up the hill.

Soapy Smith, removing his hat, the wind almost snatching it from his grasp, delivered a funeral oration, calling attention to the virtues and square-shooting character of Joe Simmons; he told how Joe didn't want prayers said over him by any strange preacher. No! All Joe asked was that his friends assemble at his "burying" and drink his health and wish him good fortune in whatever place his soul might go.

Champagne was provided, the corks popped, and many solemn toasts were drunk to Joe. A song or two were sung, the grave was filled up, and Soapy returned to Creede to open up the Orleans Club for business again.

The Silver Act of 1893 was passed; silver dropped below fifty cents in price; Creede, willy-nilly, was on the toboggan slide. Soapy got his gang together and pulled out to find another town with lots of suckers. He found one at Skagway, in Alaska, where he operated briefly, then was shot dead.

During the brief but splendidly flaming glory of Creede, Charley Thomas made trips there to take care of the law end of quarrels. During one of them he brought me along. I was then eight years old but an old stager, for he had taken me to Leadville on one short trip. This one was made at the time that Bob Ford was killed. Neither of us saw the killing (in my book, a tragically missed opportunity!) but we did see the crowds milling about and heard the shouting during the brief melee that followed. Later we heard some of the details.

Bob Ford was the Missouri "bad man" who murdered Jesse James. He went to Creede to make a fortune with a gambling saloon named the Creede Exchange. A prize fight was pulled off there and it went contrary to bets that Ford and a friend of his had made. They started drinking and then conceived the idea of hunting up the winning fighter and killing him. They didn't find him but, as a part of "their night to howl," they shot up the town. Creede was getting tired of such proceedings so vigilantes were called together and they voted to run the two disturbers out of town. Anyhow, Ford and his friend left in a hurry. In a few weeks, hoping his sin was forgotten, Ford wrote some of his friends; he said he was sorry about his bit of playfulness and would like to return to town to apologize and take up a life as a peace-loving citizen. He did not get encouraging replies, or any turndown, so, after a short while, he returned to Creede. Still he was not welcome. He tried to purge himself of his sinfulness by confessing to a misdemeanor before a Justice of the Peace and paying a fine for absolution. Despite this, the vigilante committee sent Marshal Craig to tell him he must leave. He refused to go and gathered about him some of his gambler friends, all well armed. Another warning was sent to him; he was *persona non grata*—it would be wise for him to leave before someone tried to shoot him.

The tough element of Creede backed up Ford and rallied about him. At one stage he threatened to burn the town. Coincidentally a fire did start that cleaned out all of the main part of the town, and he was accused of doing the job, or at least of having had a hand in instigating it. He still remained in town and made plans to open up a new dance hall.

All this happened just before we reached Creede. It

was a mess. We had our living quarters in a Pullman car and got our meals at a restaurant set up in a large tent.

It was not hard to find a man to do in Ford. The town marshal of Bachelor City, up the mountain, one Edward O'Kelly, was an old friend of the James boys in Missouri. He was the man for the job. He had an assistant, a man called French Joe. O'Kelly went to the new Ford dance hall and stood in the door, talking to the girls and watching for Ford. At that time he was not armed, but French Joe came along with a shotgun and passed it to O'Kelly as he walked by him. Ford was at the bar, saw O'Kelly enter, and started for the back door. O'Kelly followed and called out to him. Ford started to draw and O'Kelly let him have both barrels of the shotgun.

Excitement became acute and a mob formed, yelling out for the lynching of O'Kelly. He was then arrested by Deputy Sheriff Plunkett, who rushed him off to a cabin where he might be protected more easily. O'Kelly was tried and convicted of second-degree murder and sentenced to life. He was pardoned after ten years; two years later he was himself killed in Oklahoma for impersonating an officer.

The Creede city life was short but almost it made up in jampacked exuberance and riotous living for the short time of the boom. Cy Warman, of the *Creede Chronical*, set it forth in a little verse that swept all through the country.

> Here's a land where all are equal,
>   Of high or lowly birth—
> A land where men make millions
>   Dug from the dreary earth.
> Here meek and mild-eyed burros
>   On mineral mountains feed;
> It's day all day in the daytime,
>   And there is no night in Creede.

> The cliffs are solid silver,
>   With wondrous wealth untold;
> The beds of its running rivers
>   Are lined with purest gold.
> While the world is filled with sorrow,
>   And hearts must break and bleed;
> It's day all day in the daytime,
>   And there is no night in Creede.

This was almost literally true for the year 1892, but the day came in 1893 when the days were dull and listless and the nights were dim and dark.

Discovery of Cripple Creek was almost coincidental with that in Creede. Cripple Creek, however, was built with a new crowd. Not many of the Leadville old-timers got in on that one. So Charley Thomas took little part in it for the first two or three years. At the end of that time the inevitable controversies arose and then he was in demand for twenty years to take one side or the other of the lawsuits, mostly with Charles J. Hughes as his opponent. Among others he became attorney for Jimmy Burns, of the Portland Mine. Jimmy had a partner, Jimmy Doyle. The two Irishmen fell out, of course, and the litigation between them went on to the time of the death of Burns. It probably put me through college.

SILVER—AND BRYAN

CHARLEY THOMAS was a great partisan student of the history of silver as a medium of exchange. The more he studied it the greater was his advocacy of bimetallism. The issue came alive soon after the inauguration of Cleveland in 1893. Cleveland advocated the repeal of the Sherman Act for the free coinage of silver, and he worked diligently and successfully on the Congress to effect it. Bimetallism was anathema to him but, in ridding himself of the Sherman law by means of a most acrimonious struggle, he created a serious breach in his party ranks and made bimetallism the inevitable issue in 1896.

William Jennings Bryan,* four years in Congress from Nebraska (1891-95), was a constant champion at every opportunity for bimetallism. When he was retired from Congress he was given a roving commission on the editorial staff of the Omaha *World-Herald*. For the next two years he "roved" all over the South and West, making talks on his two pet subjects—himself and bimetallism. He invaded the East on the same mission. All this made of him a well-known and prominent Democrat.

In April, 1896, he wrote Charley Thomas, chairman of the Colorado delegation to the Democratic National Convention at Chicago, that conditions at the convention of the party might so shape up as to justify the presentation of his name for the Presidential nomination, and

---

* See Plates XXIII and XXIV in the Appendix.

he asked whether, in that event, he might rely on him (Thomas) for support. This feeler seemed to Thomas both absurd and ridiculous, but he could not say so in reply without being offensive, so he simply failed to reply at all. He soon learned that Bryan had written the same to many delegates of other states. Despite these feelers, and his careful preparation and memorizing of his "Cross of Gold" speech, done during that summer, when he made the speech he managed to create the myth that it was a spontaneous and extemporaneous expression of a dedicated man whose heart was bleeding for humanity.

Senator Teller broke away from the Republican party over the silver issue. He, no less an opportunist than Bryan, went to Chicago in the belief, certainly in the hope, that the Democrats might nominate him for the Presidency. He had many adherents, and the customary headquarters was opened up. Late in the night before the convention opened, a committee from his headquarters, made up of Thomas Patterson, and Senators Pettigrew and Du Bois, called on Bryan in Teller's interest. They told Bryan that the convention was expected to cast a few fruitless ballots for avowed candidates and "favorite sons" and then be prepared to nominate a "dark horse." They went on to say they thought Teller's nomination could be secured if men like Bryan would aid in leading a movement to Teller.

Mr. Bryan told them he thought their forecast of the voting correct but that, when the break came, the delegates would go, not to Teller, but to him. The committee was not prepared for this modest announcement; they apologized for the blunder in going to him, and retired. One of them expressed himself as thinking "the young man was nutty."

Mr. Bryan was on the Committee on Resolutions. It developed from acrimonious meetings of the committee, which brought about a schism, that a vigorous minority report was to be presented to the convention. Bryan asked Charley Thomas to urge the chairman of the committee, Senator Jones, of Arkansas, to select him (Bryan) to close the debate on the floor. Thomas did so, and Senator Jones consented. Thus was the opportunity created for delivery of the "Cross of Gold" speech. It nominated Bryan, though the absence of any outstanding candidate contributed largely to this result.

Charley Thomas seconded the nomination of Arthur Sewall, of Maine, as Vice-Presidential nominee. He returned to Denver and took up work on the campaign. The state convention unanimously tendered him the nomination for governor but, for financial reasons, he declined it.

The campaign took him on speaking tours, under auspices of the Democratic National Committee, to Maine, Kentucky, Ohio, Indiana, and Illinois. At Portland, Maine, his good friend, Mr. Thomas B. Reed, Speaker of the House, attended the rally. After the close he said, "Charley, you presented a very fine front to a very poor building." The day after the election, Reed sent him a telegram which simply said, "Thanks. Come again."

In mid-October of the campaign, Bryan wired him, asking for a meeting in St. Louis. At this meeting, Bryan called for a report of his impressions on how the campaign was going in the states he had covered. Bryan was told frankly that the situation was bad and getting worse, and, unless a quick change came for the better, he was going to get a bad licking. Bryan refused to credit this information—said Thomas was all wrong, that everything was going his way and there could be but one result—his triumphant election.

Years later, in some notes made on an appraisal of Mr. Bryan, Charley Thomas recorded:

I have many times observed that no logic or course of events ever served to change Bryan's views. He might put them aside to exploit others of apparently greater importance, but he never abandoned them. He never forgot, nor forgave, a man who crossed his purpose, opposed his ambitions, or revealed any ambition of his own for Presidential honors through a Democratic nomination. His betrayal of Champ Clark, of Missouri, and support of Wilson, in 1913, at Baltimore, was inspired by the single motive of his own unspoken, but yearned-for, candidacy. And, while his convictions were strong, and his obstinate adhesion to them are well known to his intimates, he is nevertheless the great opportunist of his time. He was always a prohibitionist, and always will be, but he became its ardent champion only when it seemed to favor his political fortunes and then, alas for him, it became an accomplished fact before he could make it the outstanding issue of a Presidential campaign. I supported him in 1896 and 1900 and, most reluctantly in 1908. I have lived to realize that his successive defeats showed that the people at large were wiser than we were, for Mr. Bryan with two brief years as Secretary of State demonstrated his incapacity and amateur status for any great Executive responsibility.

Bryan hated Cleveland; always, in his speeches, he would sneer about him. In a rally, in 1908, at Greeley, Colorado, he denounced Cleveland and posed the question, "What has Cleveland ever stood for?" A farmer, seated near the platform, took a straw out of his mouth long enough to say, in a voice loud enough for us all to hear, "Wal, he done stood fer President three times an' got it twice!" The applause that followed was most unwelcome to Mr. Bryan and, when the rally was over and a facetious reference was made to it, he became violently angry.

GOVERNOR OF COLORADO

IN 1898, CHARLEY THOMAS was nominated by the Democrats and endorsed by the Silver Republican and Populist parties. The latter still had some strength even after their honeymoon and bust-up during the administration of their governor, Waite. He was a beneficiary of the depression that followed the repeal of the Sherman Act and he was elected on the Populist ticket. During his term of office, in a quarrel with the Fire and Police Board, caused by his attempt to usurp the appointive powers legally residing in that body, he called out the militia to oust the board and its appointees who had forted up in the city hall. He announced that he would oust them even though "blood flowed up to the bridles of the horses of the troops." Ever after he was referred to as "Old Bloody Bridles Waite." United States troops had to be called in from Fort Logan to bring about good order again.

Governor Waite had a habit of profanity which punctuated his conversation even on the most trivial matters. One Sunday morning, all the preachers in Denver, in a concerted drive, took notice of it in their sermons. The Press called on him and asked for comments if he had any. He said he had nothing to say other than the statement, "It's all right, boys, I don't mind. Them preachers don't mean nuthin' by their preachin' any more than I mean nuthin' by my cussin'!"

With the help of Waite's Populist remnants, Charley

Thomas was elected governor over Henry R. Wolcott by a majority of nearly fifty thousand. His administration of the state's affairs was the most economical in its history. It had to be, for the state had not yet recovered from the depression—the treasury was empty and taxes hard to collect. His biggest difficulty was dividing a small supply of patronage among three ravenous parties without satisfying any of them.

Among other accomplishments he finished the Capitol Building, under construction for over ten years. He found it in a finished state but with odds and ends, such as a stair tread here and there, a door unhung, something else uncompleted. It still was in charge of a building superintendent with three assistants. Their employment ran to "completion" and they had been very careful to see that it was not completed. He got rid of them and, with a carpenter and a mason, finished it in sixty days.

Except for the Spanish-American War, his administration was rather uneventful. The usual battles with the General Assembly took place and he found himself exercising the veto power on many appropriation bills designed to provide jobs for deserving members of the three parties. He became so exasperated during the second session that he addressed the members in a joint session and read the riot act to them, closing his remarks with the statement, "each succeeding Legislature in Colorado seems to operate only to make its disreputable predecessor reputable."

Mr. David Strickler, of Colorado Springs, relates that when Charles Thomas was governor of Colorado he had occasion to welcome, officially, General William T. Sherman at a time the latter made a visit to the state. General Sherman had a habit, when he met people, of asking them, "Have I met you before?" On this occasion he queried Governor Thomas in this way and received the reply, "I have never met you face to face, General, but if you were at the head of your army near Macon, Georgia, in 1865, you must certainly have seen my back!"

"Oh, Governor," said General Sherman. "So you were one of those groups of kids the South put in line the last few months of the war. Well, you know, Governor, I had a lot of sympathy for those half-baked kids in those days, and I issued strict orders that where they were encountered, my troops should fire over their heads and do them no harm."

"Would that I had known of that, General, at the time! It would have saved me from several headlong dives into the swamps of Georgia!"

He was a delegate to, and temporary chairman of, the Democratic National Convention at Kansas City in 1900. Bryan again was the party nominee. On that occasion Bryan made Imperialism his outstanding issue, still harping on bimetallism on the side. True to his passion for the spectacular, he insisted on being officially notified at Indianapolis, so thither they had to go. Thomas, as temporary chairman, had to go with the party.

At Indianapolis the entire party, consisting of two committees of forty-five men each, with their wives, the nominees and speakers, were housed and fed by Thomas Taggart, as his guests. Mr. Bryan was given the most sumptuous apartments the hotel afforded, with a carriage and driver at his constant disposal. He was never known to acknowledge this hospitality. On the contrary, he never hesitated to denounce Taggart as a reproach to the party, an unscrupulous and corrupt politician, unworthy of confidence and even of respect. Openly he rejoiced in his defeat for the Senate in 1916.

Charley Thomas took an active part in the campaign of 1900 and was, himself, a candidate for succession to Edward O. Wolcott in the Senate. Wolcott was very anxious to succeed himself, partly for vindication, but largely because he found the position congenial and attractive. He was easily the most brilliant and forceful man the state had sent there, and he was, easily, first in the Senate as an orator. He was not useful in the sense of his industry there, for he was impatient of detail, disliked committee work, and was of an unusually mercurial temperament. He could be, and was, morose and disagreeable beyond endurance, and generous, companionable, and winsome to a greater degree than any public man of his time.

Wolcott, during the initial stages of this campaign, singled Charley Thomas out as the especial object of his criticisms which, as the campaign proceeded, became vituperative and highly personal. But his own record was most vulnerable, so Thomas determined to reply in kind. He chose the organization of the Democratic State Convention as the appropriate occasion. The effort was successful beyond measure; Wolcott immediately changed his "line."

Governor Theodore Roosevelt, Republican nominee for Vice-President, supplied "color" when he went to Denver in the campaign. He spoke in Omaha, eulogizing the gold standard and Governor Thomas addressed to him a courteous letter of welcome to the state, in which he suggested that his views on the money question would be highly interesting to his friends in the Centennial State. Roosevelt resented the suggestion with much ill humor. The following evening he was at Cripple Creek with Wolcott—the latter being very obnoxious to the people of that town. Their feeling was born in the circumstance that, in 1894, Wolcott, in order to assure his return to the Senate, publicly pledged himself to support, in 1896, that party which endorsed bimetallism. Instead of honoring his pledge, he defiantly repudiated it. He was scheduled to make the first address, and he confronted an audience not only hostile, but turbulent. Wolcott never lacked personal courage, and he defied them when tumult began, and the meeting soon dispersed. Republicans made political capital of the occasion, claiming it as an affront to Roosevelt. However, it was entirely a demonstration against Wolcott and, largely because of Wolcott's candidacy for the Senate, the entire Democratic ticket was elected by a very substantial majority.

Governor Orman secured his nomination entirely through the efforts of Charley Thomas and his friends. He had pledged his support for Thomas for the Senate, but no sooner was he elected than he began to plan the breaking of his pledge. With the state patronage back of him he exercised great influence. Besides Thomas, Alva Adams and Thomas Patterson were candidates. Gradually the Adams and Orman forces began gravitating to Patterson and, the day before the Democratic legislative caucus was to meet, Thomas' own supporters reported a number of unexpected defections among members elected in his interest and supposed to be loyal. Therefore Thomas withdrew from the race, and Patterson was chosen. He always felt certain that his defeat was due to Orman's betrayal. In the Senate fifteen years later, Charley Thomas joined Senator Shafroth in recommending Orman for Registrar of the Land Office at Pueblo, he being then bankrupt in fortune and prospects.

In 1902, however, Charley Thomas took the principal part in defeating Orman for renomination. James Peabody of Canon City was elected that year by the Republican ticket. The Legislature, however, was Democratic by only two votes. Contenders for the Senate were Teller and Wolcott and the votes in the House and Senate were so close that each house began a game of unseating individual opponents. At last the Senate barricaded itself in its chamber, eating and sleeping there and in committee rooms until a choice of United States Senator could be made. The absence of a single Democratic member during the ballot would tie the vote. One Democratic member of the House wilfully absented himself whenever a vote was taken. This very serious menace to Teller's choice was finally overcome and he was elected by a narrow margin of two votes. Wolcott conceded, and the excitement died out.

Charley Thomas was a delegate to, and again temporary chairman of, the Democratic National Convention at St. Louis. He had an active part in the final choice of Alton B. Parker as Presidential nominee, largely in collaboration with Senator David B. Hill of New York.

In Colorado, national issues were wholly subordinated to local ones. Industrial unrest had culminated in strikes by the Western Federation of Miners at Cripple Creek and Telluride. Violence was inaugurated at once by the striking organization—the killing of Collins, manager of the Liberty Bell Mine, in a sneak murder, and the blowing up with dynamite of a group of nonunion miners waiting at a station on Battle Mountain. The latter crime infuriated the community, and justly so, but unfortunately the community lost control of itself and became, in time, as lawless as the strikers. Governor Peabody sent in the National Guard and they, under command of a Teddy Roosevelt type of general, Bell, loaded hordes of strikers into boxcars and hauled them away and dumped them in Kansas. This line of conduct became a hot political issue and the parties lined up on a "for and against" this action basis.

The choice of a governor was a mockery in the end. Alva Adams was nominated and duly elected, though all other Republican nominees for state office won out. Adams' opponents decided to contest his election by attacking the validity of the vote in Denver and Las Animas counties. With a comfortable majority in the General Assembly, on a joint ballot, the advantage lay with Governor Peabody. However, Peabody was decidedly *persona non grata* with the Assembly majority and they were not prepared to go so far as to unseat Adams and put Peabody in his place, although that, or the alternative of confirming Adams, were the only legal actions possible. They resorted to the subterfuge of declaring neither one elected and then seated Lieutenant Governor McDonald as governor. It was a course unworthy of a great political party and wholly unjustified by the facts, as disclosed in a trial contest, in which Thomas was counsel for Adams. Adams' submission to this farce, without holding onto his office, by force if necessary, alienated a great many of his supporters.

In 1904 Governor Thomas was retained by Amalgamated Copper Company (Anaconda) as counsel to fight litigation with F. Augustus Heintze. This dispute grew out of a few acres of unlocated ground in the middle of the big properties of the company. Heintze discovered the error, located the ground, bought up some other claims, and brought suit against Amalgamated, claiming apex rights to some of their most valuable ore bodies.

Amalgamated was a tough group then, mostly of fighting Irish. They took on the fight almost with relish. Heintze proved to be a superb infighter and a shrewd man at getting the favor of people who counted, among them the United States District Judge. He had good lawyers and some good geologists. When Amalgamated found they really had a fight on their hands, they carried it underground, with organized groups of miners to harass Heintze there; he promptly adopted like tactics and there were daily battles between gangs of miners, underground. Workings, being interconnected, the gangs invaded each other's ground, worked furiously to extract as much good ore as possible before being driven out; shafts were flooded by diverted pumping lines; stink bombs were set off to drive miners out of stopes. Injunctions flew thick and fast, with Heintze's judge a great handicap to Amalgamated. The litigation ended when Amalgamated bought Heintze out at a highly inflated price.

I was in Butte during that summer and did a little strong-arm work for John W. Finch, one of Amalgamated's geology experts, and I helped to make a glass model of the Anaconda workings and vein systems for use in court. It was a fine experience for me. I met

Cornelius (Con) Kelly, then a young lawyer; Dan Kelly, a mine foreman who later became vice-president; Reno Sales, a young geologist, later chief geologist for the Anaconda Company, and many others.

## CHAPTER THIRTEEN

MINING CAMPS AGAIN

IN THE summer of 1905, Charley Thomas was retained by Senator George Nixon, of Nevada, to defend the Mohawk Mine, at Goldfield, Nevada, in a great lawsuit instituted by an adjoining mine, The Combination, which made a claim to extralateral rights on a vein then producing a lot of very rich ore. This retainer was to last for some years and take him on frequent visits there.

In June, 1906, I graduated from the Columbia University School of Mines as a mining engineer. After doing a few jobs as a budding engineer in Cripple Creek and Silverton, Colorado, I was offered a job as assistant engineer for the Mohawk Mine. I proceeded to Goldfield to remain for about two years in various capacities with this mine and its successor company. The accounts to follow immediately here will be largely from my own experience in connection, partially, with my father's career there. The account is presented more to set out the life of a boom mining area than as a biography.

It seems fitting to sketch somewhat the history of the discoveries of the Goldfield area which, after all, do not follow a pattern much different than mineral discoveries of the past. It is a story of luck, of perseverance, rewarded hardship, and—bitter disappointment.

In the spring of 1900 a burro made the great discovery of the fabulous Mizpah Lode, at Tonopah, Nevada. The burro was owned by Jim Butler, a prospector who was getting out of grub. Jim and his ass were encamped in a bone-dry hollow, set among arid, sun-baked, ill-assorted and rocky hills rising out of the central plains of Nevada. When dawn came Jim set out to catch his burro; the latter, perversely evading him, led him quite a chase. Making a sudden wheel to dodge the cursing Butler, the burro kicked loose a fragment of rock from a stony ledge. The fragment was a neat throwing size, so Jim picked it up for a throw at the burro. Before loosing it a certain quality in it caught his eye. He stopped, looked at it closely, and discovered that here was what he had been looking for for years. It was ore, rich in silver and gold.

The burro is the companion, means of transport, and patient audience for prospectors. Without him (or her) probably most mineral discoveries might still be hidden. Sam Dunham,* of Tonopah, wrote a political editorial in which he paid tribute to the burro. I am reprinting it here.

The early Christians picked the lamb as the symbol of the meek and humble. Better had they picked the ass. No lamb ever bore the burdens, or had to stand for the abuse that the ass has had to endure. Not until he has been wedded to the horse does the ass's patience break. Then his offspring, the mule, if prodded with a pick handle, will launch his rear end away from his front end and, unless his persecutor is wary, will sign his autograph on the prodder's person.

The ass has been maligned in all ages. In our own age he has been traduced as the emblem of the Democratic party. He is consistency itself, yet who can truthfully say that Democrats have that quality? He is pure, a virtue that Democrats attain only when out of office. In only two attributes is it apropos that the ass should serve as a Democratic symbol: he is unbelievably stubborn and

---

*See Plates XXV and XXVI in the Appendix.

he will feed, gratefully, on any crumb that may be offered him.

Jim Butler liked the looks of his rock but, after some consideration, he did not make any claim locations. He was not in funds and he did not want just then to lay out any money for discovery holes and recording fees. He broke off a few pieces of the ledge for samples, covered the fresh fractures with loose earth, and went home to Klondyke, a camp ten miles south of his find. He turned the samples over to an assayer there, offering to locate him "in" on the property for the assays. The assayer was busy with "cash" work and was so little impressed by the samples that he let them lie about for a while and then threw them on his trash pile.

Belmont was Butler's headquarters. Returning there, he again passed by his discovery and broke off a few more samples. At Belmont he gave these to a young friend of his, a lawyer, and asked him to have assays made, promising him a share in the claims if assays proved their value. The lawyer was possessed of a small clientele, made up of men without any money, so he had none to spare for assays. He sent the samples to an assayer friend of his at Austin, in turn promising him a "cut" for the work. After some delay this assayer reported back that the samples showed, in gold and silver, values from $150 to $800 per ton.

Even when he had this information, Butler took no steps to make locations. The news got to Klondyke, so the first assayer resurrected the original samples and assayed them with astonishing results. He and a party set out without delay for the supposed site of the discovery. They wandered within a half mile of it, but didn't find it. They ran out of grub and had to return home. At last Jim Butler took time out and went and located his claims. His lawyer friend at Belmont got a generous "cut" and he, in turn, rewarded the Austin assayer. It made them both rich. The lawyer's name was Key Pitt-man, later United States Senator from Nevada.

A rush started and the whole countryside for miles was staked with claims. Tonopah became a city almost overnight, in the usual way of such things. The ores were rich and they paid for the long haul by wagon, over sixty miles, many times over. Development exposed so much ore in a short time that a rail connection with Mina, Nevada, where the Southern Pacific terminated, was financed and built. The annual report of the Director of the Mint had in it the following paragraph:

Tonopah supports 32 saloons, 2 dance halls, 6 faro games, 2 weekly newspapers, a public school, 2 daily stage lines, 2 churches and other evidences of internal prosperity. It is a very orderly community and there has been but one stage robbery thus far.

A number of the veins in the district were "blind"— covered up and hidden by the surface wash, or detritus, Several shafts sunk blindly in this wash found some of the hidden veins. This led to the belief on the part of many people that veins of rich ore might be found over a wide area and another boom surged over the old one as a result of this enticing, if ill-reasoned hypothesis. The new boom completely eclipsed the old one. It brought in a lot of the busted Alaska crowd and a host of fancy mine-stock promoters. The latter gentlemen were quick to see the lure value of capitalizing on blind veins. A couple such had been found and this made it reasonably safe to float stocks on such prospects since the precedent set would operate against troubles with the Post Office authorities. Any old claim, located out in the wash, with-in miles of Tonopah, was enough to base a million-dollar company on.

The minimum unit of money for consideration in any deal was a million dollars. Every corporation organized used this standard. The business of organizing new com-panies was put on a production-line basis by the lawyers of the town. From the time of acquisition of a mining claim at a cost, perhaps, of five hundred dollars, until the initial offering of treasury stock at ten cents per share, barely forty-eight hours would intervene. In another twenty-four hours the stock would be oversubscribed and quoted on the local stock exchange at twice its offering price.

Claim locations spread out from Tonopah for miles in every direction. By October, 1903, they had spread thirty miles to the south and some covered the ground where Goldfield came into existence.

The town of Goldfield first was named Grandpa. One Harry Stimler, operating under a grubstake furnished by Butler and Kendall, of Tonopah, made the first location there. He found evidence of gold in the slopes of Columbia Mountain, a prominent, Gibraltar-like butte, and he made the first location on its slopes and named it the Sandstorm Mine. He opened up some nice ore which proved out quite rich on development. A stampede took place and many mineral locations resulted, but the Sandstorm ore bodies proved to be superficial and soon played out, so the rush was short-lived. Most of the newcomers left, but a few, "busted" souls—some seventeen of them —remained at the site, too broke to move out. They were able to scratch up a little ore, here and there, but it was tough going. The town was built up mostly of tents, or board shacks with canvas roofs. A general store and two saloons survived.

On October 30, 1903, these few citizens gathered on Main Street. There was no other street. They didn't like the name Grandpa for their new town—it seemed, somehow, to convey an impression of age and senility. The assembled crowd decided that a new name should be adopted and also that a formal organization of a mining district should be made. They hoped such a move might infuse new life into the area. "Goldfield" was the name these citizens adopted. A mining district was proclaimed and Claude M. Smith, ex-citizen of Grandpa and leading citizen of Goldfield, was elected recorder of the district.

For some little time the main pastime of the people of Goldfield, aside from the "solo" game, was playing outsiders for suckers. Let a man make a visit there with some real money on him, or so fixed that he could raise real money, and the camp played on him, wholeheartedly and with good teamwork, until they acquired some, if not all, of his money, while he acquired a few arid and desolate mining claims. Many a man bought claims and, hope fading out as he found himself "taken," he, in turn, laid in wait for another "sucker."

Not long after the district was organized, work on a pair of claims located about a half mile south of Columbia Mountain broke into very rich gold ore. These claims were located in May, 1903, by A. D. Myers and R. C. Hart, and were named the Combination Lodes, No. 1 and No. 2. Myers and Hart were backed by a grubstake syndicate of eight men. By November, 1903, the existence of gold ore in these claims became known and a deal was made to sell them for $75,000—$5,000 down and $70,000 in time payments. Early in 1904 the new operators began shipping ore, development showed a large ore body, and profits began to accumulate rapidly. Just to the north of the Combination claims lay the two Mohawk claims, the two groups having a common side-line together.

Later that same year, rich ore was discovered in the Jumbo, Florence, Red Top, and January Mines. The Mohawk claims were held by a million-dollar company, named the Mohawk Gold Mines Company. This company, in January, 1906, gave one-year leases on several three-hundred-foot-square blocks, and in April, 1906, one of these leases, the Hayes-Monnette, broke into rich ore at a depth of 130 feet in a shaft. It was followed by a similar rich strike in the Frances-Mohawk lease lying just to the east. These rich strikes were the cause of the

Combination suit against the Mohawk Mine for trespass, the Combination Company claiming ownership of the outcrop and the right to mine the vein where it dipped beyond the sidelines into the Mohawk ground. It was this suit—a suit involving many millions of dollars—that Charley Thomas went to Goldfield to defend. During the balance of the year 1906, the Mohawk leases produced more than eight million dollars. The miners working in them probably stole—"high-grading"—half as much as the official production and sampling works. Buying the ores for the market probably skimmed off another million dollars' worth.

Control of the Mohawk Mine was owned by Nixon & Wingfield, a partnership between United States Senator George Nixon and George Wingfield. It was alleged that many of the shares were acquired from owners who, broke at the gambling tables and wanting to continue play, sold them to get the funds. It could be true, for George Wingfield was not the man to turn down a good chance.

He was (and is) a picturesque character. A story went the rounds in 1906 that Wingfield was a cowman who had ranched in the Winnemucca area of Nevada; that he had a small herd of steers there that had been wiped out in a winter blizzard. He knew George Nixon well and had done business with the Nixon bank in Winnemucca. When he went broke, he went to Nixon at Reno and asked for a grubstake—he said he would take it and go to the new Tonopah mining camp and pick up something in the mineral line and share it fifty-fifty with him. Nixon was said to have given him a thousand dollars. While waiting for transportation to Tonopah, he got into a poker game and ran his grubstake up to several thousand dollars by train time. The story probably is apocryphal but it could be true in part.

George Wingfield was not a large man—a little under average, perhaps. He was somewhat on the dour and silent side, until one knew him fairly well, and then he could be quite expansive and very entertaining. At this time he was about twenty-five years of age, though he appeared and acted older. He was a man of great personal courage, both physical and moral. A very intelligent man, his administrative ability, while not extraordinary, was excellent for a man of his background, and he was quick to learn; he was a wonderful friend when he gave friendship, generous and kindly in every way. When Senator Nixon died in office, Governor Sparks offered him the appointment for the unexpired term, but he turned it down because, in self-appraisal, he did not feel that he could give all that it called for to the position.

Senator Nixon was a genial sort of man, very short, and quite round in figure. He was a good Senator; very easy to meet and always ready to talk. He owned several banks in Reno, Elko, Winnemucca, and other towns in Nevada. These banks were very prosperous as most of the people of Nevada were not aware of the fact that money could be borrowed for less than 1 per cent per month. He had a signature that was as big and bold as he was short and round.

Nixon & Wingfield were nobody's fools and they did a lot of trading in mine stocks around Tonopah and Goldfield, acquiring substantial interests in most of the good properties in both districts. I went to work for them as assistant mine engineer for the Mohawk Mine.

The big discoveries, particularly in the Mohawk Mine, sparked a tremendous boom. Ore was so rich that a miner could, and many did, steal the high-grade rock that showed visible gold. Everybody was making lots of money—miners, leasers, stock brokers—and few cared where the money came from or how they spent it. The high-grading miners supported hordes of phony assay offices and, with the proceeds, supported dance halls, saloon and gambling houses. The brokers put the money in circulation in fancy offices and in the purchase of advertising space; a stock exchange traded in local stocks with a larger turnover in shares traded than did the New York Stock Exchange. Nobody thought of saving any money; the gold was there in the ground and it was inexhaustible. Why save any money when life is fleeting and pleasures are many?

Grubstakes absorbed some of the free and easy money. Prospectors swarmed the whole state and spilled over into California. New discoveries created new mining camps; the speculative fever was running strong and Eastern capital was primed to bite at almost any offering. Bullfrog, Beatty, Skidoo, Manhattan, Wonder, Fairview, Seven Troughs—all these and many more were born, flamed up momentarily, and then died.* In most of them no one is left. The wind rattles the loose boards of the sagging shacks; coyotes sneak into them in the full knowledge that they will be undisturbed; in wet weather the sidewinder and chuckwalla find refuge in empty saloons of once-hopeful towns.

The populace of the region in these boom days was heterogeneous in the extreme. Disinterest, charity, honesty, virtue, kindliness, and gentility consorted with thievery, meanness, cruelty, rape, arson, and gambling. All were brothers under the skin and they got along together because they had to or get out. The town's population was about four thousand when the Hayes-Monette† lease broke into "pay"; by the end of 1906 there were twenty-five thousand people there.

The town was sprawled out like a huge rubbish heap that had been tossed about a bit by a cyclone. It lay in an arid bowl, rimmed about on two sides by rhyolite cliffs of a particularly harsh and forbidding aspect. These cliffs were called, locally, The Malapai, from the Spanish *mal pais* ("bad country"). Columbia Mountain, a desiccated rhyolite cone, hunched itself up on the west side;

---

* See Plates V, VII, and XVI.
† See Plates XXVII, XXVIII, and XXIX in the Appendix.

the fourth side was pure, unadulterated, open desert, supporting nothing but occasional Joshua trees (yucca palm) which reared up their grotesque shapes, only to accentuate the desolation.

The town had a few stone buildings, the most notable being the Nixon Block, housing a bank (Cook's Bank) and offices on the upper floors. There were quite a few adobe houses—very comfortable for living—a couple of bottle houses,* made of empty beer and whisky bottles laid up in walls of rubble masonry, the bottoms of the bottles outside and the whole agglomerated together with clay or lime mortar. There also was a barrel house, built up of the barrels that brought in bottled beer. For the rest, the town was of unpainted board shacks, with a generous sprinkling of tents and tent-roof houses.

Streets were laid out in the usual rectangular fashion, with Main Street as the principal thoroughfare. Laying the streets out in straight lines was all that ever was done to them. Their pristine desert contour was marred and churned up by heavy wagons; they were full of holes a foot deep in dust which became a gluey slime when wet. Sidewalks were of boards, of no uniformity, though some of them were wide enough to carry the pedestrian traffic. The streets were a milling mass of freight wagons, pulled by sixteen- and twenty-mule outfits, a few automobiles, many diminutive burros, and pedestrians; all colliding and recoiling, trying to make progress in all directions. Nobody gave a damn which side of the street he followed so long as progress was at all possible.

There were no water or sewer systems. Water was hauled to town in tank wagons and peddled from door to door by the bucketful. A bath was an expensive luxury, not to be indulged in except at long intervals when necessity dictated, or when your friends averted their faces.

While the boom was on, there was no doubt about it. Crowds of people arrived daily, with no place for their

---

* See Plate XI.

accommodation unless they had friends there. The saloons permitted those who could, and would, pay for drinks to sleep on the floors and on billiard tables, when these were not in use. An enterprising undertaker made up beds on the tops of casket shipping cases and these were rented out to sleepers at the rate of three dollars per eight-hour shift—and they slept people for a while for twenty-four hours daily. A few lodging houses did the same. As in Creede, when the railroad to Tonopah was extended to Goldfield, de luxe accommodations were furnished by parked sleeping cars.

Undertakers did a thriving business on funerals as well as the business with lodgers. Corpses were quite plentiful —pneumonia, acute alcoholism, and ptomaine poisoning were good producers, along with the aid of some medical insufficiency. Many a bum, having an M.D. appendage to his name, went to Goldfield. These M.D.'s let it be known that the Goldfield type of pneumonia was peculiar-ly fatal in the locality because of the high altitude and desert herbage—an alibi for the unusual percentage of fatal cases they handled.

A real good fire, with a stiff wind from the right quarter, would have wiped out the town in nothing flat. When a fire started, it brought out the whole town as volunteer firemen, not only to see the fire but to defend the unkindled part of town. An alarm was broadcast by firing pistols and a local steam laundry helped with a whistle. With no water supply system, the fire had to be localized by removing combustible material from its neighborhood. The big crowd either demolished adjacent structures, or they moved them away. Most of the houses were small board shacks, set up on blocks, so moving them was easy. It was a weird sight at night to see a house with fifty to sixty legs silhouetted against the light of the fire, tottering drunkenly to a new location. The thoughts of the absent owner, if not a spectator, trying to find his house after the event can be imagined. As soon as the fire burned out, everybody went home, but owners of shifted houses had to get them returned to the proper sites as best they could.

The litigation between the Combination Mine and the Mohawk Mine turned out to be a most tricky business. Many noted experts were called in, such as John Wellington Finch, Director of the United States Bureau of Mines under Ickes' administration of the Interior Department, Horace Winchell, J. E. Spurr, and others. Geology of the mineral deposits was most obscure and the directly-opposed opinions of experts could be had, and sustained by competent reasoning. Charley Thomas advised Nixon & Wingfield that they should take steps immediately to sidestep any future expensive litigation by negotiating for, and buying, all outstanding interests of all the adjoining claims to the Mohawk.* They took his advice and got options on the Jumbo, Red Top, and other nearby, but still not productive, properties. This was a headache to me as I had to organize sampling crews to take samples for evaluations of these properties. Time was short and we had to work long hours to get the work done in time. The purchases were made and, much later, after the costs of the Combination suit had run to high figures, it, too, was bought.

The Goldfield Consolidated Mining Company was organized, with a capital of fifty million dollars. Charley Thomas considered this capitalization too great, but as only thirty-five million dollars' worth was issued, this error was modified somewhat. Funds were needed not only for the purchase of all the properties, but to coordinate their development for economical operations and to provide large-scale milling facilities.

Senator Nixon, urged by some friends to do so, solicited the aid and investment capital of Mr. Bernard M. Baruch.

---

* See Plates XXX, XXXI, and XXXII in the Appendix.

This event is described by Thomas, in his own words, as follows:

He (Nixon) instructed me to meet him in New York at once, and take part in the negotiations. I complied with this request and met Mr. Baruch in the Fall of 1906; and thus began an acquaintance which soon ripened into a sincere and permanent friendship. I was impressed with his ability, his charm and, above all, with the deep-rooted sincerity of the man. Sincerity is a rare but noble quality of human nature. Integrity is its invariable companion, and confidence its offspring. I assured my client when our first conference had ended that Mr. Baruch's fortune and high place in the financial world were the result of his straightforward and positive qualities, and that my opinion was that he could be trusted absolutely to do and to observe whatever he might commit himself to.

Mr. Baruch undertook to supply all funds needed to secure title to the properties, to equip them with reduction works, and to carry the enterprise until it could stand on its own feet. Both Nixon and myself were astonished by the fact that he knew almost as much about the properties as we did. He told me, long afterwards, that he always acquainted himself with the details of every mining district and every mine of consequence in the United States, since one could never tell what contingency might arise to make such information valuable. And he cited our case as an example.

But for his foreknowledge the plan would have been postponed to a thorough and exhaustive investigation, requiring much time which, in our circumstances, would have resulted in the miscarriage of the entire plan.

I had occasion to see Mr. Baruch at intervals after this experience, and thus, to become well acquainted with him. With the approach of our entry into the European War in 1916, President Wilson asked him to take charge of the activities of the Council of Defense, which he did cheerfully, despite the need for complete divorcement from his business interests. This afterwards developed into the War Industries Board, with Mr. Baruch as its Chairman and guiding spirit.

Senator Thomas* was chairman of a subcommittee of the Military Affairs Committee in the Senate, organized to investigate aircraft production, then lagging badly. One day he was delegated by the committee to report,

* See p. 187.

personally, the bad news to President Wilson. His report was of serious import—failure to produce a single operable airplane. This failure, it had developed, was due to jealous rivalries, unwillingness to produce exact copies of British, French, and Italian aircraft then performing satisfactorily in Europe, preferring, rather, to try to improve them first; there was the ballyhoo of the Liberty Motor, said to have sprung, perfect in all details, from the brains of the Packard engineers in one twenty-four-hour session, ready then to supersede all aircraft motors—except, of course, for a few major defects to be cured later but about which nothing was said. The President received the report with disbelief and astonishment until proof was given; then, convinced, he addressed Senator Thomas, as the latter reports:

As we were ready to part he (Pres. Wilson) said that one who bore bad tidings ought to suggest countermeasures, and asked if the Committee had considered that. I told him it had not had time to do so, but that I would venture to suggest that the War Industries Board, whose Chairman, Darius Miller, had resigned the week previous, be re-organized and made independent of all control save Presidential control, and that aviation be separated from the Signal Service of the Army and be made a separate service, re-officered from top to bottom with the best available officers and, with the best available civilians in charge of production.

He asked if I had any such men in view and I replied that the country possessed many, though I, personally, knew but two, naming Mr. B. M. Baruch and Mr. John D. Ryan.

Within the next fortnight, and before the public had been fully apprised of the serious state of affairs, the President, by two Executive orders, established the Air Section of the War Department, placing Gen. William Kenly at its head and John D. Ryan in full charge of aircraft procurement. By the second order, Mr. Baruch was made Chairman of the War Industries Board, with his authority limited only by the President of the United States.

Mr. Baruch proved to be the man for the place and, therefore, the man of the hour. As is usually the case his effectiveness was apparent from the resentment of some of the members of the Congress and of others—many of the latter seekers of favors from the Board. There they had been most welcome if able and willing to help the war effort effectively, but were given short shrift if their motives proved to be personal and selfish.

It gave me great pleasure not only that the President had accepted my appraisal of this dedicated man, but also that I could honestly defend my choice publicly, when necessary, against any and all carping critics. In a long life, with exceptional opportunities to meet great numbers of lawyers, engineers, industrialists, financiers, politicians and what not, I have never encountered a man of Mr. Baruch's immense wisdom, capabilities, and superb qualities of straightforwardness, ability, honesty and sincerity, coupled with kindliness and generosity, and I consider it one of the greatest privileges of my life to have known him well and, in return, to have been honored by his friendship.

His performance as head of the War Industries Board is the best reply he could have to all of his critics.

Mr. Baruch's association in the organizing and financing of the Goldfield Consolidated Mining Company was effective and successful, and while the mines deteriorated after some years, the company is still operating, mostly as a sort of investment trust in mine securities.

Ever responsive to the needs of the Democratic party, fancied or otherwise, Charley Thomas attended the state convention of the party in Colorado in September, 1906. The unconscionable deposition of Governor Adams in 1904 had developed a bitter feud in the party ranks. One faction under Senator Patterson contended that the City Hall machine had, at least passively, lent its support to the crime. The other faction, led by Mayor Speer, hotly challenged his position. The latter had control of the party machinery and might control the convention unless heroic measures were taken to prevent it.

The "antis" (Patterson faction) determined to hold separate primaries and elect delegates, independent of party organization procedure, relying on the out-State sentiment to bring them success. Thomas sympathized with the "antis" but not with their plan. He was chosen a delegate by each of the two factions. On assembly of the convention, however, it was apparent the "antis" would win, without any regard to regularity or to ultimate consequences. Thomas opposed the resolution to unseat the regular delegates from Denver to the best of his ability, but without success. Riots were imminent more than once and personal encounters were too numerous to be sensational. He retired with the unseated delegation, but supported the ticket. Although unobjectional in personnel, the ticket, headed by Alva Adams, the most popular Democrat in the state, was doomed to defeat at the polls. The entire Republican ticket, with Chancellor Buchtel at the head, was successful.

GOLDFIELD

Truffles, Champagne, and Growing Pains

IN ASSEMBLING the mine properties for the big consolidation, a block of one hundred thousand shares of
Mohawk stock was bought from Al Myers, who had
acquired it as one of the original locators of the claims.
Al Myers wanted to sell his stock for enough money to
bank a system for beating roulette and, when Wingfield
offered him four dollars per share for it, a deal was made.
This sale received wide publicity and the news fanned
the fires of the boom to a greater intensity. Mohawk
stock took off and climbed rapidly on the local stock
exchange and on the exchange in San Francisco and, in
a few days, passed a price of twenty dollars per share.

George Wingfield once had committed himself to a
promise that when Mohawk stock sold at ten dollars per
share, he would give a big, free-loading blowout at the
Palm Restaurant. When the stock rose, it passed through
ten dollars like a coyote on the run.

The Palm Restaurant was the elite eating place of
Goldfield. Its name was chosen either from the dusty,
imitation palms that adorned it, or the palms were put
in after the name had been pinned on. Perhaps the Joshua
trees in the desert were the inspiration. The food there
was good, though the atmosphere was not always all that
might be desired. Prices were high, drinks were high; the
customary wine bought by the patrons was usually champagne. The newly prosperous people felt it was not fitting
to drink any other beverage. An annex to the restaurant

proper sported a little bar and quite a layout of roulette and craps tables; prospective diners always were free to try to get a dinner for nothing.

George Wingfield put on his party there and spared no expense. The place was filled until it was impossible for anyone to enter unless first somebody departed. Food and drink were unlimited to any and all able to get in and consume them. The last guests were swept out the door and carried home about 5:00 A.M.

My other number as engineer for the Mohawk, Jock Finney, was there. He could drink hard liquor for hours without batting an eye. When his capacity was reached he would quietly fold up and be "dead doggie" for half a day and then emerge as husky and vigorous as if he had never had a drink. Jock loved the girls and a great many of them seemed to love him. I left the party before he did. As I went out I saw one of his gals, and she asked me if Jock still was there. I told her he was and that he had a "load" that was getting pretty heavy for him to carry. She cheered up, laughed, and said, "I must get along home, then. He always comes to see me when he gets full!"

Jock had his women pretty well trained. If they bothered him when he wasn't in the mood, he would slap them around a bit. One time, in the Palace Bar, one of them saw him and she went in and suggested that he go home with her before he got "stinko." He pushed her aside and told her to "beat it." She tried again— telling him he would be sorry; he knew the booze was bad for his stomach. He very calmly cuffed her a couple of times and told her he would go home when he got damned good and ready. She rubbed her cheek, looked him over, and said, "O.K., Jock, I'm going. You certainly are a mean, dirty sonofabitch! Why I like you, I don't know, but I do, and I'm not letting you go to hell in a basket if I can help it."

Jock never batted an eye or changed position as she

left. He told his companion that a woman was just a woman—you want 'em sometimes and sometimes you don't want 'em. When you don't want 'em, they ought to know it and keep away. Trouble with 'em was they got mushy and thought they had rights. Only thing to do then was hammer 'em a bit—just like you had to hammer a child occasionally.

Our jobs were no sinecure. The Mohawk Mine was in full production, with six sets of leasers mining furiously to get out all the ore possible before the lease terms expired. Each of them had a separate shaft. We had to visit each shaft every day, go underground and check up on the work done, the manner of its doing, sample all new ore faces for assay, and see that adequate timber supports had been placed to prevent caving. That done, we had to make reports, plat the new work on the mine maps, and sometimes check up on the carload samplings.

Leasers' shafts were two hundred to four hundred feet deep. They had been driven hastily and timbered with the minimum amount of timber that would keep them open. No lessee went to more capital expense than was absolutely necessary, so the shafts could get in dangerous condition before repairs were made. Buckets, dangling from hoisting cables, were the only means of ingress and egress, unless one wanted to use wooden ladders in bad condition. Hoisting engines were mostly one-lung gasoline engines—noisy, clattering and jerky in operation—all of them underpowered for the work they were doing. It was a real adventure each time one made the transit of these shafts.

Underground stopes and galleries were little better. Roof supports were put in sparingly, of timber dimensions too small to be permanently adequate. Large and small slabs of rock would fall out of the roof at intervals all too frequent. Security of one's person called for continually testing the roof ahead; unguarded winzes and underhand stopes were many and must be watched for. One never could be completely sure he would not encounter an impromptu blast because of the many passages of intercommunication between leases, few of them protected by men for blast warnings. There was no regularity in the blasting—when a crew finished a round of holes they loaded them up and shot. Ventilation was poor and there always was some powder smoke in the air, so headaches were frequent. Everybody was hurrying to extract as much ore as possible in the short time left so none of the processes of ore extraction were orderly in any sense. Most of the miners were stealing rich ore (high-grading) and, if one paid it too much attention, a sock on the head in any one of the dark drifts could have been one's reward.

Prices of ordinary commodities might have stood a revision downwards in Goldfield. Water was twenty-five cents per bucketful; baths, in just enough water to moisten one average-sized man, were two dollars each; and board, at the cheapest restaurants, was twenty dollars per week. Eating cards, good for twenty-one meals had to be purchased; these were not transferable, so if one was killed just after buying one, the heirs would be unable to claim it as an asset. It was almost impossible, on my salary, to maintain a state of bodily purity and also eat, so I ate. Later the mine put in a change house with showers, and that solved the dilemma. Nothing in town could be had for less than "two bits"—even newspapers. One day I ran across my father, sauntering down Main Street eating a banana with evident enjoyment. He told me he had bought it to eat publicly because it was the only item he had seen in town to be had for only a dime.

There was plenty of liquor of all kinds in Goldfield, and it was much easier to get a drink than it was to get out of taking one. The average "desert rat," on making a stake, took immediately to champagne as his beverage. To him, drinking champagne and treating his friends to it was the quintessence of class and nobility. He really preferred "rot gut" whisky, taken straight, but there was no class to that sort of drinking, so he would stick to his champagne, no matter how he dreaded it, until he was out of funds. When this normal and natural condition overtook him, he dredged up his burro and took to the desert again, with a vague feeling of relief that no longer must he maintain "side."

Though the Palm Grill was the classy restaurant of town, the best one for good food was located in the heart of the red-light district. It was called Ajax' Parisienne, owned and operated by one Victor Ajax. It was related of Ajax that his real surname was Zeus; that he had come to the desert as chef for a traveling circus. The circus went on the rocks at Tonopah and creditors were paid off in alphabetical order. The money ran out at the L's, so ever since then Victor had adopted Ajax as his official surname. I asked him one day if the story were true, and he said that if I had heard it that way it must be true.

Meals at the Ajax always were good. Often there were also very informal and entertaining diversions during the meal. The higher class ladies of the red lights, and the gentlemen of the "bon ton" of Goldfield took their meals there. A typical diversion I witnessed was the shooting of a man, dining there with a pretty woman, by a "Russian" gentleman who laid claim to royal birth. He told the press that he had followed the pair for years, all over the world, to get revenge for something that he was rather vague about and, finally, had run them to earth in Goldfield. The press treated the affair as of secondary importance. The Russian was a mighty poor shot; he missed with two shots at very short range—got his man in the shoulder with a third one.

I was dining there with Jock Finney when this little episode took place. Jock was playing at the roulette table, trying to win the price of our dinner, just at the time of the shooting. With the first shot the croupier ducked under the table. Not so Jock Finney, for at that moment the little white ball dropped into the pocket at his number, and he dragged forth the croupier and made him pay up.

After the law appeared and dragged out the Russian, we dined. Jock was quite pensive for a while, then he began to muse aloud about the shooting and, from that topic, he went on about the opportunities that such events held out to entrepreneurs for profit. Why not go to the Chamber of Commerce and arrange for them to capitalize the disputes of mankind for the economic benefit of Goldfield. For example, judiciously advertising Goldfield as an ideal place for human triangle affairs to culminate; it could be made into an ideal spot for sensational murder trials. Subscriptions could be made for the construction of a stadium to carry on the trials, with fixed box-office prices for different classes of seats; a bar and lunchroom convenient for refreshments; boxing or wrestling matches to amuse the crowds during court recesses. What a chance for the establishment of a center of American culture and erudition! Nevada then would have two famous cities instead of one; Reno to provide the peaceful divorces, Goldfield to provide the violent ones.

"Think of the value of slogans!" said Jock. "Goldfield, the domestic battlefield of the nation. We pay more for classy homicides; to extra-sensational cases we guarantee either a lump sum, in cash, or a percentage of the gate. Service includes luring the victim to Esmeralda County jurisdiction; choice of public or private sites for the killing; free weapons—'Pistols with a Past!' 'Sash Weights in Matched Sets,' 'Knives of Damascened Steel!' 'Authentic deMedici Poisons!' "

Jock finally tired of this musing and closed the subject by saying that perhaps the idea was not really a good one, because, if it was, Tex Rickard, at the Northern Saloon, would already have it in operation.

Ajax' Parisienne was the scene one night of a domestic dispute between Mart O'Toole and his mistress, "Gold Tooth" Bess. The latter was one of the picturesque girls of the dance halls; she was about thirty and as handsome as anyone could wish for. She affected a Merry Widow style and it suited her. Mart was a snappy, reckless, and scrappy lawyer. He and Bess had been friends for years; their quarrels had been many and violent.

That night Mart shot Bess, in Ajax' Parisienne, and in her right limb. In those days it was a "limb" instead of a leg, especially where the bullet struck. Bess had wanted to sit up on the bar, a point of vantage from which she might see and enjoy the party. A man—no friend of Mart's—was very accommodating and he assisted Bess to the top of the bar with some quite unnecessary handling. A scuffle ensued and Mart, indignant, produced a gun. In the melee the gun was discharged, either purposely or by accident, and the bullet entered Bess's limb.

Bess took the affair rather lightly at first, but the county authorities for some unknown reason—a superfluous one from Mart's point of view—took a dim view of it and charged Mart with assault with murderous intent. Bess ignored the charge and seemed to care not at all whether it was true or not. Later, for another unknown reason, she changed her mind and decided the charge might be true, so she agreed to be prosecuting witness.

The night before the trial opened, Mart and Bess spent together. Next day, during the trial, Bess was very dramatic but so lukewarm that the jury disagreed. A new jury was empaneled and the trial started all over again. Again, Mart and Bess made a night of it together. During the trial this time, however, Bess poured out the phials of her wrath and damned Mart in every way. Mart retaliated, when it was his turn, by testifying to occasions when Bess had tried to put him under the sod. The judge wanted to know why she was not sure of murderous intent at the first trial but now was so positive about it. She replied that it must be on account of her temperament; confound it, it always was getting her into trouble.

The jury found Mart guilty of assault, but without

murderous intent. He was fined five hundred dollars and the jury was dismissed. As the courtroom began to clear, Bess marched purposefully over to Mart; she produced a pair of scissors and gave him a savage jab in the cheek, just missing his left eye, and said, "What the hell did you want to lie about me for, you dirty bastard?"

She was prevented from doing further injury by a man near by who reached out quickly and grabbed the scissors out of her hand. A woman spectator then took part; she crowned the man with a swipe of her handbag, and remarked, "Served him right!"

Bess turned on her, glared at her for a moment, and launched herself at her. With one expert movement she grabbed the woman by the hair with one hand; with the other hand she stripped the dress off the interloper with one long, sweeping rip. The gesture of her arm continued toward a near-by open window, out of which the dress disappeared. The woman shrieked, trying ineffectually to cover her exposed person with her hands, while Bess looked her up and down, and said, "Who the hell asked for your opinion? You better mind your own business, which probably ain't too good, and not go butting into the affairs of a lady and gent that has had a little disagreement!"

The bailiff took a hand and arrested Bess. The judge, hearing the commotion, hurried out of his chambers and charged Bess with contempt and assault. Bess was a believer in prompt action and she told the judge she didn't want no jury and would admit her guilt. The judge imposed a fine of one hundred dollars, and Mart stepped right up and paid it. Bess watched him complete the arrangement with the clerk, then stepped over to take him by the arm, and, strolling to the door, her hips swinging arrogantly, she said, "I'm sorry, Mart. It's a damn shame we have to pay so much for defending our honor. You are a good sport, boy. Let's get to hell out of here!"

They left the courtroom in perfect accord, oblivious to the invective of the incautious lady who had butted in. She was enveloped in the folds of an old man's duster and was giving full vent to her outraged feelings.

GOLDFIELD HIGH SOCIETY

I Knew She Was a Lady 'cause She Wore a Lady's Hat

SOCIETY inevitably got to be of absorbing interest with the dear ladies of Goldfield. Caste lines were set, only to be overturned and reset, time after time. The men who made stakes brought in wives and daughters, or acquired wives with or without benefit of clergy. Segregation of the sheep from the goats was a difficult process because it was hard to find anyone in any sort of social stratification who didn't have a past without at least one or two picturesque episodes in it. The dear ladies showed great genius in ferreting out lurid details of past indiscretions—and in inventing some if they were unable to secure real evidence. Social leaders proclaimed themselves, and contests for supremacy were fierce and without mercy.

These contests were very burdensome to the male members of the families entering the lists. It meant that there must be bigger and better houses built; more and larger pieces of jewelry bought; larger and gaudier automobiles became necessary. Questions of precedence and protocol were dredged up and savagely disposed of.

The wife of a local banker, largely by great energy, a keen mind, and the ruthless instincts of a jaguar, finally emerged as the "Mrs. Potter Palmer" of Goldfield; and she held sway, grimly, for months, until the big bust came. She had the best house, the biggest motor car, the most jewelry, and the best cook in town. She even had a chauffeur, a hired man who doubled in driving her car and taking care of the garden. The living room of her house was decorated elaborately with artificial plaster icicles depending from the ceiling to give an air of coolness to the room on the hot, summer days. She was a pretty good scout, fundamentally, with wit and much kindness of heart where social pre-eminence was not involved. In the heat of social battle she was picturesquely profane.

The men of Goldfield had a very nice social club— the Montezuma Club. Its quarters occupied the second floor of a stone-front building having the Palace Saloon as the ground-floor occupant. The club had its own bar for the members, and it also furnished a pool table and a billiard table. It was open twenty-four hours per day, and always had somebody in it, even if they were only a couple of late roisterers. During the cold winter of 1906-7 the club always had enough fuel for a large, potbellied stove in the center of the lounge; the heat from it was supplemented by a sheet-metal chimney from the big stove of the Palace Saloon below. The place was crowded in late afternoon and evening; parties for the commission of murder, rape, or burgling could be conceived and arranged around the bar, or one could sit down for a relatively quiet game of bridge or solo. The latter was played a great deal as everybody knew the game. Bridge was new to most people but many wanted to learn it so it was not unusual to find three or four tables in full swing.

With the spread of prosperity and the creation of a waiting list for membership in the Montezuma Club, a rival club came into existence—the Goldfield Athletic Club. The rivalry between the two clubs was quite keen, with a certain amount of "snob" social superiority claimed by both of them. A stranger in town, chatting with Charley Thomas one day, said he had heard conflicting claims made by members of both clubs and this had caused him to wonder a bit about the relative merits of the two organizations. My father enlightened him about as follows:

"I asked a similar question in a small Tennessee town once about the difference between two churches, cater-corner at a street intersection. One was the Dutch Church, the other the Dutch Reformed Church. I was told that it was not too clear, but as far as could be determined one of them believed that Adam fell from Grace, the other that he was a bad egg from the start. Well, it might be said in reply to your inquiry that the Montezuma Club is a home for falling men; the Goldfield Athletic Club is a home for fallen men!"

The society ladies of Goldfield, of course, had the gambling fever, especially for stock-exchange securities. Women usually are the most intelligent speculators in stocks because they make no attempt to try to appraise real values. The woman who bets on a horse-race selection by punching a pin through the program usually is wiser than her husband, who studies the form sheet.

The dear ladies were quite successful at stock trading on the Goldfield Stock Exchange. Being realists, they began to question the commissions they had to pay for brokerage, so a group of them, finding no chance to make bargains on volume transactions with the brokers, decided to organize a stock exchange of their own. They rented quarters and, after seeking and getting some expert male advice, most of which was disapproving, they organized and opened for business.

Individual, factional, and general troubles plagued the ladies right from the start. Seats on the exchange were sold on time payments. One lady threw a monkey wrench into the gears when she said her husband told her they should pay cash for the seats since they had to have assets back of them to insure trading commitments. She got a dirty look from another lady member who said that was ridiculous; that everybody knew that cash was money and couldn't possibly be anything else, such as assets. Assets, she went on to say, are things like tangibles and intangibles. This statement impressed quite a few of the ladies until one curious soul wanted to know just what tangibles and intangibles might be. The first lady tried a withering look, without success; she tried a sneer, with less success; finally, collecting her wits, she said everybody knew what was meant by the word "unmentionables"—that meant ladies' underwear. Well, tangibles and intangibles, were in a like category. The other lady said that didn't help any; she, for her part, thought the members should furnish their own underwear. The first lady took refuge in an attempt to assume that she was being insulted, so she refused to discuss the matter further, and changed the subject by announcing she had an important and constructive proposal to make. She turned and addressed the Chair.

"Madame President and ladies. Why do we not list our seats on this exchange and trade with them? There is a perfectly adorable little phrase the brokers use— "when, as, and if." They get an option to buy something they want and then they put that phrase in to make the price go up. Why don't we take an option to buy the president's seat, since she wants to get out, put in that phrase, and make it go up?"

This proposal almost caused a panic. One lady, when she could make herself heard, said that she always thought that "option" had something to do with one's eyes and she was unable to make out how eyes came into the matter at all. Her observation got lost in the tumult and she was too uncertain to press the question. The exchange members voted to take an option on the president's seat (her stock-exchange seat), "when, as, and if" it should go up in price. The lady president agreed to the option, but she put the members on notice that if the price went up she wouldn't sell.

Two events transpired which permitted the suspension of business permanently without much public notice, other than a report in the press of Los Angeles.* The first event was that the lady president's husband—the brute —told her to stop making a fool of herself. She offered to sell her seat to him; he accepted and said he would give her fifty dollars for it if she would promise to quit for good. She told him she had optioned it ("when, as, and if," or "as, if, and when," or some such way) and she wasn't going to let him make all the money on it. He told her, explosively, that her seat wasn't worth the price of a drink, either "if, when, and as" or "where, why, and because"; that it was worth fifty bucks to him to have her out of the damned affair and paying some attention again to his socks. She agreed to get out if he would give her the hundred dollars it had cost her. She neglected to tell him it wasn't yet paid for. He consented readily enough. She explained to her friends that her husband had taken over her investment and she was re-tiring because, after all, the business was pure, sordid gambling, and not at all fit for those ladies who stood for the better and higher things of Goldfield. The other ladies took the cue and shook down their husbands like-wise.

The other event was the arrival of Nat Goodwin and his entire New York Company to play repertoire. Nat's "bids and asks" in the matrimonial field appealed much more to the ladies than "bids and asks" on mining stocks. At that time, Nat was rumored to be about to embark again on the ship of matrimony, his appearance in Gold-field chancing to be at a time when he was having a shore-leave interlude from that blissful state. The lady of his troupe broke up the schedule a bit, however, by deciding to have a little interlude of her own. Quite a number of unattached males were on deck and willing, so the pickings were easy for her. She settled on one of them and became publicly engaged to him. He was in

---

* See Plates XXXIII and XXXIV in the Appendix

the money at the time, but he found her an expensive bit of fluff and, before marriage took place, he found himself floundering on the rocks, sans money and sans gal.

My father saw this swain later in San Francisco, quite down and out. He asked for the loan of a few hundred for a short time while he put over "an important and profitable deal." Father passed up the loan but agreed to pay his restaurant checks for a few days and, each evening, buy him a drink and a bottle of whisky to carry him to the next day. He was very grateful and, in return, related how the lady had taken him for a "ride." She was no sloppy worker. Father suggested to him that he get revenge on the daughter of Eve by finding himself a rich widow and marrying her. But he could only shake his head, and say:

"Governor, I'd like to do just that but it's no use. Every day is the same; mornings I'm too tired for it; afternoons I don't want to; nights I'm just not able."

Nat Goodwin would have been better off if his girl had stuck to him while he was in Goldfield. But when she went off on her own he had nothing to do but get in trouble. He met George Graham Rice, a slick, smart promoter if ever there was one. Rice was operating in Goldfield as the L. M. Sullivan Trust Company. Larry Sullivan—"Shanghai Larry," as he was called, because of an activity of his past along the sea front of San Francisco —was a well-liked, sporty gentleman, stupid enough for Rice's purposes, and he acted as "front" while Rice conducted the business. Occasionally, in some moment of unusual sobriety, Larry tried to help out the business. One of these moments, when a customer evidently tried to arbitrage on one of Larry's pet stocks, resulted in an amusing exchange of telegrams, reproduced herewith.* Another time, a new customer in Denver, lured by the respectable name of the firm in an advertisement, wired

---

* See Plate XXXV in the Appendix.

the company to buy him five thousand dollars' worth of stock in the "Coming Nation" Mine, stating that a check was being dispatched in the mail to cover it. Larry knew how to handle this one. He was certain the man wanted stock in the Combination Mine, a good producer, but Larry, the meticulous broker, would not assume anything. No, sir, not him! Larry incorporated the Coming Nation Mining Company, bought some sagebrush and sand mining claims, printed certificates, and, in forty-eight hours, had the stock in the mail for his customer.

At the time of Nat's visit, the L. M. Sullivan Trust Company was getting known for the unsavory outfit that it was. Rice laid himself out to be nice to Goodwin. He was careful to give him good market advice on local stocks and to steer him away from bad actors. The two became buddies and soon a new brokerage firm appeared at Reno—Nat C. Goodwin & Company. Nat replaced Shanghai Larry as front for Rice, furnished capital, and didn't have to do a lick of work—Rice generously agreed to run everything. When the Rawhide boom had its short-lived headlines, Nat C. Goodwin & Company opened branch offices there. In a little while Nat C. Goodwin & Company got to smell pretty badly, so a new firm was born—B. F. Sheftels & Company. This one opened up in New York on Broad Street. There, at No. 44, they occupied an entire floor, with hundreds of clerks and typists. Rice published a newspaper called the *Financial News* and in its columns he took some shrewd whacks at the large banking houses of New York, at the same time boosting his own wares. He cried out to the world that he was a crusader, bent on reform of financial practices and giving the small investor a chance to make money safely; his advertising bills ran in excess of two hundred thousand dollars monthly. He got away with it for a while and sold enough securities to carry his huge overhead, but it is doubtful that he made much take-home pay from it. He kept a very pretty blonde in grand style and she, of all his associates, was the only one to stick by him when the boom was lowered. She defied the grand jury when they tried to get damaging evidence of fraud out of her.

The United States Post Office Department moved in on Rice, the B. F. Sheftels Company, and Nat C. Goodwin & Company. Nat himself escaped indictment by an eyelash. He was called before the grand jury and quizzed unmercifully; frightened almost into a stroke. His obvious fear and lack of knowledge of the business stood him in good stead for he convinced the United States Attorney, Henry Wise, that he was the worst sucker of all the lot in Rice's net because he not only lost a lot of money but he lost caste and his own self-respect.

I was employed by the United States Attorney to examine and report on many of the mining properties touted by Rice and had to attend the trial and give expert testimony as to proper appraisals of them against the florid claims made by Rice in his *Financial News*. It was a huge headache. The volume of evidence introduced was tremendous; trial of the case dragged on in New York for four months and then was not finished. The United States Attorney finally compromised the case by accepting a plea of guilty from Rice and arranging for the Court to give him only three years.

I was asked, among other things, to define a mine, which I did to the best of my ability, and I think I gave a good one, though perhaps it was a little windy. The Court asked me if I couldn't draw a shorter line between a real mine and a rank prospect, so I told him that Mark Twain had given out the shortest definition of a mine —"A hole in the ground, owned by a liar"—and I said he could apply that definition to practically all the mines that depended on extravagant advertising for financing. Good mines needed no advertising. The press in New York seemed to enjoy this part of the testimony.

HERE COME THE WOBBLIES
Labor Takes Over

LABOR UNREST was a constant source of trouble; with the Wobblies, labor peace was an impossibility; it would have been so even if they had attained all their objectives of communism and socialization. With this unrest went "high-grading," hand in hand. The quantity of rich ore stolen by miners underground reached fantastic figures and any effective curb on the practice brought labor trouble.

Wobblies—this was the name given to the I.W.W.—Industrial Workers of the World. They were firmly entrenched in Goldfield in 1906-7. The old organization, Western Federation of Miners, formed in Leadville in 1880, was the official labor union operating there, but the I.W.W. was running the show. The W.F.M., as an organization, had been badly bent, if not shattered, by their anarchy in Colorado, in which they had come off second best. Their leaders were "Big Bill" (W. D.) Haywood and Vincent St. John. These two precious pirates held to the W.F.M., but they also hitched to the coattails of the I.W.W. Following policies laid down by Big Bill, the local leaders began the unionizing of the entire area, regardless of the trade or skill of the worker. St. John was the active agent in the field. He had been president of the W.F.M. local at Telluride, Colorado, during the labor war in that area ten years before. He decamped after the assassination of Arthur Collins, superintendent of the Liberty Bell Mine. A suspicion of complicity in the murder hung over St. John—probably rightly so.

The Miners' Union Hall occupied the second floor of a large frame building on Main Street. In the front of these quarters were the executive offices, with a hall opening off them to the meeting room at the rear; a room that could not accommodate more than a hundred men. The walls were hung with banners carrying the trite catchwords of communism. The Stars and Stripes flew from a staff above the building, but it was absent inside the hall; there the rostrum was draped with a solid red flag.

Haywood and St. John lay low until after the state election in November, 1906. At this election the Wobblies captured most of the county offices; they got all of the important ones—sheriff, county judge, jury commissioner, and also the city government; with all serene they could stir themselves and get busy. The election was a good deal of a farce—a tragic one. The best elements of the town were too busy making money to pay it much attention; they took no interest in the candidates, except to mumble a bit about them. In this respect they showed, as they do in many communities, their own complete disqualification for self-government.

I was working in the drafting office in Columbia on election day. The polls were in an empty store next to my working place. A large, tough gentleman was in charge there with two others, not large but still tough. When it came time for lunch he took the ballot box and registration book to the restaurant. He set the box on a chair beside him on his right—sort of as guest of honor. The registration book was superimposed on it, and, crowning all, his big slouch hat. He then ordered and leisurely ate his dinner. During the meal several irate voters sought him out at the restaurant, demanding to know why the polling place was closed, contrary to law. Not closed, at all, the man let them know; just temporarily moved to the restaurant; and he "reckoned" he wasn't going to go hungry just to wait and serve a lot of galoots who wanted to be ornery and vote at dinnertime. If they were in such an all-fired rush to vote it was O.K. by him; he would give them ballots and they could mark them up and leave them with him then, and when he got done with dinner and had picked his teeth, he would be going back to the polls, check up on the ballots with his confreres and, if O.K., they would go into the ballot box; if not, he would simply tear 'em up. They could take it or leave it.

One or two kicked vigorously at this procedure; they called it crooked and outrageous; all without effect on the diner. He calmly buttered his bread, swabbed up gravy with it, and, after transporting it to his mouth, together with a huge load of potatoes balanced on the end of his knife, he told them to go and entertain the Marines with that crooked-business talk; he just wasn't interested one little bit. He was running the show, he was, and he would run it his way; if they didn't vote then and there, the way he said, they had better make up their minds they weren't going to vote at all; if they showed up later at the polling place he'd be damned if he didn't throw them out. That was that! The applicants marked up some ballots and turned them over to him; he stuffed them in his pocket without looking at them. Doubtless he put those in the box that met with the specifications of Big Bill; those that did not, probably were destroyed. However it was, Big Bill's slate swept the field.

Incidentally, this informal poll judge amused himself during the voting with practical jokes on some of the voters. A Jewish merchant of Columbia appeared to vote. The playful gorilla affected not to know him and challenged his vote on the grounds that he was a Jew and, therefore, not a citizen. The merchant was furious and sputtered imprecations in a flow of disjointed words; all to no effect—he was required to swear in his vote. When the formalities were concluded, the Jew went over to the big jokester, rose on his tiptoes, shook his fist in his face, and sputtered, "You tink you are a sonofabitch! But you ain't!"

Wage scales at that time did not suit Big Bill, either in size or equality. There was a differential of a dollar a day between skilled miners and unskilled, for example. One big union, the I.W.W., was his idea, with equal wages for all, regardless of skill. Big Bill called a strike to enforce his ideas.

Everybody was to get five dollars for an eight-hour day; all grades of miners, dishwashers, cooks, waiters, bartenders, roustabouts, the butcher, the baker, the candlestick maker—all the same.

Big Bill won his strike because of the cupidity of most of the mineowners and leasers. Ore was rich enough to stand a much higher scale of wages so, in order to continue production, operators conceded the scale demanded and, to save face, got acquiescence of the union for the establishment of change houses. These change houses were not the usual locker rooms in ordinary use; they were devised to prevent theft of high-grade ore. They were built in two parts, a narrow connecting passage between. Street clothes had to be removed in one room and left there; the miner then had to pass into the other room under the eye of a watchman, and then there put on his work clothes. When he came off shift the reverse procedure took place. The watchman was in a position to intercept stolen ore. Big Bill consented to the change houses because he intended to incorporate watchmen in his union, and because he controlled all the law-enforcement officers authorized to deputize watchmen. In any event, if burdensome, he always could call another strike to abolish them.

The men went ahead and high-graded just the same; no one was able to stop it. High-grading was real big business; ores were very rich, with high-grade streaks in the veins up to eight or ten inches wide that would carry ten dollars to twenty-five dollars per pound. It was common practice for the miners to carry out ten to twenty-five pounds of such ore. Most of them looked on it as a right and perquisite, and they resented any interference. Big Bill worked out a sophistic philosophy for the practice; he contended that God (he had no other use for God in his business) put the gold in the ground, not for any one man, but for all men. The mere title to the ground did not alienate the individual's right to a share in the gold, therefore, if a miner worked for wages, ore broken while not drawing pay belonged to the man who could dig it out of the place where nature deposited it; ore broken while drawing pay belonged to the man who paid the wages. Hence, technically, all a miner had to do was break out some high-grade ore after his eight-hour shift was complete, and such ore was his. This would take but a few minutes, especially if the miner spotted his place to dig it out while putting in his shift. All according to the gospel of Big Bill. Of course, no miners were fussy enough about the morality of the business to follow this program literally. Some miners used to wear two shirts, sewed together at the tails, to be used as huge pockets for high-grade ore.

High-grading miners disposed of the ore to the assayers of Goldfield. At one time there were forty-seven assayers in business, all prospering, even though there was not enough legitimate business to support three shops. A miner who couldn't steal a hundred dollars a day wasn't much of a miner. Assayers bought this ore at 50 per cent of its value; when the miner had the money for it he usually blew most of it gambling at one of the saloons. What matter if he lost? Lots more in the mine for to-morrow.

George Wingfield had Charley Thomas get him an injunction from the United States District Court at Reno

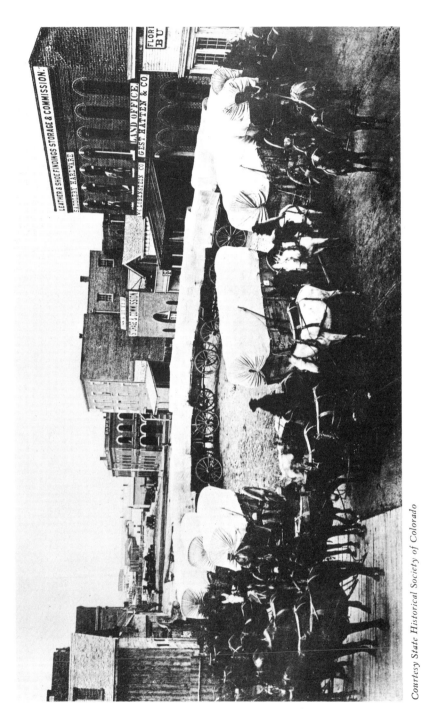

Courtesy State Historical Society of Colorado

ELEPHANT CORRAL AND WAGON TRAIN, DENVER, 1868

Plate II

CHESTNUT STREET, LEADVILLE, COLORADO, 1877

Plate III

MAIN STREET, CREEDE, 1904

Plate IV

EARLY RESIDENCES (SAHARA RENAISSANCE) OF GOLDFIELD, NEVADA, 1904

Plate V

CLARK MULE OUTFIT, 1906

Plate VI

MAIN STREET, MANHATTAN, NEVADA, 1906

Plate VII

TWENTY-MULE FREIGHT OUTFIT

Goldfield in background

Plate VIII

RED LIGHTS!

Goldfield

Plate IX

CASEY'S MERCHANTS' HOTEL, GOLDFIELD, 1906

Plate X

BOTTLE HOUSE, GOLDFIELD

Plate XI

AUTHOR IN HIS 1906 OLDSMOBILE
Note the acetylene gas generator for lights and the extra cans for gasoline

Plate XII

NIXON BLOCK CORNER, STRIKE OF DECEMBER, 1907

Plate XIII

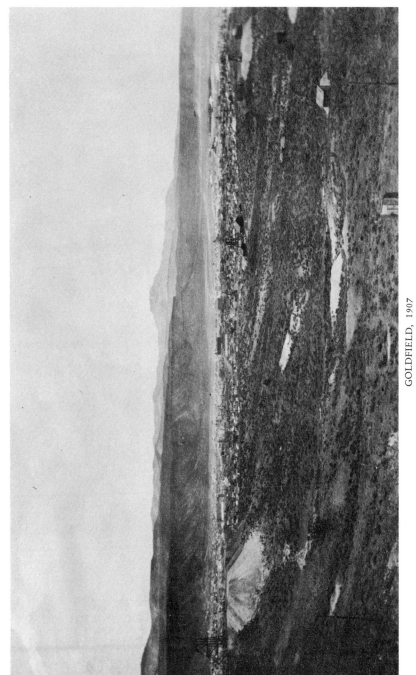

GOLDFIELD, 1907

Plate XIV

CAVING STOPE, FRANCES MOHAWK LEASE

Photograph made for evidence by the author

Plate XV

FAIRVIEW, NEVADA, 1907

Plate XVI

LOOKING NORTHWEST FROM BALLOON HILL AND SHOWING GRUTT HILL AND THE TOWN OF RAWHIDE

Plate XVII

restraining the miners from stealing ore; under this injunction he could secure its enforcement by means of
Deputy United States Marshals. Such officers were appointed and worked in Goldfield on the business, but a
few of them who resisted corruption were blown up
and the game went merrily on. So he decided on another
course; take a whack at the assayers and try to take away
the miners' market facilities. He wished part of this job
on me. I had to find out all I could about where, when,
and how sales of stolen ore were made; to learn, as near
as possible, when shipments went out from the assayers.
We hired agents, put them to work as miners, letting
them high-grade and sell ore and, in time, they were
able to give us information.

George Wingfield went to Reno and waited there while
I followed ore shipments made by express. At Reno,
Wingfield, with the sheriff of that county, met the train
from Goldfield, and swore out a writ of replevin and
took the ore off the train. We could not seize the ore
at Goldfield because the sheriff and court there were in
the control of Big Bill. In this way we grabbed three
shipments before the word got around and shipments
stopped.* We started then to find shipments made in
empty beer kegs, in nail kegs, in champagne boxes, in any
container that would stand up under the heavy weight.
One lot grabbed at Las Vegas had been put in stout
trunks and hauled there by wagon. We got one big lot
shipped to Burlingame in Denver, and we proved ownership for all of it.

On ownership we had one lucky break. The Goldfield
ores had in them a complex and new mineral—a chemical combination of gold with tellurium and bismuth.
It was not known to exist anywhere else. It was named
Goldfieldite. Samples of the seized ore were analyzed and
then used in court to prove ownership. We must have

---

* See Plate XXXVI in the Appendix.

missed many lots of ore, but the ones we did seize were worth over five hundred thousand dollars.

One assayer, more enterprising than the others, put up a small reduction plant, calling it an "ore testing laboratory." It was fully equipped to take crude ore, concentrate it, and extract the gold as bullion. We couldn't identify the gold from any other gold in the world, so a little arson party was organized one night and his plant burned down. Too bad!

The next strike was a jurisdictional one. The Wobblies attempted to force the building trades to join up with them. These organizations, backed by the American Federation of Labor, stood pat and refused, so all Wobbly members went out on strike. An uncompromising, bitter fight started; Union conditions in camp were fast becoming intolerable, no matter what the cost in loss of production might be. It was such that no merchant dared discharge a clerk, no matter how incompetent, dishonest, or lazy he might be; discharges, even for dishonesty, had to be referred to agents of the Wobblies by employers and, in practically all cases, the employer was informed that he would have to reinstate his employee or face a boycott.

Local newspapers were restrained from publishing any adverse facts about the I.W.W. by means of boycotts. The Goldfield *Sun* once had criticized the Wobbly policies and immediately had suffered from a hard, vicious boycott. Every member of the union stopped his subscription; advertisers who continued to use its columns were boycotted; men of the union were set at the job of keeping tab on every man who, in any way, patronized the paper. An Associated Press man called on the editor during this time; he was informed before night, by I.W.W. goons, that in the future he was going to find the Goldfield climate very pestilential as far as he was concerned. Soon the *Sun* gave up the ghost and died. The owners had to sacrifice the paper and leave town. New owners had to change its name.

Brokers and promoters had been accustomed to employ school children to fold and address circulars for mailing. The I.W.W. took notice of it and demanded that the children should join the union and receive five dollars per day, whether working two hours or eight hours. Boys, employed to strap on roller skates for patrons of a skating rink, had to be made union miners at five dollars per shift.

Anyone "bucking" these extortions was subjected to all sorts of annoyances, with a possibility of injury, or even death, as a result of any sustained obstinacy. The favorite routine for ridding the camp of those marked "undesirable" by the Wobblies was carried out by a group of sweet-scented goons. They would quietly surround a man and, either peaceably or forcibly escort him to the edge of town after dark. There he was ordered to keep going and to be sure not to return. Often the group would indulge themselves in a bit of amusement and get playful; perhaps they would remove the clothes of the victim and give him a more or less bad beating before he started his trek. If in good humor, they might omit the beating and only take his shoes away from him.

There were plenty of authenticated cases of this practice, perpetrated on prominent people. There was F. J. Campbell, an owner of the Vindicator Mine at Cripple Creek; he was beaten after seizure by goons on his arrival at Goldfield and forced to hike out. Richard Curry, whose crime was being dubbed a "scab" without cause, was knocked in the head. Thomas Woodbridge, an "unfair" assayer of Cripple Creek (he wouldn't buy highgrade), and Walter Schilling, agent for a powder company, both disappeared from town for such varying crimes as working for "unfair" mines and establishments, for putting out an honest day's work, and other similar causes.

Not a ripple was raised by these deportations and this

wanton violence; they had no written history or police-blotter existence. The authorities were all good union members, 100 per cent Wobbly, vouched for by Big Bill. For a little time they had the effect of keeping enemies of the Wobblies quiet—all but George Wingfield. He had plenty to say and said it, but his voice was a voice in the wilderness.

I was driving one night with Lovell, one of our United States Deputy Marshals, at the wheel of the company car. Near Goldfield we were confronted by a party of three I.W.W. goons who stood near the roadside. They had guns and signaled for us to halt. Lovell held a fair speed and swerved just enough to knock two of them down, good and hard. We didn't stop to investigate and never a word was heard in Goldfield about the episode, other than a couple of whispered warnings to Curly Lovell that "they" would soon get him. But they never did.

This strike really caused the mine operators alarm, so they settled down to get organized against it with grim purpose. A committee of vigilantes was formed; all arms and ammunition in the stores of Goldfield and Tonopah were gathered in and taken to the Montezuma Club; guards were posted there, day and night. Down the street from the club, one block, was the headquarters of the union; they, too, were well armed with firearms and ammunition secretly brought in (as they thought) in a mock funeral. Three caskets were brought for services at the Union Hall. Services, with bareheaded pallbearers, were held and the caskets brought out again and solemnly buried in the cemetery. The fact that the caskets held arms came to us from one of the secret miners we had for reporting high-grading.

The mineowners' organization was solidly formed, all but one man. Tom Lockhart, owner of the Florence Mine, was a lone wolf. He had been a prospector for twenty-five years before he got in the money and he was shy and did not mix well with anybody in the camp.

His mine "made" a little water and he was afraid the shaft would fill up if it wasn't pumped every day. I fixed that up by offering to go with him, daily, to the mine; operate the hoist to lower him to the pump, and stand by to bring him out after he had pumped the sump dry. He joined up then, and the organization became 100 per cent.

We got well acquainted and he would talk to me quite freely after a week or two of this mutual labor. He told me how he located the Tonopah Extension claims out in the wash and started his shaft with everybody laughing at him for a big "boob" who didn't have good sense. But he hit good ore in a blind vein and the tune changed. He got "stung" in Goldfield by having the Florence claims sold to him as a "sucker." He, too, thought he had been a sucker when he started to prospect the ground, but Lockhart, once he had put money into something, would never let go of it. He gave a lease to an Irishman by the name of Jack Sweeney who opened up a good, small-ore body and made a stake for himself and a mine for Tom Lockhart. Sweeney immediately became an insufferable snob; he was called Gentleman Jack—and loved it—and he got very upstage and carried, permanently, a malacca cane. He was one of those men designated by Charley Thomas as "able to strut in a seated position."

Tom Lockhart got quite confidential with me one day. He had just come to the top after pumping and he had a few odds and ends he wanted to tend to in the shop. He told me that everybody considered him just a lucky accident; he wanted to tell me that he knew he had been lucky, but, after all, he had worked, and denied himself, prospecting for twenty-five years; he felt he had earned some of his luck. He said, "Why, when I sunk that shaft at Tonopah, they all shook their heads and said, 'The poor goddam old idiot!' When I got the pay there they said, 'God sure looks after fools, children, and drunks!' When we got ore in the Florence they all just

hunched their shoulders and said, 'The lucky sonofabitch!'
Well, anyway I got it, and some of those old stiffs jeering at me are out at the ass."

Conditions at Goldfield made for tenseness for two or
three weeks; the whole town was armed, and any incident might have set off a real battle. George Wingfield
was a walking arsenal. He carried a sawed-off shotgun,
loaded with buckshot, slung by a strap from his shoulder
with the butt under his armpit, ready to swing up into
action. To infuse nerve into his associates and to show
his contempt for the goons, he procured a bundle of boycotted newspapers, took them out on Main Street, and
sold them openly and defiantly. The street was crowded
but no one made a move to interfere with him, even
though he was arrogance personified and shouldered men
out of his way as he walked.

Among other classes of labor the Wobblies organized
the ladies of the dance halls and the red-light district.
These individuals were, presumably, forged into a weapon
designed to hold male members of the union in line. Not
all of them, by any means, proved faithful to the cause
because, after all, these ladies, like their sisters of high
moral conduct, were realists. The principal union crimes
committed by them were cutting prices and the failure
to discriminate between the sheep of the elect and the
goats of the proscribed when selling the wares they had
to offer. There was frequent strife between those who
remained true to union precepts and those who were
opportunists. Some hair pulling resulted, but the union
weapons favored were the boycott and the picket line.

In the city of Bullfrog—the Chicago of Nevada, according to the ads—the Concert Hall Girls thought they
had reasonable complaint against the girls of the Unique
and Adobe Dance Halls,* so they put in motion a boycott of these two establishments. Zealous girls picketed

---

* See Plate XXXVII in the Appendix.

the two places of entertainment and had posters printed naming the "unfair" girls, pleading that they be denied patronage. The posters were liberally tacked up on fences, poles, walls, and other conspicuous places.

It was dead-serious business; a principle was at stake, though it seems incredible that the oldest profession in the world ever might be harnessed to the chariot of communism and subjected to union discipline. Nevertheless, the attempt was made at Bullfrog. In Goldfield we had the spectacle of a similar boycott instituted against the girls of Ragtime Kelly's Dance Hall. No bills were posted there but girls, as filling for sandwich boards, paraded for several nights in front of the dance hall, proclaiming, vocally, the unethical conduct of Kelly's girls. They were cheered by enthusiastic members of the Wobblies and jeered at by others. Just what doles were given the pickets to compensate them for time thus taken from regular pursuits at the hours when their work would normally be at its peak, has not been revealed.

Because of the stiff attitude of the mineowners, plus some counter-goon work by the A.F.L. unions, the strike was a failure. Big Bill slipped on this one. Even the social ostracism of Skidoo Babe and her sisters in Bullfrog was unable to force an adjustment of their "unfair" practices, and this boycott fizzled out in less than a week.

Panic conditions in the fall of 1907 brought on another strike, and this strike put the Wobblies clear out of business in Nevada.* The official, public reason for the strike was a protest against the use of the "Christian Science" money, issued in lieu of currency for a short time. The union demanded legal tender for their work, despite the fact that the scrip was usable freely in the area and any man wanting to quit and leave town could ask for and receive currency. The real reason for the strike was the great difficulty in getting away with high-grading. A

---

* See Plates XXXVIII and XXXIX in the Appendix.

protest, couched in noble and indignant terms, was made against the change houses; it set forth that these devices were an insult to every man required to use them, a standing accuser of his moral degeneracy. How easy it is to insult a man who has in mind the very thing you prevent him from doing!

There was another reason for the strike: the Wobblies had an idea the financial panic had embarrassed the operators and, therefore, they would be hard put to raise the funds for an effective fight against it. Just the opposite was true; the operators were fed up with the Wobblies and they were very happy that the Wobblies took the initiative in shutting down the mines. The operators organized themselves tighter than ever, appointed active committees, and proscribed rigidly all of the camp malcontents. They played on Teddy Roosevelt's love of fire and thunder and prevailed on him to send United States troops to preserve order after forcing the governor to declare, publicly, his inability to maintain the peace. No overt act, up to then, had taken place; even if it had, the operators had enough plug-uglies of their own to clean up the bad boys of the Wobblies.

Economic conditions worked in favor of the operators and the Wobblies lost out in a big way. No man could get a job of any kind in Tonopah or Goldfield until his record had been searched and found to be snowy white and not entangled in any way with the I.W.W. And so the Wobblies passed out of Nevada; their professional members drifted to California and made trouble for the people there in the agricultural areas. Nevada settled down to the steady mining of gold and silver by quiet, industrious miners—and dullness reigned in the land.

INDOOR SPORTS

The Boys Amuse and Refresh Themselves

GAMBLING, as a vocation or an avocation, was the most easily gratified desire there was in Nevada.* Every saloon was a gambling house, with faro, roulette, stud poker, blackjack and craps setups. The "old-timer" hadn't much use for anything in the gambling line other than faro or poker; he passed up the fancy roulette wheels and craps table—they were for the effete boys who have been to Europe, or to the East, which is just as bad. Goldfield had many saloons, all interesting. Names were picturesque—the Northern, Palace, Elite, Bonanza, Del Monte, Bank, Hermitage, Gold Dust. In the red-light district was a Negro saloon called the Needmore.

The Northern was the largest and best known of them all. The Alaska crowd, headed by Tex Rickard, owned and operated it.† Practically everybody in town, at one time or another, visited it and took a whirl at the games. It was reputed to have a million dollars in gold coin in the big vault; a bank roll big enough to tide over any adverse run of bad luck. For more than a year it ran twenty-four hours per day; three shifts of croupiers, and four roulette wheels which never stopped spinning except for repairs. Service was the keynote of the Northern. Want a hack? Call the Northern. Want to cash a check? The Northern will cash it. Need a cook? They'll get you one at the Northern. Want a "cutie" for an

---

* See Plate X.
† See Plates XL and XLI in the Appendix.

evening? Call the Northern. The place prospered beyond measure for two years in Goldfield, gradually faded
as the town faded, and then Tex went on to New York.

One of the original locators of the Mohawk Mine sold
his interest for a considerable sum of money. After a
while he found his newly acquired state of affluence
boring; he yearned for some excitement and this, in his
case, meant bucking a faro bank. So he eased himself
into the Northern Saloon; bought himself a drink and
invited the barkeeper to have one also. The latter, according to long custom, accepted; he took a pony of
mineral water and rang it up as a real drink. Our *hombre*
then looked up the boss and asked his indulgence; he
wanted to play a no-limit game so he could really amuse
himself. He was accommodated. "Play it any way you
like, old-timer. Stack your chips to the roof; if that
ain't high enough, we'll cut a hole in the roof!"

That cheered him up. He eased himself into a chair
in front of the faro layout and called for a five-thousand-
dollar stack of chips. The play began and he was happy;
a gallery of kibitzers gathered to give him courage and
moral backing. The "ahs" and the "ohs" and the "Jesus-
es" of this gallery when he won or lost a bet was music
to his ears. He played all afternoon and all night, with
a continuous, though changing, gallery at his elbow right
to the end. The house furnished him with all the food
and drink he wanted for his physical comfort; the game
sustained his mental appetite. Satisfied at last, he rose
from the table, counted his chips, and wrote out a check
for sixteen thousand and some odd dollars and went home
to bed. He was content—what the hell good was his
money to him if he couldn't buck faro with it—or poker,
for that matter?

The end of the year found this *hombre* broke. He
wasn't too downcast about it. He had his burro, tent,
pack saddle, a few hand tools, a gold pan and some cooking pots; the whole desert was his for the taking—as

much as anyone else's at least. Somebody always would grubstake him—and somebody did. He would just mosey out and get him another good mine, pronto. *Hasta mañana, amigo!*

A professional colleague of this man—that is to say, a prospector—owned control of two properties he sold to Wingfield for several hundred thousand dollars. His basic needs were the same as his colleague's; he liked faro and poker. He played the games quite steadily for two or three weeks; found himself in the hole for something over one hundred thousand dollars as well as somewhat sated with the games. Also, he seemed to be off his feed a bit. He was heard to remark, "Effen I had hell and the desert, all fer my own, I'd rent out the desert and go live in hell. Just supposin', in course, I'd find some Paiute damn fool enough to rent it!"

He went on to observe that he had had his fill of faro and poker; he was sick and tired of the looks of all the saloons in town—all alike as two peas; a long bar, two-three roulette wheels, faro bank, tables for other games, all crowded with a stinkin' lot of unwashed loafers millin' around the games; floors unswept; stale smells of bum booze, cheap cigars and sweaty people. He was tired of havin' a crowd of dirty loafers watch him play; too damned much free advice out of 'em; every odd one cadging for four bits when he won a bet. He 'lowed he had played poker before the day Moses led his rabble into the Red Sea; he just didn't want no advice. He also wanted to tell the cockeyed world he would like to get shut of it if he only could know where the hell to go!

The faro dealer suggested Monte Carlo.

"Well, mebbe you said somethin'. I've hearn tell of that place. Where the hell is it? Mexico? The name has a sort of spiggoty sound to it."

He was told where Monte Carlo was located and all about how to get to it; its beauties were described; its gaming opportunities outlined; people broke the bank sometimes and then everybody acted up like mad. This all appealed to him—all but the need to cross the ocean to get there. He had gone once to San Francisco and tried out sea fishing, but he got so damn sick he never again wanted any ocean. The dealer told him it wouldn't bother him on a big boat, so he said he might try it, adding, "If any cockeyed native cockroach can bust thet bank over there, by God! I can do it with one eye shut. It'll be like takin' bird seed from a cuckoo clock!"

He left next morning and it was the last that Goldfield ever saw of him. There were never any press notices that any old Nevada angora goat had busted the bank at Monte Carlo, either.

Prize fights and battles royal were a common form of amusements. The Gans-Nelson fight had been held there with much excitement and ballyhoo and, following it, the town had burgeoned with quite a number of colored fighters. They were recruited for the battles royal —five of them put in the ring to battle until only one was left on his feet. A better show than any prize fight between a pair of pugilists and with chances to bet all through the battle at changing odds.

We had Mexicans in town and there was a cockpit where cockfights were staged regularly. These drew large crowds of miners with their pockets full of money from high-grade ore. The Mexicans knew this game better than they did and they were mostly well "taken."

THE UBIQUITOUS BAD MAN
Same Old Fraud Pattern

GOLDFIELD had its share of professional bad men, plus those who became bad by accident. There were many shootings as a matter of course, since many people carried side arms and pocket pistols. Most of them knew no particular reason to carry a pistol or two; it simply was done and that's all there was to it. Sort of traditional.

The rugged Westerner over the age of ten always was pictured as having the ability to unlimber a pistol with the speed of lightning and shoot a bull's-eye from the hip. The idea is pure fiction; history takes no notice of the missed shots. Nevada shooting was just plain rotten, but about on a par with most Western shooting. Chicago gunmen could have shot rings around most of them.

The bad men themselves mostly were fakes; a swindle on the credulity of small boys and grown-up morons. They were swaggerers; one part head and ten parts mouth, with a happy faculty for being absent from scenes of real strife. Some of them had the courage to shoot men from behind; preferable targets were men when asleep.

The counterpart of the bad man is the noble sheriff or town marshal; in real life he is a politician willing to do the dirty work of the boss. In Goldfield he was the tool of the Wobblies. Such men have the nerve to arrest an ancient prospector on an innocent jag, but his deputies have to handle the tough cases. One of the Goldfield boom sheriffs was a big hulk of a man, fine physique, handsome as a prize bull at a county fair, and nothing above the neck. He was a Wobbly because Big Bill told him to be one; he was sheriff because he was stupid enough to take orders from Big Bill. He knew which end of his pistol was the business end but he hadn't the slightest idea where a bullet he fired from it would wind up. He could pick up a one-hundred-pound sack of high-grade ore in each hand and walk away with them—he was known to have done that very thing—but in an argument with a fly-weight pugilist he walked away. Elinor Glyn visited Goldfield, looking for the "perfect man"; she picked this sheriff as "it" shortly before he had the top of his head shot off by a shotgun blast when he was engaged in stealing gold amalgam from a mill.

An assayer had an argument with a miner over the purchase of some stolen high-grade. It resulted in the miner telling him that he was going home for a gun and would return to fight it out. So the assayer was warned and prepared himself. When the miner hove in sight, lugging a shotgun, the assayer opened fire with a Colt automatic. The miner kept advancing stolidly in the face of the fire; out of six shots only one nicked him slightly on the hip. When within ten yards of the panicky assayer he upped the shotgun and fired. His first shot missed but he got the assayer with the second. That was shooting as "she is shot" in Goldfield.

One of those rearing, tearing he-wolves of the Southwest, who ate a man for breakfast every morning and picked his teeth with the victim's ribs, blew into town. He wore a pair of well-notched six-shooters (probably went to bed with them on); he had the traditional smooth voice with a Southern drawl, and he took his "likker" straight with his eyes shut. He wanted it truly straight and if he looked at it, it made his mouth water! He wasn't shy about letting the world know that he was a bad man from the badlands; he gave this information to Jock Finney one day in the Star Saloon. Jock looked up at him, quizzically, and said, "So what?" and then went on with his chatter with a friend. The he-wolf was quite upset at this noncommittal remark, but he hitched up his belt and said it was nothing; he just wanted him to know it. Jock paid him no more attention, so he started to load up on hootch and, later, started in to shoot up the town. He had to recover face somehow. He picked up a mild butcher from Saxony to start in on; the German took him seriously and went for him with a meat cleaver. The bad man had to shoot then in dead earnest, but he didn't score a hit. The butcher threw the cleaver in his face and put him out of business and, after he got out of the hospital, Goldfield didn't see any more of him.

The prize bad man of Goldfield was quite something. He looked fierce enough to scare an automobile out of a bog. He was of medium height; always dressed in black broadcloth, wearing a black sateen shirt under it; he wore the traditional mustachios, grown long enough to chew on when angry. He carried two pistols, one stuck in the front waistband of his pants, the other in a shoulder holster. He had a mean-looking bowie knife, exhibiting it at frequent intervals as a slicer for his chewing tobacco. He was known locally as Malapai Hank.

Malapai Hank claimed that he had shot and killed three men in Idaho because they had taken him for a tenderfoot and tried to make sport of him. For this mistake, justifiable and laudable in the upholding of his dignity, he was arrested, tried and "unfairly" found guilty of murder and was sentenced to be hanged. Now he didn't mind being hanged one little bit—not he, no sir! That was an injustice a man must be prepared to face at any time. But he did object to being hanged for murder. Now, for cattle rustling, or horse stealing—that would be all right and proper—but for murder—no, sir! All his killings were on a high plane, depending solely on his speedy "draw" and calm, cool aim. Nevertheless, he had to be hanged and he had a speech all fixed up for the occasion, so the ladies would weep for him as he spoke it from the scaffold. But the governor of Idaho spoiled it all by sending him a pardon just as the sheriff was about to adjust the noose to his neck. He had the rope to prove this story. To show how tough he was, he had this rope draped, in sinister loops, the hangman's knot in full view, on the wall above his bed. The black cap was there, too. It looked suspiciously as if it had been fabricated from an old discarded sateen shirt, but it lopped gracefully from the top of a bedpost.

A table in his bedroom was adorned with a human skull, with a bullet hole in it. This, he explained, was the head of an enemy he had killed. The man had tried to shoot him in the back, but he had been too smart for him. Because of his foul, underhand attempt on him, Malapai, after he shot him dead, with one, quick, well-aimed shot, decapitated him with his big bowie knife and buried the head in an ant hill to be picked clean; then he had disinterred it and kept it on his table as a warning to others. Even the tears of the man's widow had failed to move him from his purpose.

It was fortunate that this formidable man was always on the side of the mine operators during strikes. He was full of advice about "getting" your man; about how to call out, "Hands up!" and then, before the man could get them up, to shoot him down for being too slow about it. But the mine operators were very unlucky; at every occasion when he could put his advice to some good use he was away somewhere else and doing something else.

At a meeting, one time, during the second strike, when things were tense and it looked as if trouble was close by, Malapai Hank was laying it on the line about how to post guards at strategic places. He, himself, would take the most strategic place of all—the third floor of the Nixon Building,* which had such nice, thick stone walls. I got a little facetious and told him that the building also was one that might be attacked among the first,

---

* See Plate XIII.

and that I thought there should be another guard to guard him. With his characteristic scorn for his own safety, Malapai repudiated this.

"I don't need no guard—don't want none. My two guns is all the guard I need. Does anybody here think I'm scared of these sonsofbitches? Why, gentlemen, I could eat a dozen of them fer breakfast every mornin' an' then cry fer more. To show you how scared I am, I'll tell you boys that I let my wife—my wife, boys!— walk, all alone, at night, from here to Columbia. Me scared? That's too funny fer a laugh!"

Of course he wasn't scared; his wife absolutely spiked any such idea. Jock Finney told him so and added that, if he had a wife, he would be too scared to let her do any such thing.

Poor Malapai Hank! He did die a violent death. He fell on hard lines when Goldfield deflated. In desperation, one day, he tried to rob a ranch out in Nye County, when the men had all gone to town. One of the women there resisted him; he tried to scare her with his big bowie knife. She grabbed at his arm and received a cut from which she bled to death. The ranch crew caught him and strung him up on a big cottonwood tree. A card was pinned to his swinging form, which read, "This man was a damned bad man in some respects, and a damned sight worse in others."

WALTER SCOTT
Alias Death Valley Scotty

WALTER SCOTT may have been a descendant of Sir Walter Scott. They had one thing in common —both were novelists, with Scotty a superb mystery novelist. In 1904 he blew into Barstow, California, with his pockets full of gold. Barstow was a town he had lived in, off and on, for some little time, but never, theretofore, had he done anything to excite comment. On this trip he made the rounds of the saloons there and "set 'em up" for all inmates in each and every one. He spent several thousand dollars within forty-eight hours; then the press took notice.

Mr. Scott was cagey; he let it be known that he had discovered in Death Valley the greatest gold mine since King Solomon; probably one greater than any of the ones that king had. Where in Death Valley might it be? Well, he wasn't yet prepared to record any claims and he just couldn't reveal its location until they were of record. It was so rich he didn't need a mill—all he had to do was dig a few hundred pounds of rock, bust the rock away from the gold with a hammer, and there he would have a couple hundred-weight of gold!

Following his press conference, Scotty chartered a special train to take him to Los Angeles. The Santa Fe railroad people insisted on cash payment before assembling the train and Scotty dug deep and paid. He affected the garb of a prospector; faded blue flannel shirt, high boots with his pants stuffed in them, droopy slouch hat.

He wore this same garb to Los Angeles and checked in at the Alexandria Hotel. By the time he reached town, the press had a vivid story on front pages and he was besieged at his hotel by all kinds of seekers of knowledge. He bought drinks for all of them, fishing currency out of his boots, pockets, and the front of his shirt. Yes, he really had the gold strike of the era; it was in Death Valley, a very large and arid stretch of desert and desiccated mountain lands. No, he wasn't ready yet to pin point its location but some fine day they could all see for themselves.

He spent a few thousand dollars in Los Angeles and then returned to Barstow—by special train. Meantime, hordes of prospectors, both professional and amateur, were pouring into Death Valley to find his mine. Scotty let them get a bellyful of the arid search, then bought himself some good mules and a horse; loaded them up with tools and supplies, and set out for himself. Attempts were made to follow him, but he shook off all trailers. At the end of a month he reappeared, with a fresh supply of gold.

He returned to Los Angeles and had another press conference; informing the press that he was going to make the fastest trip ever made to New York by special train. He set the time at forty-five hours to Chicago and fifteen hours from there to New York. The Santa Fe officials scoffed at the idea, but he insisted that if they would sidetrack all traffic for his train, even the Limited, that it could be done. They agreed to try it, provided he would pay a 50 per cent premium over the regular price for a special train. Scotty agreed and a deal was made.

The trip is history now; it made Scotty famous, the world over as "Death Valley Scotty." He always was importuned by people offering to buy his mine, by others wanting to find its location. Whenever he set out on a trip he was followed. He knew the Death Valley terrain as no one else knew it; he had hideouts, from many of which he could spy on his trackers without himself being seen; he established caches of water and supplies which enabled him to lead his trackers over impossible terrain where he could refresh his livestock and himself, and they could not. It got so a great many people hated him and sought to kill him, even though a successful murder would have ended all chance of finding his mine. One time he was followed so closely that he could not shake off his pursuers; he was ambushed and shot through the leg. He returned to Barstow for treatment. On another occasion he was shot in one arm and, still later, was shot in the body. He survived all of these injuries and, progressively, he became embittered against everybody. He reached a point where he would go out of his way to do injury to all and sundry, but especially he enjoyed putting one over on a rich man.

He ended his life—by a natural death—at his castle at the upper end of Death Valley, in January, 1954.

Periodically Scotty liked to visit Goldfield; always unheralded, and always with some sort of drama to point up his visit and draw a crowd. One time, for example, he would appear, driving a new automobile, not just a plain one but one to attract attention. In those days autos were sold without a top or windshield—these were extra. His car was a flaming red, in color; it had a glittering windshield that folded down forwards; the top was low and rakish and had long yellow straps, fastened to the front of the frame, back of the head lamps, to hold it taut and in place. To cap all, he had a newfangled compressed gas tank for his lights, instead of the temperamental gas generator everybody else had. When he appeared in his exotic car a crowd collected and shouted questions at him.

Scotty could, and would, indulge in good-natured badinage before he got completely soured; he would buy drinks for everybody and take drink for drink himself. But he never became talkative with much drink; so nothing ever was learned from him by the flowing-bowl route. He liked a game of poker well—not the game against the "house" in a saloon but a private game with friends or chance acquaintances. He was absorbed in such a game one night, in the Elite Saloon, when an itinerant evangelist came in, distributing religious tracts. He approached the table where Scotty was playing and timidly laid one of his tracts at the elbow of each player. Scotty was engaged in scanning his hand after the manner of the cagey poker player; just sliding the cards far enough to see the corners. He brushed his tract to the floor with an impatient movement, without even glancing at it. The little man picked it up and laid it on the table again, only to have Scotty brush it off and remark that he would kite the opener five bones.

The man picked it up and tapped Scotty on the shoulder, and asked him, "Brother, don't you love Jesus?"

Scotty looked up in astonishment. He laid down his cards, face down and still covered with one hand; looked the little man up and down, then said, "Yes, I love Jesus plenty. And I want to see the bastard son of a Cousin Jack who loves him more than I do."

That was that—and then the game went on.

LOST MINES
Hallucinations of Weak Minds

THE AVERAGE prospector would rather hunt for an alleged "lost mine" than for anything else. Scotty's mine, of course, was nonexistent, but it popularly was supposed to have been one of several legendary lost mines of the Death Valley region. One thing, common to all the legends of lost mines, is the simple-mindedness and credulity of all the main actors in the play. The original finder always goes crazy, either from excitement or privation, and he always succeeds in dying without giving away the secret. Anyone who has ever seen the painstaking care of an old prospector, while methodically tracking down a mineral deposit, could not help but know that lost mines would have been found long since had they been real instead of mythical. Coincidence cannot be so unrelenting or make such a perfect score as to strike dead every man who ever found one of these mines; nor can average human nature render all discoverers so close-mouthed as to be able to keep the secret right up to death's door.

Listen to the tale of the Breyfogle lost mine. Near Daylight Springs, where the Grapevine and the Funeral Mountains meet, there are five crossing trails. This crossing will not be found on maps of Death Valley, but any old-timer can take you to the place. In the desolate and desiccated mountains of the Funeral Range, near this crossing, lies the alleged lost gold treasure of Breyfogle's mine.

Anton Breyfogle, traveling alone in the 1860's, came upon Daylight Springs. He traveled thence to the south and east into the hills; he observed a number of trails going in different directions and noted that there were five of them and that they crossed like a star at one place. He hadn't yet found the rich gold deposit so he did not take particular note of the cross location. He followed one of the trails, which led up a canyon for a few miles, then, suddenly, he observed gold ore float in the bed of the canyon. There was a lot of it. It was a dark quartz, seamed with metallic gold to such an extent that it was more than 50 per cent virgin ore. It was heavy, of course, so he could not carry much of it. It seemed to have come from a huge outcrop that showed up in the canyon wall. Breyfogle was an experienced prospector and, though excited by this fabulous discovery, he knew he had to get help to stake and develop this rich mine. He had come into the area from Austin, but that town was several hundred miles to the northeast; Ash Meadows, he knew, was about sixty miles away to the southeast, so he headed for that settlement with as much of the ore as he could carry.

He was unfamiliar with the country so, without a knowledge of water holes and distances between them, the crossing of the Amargosa Desert was a dangerous undertaking. He escaped death by some miracle after five days trudging and stumbling to Ash Meadows, which he reached, more dead than alive. Indians there gave him the help needed for him to recover from his ordeal. When able to travel again he set out for the white settlement of Manse, some thirty miles distant. An Indian, from Ash Meadows, covetous of a pair of new boots Breyfogle had in his pack, followed him and tried to murder him. In some way, which he was never able to explain, he escaped this fate. He reached Manse in as poor condition as that in which he had arrived at Ash Meadows. He still had his gold specimens, showed them to covetous men, but refused to tell where he had gathered them. The men at Manse threatened him; they coaxed him, to no effect. His suspicions of all men now caused him to show his German stubbornness and he gave them not even a hint. When he had recovered his strength, he left Manse, secretly, one night. The following day some of the men tried to pick up his trail and follow him, but with no success.

Some months later he turned up again at Austin. He still had his gold specimens (suspiciously remarkable in itself) and showed them to his friends there; describing the mineral deposit but without giving its location; and related his experiences. He still refused to take partners and lead an expedition to his discovery and, very quietly, he again disappeared. It became known later that he went again to Death Valley by way of the Owens River Valley and across the mountains from Keeler. He had failed to find his discovery again.

After a month at Austin, he again left secretly (as he thought) for a third attempt to find his mine. This time he was followed by a party of men who picked up his trail and followed it to Daylight Springs. There they found evidence of a recent camp, but here they lost his trail. They cast about to find it again when, by accident, they came across the man himself. He said he was again disappointed, but the men of the party, disbelieving him, forced him to take them along the trail he had been following. They came to the five-point crossing of the trails, but Breyfogle told them it was not the right one —he had been seeking it without success. He was not believed and the party explored each one of the five trails, but they failed to find the mine. Provisions gave out and they all had to return to Keeler.

Breyfogle now was willing to share his discovery with partners. He told them they had to locate the proper five-point crossing of trails in order to find the gold. Two or three more attempts were made without success and, finally, Breyfogle died at Austin about 1870.

Prospectors, for fifty years after, have searched diligently for the Breyfogle Mine. They haven't found it,
of course, because it doesn't exist. All of the gold specimens he brought out also have disappeared—because, of
course, they never were.

Then there is the Gunsight Mine. In 1847, a group
of Mormon emigrants started out by wagon train for
California. After some weeks of travel, with not too
much hardship, the train reached Las Vegas. There they
rested up a bit and then resumed the journey with an
Indian guide, reaching the eastern border of Death Valley
in due course. The Indian, knowing the country, wanted
to lead the party south around the southern end of the
desert, but the emigrants, knowing that California lay
west, thought the Indian was leading them astray. A
powwow caused a split in the party; one part went
southward with the Indian and reached San Bernardino;
the other party went west across the valley. This party
spent themselves considerably in trying to find a pass
through the Panamint Mountains. One day they reached
a place in the valley where they sunk some wells and did
find water. This place now is known as Bennett's Wells.

The party remained several days to recuperate. Young
men of the party wanted to press on to California, but
the elders wished to wait, so another split in the party
took place, and about forty young men started across
the Panamint Mountains. They soon ran out of water
and tried to return to Bennett's Wells. Almost dead with
thirst, they finally found a spring, now known as Bitter
Springs. Incautiously they drank deeply of this water
and soon the whole party was dead—poisoned. Their
bones, picked clean and bleached, lay where they died
for some years before they were found and properly
buried.

The rest of this party decided to play safe; stay with
the water while a scouting party could lay out a satisfactory route through the mountains. A party of three

young men was selected. They carried as much water as possible and each one carried a gun, both for protection against Indians and to use for killing game if any should be found. Two of the scouts lost the front sights of their guns so, as they proceeded, they looked out for something with which to fashion new ones. In this search they discovered a mineral ledge with pure silver in it; from it they made front sights for the guns. They tried to mark the location of the vein by bearings on prominent features of the landscape before proceeding on their way. They finally reached Newhall, California, then a ranch owned by a man of that name. There they obtained help and returned to the rest of the party at Bennett's Wells, and led them out to safety at Newhall.

These three scouts were fired by the silver discovery and didn't want to settle down; they preferred to return to their Gunsight Mine, as they now called it. They searched for several months, returning only when in need of supplies, but the bearings they had taken were either wrong or the ledge of silver had moved itself to another location—they did not find it. Other prospectors tried to get the bearings and find the mine, but these boys kept their secret to the day they died. Many seekers have died in this search and never has it been discovered. Interesting fiction again, of course. Also, the guns with the solid silver sights have been lost!

Another of these rainbows is the Peg-leg Mine which was said to have been discovered by a certain Peg-leg Smith, a gentleman possessed of a wooden leg, a marvelous lack of knowledge as to what gold looked like, and a very weak head. This mine is supposed to have been found in the 1830's.

Peg-leg Smith, so the story goes, was crossing the desert between old Fort Yuma and the Pacific coast; he tried to make a short cut and got himself lost. Distracted with fear and tortured with a burning thirst, he sighted some yellow and peculiar-looking pebbles, quite heavy they were; he picked up a lot of them and put them in his pockets, but he was quite ignorant of what they were. He stumbled somehow onto the right trial before being overcome by his thirst and reached his destination. A year later, still ignorant, he showed his pebbles to somebody who told him they were gold nuggets. When he realized this, the weak head exploded and he had a fit of brain fever. Though a brain fever had very little to work on in Smith's head, nevertheless it killed him off; he died without divulging the location of the gold. Some fifty or sixty men tried to find his mine and over half of them died out in the desert.

Many years later another miner is said to have come out of that desert area with nuggets like Smith had. He had found the mine but he, too, died of his sufferings and failed to reveal its exact location. A few years passed, then an Apache squaw, almost dead of thirst, staggered into a camp near the Salton Sink; she had lost herself and, in her wandering had found the Peg-leg Mine. She knew what gold was and she had several pounds of it; she repulsed all efforts to pry the secret of the location from her.

In the nineties a Mexican *vaquero* came in from this same mysterious desert with nuggets worth ten thousand dollars. He returned to his find several times and always came back with more nuggets. He was a gay bird— gambled and drank and played with the girls, and he spent money like Scotty did. The nuggets were just like the Smith nuggets. No one ever got the *vaquero* to tell where he found them and no one was able to follow his trail to the place. Finally, he was knifed to death at a Mexican *baile* and, since then, the Peg-leg Mine has rested in peace.

There are tales of lost mines ad infinitum, but these are good samples of them all.

PROSPECTORS
Optimists, Philosophers, Ingenious Liars

A mine is a hole in the ground, owned by a liar.
— MARK TWAIN

THE TALES brought in by prospectors about their "finds" usually were fantastic; the size of the relation was proportional to the distance to the discovery. If one went with a prospector to examine his discovery he would start to hedge a bit; more and more as you approached it, the tale would curl up and roll in on itself. By the time one got close to it, the old bird would have hedged very materially and then he would begin on stories about good mines that had had poor showings on the surface. Another thing about prospectors, they always think their property is equal to the best there is and, frequently, they will make it impossible to deal on it because of their inflated views.

When things were running smoothly at Goldfield I was often sent out to look over new discoveries and report back on them. Wingfield was sympathetic with prospectors and would always take a look at a discovery —there was slim chance of a good bet in it, but he didn't want to miss any.

Automobiles were used for transportation; the roads left much to be desired, but one could usually get to the prospect in a car.* Occasionally one needed a horse or mule for the last five to ten miles. Henry Ford was in business in those days with his early Model T. His

---

* See Plate XII.

output was small then so one could travel for hours and not see another car; choice water holes were not littered with empty cans and picnic remains, and high speeds were not possible. A day's run of two hundred miles was excellent. The automobiles used were mostly surprisingly good for the times. The most popular ones were the Thomas Flyer, Pope-Hartford, Pope-Toledo, Pierce Arrow, Royal Tourist, and Dorris, none of which have survived to this day. Fords were not in much use in the desert, largely because they boiled water out of the cooling system too quickly.

Travel by motor car in the desert during the first decade of the century was quite delightful. There were no filling stations; the general stores at the few crossroads and little towns sold gasoline in cases; two five-gallon tins to a case at fifty cents per gallon. Car radiators were not as efficient as they became later, so the empty gas tins were handy for carrying water. There were no garages or repair mechanics except in the large towns; a breakdown on the road was something one had to fix himself on the spot—or one just stayed there until a car or wagon came along. A puncture was a calamity; the cars had clincher rims on fixed wheels; a "flat" meant an hour's hard work prying the tire from the rim, changing the tube, jamming the tire back in place; agonizing work with a hand pump to reinflate it, not to twenty-five pounds pressure but to eighty or one hundred pounds. It meant torn fingernails and lacerated hands and, as often as not, one would have pinched the tube someplace, and the pressure would rupture it just about the time the pumping job was done. Then—do it all over again. Two thousand miles of life for a tire was good in those days.

During the summer, when days were hot and glaring, I usually tried to make my motor trips at night. There is nothing that still retains the pleasure in pleasant memory as the still, weird beauty of those all-night rides in the desert. In the rarified air—dry, crisp and cool—even a half moon gave light sufficient for driving.

Desert hauling was done for the most part with sixteen- or twenty-mule jerk-line outfits.* These were driven by a man who rode one of the wheeler mules; he controlled the long, eight- or ten-span line of mules with a jerk line attached to the lead team. Handling the outfit was a real art and the jerk-line skinner was an artist and a real he-man. A meeting with one of these outfits in a narrow canyon, while driving a car, was an adventure —an especially memorable one if the mules got skittish and called forth the sulphurous remarks of the harassed skinner. One of the finest sights ever was to see an expert skinner maneuver his long, stretched-out teams and double wagons in tandem around a sharp turn.

The old-time prospector was as queer a fish as his burro. Superficially each one was as like his brother as he could be; actually, each one was an individualist and as un-like his brothers, in temperament, as could be. It is a matter for wonder how a prospector gets his training; he is always alone, with no apprentices along. Each one seems to be old—at least each one looks old—and all are of a distinct type. And now they are as extinct as the dodo bird.

Usually the prospector is a simple, kindly old soul, given to soliloquy and conversation with his jackass. The latter would understand him and would reply, either in agreement or contradiction, by semaphoring with his ears, or the movement of his tail, or by his stance. Most pros-pectors were adorned with a straggly beard, white usually —shaving is too much of a chore in the desert, with no one to see you but the jackass—and many of them looked like old patriarchs. Their eyes held a steady, unblinking, faraway look, as if always ranging the landscape for "color" in the distance; they frequently were a bit watery from the desert sun and the stiff, dry winds. Their lives, so

* See Plates VI and VIII.

much alone, tended to make their minds indulge in strange
fantasies.

During the boom period of Tonopah and Goldfield,
grubstakes were easy to come by, and many prospectors
ranged the country. In the fall the old buzzards drifted
into town almost every day and most of them went to
the Nixon & Wingfield offices to see the town "big
shots" and try to get their discoveries financed. Listening to them was part of my job. Each old man would
sit down and produce a sack of rock fragments—his
samples. They usually would be right good-looking rock
with various minerals—gold, silver, lead, copper, or a
combination of two or three of them. The old boy would
swear by the tail of his jackass that they were not selected
pieces but had been knocked out of the vein "jest as they
come"; the vein would be described as a ledge of quartz,
traceable for miles across the country. This ledge was
always at least "ten foot wide," with values "clear acrost
it" and he would bet "it was good ore from grass roots
clear to hell."

One old fellow blew in one day from a long sojourn
in the desert south of Goldfield. He parked his burro,
still laden with his tools, skillet, gold pan and all the
whatnots of a prospector's equipment. The pack was
collapsed, indicating his grub was all gone. The burro's
head hung dejectedly, one ear lopping well forward and
cocked a bit expectantly, the other one well down to one
side and his eyes half closed. When the old man entered
the building the burro never moved except to allow both
ears to lop down in utter dejection.

I indulged in the amenities—asked the old man where
he had been prospecting, what sort of luck he had had.
He said he had been down in the Panamints, but his luck
mostly had been bad; one reason for this was that the
country was getting so crowded a man "didn't have much
chanct any more to turn up a good lead 'thout some
galoot breathin' down his neck."

"You know somethin'," he said, "durin' the summer I run acrost two other outfits, prospectin'."

There were other amenities; the old man must spread out his samples for inspection and give a description of the vein and its location; tell how many claims he had located; where they were recorded; and something about the water and timber. After that I had to invite him to have a drink. With a "Don't keer if I do," he went with me to the Palace Saloon, across the street, his burro giving him a reproachful look when he saw where he was going. We solemnly had a couple of "shots," then seated ourselves in a booth and had a couple more. Then the trading started and progressed until a reluctant agreement to terms for his discovery was reached. This was sealed with another drink, and then I asked him if anything unusual had occurred during his trip in the desert. The old man delivered himself as follows:

"Yes, sir, a right amoosin' thing happened. Whilst I was gettin' ready to move outta the country to get me some more grub, a heavy, wet snow come down. It snowed all night. In the mornin' I get me started fer Bullfrog. The sun was up and shining brightly an' off in the distance suddenly I seen a couple rows of dark things in a flat below the Malapai. When I got closter I could see they was twenty-five, thirty jackasses, lined up in two sides, with their rumps facin' inward and their heads facin' out. They all was kickin' up their heels like crazy. As I got closter I could see the air was thick with flyin' snowballs. Them jackasses was stompin' their feet in the wet snow and when they gets a good gob of snow balled up on their hind feet, they let fly with it at the other line of jackasses.

"This amazin' business went on till one side had enough and broke off and run away. The winnin' jackasses then got theirselves in a huddle, heads to the middle, and then whadda you know? They brayed out a lotta big cheers.

I reckon them jackasses musta been handled sometime
by some of these yellow-legged college engineers!"

I looked down at my yellow-laced boots and told the
old codger that maybe he was right but for me I'd say
that it was desert whisky that had got him.

I had just returned from a trip East and I had some
paper currency left over. I fished out a couple of one-
dollar bills to pay for the drinks. The old man observed
them and he asked me what kind of money that might
be. I told him it was Eastern money made of paper—
Eastern people were too weak to carry hard money around,
but that it was just as good U.S. money as the hard kind.
He picked up the bills and looked them over with great
surprise and wonder; then he remarked that there "warn't
a hell of a lot of use prospectin' if people were agoin' to
use trash fer money." He asked me what I would take
for the bills. He " 'lowed he wanted them fer souvenirs."
I sold them to him for two big silver cart wheels. He
produced an old, beat-up, gnawed pencil from some inner
recess of his clothing, carefully rolled the dollar bills
around it, "borried" a rubber band from the bartender
to hold them snug, and secreted them in his clothes.

I arranged with the old boy to go with him the next
day to look at his prospect, remarking, facetiously, to
him that I hoped the big crowds he reported to be in
the country would not impede our work. He said, "Well,
I done tole you they was at least two outfits workin' the
country besides me. I jest don't like crowds, nohow.
I kin stand to see one outfit workin' the same country
as me, but two—too damn many. Why, mister, I sometimes gets crowded when I'm alone!"

We drove to his locations and I found some fair showings, but it was a mediocre vein and of no great interest to Wingfield. I let the old man down easy—he was
accustomed to adverse judgments—told him it was not
our type of a mineral deposit, but that I'd introduce him
to a man who might buy it from him. I sent him, with

a note, to Larry Sullivan and there he made a deal to sell it for a thousand dollars. The old man took five hundred dollars of the money and brought it to me, asking me to hold it for him for a grubstake.

"Don't you give it back to me, young fella, ontil I'm plumb sober an' ready to take to the hills agin." Then he went on a big binge.

Late the next day he staggered into the Elite Saloon, where I happened to be sitting at a table with a group of friends. He weaved over to the bar, grasped it firmly with one hand, eyed the bartender and the row of bottles on the buffet, jingled the money in his pockets, and turned to a man near by and asked him, with extreme courtesy and solemnity, to join him in a drink. The man decided the old boy had had enough and he declined the offer, with thanks—said that he had just had a drink and must go home. The old man was annoyed and displeased, but he said nothing; he surveyed the room slowly, spied me and my group at a table, then left the bar and, uncertainly, made his way toward us.

Leaning on the table as an aid to his equilibrium, he said, "My frens, please excuse an old desert rat; I hate like pizen to drink all alone. I'm alone most of the time, but I'm a gre—gregar—gregar—hell! I'm an old coyote that likes to mix up with lotsa comp'ny when I'm in town. On the job I don't wanta see nobody. Please won'tcha all have a little shot with me? That bird with you"— pointing to me—"that bird put his thumbs down on my location, but hell! I ain't got no hard feelin's 'count o' that."

We all tried to talk him into going home and saving his dough for tomorrow—then we would be glad to drink with him—help him drag out his good time a bit and make it last longer. This only exasperated him; he jerked off his battered, dusty old hat, slammed it down on the floor, and exploded.

"This shore does beat the dutch! Ain't they nobody

will have a shot with me? Then I'm goin' outside an' bring in th' bums, an' th' whores, an' anybody I kin find, jest like that ranch galoot down there in Galilee that the Bible tells about. He was my kind of a coot. When he put on a party it reely was a party!"

"What galoot is that you're talking about?" I asked.

"Well— I ain't much of a Bibler, but I got th' Book in my outfit an' I like to read it. I did read in it one time 'bout an' ole cock that had him a ranch down in Galilee. I don't rightly know whereabout thet is, though I've prospected a hell of a lot around this crazy man's country. This galoot married off his oldest gal an' fixed it up to have him a big blowout to celebrate. He killed off a lotta his livestock fer a big, ripsnortin' barbecue. He ast in all the neighbors, but they was snooty; thought they was too high-toned fer the likes of him, and nary one showed up to the party. The old boy got on his ear 'bout that, an' he cussed, an' he stomped, an' he yanked at his hair, an' he vowed as how he was goin' to have him a party, spite of hell. So he calls in his ranch hands an' buckaroos, an' he sends 'em out to bring in all the bums they kin find. They got a plenty of 'em—from the sagebrush, back alleys an' lumber yards, an' th' hooker joints—an' what thet gang did to thet chuck was a plenty. They cleaned up all th' lunch, an' they guzzled all th' hootch an' beer, an' then they danced an' played poker, ontil the whole shindig broke up in a tearin' row. Thet gal had a lively weddin' after all. Now I'm kinda kin to thet ole galoot, I am; I'm goin' out in th' sand an' th' sagebrush agin, jest as soon as I kin travel, but I'll be all-fired goddamed ef I ain't agoin' to have me a bang-up weddin' feast first!"

The old boy had his wedding feast. We all pitched in and drank with him; he was jubilant about it, and he informed all and sundry that he was a gold hound for fair; could smell out gold any time where it wasn't. Anybody, he said, can find gold where it is, but it takes a regular hellcat to find it where it ain't! And after a short monologue on this subject he went peacefully to sleep on the floor in a corner.

Another old prospector, and he really was an old one, named Joe Fisher, came into Goldfield with a tale of a new prospect of his that was "jest lousy with gold." "Panamint Joe," as he was called, showed me a few interesting-looking pieces of gold ore he claimed to have broken off his vein. His locations were in the Bullfrog area, and I went with him to look at them via the motor stage to Beatty. I took samples from his vein, crushed them in a mortar, and panned them on the spot. They were very disappointing in yield. After each sample was panned, Old Joe would shake his head sadly and exhibit the utmost contempt for my panning technique, but I couldn't persuade him to do some panning himself. I asked him where the gold was that he had been talking so much about; he replied with the cryptic remark that any fool knows that almost all of the gold of Nevada and other places is back East.

There was a shaft on Joe's prospect that had been sunk about twenty-five feet deep. Some of my samples I took from this shaft—halfway down and at the bottom. The bottom rung of the ladder had been damaged by the last round of shots and, when I was descending on it, another rung gave way and I landed in a heap at the bottom. In falling my face scraped against the rock wall and one side of it was lacerated from chin to scalp; it looked terrible but actually was superficial. Old Joe patched it up with some mercurochrome and then I looked like nothing human.

Back at Beatty I got my lunch and then sat on the hotel veranda to wait for the northbound stage. A man, driving a nice-looking horse, drove up to the hitching rack and tied up, then started into the hotel for his lunch. As he passed me he looked me over with more than passing interest, but he said nothing until he came

out again. He stood a moment, lighting a cigar and eye-
ing me. Then he said, "Beg pardon, mister. That's a
pretty raw-lookin' face you got for yourself. I'd like
to ask a favor; would you mind steppin' out in front
where my horse can see you? He's a high-sperited anni-
mile, new to this country, and I'm a-tryin' to get him
used to everything."

Why not? So I stepped out, looked the horse over, gave
him a tentative rub on the nose, and stared him in the
face. He looked me over, but my face didn't excite any
reaction in him at all—I didn't look anywhere near as
bad as his owner thought. The latter didn't show any
disappointment, but he thanked me and gave me a first-
class cigar.

A month later, Panamint Joe sold his prospect to an
Eastern man for fifteen thousand dollars. He told this
man that only very large samples would show the true
worth of the ore—at least one-hundred-pound samples,
shot out of the vein with dynamite. He agreed to do
the drilling for blasting, and to furnish the blasting
powder. The prospective buyer liked the idea, and so
it was done. Joe privately introduced some gold dust
into the sticks of powder and, by this means, thoroughly
salted each sample with enough gold to make it assay
well. It was Eastern gold, after all, that Joe got for his
mine. Little good it did him—the Bullfrog faro layouts
took it all away from Joe in six weeks' time.

Joe was a little, wizened old man, his skin dried up
like parchment; his bones showed at the joints in twisted,
gnarled shapes from the arthritis that plagued him. His
thin hair was completely white; he had a straggly white
beard. After he had been well "taken" in Bullfrog he
went out in the desert again with his old burro, which
looked as old as Joe. The winter was a hard one, even in
the south where Joe did his prospecting. He showed up
in Goldfield in the early spring, apparently having just
been able to make it to town. Two days after his arrival

I discovered him in a state of near collapse at the Bank Saloon. The people there thought he was only drunk— he was well known there—and they just let him lie down to sleep it off. I thought also that he was drunk, but I liked the old man and thought I'd get him up and put him to bed somewhere. As I started to rouse him, he opened his eyes, sober as a judge. He recognized me and said, "Hello, you old Cousin Jack! Go easy there in the way you handle me. My rheumatiz is somethin' fierce; I jest cain't seem t' stand on my laigs. Reckon Ole Joe has done finished up with his last trip."

I asked him where he was lodging and he replied, "No place." He had had a fruitless trip and had returned when his grub ran out. No, he didn't have a thin dime; ole Bill MacPherson, who could have taken him in, had died of the pneumonia fever a month back, and he didn't have anywhere to go.

It was apparent that he was in a bad way, so I went out and got a car, got him to his feet very carefully— he was pitifully skinny, couldn't have weighed more than ninety pounds—put him in the car, and drove him to the hospital. There they installed him in a ward and I went out to find a doctor. The doctor examined him and then told me that he didn't think Old Joe would last more than a week or ten days; his heart was getting all ready to quit on him.

Old Joe knew it, too. "I know the answer, Doc. You don't need to make it soft fer me, 'cause th' way I feel now I'm all ready to get clear of it. I'm reely glad fer somethin' sartin to go on."

The doctor nodded, gave some instructions, and left. Joe then told me he had his burro, and a mean, scrawny horse—"name o' Swipes"—that he owned over at the Palace Stables. He asked me if I would hunt up John Browning, another old prospector—they would know about him at the Bank Saloon. If Browning should be in town, would I "get aholt of him and ast him would

he either buy his livestock or sell it fer him." Maybe,,
he thought, that his outfit and his "ornery annimiles"
might bring in enough to pay his hospital bills and bury
him.

I found Browning at the Bank Saloon and told him
about Panamint Joe's plight and what he wanted of him.
He listened without a word; my tale finished, he looked
at me quizzically, cocked his head sidewise toward the
bartender, assumed a hopeful look, and, tentatively, shoved
his empty shot glass down the bar a few inches. I bought,
of course. Browning took a large slug of "redeye," gulped
it down with approval, smacked his lips, and passed his
sleeve over his mouth. Then he was ready to talk.

"So Old Joe is ready to cash in! That old bastard
must be a hundred years old. Time he left things to
us young fellers (Browning was seventy-five if he was
a day). I've known him fer uppards of thirty-five year
—ran acrost him in Mexico first. Him an' me been
buddies an' enemies, an' everythin' in between. I mind
the time he almost chawed an ear offen me in a little
argyment we had over sidelines to a hell of a good location. Both of us got chawed up so bad that time that
we was laid up a spell an' a bastard of a Cousin Jack
jumped the claims an' got recorded before we did. But
we made it up then pronto an' then made hash outta
him an' got th' claims back. Made a nice little stake
outta them, too. Them was the days, them was. Things
is punk now; Joe oughta be glad he's gittin' out of it.

"I can't buy his outfit, though; I'm about six hundred
dollars short of nuthin'. Fact. I'm flat an' lookin' fer
a grubstake. But we kin raffle off th' outfit if we make
a right tony raffle outta it! I'll git up a snappy dodger
advertisin' it an', effen you'll git it printed, we'll do some
right-good business.* What say?"

Having said his say, he cocked his head again at the

---

* See Plate XLII in the Appendix.

bartender and again it paid off. When he had done the needful to his drink he told me to meet him in a half hour and he would have his "copy" ready for me. He composed a notice that woke up the town and produced $423 for Joe's outfit.

The Salvation Army took official notice of Panamint Joe on account of the publicity attending the raffle. A well-meaning member called on him at the hospital and reproached him for allowing such a lewd notice of his raffle to be broadcast. This was the first notice to Joe of the raffle; he was mystified and explanations were in order. John Browning brought him a copy of the notice; he read it over painfully, spelling out each word as he went along. He chuckled softly and observed: "Why, John, damn your rotten old gizzard. That's a hell of a way to talk about my horse!"

"Now, now!" said the Salvation Army man. "My good man, how can you speak in that way with death staring at you. You should be thinking of your salvation and praying to reach that happy bourne of the dead."

He continued urging Joe to fix his thoughts on his sins; to ask contritely for forgiveness, and prepare his soul for redemption. Joe listened patiently and, when the man stopped to get his breath, he said, "Parson, you shore do sling a pow'ful lot of persuasive and heavy words. But, thankee, I don't reely think I'd feel easy like an' homey in a place like thet there bourne you bin talkin' about. I'll jest have to kick in, in my own way, an' trust to th' Almighty like I always done, out in the hills. Course I don't know nuthin' about the lay o' the land in that there bourne; mebbe it's good live country fer prospectin' an' agin mebbe so it's not. Effen I could have anythin' to say about it I'd take along Swipes an' Old Grouch—them's my horse an' burro—an' I'd choose to settle down in a good mineral country with lotsa elbowroom; with nice water holes an' with all the beans an' sowbelly an' eatin' tobacco thet I'd need fer so long as I'd be set down there. Oh, yes—an' a good drink o' good whisky onct in a while."

"I'm sure you don't realize it, Mr. Fisher, but it is wicked to talk as you do—it's sinful—and I cannot sit here and listen to such depraved ideas. If only I could make you see the error of your ways I'd have great happiness."

"Well, parson, you means well, I know. Ain't nobody called me Mister Fisher 'cept galoots thet wanted to do me fer somethin', an' I thank you. But I jest don't know of any error in my ways; I gotta die an' I ain't sorry fer it. Now that ain't no error neither—nohow. Effen I'm goin' someplace after thet, all I want is a place where there ain't no rheumatiz, an' where a man's teeth don't bother him none. I done a little hell raisin' an' had a few fights, an' I done a little sample saltin' onct in a while, but I ain't ever done nuthin' as I kin recollect thet I oughta be special sorry fer. I kin leave it to God, I guess, an' I'm plumb satisfied to let all my bets ride jest thataway."

Old Panamint Joe slept his life away one night. He had asked me, "effen it ain't too much trouble" to have his old "carcass" burned up and "effen it makes any ashes, jest take 'em somewheres on the Malapai an' spread 'em out on the ground. Thet's funeral enough fer me!"

His wishes were carried out.

GOLDFIELD AT FLOOD TIDE
Tex Rickard Brings Civic Beauty

GOLDFIELD* was a town without trees or grass; or any running, walking, or standing water. No vegetation but Joshua trees and sagebrush would grow naturally. When water finally was piped into town from springs thirty-five miles away, a few small trees were planted and, with care and liberal watering, they did pretty well. The soil was a barren, adobe clay; it wouldn't support much plant life without heavy fertilization. The population was a shifting one, uninterested in beautification; just make a stake and blow. Tex Rickard, however, made up a seedbed around his house and planted grass, put in a few trees, and had a colored factotum from the Northern Saloon put in a lot of time watering the place, spreading horse manure from the livery stables, and picking up the debris the wind blew in every day. It was a moot question whether Tex did this from a sense of civic pride or because he had a bet on it. The Northern Saloon saw but little of him while the grass was nursed through childhood into adult life. Cutting the tender young blades was a difficult process; Tex didn't want to run a standard lawn mower over it until it was hardy enough to stand such brutal treatment. It was suspected that the first cuttings of the tender grass were done by Tex, himself, with barber clippers, in the dark of the moon. There came a day, however, when Tex wheeled out his new, red, shiny lawn mower and had it

---

* See Plate XIV.

really cut. The whole town turned out and the press attended and featured the event as front-page material.*

Goldfield had a chamber of commerce, with all the trimmings. It was a hothouse and forcing bed for a lot of only-just-give-us-a-chance senators and governors. The town had simply to be carefree and gay merely to tolerate these ponderous and complacent bores. Fortunately for the city, county, and state, their ambitions to serve the public on the public payroll remained unacknowledged. The only thing the chamber might have been useful for was to show up the thievery and chicanery of the crooked promoters and stock jobbers who had flocked in by the hundreds. They, of course, took no action at all because it would be bad for business.

The press was well represented; at one time there were two morning and one evening daily papers, a couple of weeklies, and a few monthly magazine-type papers. The latter were mainly used to boost new mining camps; such a one was the *Death Valley Chuck-Walla*. It was launched with some fanfare, announcing that it was "Published on the desert at the brink of Death Valley. Mixing the dope, cool from the mountains and hot from the desert, and withal putting out a concoction with which you can do as you damn please as soon as you have paid for it." It's theme:

The men and the mines, the life and the lore, the wealth and the wisdom of the Western Desert comprise the theme of the *Chuckawalla*. Born on the Desert and versed in all the things of the Desert, it carries to the world the knowledge of what is here (slickers for one thing). If you don't like it, don't read it. If you do read it, remember these facts: what it says is true; what it does is honest; it will call a liar a liar, a thief a thief, or an ass an ass, as is justified and, if you don't like it, you may kick and be damned. Its editors are its owners, and they will do as they see fit with their own, restricting themselves only in so far as they are restricted by their demand for the truth, the whole truth, and nothing but the truth, and their wish to give the devil his due.

---

* See Plate XLIII in the Appendix.

How noble! The dues for the most part were only the devil's.

Goldfield Gossip was a weekly set up by the head of the chamber of commerce. It had a dual purpose—to put the Western Federation of Miners in its proper place and to purvey the tittle-tattle of the society of Goldfield. It was supposed to perform this latter function in much the same way that *Town Topics,* in New York, was doing it in the effete East. The elite in Goldfield thought that *Town Topics* was the official society journal of New York, and they were irked no end by the indifference of that publication to the doings of Goldfield's upper crust. This was *Town Topics'* loss, however—they could have sold thousands of copies in the town with just a few spicy, personal notices—and there was a vast quantity of spice to be noted there.

Goldfield Gossip also was a vehicle to boom the editor for the United States Senate; to the credit of that august body, he failed to make it. Jock Finney once made a bet with me that he could write an article of complaint about Goldfield and get it published, despite the booster line of the periodical. He picked on the wind, always blowing there, and treated in the columns, when mentioned, only as a "gentle zephyr." He wrote in the form of a diary, as follows:

May 1. Sun shining, wind blowing like hell.

May 2. Wind blew all day. Changed direction 7 times.

May 3. Blowing up a good stiff breeze. Hat blew off en route to mine. Chased it hard but unable to gain on it. Bought a new one.

May 4. Cloudy but plenty of wind. My house door blew open. Sent for paper hanger.

May 5. Still blowing. Flying empty bean can hit me on cheek. Doctor bill and 7 stitches.

May 6. Blowing moderately, no clouds and looks like wind might let up and take a rest.

May 7. Blowing up again; tempo crescendo.

May 8. Ditto. Got into a twister, an association forced on me. Found in it fragments from prehistoric times.

May 9. Ditto. Wind reversed direction, apparently in order to return dust and trash heretofore borrowed.

May 10. Blowing. Paint coming off my house.

May 11. Blowing from southeast. Neighbor's panties blew off her clothesline. Chased them for her—a vain effort. My pants torn by sagebrush. Bought another pair—for me.

May 12. Windy. Man dropped into mine office; said he could not remember any time when the wind did not blow. He has been in this section for 12 years.

May 13. Blowing. Blanket and 2 sheets blew away from clothesline. Hope they reach deserving party.

May 14. Wind slacking up; must be nearly blown out.

May 15. Blowing up again.

May 16. Sunny day. Blowing in gusts. Bet $5 it will stop blowing tomorrow.

May 17. Lost $5.

May 18. Wind, sun and debris. My house chimney toppled over. Well—not needed till next winter.

May 19. Bet $10 it will blow until June.

May 20. Blowing harder. Looks good for the money, so I doubled the bet.

May 21. New hat blew away. Let her go! My bet will buy a new one.

May 22. Something wrong with the wind works. Lost $20.

May 23. Fair and calm. Bet $25 the blow is over for at least two days. Nature must be out of breath.

May 24. HELL!!

I won my bet. The *Goldfield Gossip* said this little effort was "frivolous."

That is the Great American Desert at its most capricious. Forbidding in every aspect by day; hot, dry, and most of the water, when one finds it at all, is charged with salts, or stagnant; little, or no vegetation; the earth alkaline; the very rocks seeming as if seared by fire. By night, under a full moon, it is soft and lovely, cool, the mountains fairylike and weird, with sharp black shadows and ghostly, whitish high lights; dry lake beds in the distance like silver pools of clear water; the sagebrush, with distance to blend the plants together, like a velvet lawn. Despite its lack of the greens and softness of Atlantic seaboard countryside, it is vivid with reds and yellows, with a fascination that holds one. Even Death Valley, that dazzling, burning hot waste of sand, borax, and alkali, and hot, stark rocks, is enchanting by moonlight.

The Montezuma Club found its quarters over the Palace Saloon cramping as to room and undignified as to location. A new and palatial stone clubhouse was built, with a generous mortgage, in the summer of 1907. The cornerstone was laid ceremoniously; a large gathering attended. Facetious and serious speeches were delivered for the occasion, the former by the professional funnymen, the latter by members having ambition for political preferment. The cornerstone hollow was provided with copies of the daily newspapers, charter and by-laws of the club, marriage certificates of the most often married members, a replica of "Gold Tooth" Bess's gold tooth, one of Tex Rickard's little ivory balls, a pair of dice, and other mementos. The serious speeches all hailed the new era of expansion for Goldfield, making of it a greater center for industry, banking, and "cult-your." Who said there were clouds coming up over the Malapai? Let the cantankerous croaker beware! Let him show himself and be blasted off the face of the earth where nestles the blooming, fair city of Goldfield.

Many fine—that is to say, expensive—residences had been built of stone, imported brick, stucco, and wood. Those on whom Fortune had smiled vied with each other in erecting houses, always for the dual purpose of shelter and opportunity for social display. There were two-story houses, castles off the Rhine (and glad to be off), Spanish Renaissance, Norman-French, Elizabethan; also Mormon, Paiute, and Renaissance Sourdough. Usually one had to be told by the owner just what period his house typified.

The hitherto half-clad, shivering, unwashed desert rat took on, with amazing aptitude, all of the appurtenances of the effete civilization which theretofore he had loudly denounced.

In the saloons life was just one long, hearty laugh. Men poured into and out of them all day long and all night; crowds, three deep, stood around the roulette wheels, scrambling to get bets down. Always there was a hilarious crowd at the craps tables, taking turns at the "bones" until someone would get "hot" with them; he then kept the bones; no one would touch them for fear of putting on a "hex," and everybody hastened around to ride with Fortune on the "hot" coattails. Three shifts of croupiers and lookouts ran the games twenty-four hours a day; at the bar there was a continuous, shifting crowd, always somebody to buy for all who could stand to the bar and get a drink. Waiters were always busy carrying drinks and eats to the men bucking the games. Who said hard times were coming; that open gambling would be outlawed by a lot of bluenoses? Bring in the sonofabitch and pump him full of hootch.

The red-light district* tinkled with pianos and fiddles; it was uproarious with laughter and the shrill, profane chatter of the girls; it glittered with the tawdry, artificial show of Oriental splendor. Dance halls were crowded with customers enjoying very bad and expensive drinks, while the music alternated between waltzes and two-steps. Who said the high-grade ore was petering out and that miners soon would have to work like hell just to keep a job? Bring in the ornery stiff and we'll spank him with pick handles.

The City Fathers were collecting big taxes with hardly a whimper from the taxpayers; lots of superfluous employees were enjoying sinecures on the city payroll; they were busily engaged in letting the streets and sidewalks get in just as bad condition as obtained in any other thriving community. Main Street was crowded and seeth-

* See Plate IX.

ing with automobiles, wagons, mules, burros, dogs, and whatnot; brokers were rushed to death with stock selling; the local stock exchange had so many issues listed that a lively curb market had started. Merchandise stores could not keep inventories up to demand; jewelry stores did a rushing business in diamonds; the banks piled up deposits and loans at 1 per cent per month.

Social aspirations, pleasures, combats and triumphs boiled and fermented, foaming out over the top. One triumph succeeded another with dizzy speed; there were five hundred and euchre parties, and some of the elite took up duplicate whist and the new bridge game. Social lions were in demand; Nat Goodwin and his leading lady, Edna Goodrich, were the prize animals of the menagerie; the man from Boston who called stocks briefly at the women's stock exchange—he was at least a bobcat. A French costume ball, given by the local Mrs. Potter Palmer, was the crowning affair of Goldfield's brief social season. Any scoffer who designated Mrs. Malaprop and the Dutchess of Danzig as overdrawn characters would have had reason for sober thought had he been at that ball. The costumes were out of this world—or any other world! Potential statesmen were there, seizing on every opportunity to toast the hostess and get in a little ponderous oratory; drinks were served in the most liberal fashion, and, at five o'clock in the morning, more drunks had to be swept out the front door than at any time in the history of the camp.

## CHAPTER TWENTY-THREE

EBB TIDE
Where Did the Money Go?

IN THE FALL of 1907 the prelude and the main movement were finished; it had been a gay, melodious symphony that had worked up to a fine point. Now the violins began to shiver gently; the drum whackers tightened up the wing nuts on the drums preparatory to the final movement. This broke out into music 'way off in New York, with a great assemblage of people at the doors of the Knickerbocker Trust Company.

The picture changed quickly. Main Street, physically, was the same old street, just as wide and just as long as before, with the same chuckholes full of dust; the same clattering, loose-board sidewalks, with nails and knots in their accustomed places; the same signs proclaimed the excellence of this or that beer, whisky, broker, bank, or store; the same throng of people, dogs, burros, and mules milled about; but there was a vast difference. It was a difference in morale. It was shown visibly in the way people walked; the way they leaned against posts or buildings; the way they entered or exited from places of business or of refreshment; the way they looked and the manner in which they greeted one another; in the very way of expectoration.

As time went on the crowds perceptibly thinned and metamorphosed, consolidating from a large number of types to only one or two predominating ones. The congenital loafers became all of one kind; the businessmen were all typed in one category, the eggs all in one basket, inventories swollen and customers missing. The swinging doors of the saloons flapped open and shut much less frequently; plate-glass windows got streaked and dirty, first those of the brokers, most of them posted with "For Rent" signs, followed by those of stores with signs reading "bankrupt sale" in them. There were mass sales by trustees in bankruptcy; the bidders were nearly all Jews from the West Coast. Lastly, the saloons began to close, reluctantly, one by one. When this stage was reached, there could no longer be any doubt at all about the descent on the slide.

Soon the streets returned as near to original patterns as possible. One cannot say dust unto dust; that implies an intervening condition alien to dust. Dust always was on Main Street, except for very occasional wettings; now it was almost undisturbed dust, except for the wind which whirled it about as usual; the dogs collected fleas from it as usual; but seldom was it ruffled by contrivances of transportation. Signs fell down and lay as they fell; broken glass windows stared in the mournful way peculiar to them; trash of all sorts gathered in corners where the wind formed eddies; tin cans and empty bottles lay about everywhere.

Taxes were collected with difficulty or not at all. The city administration got hard up and many a man who had fattened on the public purse had to jar loose and rustle for his ham and eggs. The newspapers carried increasingly long lists of property for sale or for swap, sales for taxes or mortgages, or both. The full-page ads for sales of stocks stopped altogether; gloom shouldered out everything else and usurped the editorial page.

Burros, skillets, tents and pack saddles again were in demand—a regular bull market. Half of Goldfield's upper crust had to fall back on the only work they knew anything about—prospecting. The other half of this crust didn't even know prospecting; they rode the freights out.

The Montezuma Club members would have been glad

to get half the cost of the new clubhouse and go back
to the rooms over the Palace Saloon; the saloon would
have been glad to have them back at half the rent they
had paid before. The mortgage on the new building was
held by one of the mining barons; sort of a *quid pro quo*
for his election as president of the club. When the bust
came, everybody was glad that he held the mortgage
and also was president. The place was transformed from
a roaring place of joy unconfined to a gloomy retreat
where one might contemplate suicide and find it quite
attractive. The mine operators kept it alive for a while
during the strike as their headquarters. It began to get
shabby and slowly declined. Finally the president bought
it in at a foreclosure sale with no competing bidders and
nobody to supply funds to pay any deficiency judgment.

Gradually people who had the price moved away, some
to the desert to prospect, some to Southern California,
the home for the idle poor. If possible, all left as many
unpaid accounts as they could get by with; if not possible, they took as large discounts as they could wangle.
"Pay as you go—unless you're going for good." They
all were going for good, and the sheriff had his own
troubles.

The fine houses were still fine for a little while, but
no one could or would buy them. Their windows got
broken; roving parties in need of cash or spare parts
took out fixtures and lead pipe in the dark of the moon;
vandals committed obscenities in and about them; for-
lorn cats, wild as forest animals, lived, fought, and littered
in these houses; birds nested in living rooms not so long
ago the glittering scenes of social triumphs. Gradually
the wind filled these houses with sand, dust, and trash,
tumbleweeds, all blown in through the broken windows.
Roofs fell in or were blown off; a merciful fire cleaned
out quite a lot of them.

The saloons became very depressing; instead of a crowd
milling about there would be only two or three dejected

men at the bar, idly picking teeth that hadn't had a decent meal in weeks. Every man now entering a saloon looked hopefully at the men already there to see if, perchance, he might get an invitation to "have one on me." Usually there wasn't any such liberal spender within a mile of the place, so he would buy for himself, if he had the price. No longer did the mere order of a drink suffice; the bartender had first to know whether or not the drink could be paid for; if so, you got served; if not, nothing doing. A sign over one bar read, "No jawbone taken for service." The free lunches shrank up to a few dusty crackers and rat cheese, kept back out of reach, and passed out only after a drink was bought and paid for. The house now never "set 'em up"; you had to lose about fifty bucks at the games in order to get one on the house. All the roulette wheels but one were shoved to one side and covered with a brown canvas, like a shroud. The green broadcloth on the craps table was dirty and snagged in places; repaired in other places with a dirty piece, glued on. Evenings a few miners with jobs might enter and play solo for the drinks under a dim light grudgingly furnished by the house. Habitual loafers were always about hoping to cadge a drink.

The "red-light" district became indescribably bedraggled and unkempt, especially as the hard, bright sunlight showed it up. Most of the houses and cribs were empty and windowless, the dance halls closed. Victor Ajax was busted again and his Cafe Parisienne closed. The only women left were a scattering of slatterns without money enough to leave; they were doomed probably to end their days in Goldfield either through hardship and destitution, or suicide.

The sun beat down hotly at noon; it shone on a different town; petulance and the curses of frustrated men and women greeted the dawn. And the wind—it blew in the same old way, but now it lacerated the nerves of a chastened people and became an irritating and monotonous nuisance. The dust that it swirled about, and transported from one end of town to the other and back again, suddenly became noticeable and was now rated as almost unendurable. Society folded; Goldfield women had to give up the book on etiquette for the cookbook, the evening gown for the bungalow apron, the piano for the carpet sweeper. Potential statesmen blew up like punctured balloons; the desert air dried up their vocal chords with the vanishing of auditors; frock coats became cloaks only for ragged shirts, or to cover pants out at the seat.

Frantic efforts were made to revive the boom. The town of Rawhide* furnished a momentary flare that was nursed in the hope that it might become a conflagration. It was born of some small, rich pockets of gold ore; it grew magnificently from the hegira of people leaving Goldfield and Tonopah; from the hobos kicked off Southern Pacific trains at Hazen; from bums from other scattered settlements of the area; and by a few badly bent promoters who still had a little money or credit for a last despairing call on the public purse. The gold didn't last very long and the public proved unable, or unwilling, to crash forth with money in support of stocks that had no dissimilarity from the ones that so recently had buncoed them.

Charley Gates, son of "Bet a Million" Gates, and a party of Eastern friends visited Rawhide under the auspices of a group of owners of properties who were eager to unload. Charley was willing to buy a little something if that was the only way to get a bit of amusement. This, however, was furnished to him by the grand opening of a new saloon and gambling house—much better than the purchase of a mine prospect. He "set 'em up" to the whole town and, when the proprietor got annoyed by the boisterous behavior of the crowds and the general rough character of the proceedings, and made objections, Charley asked him to put a price on the place. He did so, and made an immediate sale. When Rawhide blew

* See Plate XVII.

up shortly thereafter it is to be hoped this man gave thanks to his good fortune in getting out with a small profit. Charley Gates had the liquor served out as long as it lasted; first come, first served. Champagne was poured out into a large, galvanized tub with ice in it, and dipped out with tin cups. Quite a party!

Elinor Glyn visited Rawhide and gave it some good notices and free advertising—too late to help it, however—in her book *Elizabeth Visits America.* Her *Three Weeks* was a best seller at this time so that made her a VIP out in the Nevada wilds, worthy of special entertainment. A series of wild West episodes were rigged up for her—a midnight holdup of the hotel which sheltered her; a shooting affair in a saloon, in which a couple of men were "killed" with lots of catsup gore. She was thrilled no end and the episodes were faithfully reported in her book.

Nat Goodwin and George Graham Rice spread Rawhide's name across the continent in lurid, gummy, flamboyant advertising. This only brought jail for Rice; a near-indictment and loss of considerable money for Nat, who proved himself the prize sucker of them all.

A song then current was "School Days." The chorus was paraphrased by some unknown wit of Rawhide, giving an admirable picture of the final condition of the place. It almost fitted Goldfield, except that the mines in Goldfield did produce profitably for some years more. It ran thus:

> Rawhide, Rawhide, poor old busted Rawhide;
> I been workin' and diggin' like hell for gold,
> With never a dollar in sight—I'm sold!
> Scotty was there and so was I,
> I'll dig and starve there till I die;
> And all men will say, as I die with the itch,
> The poor, busted sonofabitch!

Sic transit gloria!

## CHAPTER TWENTY - FOUR

ADIOS GOLDFIELD

A Damn Good Wagon but She Done Broke Down!

WITH THE completion of the organization details of the Goldfield Consolidated Mining Company, and its listing on the New York Stock Exchange, there remained nothing more to be done, legally, except to attend to the dismissal of the various lawsuits settled by the merger. So Governor Thomas returned to Denver. I followed him there a few months later because I was able to see that the life of the mines would not be long and thus I would have no great future by remaining with the company.

A part of my work before I left was to make a detailed examination of the underground workings of the Mohawk leases to provide a basis for later damage suits for the failure of the lessees to comply with convenants for proper roof support of the leased premises. During the last two weeks of the lease terms, lessees worked around the clock to get out all ore possible, and they failed to put in any timbering at all. One lessee remarked that so far as he was concerned, the last man out of the shaft at shutdown time could get his foot caught in the cave-in.

Jock Finney and I made the survey of the workings; we took flashlight photographs* to use as evidence of the neglect of the lessees. It was a wild and harrowing experience; timbers broken and squeezed, slabs of roof rock peeling and falling, and the constant sound of timber everywhere giving way as the heavy ground pushed steadily and inexorably on the few remaining supports. We

---

* See Plate XV.

completed the job in a week of work—and I never want another one like it. Suits aggregating several hundred thousand dollars were filed against the two principal lessees—Hayes & Monette and Frances Mohawk Mining Company.

The Democratic National Convention was held in Denver in 1908. Governor Thomas, as usual, was a member of the Committee on Resolutions. Bryan again was in the driver's seat and succeeded in getting Governor Haskell, of Oklahoma, made chairman of this committee to aid him in putting in the platform his own pet plank —this time it was to be the "trust problem." Bryan proposed to treat it mathematically—any corporation having 50 per cent or more of production in its line of industry automatically was to be "busted."

Governor Thomas spoke his opinion, saying that no more ridiculous or impracticable proposition could have been evolved by the wit of man. Fully three quarters of the committee agreed with him and, when Bryan learned of this, he served notice that he would cause a minority report to be made and move its adoption instead of the majority report. This would split the convention wide open and the move probably would succeed. So the majority gave in, but each member of it recorded his protest against conditions requiring self-stultification, if complied with without reservation.

Governor Thomas remarked during the tumult caused by the Bryan ultimatum that if "the Heavenly Father should offer a prize for the worst damn fools of record, Democrats would win it by acclamation."

Governor Hughes, of New York, made a speech in Youngstown, Ohio, which completely demolished the Bryan antitrust plank and paved the way for the election of Taft. Bryan then announced in the press that he would reply and smother Hughes "very shortly." However, up to the end of his life, Bryan never refuted Hughes nor made any effort to do so. Governor Thomas characterized the plank as a "brain storm the like of which was never equaled, even by old Wouter van Twiller who evolved a system for administering justice by weighing the documents of plaintiff and defendant and awarding the verdict to the heaviest side."

The Colorado state convention nominated John Shafroth for governor, with a strong supporting ticket, and he was elected handily despite the Bryan debacle. Under Shafroth the primary system of party nomination and the initiative and referendum were adopted. Governor Thomas espoused this cause and supported it at first because these measures seemed to afford the only escape from a situation which had become intolerable. The notorious subserviency of the General Assembly to the combinations of business and labor, and the complete domination of the machine over party policies and nominees, made resort to other methods necessary. Those advocating this reform assumed that the people, given an opportunity to exercise their authority, would avail themselves of it; but without considering that they could have done so before if they would. But the substitution of the primary for the convention has only revealed the unpleasant fact that the faults and defects of free government are due not to systems, but to the people themselves, and that those who make politics their business will manage to control affairs political, whatever the system, so long as the people permit them to do so. And the plea that the primary offers opportunity to ambitious but poor aspirants for office is the grimmest of all political farces. The cost of a primary campaign is, relatively, very great, and it becomes greater as population increases.

Governor Thomas, after a ten-year trial of these changes, stated: "I do not think these innovations will ever be displaced, nevertheless I regret that I advocated them and aided in securing them."

During 1909 I returned to Goldfield with my father for a brief spell—he to lead the trial of the damage suits against the Mohawk lessees and I to furnish expert technical testimony in support of the complaints. The suits were fought with vigor but we won them handily, and heavy damages were awarded our client.

Goldfield had settled down to a humdrum existence based on a steady operation of the few good mines there. To us, it was not the same place it used to be by far, and we left again at the conclusion of the trials with no regrets.

## CHAPTER TWENTY - FIVE

U. S. SENATOR FROM COLORADO
Charley Thomas Makes It

IN JANUARY, 1909, Charles J. Hughes was chosen United States Senator from Colorado, to succeed Henry M. Teller. Hughes came from Missouri in 1880 and quickly demonstrated great ability as a lawyer. He and Governor Thomas were often engaged as associates or opponents in most of the important mining controversies in the West, particularly in Colorado and Montana. As time passed the two men grew accustomed to differing temperaments, tendencies, and opinions, and they became very good friends. When, in 1901, Governor Thomas aspired to the Senate, Hughes and his friends favored his candidacy and worked for his success. He appreciated it and therefore he willingly reciprocated in 1908 and was pleased to be able to contribute materially to the success which Hughes attained.

Hughes was a man of ripe culture and surpassing abilities, a powerful advocate and possessed of courage and conviction. Unfortunately for Colorado, he did not long survive his election, but died in January, 1911.

The General Assembly was then in session and the choice of Hughes's successor became a hot topic of interest. Mayor Speer, of Denver, was eager for the place and had control of a strong city machine. Nevertheless, Governor Thomas decided to enter the lists. Thomas had excoriated the Assembly several times for the abandonment of party pledges and he, with some others, had revolted against the local ticket in 1910, so he was *persona non grata* to many of the members of the General Assembly.

Mayor Speer sought and obtained a conference with him regarding his own candidacy. He said that he wished to round out his career with a seat in the Senate and that he felt, with Thomas's assistance, he could do so. He told of pledges he had from members of the Assembly, with only a few lacking to give him the election, and said that he thought Thomas might aid him in securing what he needed.

Thomas then told him he was himself a candidate, and asked him for support, telling him he could not be both mayor of Denver and senator and, to resign as mayor would give over the city to the Republicans. Governor Thomas added that he considered his claim on the party for the place was superior to his own. At this the conference ended abruptly.

The Assembly was deadlocked when adjournment came. Speer reluctantly gave such aid as he could to Governor Thomas, and Gerald Hughes, son of the late Senator Charles J. Hughes, labored mightily for him but, because of the Thomas stand for free trade and reduction of the tariff on sugar, the Boettcher interests worked mightily to prevent his choice. In January, 1913, the new Assembly gathered in session, with Governor Thomas holding the pledges of sufficient votes for election, but a new contest was started by the Boettcher interests in which a determined effort was made to obtain sufficient legislators to violate their pledges and throw the election to a "dark horse" of Boettcher choosing. One of the leaders in this contest was State Senator Hume Lewis, himself under pledge for Governor Thomas. The attempt failed and, before the month of January had passed away, Governor Thomas became United States Senator from Colorado.

In February, 1911, Governor Thomas was in New York at the invitation of the National Woman's Suffrage Association. While there he took occasion to seek a meeting with Woodrow Wilson, in New York at the same time. This meeting took place with great cordiality on both sides. He told Wilson that Western Democracy was seeking a man of his type and would like the opportunity for coming more closely in contact with him. He replied that visions of the Presidency were alluring, but that just then they were not rosy as he had broken with the New Jersey machine and it threatened him with a hostile delegation from that state. Tammany, he thought, was inevitably against him, Bryan doubtful, Champ Clark a probable popular choice, while the so-called Cleveland branch of the party was unfriendly and apparently favorable to Governor Harmon of Ohio. He asked the views of Governor Thomas.

He was told, in substance, that the Rocky Mountain West was friendly to Clark and, as a consequence, Bryan would be for someone else, including himself; that Bryan would not support Harmon and would not favor Underwood, hence he (Wilson) would have a chance for Bryan's favor, though a remote one. Wilson told him that he thought his previous criticisms of Bryan probably had alienated him. He (Thomas) went on to tell him that he could not rely on the delegation from Colorado as it was split evenly between Clark and Harmon, but by pitting them bitterly against each other the chances for a Wilson compromise might be fair. He went to to suggest that Governor Wilson make a visit to Colorado and the Pacific West, assuring him of a rousing welcome and much good publicity in Denver. This talk resulted in Wilson falling in with the idea and promising a visit in May.

This trip was an immense success. It was arranged for Wilson to address a very large audience at the Denver Auditorium in celebration of the tercentenary of the King James Version of the Bible and adroitly he was to bring in his availability for the Presidential nomination.

Governor Thomas arranged a number of private lunch and dinner meetings, one of them at his own house, during which Governor Wilson could meet and talk intimately with influential party men. He went on to the Pacific coast, Governor Thomas accompanying him, and there he had equal success. It is more than likely that this jaunt had much to do with his ultimate attainment of support by delegations from the Western States.

The Baltimore Convention of 1912, at which Woodrow Wilson gained the Presidential nomination, was historic in respect of the tumult and the number of ballots it required to secure a candidate. Governor Thomas has recorded some comments on the Champ Clark phase of it that are of interest.

> Champ Clark's defeat after recording a majority of the vote broke his heart. I knew him well since 1892. After this defeat he became morose, absent-minded, indifferent to the ordinary amenities and mournfully conscious of the fact that his star had set. Personally, I rejoiced that Wilson was the nominee but I wish the result could have been accomplished otherwise than through the unpardonable treachery of a party leader, instructed by his constituency to support Clark and therefore duty-bound to obey orders. Mr. Bryan knows that his flouting of his instructions was not a preference for Mr. Wilson, nor yet because Clark stood condemned by the support of Tammany Hall; Mr. Bryan hoped, by assassinating Clark to secure the prize himself.

Senator Thomas became quite bald early in life. He was very sensitive to the cold air of winter on his head, and a year or two before he went to the Senate, he took to wearing a toupee during the winter months to protect his bare scalp from cold draughts. When the warm days of spring came he discarded it, to be put away in moth balls until winter should come again.

He was sworn into the Senate in January, 1913, wearing his toupee and, apparently, endowed with a fine, full head of hair. With the arrival of the first warm days of April he put away his toupee one morning and walked as usual to the Hill to attend a session of the Senate. The Sergeant-at-Arms barred him at the door of the Chamber —would not let him pass.

"But, my friend, I have a right here. I am Senator Thomas of Colorado."

"Oh, no, sir, you couldn't be. Senator Thomas has a wonderful head of hair!"

Senator Shafroth, his colleague from Colorado, came along just then and explained to the guard. Later that day, he was observed at his desk in the Chamber by Senator James (Jim Ham) Lewis, of Illinois. Senator Lewis asked for the floor, got it, and begged the assembly to take note of a phenomenon that was on a parallel with the first robin, bobbing over the grass; the first stirring of life in the roots of the trees and the rising of the sap in them. He spoke for a few minutes, aided and abetted by three or four more Senators; then the Senate got down to business again.

Until he left the Senate, each fall, when the toupee first appeared; and each spring, when first it disappeared, the Senate put aside other business to hail the advent of the seasons, never again officially at hand until Senator Thomas wore or discarded his head adornment.

His induction into the Senate was nearly two months prior to the inauguration of President Wilson. Very soon he was to suffer the first of many delusions he had regarding the purity of the motives of most of his colleagues, and even of the integrity of the President himself, where political expediency clashed with proper and straightforward action.

Firstly, he made a speech against an item in the appropriation bill for Public Grounds and Buildings. This item was eighty thousand dollars for the purchase of a building at Sundance, Wyoming, a town of less than two hundred people. In the cloakroom he was solemnly warned by several Senators of the unwisdom of opposing appropriation bills; he was told the people want money to be expended among them and, this being the case, he might head himself for unpopularity with his colleagues if he continued the practice.

Shortly after this, the Clayton Antitrust Act came before the Senate. In this matter, to his disgust, he noted President Wilson eagerly second the demand of Mr. Samuel Gompers for the exclusion of labor unions from the effect of the bill and, to compound this political expediency, the President went on actively to encourage the grouping of Federal employees in labor unions affiliated with Mr. Gompers' A.F. of L.

He was disillusioned by such revelations, but he determined, nevertheless, to persist in his attitude, despite the certain collision with the forces advocating one thing and taking action on another. He felt he could not be, at one and the same time, against these forces and in favor of them. President Taft had just vetoed a bill prohibiting certain appropriated moneys to be used to prosecute labor organizations for violations of the Sherman Antitrust Act. These provisions were incorporated in the new Clayton Act and he and Senator [Secretary?] Ballinger moved to eliminate them. The motion was beaten, with many rabid antimonopoly senators voting against it. Of course he soon alienated the political friendship of the labor interests, but he felt keenly that monopoly of every sort should be subject to the laws.

Senator Thomas was greatly disturbed when President Wilson made Mr. Bryan his Secretary of State and he was still more disturbed when he observed the apparent influence the new Secretary had over the President. He attributed this latter condition to the vigorous persistence of Bryan, whose determination was always stimulated in proportion to the grotesqueness of his purpose. When his resignation finally came it was a relief to him. It came about when President Wilson demanded that Germany disavow the sinking of the SS *Arabic*, the facts having been related to him later by Secretary Garrison.

The note to Germany, prepared by the President, was discussed at a full Cabinet meeting, and was unanimously approved. The President then said it would be delivered to Ambassador von Bernstorff the following morning. Secretary Garrison, as the Cabinet was about to adjourn, remarked that everybody seemed most unconcerned over the fact that they had just agreed to declare war on Germany. Bryan at once became alert and asked what he meant. Secretary Lane replied that the *Arabic* note meant war unless Germany yielded to its demands, which she would not do, in his opinion. Bryan then became much agitated and said if that were true the note should be held up and reconsidered the next day. This request was granted.

The following day Mr. Bryan wrote the President, suggesting two or three modifications of the peremptory clauses of the note, greatly altering its tone, and practically shearing it of its sharp nature. He told the President that unless his modification was adopted he no longer could remain in the Cabinet and, therefore, he enclosed his resignation, to be accepted in case his suggestions were not adopted.

Thereupon, to Mr. Bryan's consternation, the President accepted both his suggestions and the resignation. At the next Cabinet meeting, unattended by Bryan, his letter and the new draft of the German note were read, and these the Cabinet approved. The resignation was then referred to, the President announcing that he was accepting it, and suggesting that Mr. Bryan be sent for to inform him about the meeting. This was done and, after the usual regrets had been expressed, the meeting adjourned and the matter was given to the press. Mr. Bryan found that he had ridden roughshod once too often; that he had been duped by the President was brutally obvious.

In this affair it must be conceded that Bryan's conduct was vastly superior to that of Mr. Wilson; the action of the latter being indefensible from any standpoint. Its duplicity was perilously near the line of dishonesty. It can be explained only by an assumption that Mr. Wilson wished to get rid of Mr. Bryan and probably felt it was easier for him, and less offensive to Bryan, to act upon his counsel and let him out than to reject his counsel and accept his dismissal. One thing there can be no doubt about; the whole country drew a long breath of relief when it read the news that he had resigned.

In the organization of the Senate in 1913, Senator Thomas was assigned to the Finance, Military Affairs, and Foreign Relations committees. He also was chairman of the Committee for Interoceanic Canals, an assignment that required no work to speak of but which entitled him to another secretary and additional allowances for stationery, telegraph service, and other perquisites. However, his membership in the first three committees named was to result in a great deal of very arduous work, especially when the United States became involved in the war in Europe. He always took his work seriously and he made no exception in respect of the Senate's business.

Hard work was occasionally relieved by a bit of horseplay. One day Senator Thomas described a meeting of a subcommittee of the Finance Committee. He and Senators Stone (Missouri) and James (Kentucky) were the members of this subcommittee which had charge of the earthen, metal, and free-list schedules of the Underwood tariff bill then under discussion. The three Senators separated about 5:00 P.M. with an understanding to return at eight and work until ten. He and James met promptly at eight, but Stone was late. They waited patiently until 8:30 for him and then Senator Thomas proposed they arrange a surprise for Stone and suggested that they tell him that they had gone ahead without waiting for him and had determined that a duty of 25 per cent ad valorem should be placed on all Bibles valued at more than $2.50, thus rating the more expensive ones as luxuries. James was agreeable so, when Stone came in a little after nine with profuse apologies and expressing the hope that they had gone ahead without him, Senator Thomas told him they had done so, and told him about the taxing of the Bibles. Stone asked James if he had agreed to do this and James replied that he had done so. Stone remained silent a moment, then said:

"Well, gentlemen, in a body of three men the vote of two of them constitutes a two-thirds majority. Therefore, I cannot hope to change the result, but I'll be God damned if I'll ever vote to put a tax on the Word of God!"

So Senator Thomas told him he was surprised to find that he felt so strongly on the subject and, most solemnly, offered a motion to reconsider. Put to a vote, the motion was carried solemnly without a dissenting vote.

The Federal Reserve Act was the work of the Finance Committee of this Congress. This act was drafted by Senator Glass, but the credit for its adoption must go largely to Senator Robert L. Owen, then chairman of the Committee on Banking and Currency, aided by Senators Hoke Smith, Pomerene, and Weeks. The act, when the European War started, saved the country from a most disastrous panic; under its provisions the Secretary of the Treasury was empowered to provide currency ample to care for any emergency. But for this the deluge of American securities held in Europe and thrown on the New York market would have closed all the banks. Secretary McAdoo was prompt to avail himself of this power and, even so, the Stock Exchange had to be closed for some time.

Senator Thomas saw only one danger to threaten the efficacy of the Federal Reserve Act—politics. He called attention to the fact that the President approved the act, providing for the placing of a dirt farmer (whatever that may be) upon the Board. In a speech on that subject he said that this would no doubt be followed by additional legislation to fill the Board up with a day laborer, a pill doctor, a country lawyer, an able seaman, a veterinary surgeon, a locomotive engineer and a typical pawnbroker, thus making the Board look like a Tammany caucus. Its course, when thus doctored to suit the clamors of a Congress skilled in the art of keeping ears to the ground, may be easily foreshadowed.

Senator Thomas refused to vote for the Clayton Anti-trust Act, although he attended two White House conferences and all the caucuses where it was considered. His objection to it was to the clauses exempting labor, agricultural, and horticultural organizations from its operation and this he publicly denounced as wholly indefensible. He felt strongly that if trusts and combinations are a bad thing for the public they should be checked and regulated, whether composed of bodies of industry, of banks, railroads, or labor unions, that laws in a free government must be general in their application; that laws creating exemptions are laws which create privilege and establish classes. Such laws as the latter impose severe penalties for their infraction by one part of the community, but expressly exclude another part from its penalties, thus encouraging the latter to create evils calling the law into being. He gave public expression to his reasons but the law, nevertheless, was passed easily.

The President favored the bill and even urged the exemptions to which Senator Thomas objected. He was a determined foe of the trust combinations but he could not (or would not) perceive that it was equally reprehensible in a large combination of laborers and farmers as of financiers or manufacturers, and that once such a principle was established, the battle against the system of monopoly was lost. It was thought that all contradictions and inconsistencies would disappear if Congress declared that labor was not a commodity; and this was done. What a pity it is that eternal verities, when they become embarrassing, cannot summarily be disposed of in such an easy and simple manner.

AMERICA GOES TO WAR IN
A BIG WAY

AT A SPECIAL session of Congress, called for April 17, 1917, and advanced to April 2, Senator Thomas joined his colleagues in a vote to declare "the existence of a state of war with Germany." Washington, overnight, changed tremendously; grounds of the White House were closed to visitors with a twenty-four-hour Marine guard patroling outside the iron fence; passes had to be obtained to visit any of the departments; temporary housing started up on parkways to care for the expansion of offices and help, and the Senate committees of Finance, Foreign Affairs, Military Affairs, and Navy Affairs, with Senator Thomas a member of the first three, began to receive a deluge of bills of all sorts, all considered urgent. In a letter to me he observed:

Men, women and even children filled the outer offices of Senators, seeking aid and influence for places in the rapidly enlarging bureaus and agencies; for positions, civil and military, across the sea; for exemptions from military service; for commissions in Army or Navy forces. They sought contracts for supplies; had schemes and devices for immunity from submarine attacks, for air defense and attack, for detecting enemy movements and the thwarting of them; for camouflage, for new types of guns, bombs, grenades, aircraft engines and explosives. They are merry days for us poor fellows, busy as hell with the many legislative tasks upon our shoulders! Our solicitous friends followed us into our committee rooms, waylaid us in the streets, telephoned our houses, rang our doorbells at all hours, wrote and wired us without cessation. The business of each one seems to be, in his eyes, the most momentous and all-important thing of the hour. We manage to live through it all and indeed to survive this ordeal of several months, but may the Lord deliver me from any like experience. Every soul whose request has been denied, or whose invention has been rejected, or even questioned, has become an embittered critic or opponent of the Administration; while the particular official passing on the project is characterized as prejudiced, ignorant, or a secret agent of the enemy. Many times he is declared to be all three.

In early summer of 1918, Secretary of War Newton D. Baker set up a custom under which he received members of the Committee on Military Affairs every Saturday morning in the rooms of General Peyton C. March, Chief of Staff. There, with charts on the walls provided by General March, many of the phases of the war and the preparations for personnel, weapons, housing, and transport were threshed out informally. It was most helpful for the work of the committee during the rest of the week, and Senator Thomas made a practice of attending this session regularly. He fretted a great deal about the slow motion of most of the branches of procurement and construction and, by January, 1918, he began to take a specific interest in aviation procurement. At his insistence the committee began an inquiry into it early in March.

The air forces then were under General Squier, head of the Army Signal Corps. Howard Coffin, of Hudson Motor Company, with Colonel Deeds, of Dayton, Ohio, as deputy, was at the head of the construction section. The Congress had appropriated over $600,000,000 for aircraft motors; the Liberty engine had been designed, tested, and pronounced perfect. Mr. Coffin had contributed an article to the *Saturday Evening Post* entitled "Ten Thousand Cavalrymen of the Air." Both General Squier and Mr. Coffin entertained the committee with detailed accounts of the remarkable progress made in the production of planes and motors, including machine guns, cameras, compasses, and all the essential paraphernalia required. They even gave out the number of motors and airframes to be completed that month, and they declared that America would have, on the coming first of July, 1918, 2,500 fighting and bombing planes assembled and ready for action at the French Front, and that they had so notified General Pershing.

A few nights after this bouyant meeting, Senator Weeks attended a dinner at which Mr. Gifford, the capable secretary of the War Industries Board, was a fellow guest, sitting opposite him at the table. Senator Weeks, in conversation, told the guests about the wonderful progress of the air service construction, but he hadn't proceeded very far when Mr. Gifford caught his eye and shook his head ominously. Senator Weeks deftly turned the conversation and, after dinner, he took Mr. Gifford aside and asked him why he dissented from his remarks about airplane procurement. Mr. Gifford told him he wanted to spare him future embarrassment, because he knew the condition of the aviation section could not be in worse condition; that if he (Weeks) would go to his office the next morning he would give him the cold and dismal facts from the files of the War Industries Board.

Senator Weeks was promptly on hand in the morning. The daily records from all over the country were produced; there was no "guesstimate" in them. No planes even in sight; nothing but experimental work being done. French and British plane models, approved by the Advisory Board on Aeronautics, were being revised continually by the engineers of the companies with contracts, until the originals which were in service in France had long been lost in complicated changes. On the Bristol fighter, for example, over 1,500 changes in its design had been made, some of them after production had started. All this had been done to a proved and tested plane, daily being flown in combat. A British model had been substituted for the French Spad after contracts to build the Spad had been partly performed on material and parts. The Italian models, with their staffs of experts and engineers, had been shunted off to Mineola to vegetate—an inexplicable performance—as the Italian planes were the best of the lot.

Senator Weeks very promptly imparted this information to the Committee in executive session. Mr. Gifford attended also with all his data. To make the picture complete, Mr. Gifford produced a letter from Mr. Coffin addressed to him in which he acknowledged he had misled the committee, excusing himself with the plea that he had allowed himself to become over-optimistic. Mr. Gifford's revelations were paralyzing; he warned that instead of having 2,500 planes in France in July we would be lucky to have fifty. It was necessary to notify General Pershing and our allies that our air program was as elusive and invisible as the air itself. It was needful as well to notify the President, who was also riding on a rosy cloud.

Senator Chamberlain, chairman of the committee, was the proper one to give this notification but, as he had quarreled with the President, he would have none of it. Next on the committee was Senator Hitchcock, but his strictures upon certain contractors and officials had displeased Mr. Wilson, so he declined the "honor." Third and fourth in line were Senators Fletcher and Myers, but these two men headed other committees which kept them too busy for the meetings of the Military Affairs Committee. So, as fifth in line, Senator Thomas was chosen to be the "goat" as bearer of ill tidings to the President.

He at once called the Executive Offices and informed Mr. Tumulty that the committee had a most important communication for the President which must be made to him in person and that an early appointment was necessary. He waited on the phone while Tumulty conferred with the President, then was informed that Mr. Wilson's engagements covered every minute of the next four hours and therefore he couldn't see him at once unless the news he had was of the utmost importance. He replied that nothing could be more important. After another wait he was told Mr. Wilson would see him at his dinner hour for fifteen minutes at 7:30 P.M. At that time the President appeared promptly and greeted him with an air of ill-concealed impatience.

Senator Thomas told the President as briefly as possible all that had developed from the Gifford figures on the progress of airplane procurement. Mr. Wilson listened patiently but with patent incredulity. On conclusion of the relation he said, very bluntly, that the committee was too credulous; he had himself gone over the matter with Mr. Coffin, in whom he had full confidence. Senator Thomas then handed him the letter from Mr. Coffin to Mr. Gifford. As he read it the color began to leave his face; he finished it convinced that the bad news he had received was true after all. He then asked many questions and the fifteen-minute interview stretched out for an hour and a half. It was then that Senator Thomas suggested measures to speed up procurement, as previously covered herein.*

The War Department did not take kindly to the aircraft activities of the committee, nor to the personnel reorganization by the President. It showed its opposition by primed releases through the Bureau of Intelligence, under the direction of Mr. George Creel. This bureau was designed to secure, systemize, and distribute (or suppress) information during the hostilities as public welfare might require. But, unfortunately for it and for the public, under Creel, who was operating on his own with no one to hold the check rein on him, discretion was cast aside and, if facts obstructed his purpose or theory, so much the worse for the facts.

Primed by Army "brass," Creel saw the need for neutralizing the public wrath, if possible, when the collapse of aircraft procurement should come into the open, and he set out to forestall it by challenging the facts. He announced these facts were both exaggerated by German sympathizers and were engendered by apprehensions of

---

* See pp. 89, 90, 91.

the timid and ignorant. He followed this with pictures illustrating production in the factories of contractors. Among them was a photograph showing a large store of planes in a manufacturer's warehouse; it was captioned, "Planes actually completed and ready for shipment to the Front." This fictional caption conveyed the impression that the planes were combat materiel. But the fraud was too coarse to succeed. The photograph was made of a number of rudimentary, or Penguin planes, not even capable of flying, but designed for elementary training of pilots.

Creel was called before the committe but sent an aide instead of appearing himself, a young Russian named Strunsky. This man knew only that the Signal Service had furnished the photographs; he didn't know who wrote the captions. Blame for the fraud was placed squarely on the Bureau of Intelligence; Strunsky was either fired, or transferred, but despite the perversion of truth, Creel's tenure and control were not disturbed. The War Department claimed the episode was not important, and considered the pictures as not especially misleading. This raised the wrath of Senator Reed (Missouri), who asked the War Secretary (Baker) how long he proposed to permit "that licensed liar" to impose upon and deceive the public.

In May, 1918, the Committee on Military Affairs appointed a subcommittee of five—Senator Thomas as chairman, with Senators Reed, Smith, New, and Frelinghuysen. Paralleling the work of this subcommittee, the President ran an investigation of his own under the leadership of Judge Charles E. Hughes. The two committees got together and dovetailed their work, Hughes confining himself to legal and contractual phases while the Senate subcommittee dug into the production end and the causes of the inefficiency so painfully evident.

The committee ranged far and wide, traveling to all centers of production for aircraft and motors; they took reams of testimony for the record and, while they found appalling conditions in some of the production, their work was valuable in the reinvigoration of the program.

Senator Thomas said that the most difficult part of the investigation was to overcome the infatuation of the designers and manufacturers of the Liberty motor. Their idea was that this development was perfect from its inception and therefore further improvement was impossible. They turned a deaf ear to all criticism of the engine and to all suggestions of changes, although for the most part these criticisms came from the pilots and instructors who had to handle them in the air. At Wilbur Wright Field, pilots and mechanics appeared before the subcommittee and related these troubles and said that their requests for improvements had not only been ignored, for the most part, but had been received with ill-concealed disapprobation.

As a member of the committees on Military Affairs and Foreign Relations, Senator Thomas had the opportunity for meeting and talking with many of the great and near great of the Allied nations who visited the country during the war on "missions and commissions." One of these was Admiral Jellicoe, who came to the committee rooms unannounced, and in company with Vice-President Marshall. The British Commission, headed by Balfour, was another visitor to the committee, and later Senator Thomas was able to have a long chat with him at a reception given by Senator Saulsbury. He told him that he and the people of Colorado felt an unusual interest in him because of his advocacy of bimetallism; that if he would but go to Colorado he could guarantee him a hearty reception. He seemed much gratified but pleaded press of business as an excuse for not making the trip. Senator Thomas described him as "stately; every inch a Briton, speaking like one, very deliberately, very monotonously, each sentence perfect in itself and all of them uttered without inflection or fervor."

The big event of this sort, however, was the visit of General Joffre and René Raphaël Viviani. Senator Thomas described the two men: "Gen. Joffre was not the ideal type of a hero—a big beery sort of man, more German in physique than French; red face, white mustache and bull neck. Viviani, more perfect in figure, tall, graceful, eloquent, addressed us. But 'Papa' Joffre was the man we looked at, even when applauding Viviani. We finally forced him to his feet and he said, 'Senators, I no spik ze Engleesh. *Vive les États Unis!*' and with that we had to be content."

Members of the committee had to put up with all sorts of annoyance from the importunities of inventors. They thronged the anterooms of the committee at all times. Mostly they were made up of a cross section of the partly sane partly nutty segment of the population. An occasional good idea would be advanced, and these were exploited, but for the most part they were fantastic and chimerical. None could be rejected, however, without mortal offense, in which case they would go from the committee rooms to those of the House, and from the House to the newspapers with strictures on the ignorance and dishonesty of their public servants.

## CHAPTER TWENTY-SEVEN

THE WAR IS OVER

Peace Treaty and League of Nations

AS A MEMBER of the Senate Finance Committee, Senator Thomas was active in the drafting of the Revenue Act of 1918. It may be of interest to quote some of his notes with respect to this legislation because of his stand on matters that today have become acute and dangerous to an unorganized public.

The Committee was beseiged by all sorts and conditions of man, each possessed of some proposition pregnant with prospects of easy revenue, and all stimulated by the desire to impose the burdens of taxation upon the other man. It may be asserted that the individual motives of taxation, even though unexpressed, were so to frame the measure as to delude the taxpayers into the notion that the burden was so imposed as to fall chiefly upon the shoulders of great wealth. As camouflage, use of the term "profiteer" was most effective. While there were a few profiteers in the strict sense of the term, as there always will be, the great mass of those engaged in war production were doing so legitimately and with profit suited only to times and conditions. On the other hand labor organizations did not hesitate to hold up industries pressed for time and for men; nay, the Government itself, and to force the hand of the employer without regard either to their duties as citizens exempted from active military service, or to the needs and exigencies of the Government. In one of their conventions they were exhorted to attune themselves "to the beautiful music of more," and the Labor Department not only backed men in their exorbitant demands, but frequently encouraged the making of them in the first instance. No man had more influence with the President than Mr. Samuel Gompers, and always he used it for furthering the demands of organized labor, however unconscionable it might be. Indeed, Mr. Wilson sided with Gompers in my effort to amend the Army Bill of 1918, by requiring that all men exempted from army service for their work on war production should have their exemption cancelled when demanding increased wages under a strike threat. Gompers said this was a reflection on organized labor and Mr. Wilson agreed with him. Neither of them challenged my assertion that the evil aimed at was an actual and increasing one.

So, in framing revenue legislation, we could take no note of the profiteer who worked with his hands, but we must spread the much dreaded appellation over the entire field of production and exchange. Some of us predicted consequences, now perceived to have been inevitable. For men pay taxes reluctantly and evade them wherever possible.

It is as true as gravitation that every charge against production or distribution is passed on. Hence the consumer, who resents every direct tax, bears his indirect burden, plus additions of overhead, with cheerful indifference in his ignorance, and persists in the continuance of the system, because he will not believe, much less admit, the consequences to himself. Plucking the goose by causing him as little pain as possible is thus reduced, not to an exact science perhaps, but to a successful system. I doubt if the supreme injustice of these methods of taxation will ever penetrate the heads of its victims. And if they do not, scientific taxation based on the essential principle of equitable distribution of the burden will never be anything more than a dream.

Senator Thomas, because of his deep and firm convictions regarding the inextricable fusion of the League of Nations into the Treaty of Peace with Germany, caused him to be one of the group in opposition to the President and the matter of its ratification. As a member of the Democratic party he was naturally expected by the President to support him in what he considered the greatest work of his life, and because of his inability to do so he was subjected to condemnation by the President, and to the abuse of those League enthusiasts, aptly described by Lowell in the Bigelow Papers:

> He couldn't see but jist one side;
> If his, 't was God's, and that was plenty.

Most of these enthusiasts never read the treaty but accepted the versions of its supporters and allowed emotions to dictate to reason. In his own words, the story of his opposition unfolds.

I must chronicle the fact, a consoling one, that the differences between Mr. Wilson and myself, so far as I was concerned, were entirely impersonal. He, on his part, never evinced any feeling towards me other than one of warm friendship, tinctured with regret that my obtuseness seemed impervious to argument and considerations which were, to him, convincing and persuasive.

* * *

Congress met on the first Monday of December, 1918. The next day the Republican members whispered that the President would name himself for the head of the delegation to the Peace Conference and go to Paris in that capacity. Democratic Senators had heard nothing of the sort, yet they did not feel safe in either affirming or denying the rumor; we had long been painfully conscious of the President's indisposition to confer with members of the Senate as had been his wont before the war.

Next day the rumor was confirmed by an article from the pen of David Lawrence, then the journalist spokesman for the administration. Our side of the Chamber was amazed and aghast. We felt instinctively that it was a blunder of the first magnitude; and the other side were of the same opinion if one might judge from their jubilant attitude when the fact was known. We, of course, could not censure our President, but in the cloakroom we could and did say what we thought about it, and we knew instinctively, and from news from home as well, that public opinion was against it.

Apart from the custom established by all his predecessors was the conviction that the President could not lawfully absent himself, even temporarily, from the country during his term of service. At El Paso, President Taft met President Diaz at the center of the International Bridge, and then crossed it for a hurried and formal call, and Diaz did likewise. President Roosevelt (Teddy) had visited Panama, but the Canal Zone was American territory. The country, moreover, sorely needed the Executive; there never was a time when all the agencies of the Government were more essential to the public welfare and the idea of a President, 3,000 miles away, with an ocean between him and his country, engrossed in the tremendous problems of a world's reconstruction, and thus disabled from the discharge of his equally imperative duties at home, was decidedly unpalatable. It was resented and properly so.

The day after the Congress assembled, Mr. Tumulty informed me that the President desired me to call upon him the next afternoon at 1 o'clock. I communicated this fact to Senator Martin, and discussed with one or two others the expediency of suggesting, if opportunity offered, the selection to the Peace Conference of a delegation composed of statesmen of both Parties, directed and controlled from the White House. I thus learned that other Senators had been requested, like myself, to see the President, but at other hours; indicating that no general conference was contemplated.

At the appointed time I went to the White House. The President met me in the Blue Room and, without any preliminaries, made a statement regarding his proposed journey to Paris. I cannot give his exact language; if I could do so, it would lack his fervor of expression; for he spoke with all the zeal of a convert to a crusade. But I think I can reproduce it in substance. He said:

"Senator, I have determined to acquaint some of my personal and political friends with the reasons which impel me to head the American Delegation to the Peace Conference, and to absent myself from the United States for an indefinite period. My action is without precedent; perhaps forbidden by the duties of the office which I hold, but not so, as my advisers assure me by the Constitution and the laws. If it were I would not go.

"This war, horrible and devastating beyond all other wars, has produced one far-reaching and beneficent result, which perhaps could have been reached in no other way. It has awakened the peoples of Europe to a lasting realization of the inadequacy and ineffectiveness of their methods of government, and to the need of permanent and far-reaching changes in these methods, if the scourge of war is to be avoided in the future. Governments are worse than failures if they do not secure justice, tranquility, protection, and a reasonable degree of happiness to the peoples which they rule and whose dependence upon them is absolute.

"These stricken peoples are now struggling slowly to their feet, at the end of the most terrible war in history. Its desolation has been superlative, and its destruction of life, of property, and of what we call civilization has been most extensive and almost universal. But it has taught the suffering nations a lesson which their peoples realize and, for the first time, understand. Their hearts have been purified and their minds clarified in the crucible of conflict and disaster. Their illusions have been cruelly but effectively dispelled. The scales have fallen from their vision and now they realize the vanity of racial prejudice and religious fanaticism; that national ambitions and resentments, the coveting of dominions, the practice of dissimulation, the crooked intricacies of diplomacy and the overreachings for trade, all lead inevitably to misunderstandings, to large standing armies, to huge navies, to burdensome taxation, to increasing animosities, to strange relations, to rupture, violence, and bloodshed. And all these things they want to repudiate and destroy utterly. They have discarded for all time those ignoble traits of human nature which degrade it, and which find expression in chicanery, overreaching jealousies, heartburning, envy and malice. They will have none of resentful memories and of revenge awaiting on opportunity for fulfillment. Their renovated governments, if they can accomplish it, shall be founded upon the broader and surer foundations of fraternity, equity, justice, and democracy; so that nations, like individuals, may recognize and apply those principles, not from sentiment, but from the obvious utilitarian considerations to nations as they have heretofore been related in theory, at least to individuals. This situation and determination is quite as apparent among the vanquished as among the victors.

"But the governing powers of the recently warring nations are still the Bourbons they always have been. The new dispensation has not penetrated the consciousness of the Kings, Presidents, and Premiers, whose authority, for the time being, has been strengthened by the war. Their view of European politics is precisely what it always has been. Tradition, balances of power, ambition, land hunger, national supremacy in politics and commerce, jealousy, rivalry in deception and intrigue, if these can have their way, will mark the events of Europe's future precisely as in the past. If the Allies thus resolved have their way, the aspirations and purposes of Europe's humanity will be stifled, the lessons of the war will go unheeded, the new Europe will be modeled upon the old. France will succeed Germany, Italy will succeed Austria, the old order will continue, wars will supervene, and their exasperated subjects, despairing of their emancipation from the inevitable consequences of reorganized greed and injustice, in their despair will be driven to revolt, imperiling all governments and menacing the existence of civilization.

"These peoples, now of one mind as to what the terms of peace and the constitutions of their new governments should be, are both unorganized and inarticulate. Someone must speak for them and speak with authority. Someone must translate their blood-baptized aspirations into definite and effectual terms of national and international understanding. Someone must read into the treaty settlements those new terms of policy and of government, or the war will have been fought in vain.

"Providence, or destiny, or both, have so shaped events that peace finds America the most potent and influential of nations. Her entrance into the conflict determined its results. Her resources alone were un-exhausted by the struggle. Her power as a fighting unit was tested, but hardly fully revealed; her purpose was clearly outlined and thoroughly understood. She has no demands upon the coming peace conference save those making for the welfare and benefit of all the nations; she wants and will accept neither territory nor reparations. She would be the friend of the small nations if her friendship were needed to secure justice or proper recognition: her disinterestedness and nobility of purpose, coupled with her power and incomparable prestige, would give her representatives a deserved preponderance at the council table of the nations, which should and would be exerted for the peace and well-being of all mankind.

"The exalted place thus occupied by our country at this crisis in world affairs finds me as its chief magistrate. The nation voiced its policies and made its declarations upon all matters of international concern through the Presidency. That great office has been vested, *ab initio,* with full control of foreign affairs. Not only the Republic, but all the nations, want for me to voice the national policy and then act to make it effective. Such a power carries with it corresponding responsibility. That policy, I am convinced, harmonizes fully with the needs, the aspirations and the demands of Europe's stricken millions. It might and probably will conflict with the purposes and ambitions, if not with the treaties and understandings of the Allied Powers.

"Providence having decreed that I should be at the head of affairs during this great emergency, I feel that it is my unavoidable duty to meet the responsibility whatever its personal consequences may be. I feel that not the least part of this responsibility is that which compels me to go to Paris and there voice the hopes and the desires of inarticulate Europe; the stricken people are imploring me to do so. They say, perhaps truly, that if I refuse they are forsaken, that if I deny them they are wholly abandoned. I cannot turn aside. I must go and trust to the future for my vindication and, I hope, for theirs."

Mr. Wilson made this statement like a man inspired. That he believed absolutely what he said was beyond all question. He spoke as an enthusiast; as a convert to a great cause; his eyes, at times, glistened with the fervor of a crusader. His emotions, at times, betrayed his extreme earnestness, and I knew, long before he finished, that my effort to change his purpose would be useless, if indeed it might not be misunderstood or, perhaps, resented. Nevertheless, I determined to give him my opinion and to urge him not to leave the country on that, or any other mission, especially at that time, and to give him my reasons therefor as fully as he would permit.

But upon the conclusion of his discourse he summarily revealed to me that I was there to listen and not to comment: much less to counsel; for he rose at once and extended his hand, with a "Good-bye, Senator; I am greatly obliged for the opportunity you have given me to tell you all this," and he was gone. I now knew his mind on the subject; he did not know and evidently did not care to know mine. My views, perhaps, were of no consequence, but since they were shared by the majority of my colleagues, I may give them.

I thought, and have never changed my mind about it, that the President could commit no greater mistake than to go to Paris as a treaty delegate. Apart from the very weighty reasons which should deter a President from leaving his country during his term of office, which I will not consider, was the inevitable result of such a step upon Mr. Wilson's influence and that of his country upon the Treaty Powers. He was at the head of the nation which should be, and but for his blunder, would have been the decisive factor in every dispute so certain to arise in the discussion of terms, conditions, limitations of territory, creation of new nations, etc. Wilson, as President, would have been the arbiter of the world's peace by virtue of a common consent based upon the recognition of power, coupled with capacity and disinterestedness by remaining at home.

One cannot, at the same time, be arbiter and advocate of any cause. If the arbiter voluntarily assumes the role of advocate, whatever the motive or the necessity, he abdicates *ipso facto* the FORMER ROLE. As an advocate he must take sides as to issues, if not as to contestants, and this brings him into a controversy-provoking opposition, arousing resentments, minimizing influences and creating, if not justifying, suspicions of motives, or prejudice and of ultimate purpose. All this did follow Mr. Wilson's course as he should have foreseen. He became personally involved in, and was personally praised or blamed for, every squabble and controversy precipitated upon the Conference by the selfish differences of the signatory powers; a condition emphasized, of course, by the ultimate concentration of all authority into the hands of four men, of whom he was one. And very naturally every challenge to his judgement, however exercised, was a challenge of the disinterestedness of the country he represented, not as President, but as a self-appointed delegate.

Moreover, he had to match himself against the most experienced and practical practicians of diplomatic intrigue of his generation; men thoroughly conversant with what they wanted to accomplish, or to prevent; men devoid of sentiment and versed in all the kaleidoscopic elements of human nature. Mr. Wilson had no training in this fascinating and conscienceless field of intellectual gymnastics. Moreover he was completely engrossed in his belief of the practicability of his Fourteen Points, one of which—Freedom of the Seas—he surrendered before the Peace Conference even convened, and in his conviction that human nature had been changed and exalted by the experiences of the war. Sentiment and emotion have little place at the council tables of diplomacy. McCauley [Thomas B. Macaulay] says the Catholic Church has always known just how to deal with the religious enthusiast; the diplomat long ago had learned the same lesson. It is not surprising, therefore, that the President—able, conscientious, and alert—at the end of the conference should have found himself stripped of all things substantial, retaining only a dead skeleton of the things he had envisioned so fondly.

Neither Senator Thomas, nor his colleagues of both parties in the Senate, thought much of the President's selection of his delegation. Aside from Secretary of State Robert Lansing, a "natural" because of his position, the rest of the delegation was made up of mediocrities. The Senate, particularly, always found Colonel Edward House an enigma in whom they could discover no reason for the President's great trust in him. The Republicans all felt that Colonel House had never given any indication of fitness for the position he occupied as a member of the delegation; they disavowed his selection as one of the Republican members and charged the President with choosing him because of his willingness to serve as cipher, do as he was bidden, and second whatever the President suggested. Senator Thomas, who had met Colonel House many times, has said he was inclined to agree with the Senate appraisal and that, whatever his (House's) abilities or personal opinions might have been, he certainly always acted the role of "me, too, Mr. Wilson" in all things having to do with the President.

The President returned to America early in March of 1919 for a brief visit. Prior to his return a draft of the "Constitution" of the League of Nations was sent to the Senate. At the time American sentiment was definitely in favor of such a league; no plan having been definitely outlined, no opposition had yet built up. The suggested "Constitution" was printed at once by the Senate as a

public document and a careful study of its details began.
Senator Thomas notes:

Very shortly after the arrival of the President, he invited members
of the Committee on Foreign Relations, including the same committee
of the House, to dine with him and discuss the League at length. The
dinner itself was a social event and no discussion took place until
afterwards. Many queries were then propounded to Mr. Wilson,
who replied to them promptly, though not always satisfactorily.

Upon three propositions the majority of the Committee was in-
sistent—the Monroe Doctrine, the right to withdraw from the League,
and Article X. The President asserted the principle of the Monroe
Doctrine not only was in the League but was extended to both hemis-
pheres; that the power to join the League included the power to withdraw; that Article X was essential to the League's success if it were
to be anything more than an association without effective sanctions.

He was reminded that the Monroe Doctrine ceased to be a dis-
tinctively American policy; if carried beyond the Western Hemisphere,
it committed the United States to an insistence upon its observation
everywhere, thus defeating that part of it which required us to abstain
from all participation in cis-Atlantic affairs; that acceptance of the
League, like acceptance by the States of the Federal Constitution,
would be final and could not be canceled or withdrawn; that the
guarantees of Article X place our country legally and morally behind
every member of the League whose status might be threatened or
imperiled.

I determined to play the role of a good listener, and did so, con-
tenting myself with a single question. The draft of the League
provided that if the tribunal, or commission given jurisdiction, of any
controversy or question arising between two or more members, should
be unable to agree unanimously as to its disposition, it should report
the fact to the Council with a statement outlining the points of disagreement. The draft being silent as to further proceedings, I asked
the President what the League would, or could, do with or concerning
such an impasse. He promptly answered, "Nothing." I then asked
what would become of the dispute and how the League could adjust
it. He replied that the blood of the disputants would cool by the
time such a report was made, and the public opinion of the world
would set itself against an appeal to arms. The answer was not assuring.

The President did not commit himself to any suggestion made
by members of the Committee, but the world knows that upon his
return to Europe the "Constitution" was rechristened the "Covenant,"
the Monroe Doctrine was expressly recognized as a "regional under-

standing," and the right of a member to withdraw after a specified period of time was expressly reserved.

The famous "Round Robin" of 38 Republican Senators, more than one third the total membership, virtually pledging the signers against the League principle, and designed to serve notice on the world that the Covenant would not be accepted, appeared within a fortnight of this dinner. The failure of the Allied Powers to give that document the importance its formidable character deserved was one of the amazing features of the Treaty Conference, especially in view of the conclusive authority of the Senate to ratify or reject treaties—a fact well known to them. Certainly the President treated it in an ill-advised and most unfortunate manner.

On the night of March 4th he addressed a large audience in New York City and stated that the Covenant of the League would be so interwoven into the body of the treaty that it could not be dissected without destroying both. This was properly interpreted by League opponents as a threat to cram the League down the throat of the Senate and force it to take the responsibility of rejecting the treaty "in solido" rather than accept the League in any form. Doubtless the President assumed the Senate would not dare to "call" him—but it did! He supplied his opponents with a weapon of attack more formidable than any of their own fashioning.

*   *   *

At the time I made the following note of the situation: "Mr. Wilson's speech may mean the doom of the treaty if he accomplishes what he has outlined. No League for peace which is made the instrument for enforcing the penalties of a victor's treaty, in my judgment, will receive the approval of public opinion. Such a contrivance inevitably will strengthen the hands of the Senate and justify its opposition."

About this time the dispatches began to inform us of the doings of the International Labor Commission of the Versailles Conference— a sort of side congress engaged in the preparation of a labor code to be incorporated into the treaty as an integral part of the League, and of which Mr. Gompers was chairman. As usual, Mr. Gompers and his associates were taking advantage of the opportunity for the furtherance of their own ends, to secure the establishment of a permanent International Bureau and Congress for Labor with the League, endowed with quasi legislative authority. It seemed to me to present problems quite as serious as, and in some respects, more important than those affecting the fundamental covenants; yet little, if any, attention was paid it by the press or the Senate. I kept in touch with it as closely as I could, and referred to the subject in March in a speech in Tremont Temple, Boston.

In May, the President sent a cable to Tumulty announcing the acceptance of the Labor program by the Plenary Council, and followed it with a fulsome adulation of accomplishment. Shortly afterwards the so-called program was published in *Current History,* together with the report of Gompers to the A.F. of L., and the remonstrance of the German commissioners because of its conservatism; also the reply of Premier Clemenceau to it.

From all this it appeared that the work of the Gompers commission had been incorporated into the text of the treaty as Part XIII. Part I constituted the League, proper. Since the Labor schedule was quite as much a part of the League, it should have followed it as Part II. The reasons for this have never been explained. It may not have occurred to the BIG FOUR, or to the draftsmen of the treaty or, it may have been done with the deliberate intent of diverting public attention from it as a part of the League—this was the effect, whether intended or not.

Gompers' report was largely apologetic and explanatory. He evidently was disappointed by what, to him, was the conservative character of Part XIII, but he assured his brethren that the camel had inserted his nose into the tent of internationalism and its body would, in time, follow the nose. The German commission protested that the draft of the Labor Report failed to invest the International Labor Conference with unconditional and unlimited powers of legislation as to all subjects affecting labor among the members of the League, and they demanded that the report be enlarged so as to accomplish this. Clemenceau replied that such was the ultimate goal of the movement, and that the suggestion of the Germans would be accepted ultimately by the members of the League but, for the present, all must content themselves with the modified legislative power conferred by the treaty upon the conference. Even this astounding assurance caused neither criticism nor attention in America. This was due, in Congress at least, to the fear of the members of the political power of the American Federation of Labor. No more signal illustration of the moral cowardice of our public men can be found.

Here was a movement of the most far-reaching and stupendous character, infringing upon the fundamentals of self-government and threatening a transfer of national and state jurisdiction over one of the mightiest subjects of present and future concern; a movement potentially allied with every demogogic suggestion of private benefit; possibly commanding influence tempted by the opportunity for political bargaining and which placed a seal upon the press and a gag upon the lips of the people's representatives through the mere inertia of its possibilities. Frankly, the press, partisan, pro- and anti-league, shied at or stepped over it lest its proponents be aroused to oppose what they respectively desired, while Senators, equally concerned and prone to regard their continuance in office as the *sine qua non* of their political activities, were in a nightmare of apprehension lest this ghost should walk.

To emphasize this attitude of obsequious respect for things political, and their pre-eminence over things national and international, the Committee on Foreign Relations, by its chairman, Senator Lodge, presented a resolution and asked for its immediate consideration.

This resolution, after expressing sympathy with Irish efforts for independence, requested the American delegates to the Peace Conference to use their best efforts for securing to the American representatives of the Irish Republic, a hearing in behalf of Irish Independence. Thus, the American Republican members of the committee, for partisan advantage, were willing to jeopardize the success of the peace conference by injecting into its deliberations a movement grossly offensive to one of our allies, and certain to disrupt it if successful— if, indeed, the mere bringing up of the proposal did not do so— while the Democratic members were afraid to oppose the resolution and thus jeopardize their share of the Irish vote!

In my judgment this was the smallest and most contemptible incident of the treaty debates. It was emphasized by the adoption of the resolution, Sen. Williams alone voting "nay." Unfortunately I was absent from the chamber at the time; I nevertheless referred to the resolution on the succeeding day and announced that my vote would have been nay if present. The only effect of my declaration was a storm of epithet and denunciation from the Irish-American press and organizations of Hibernian societies.

The resolution was ignored by Mr. Wilson as everybody knew it would be when it passed, and none better than Chairman Lodge. But his aim was accomplished. Abuse of Wilson formed the refrain of every Irish speech and every Irish meeting from thence forward. I think this was emphasized by the subsequent action of Democrats in the chamber who unwisely sought to neutralize the situation by a very crude and obvious counter legislative antidote. I will refer to this later.

Such was most of the business of the Senate until the President returned with his treaty early in July, 1919. He returned to a Senate with a hostile attitude that was sufficiently evident for him to be conscious of it. He laid his treaty before the Senate in a carefully prepared speech; he spoke resolutely and confidently, urging early ratification. The Senate was full and the galleries crowded and a considerable portion of his audience applauded him. All gave him respectful and undivided attention, but his appeal had no effect upon a single Senator. Senator Thomas resumes his story:

I did not commit myself for or against the treaty, despite questions in my mind of the wisdom of many features of it prior to its possession by the Senate. I then read it with care, critically and prayerfully several times. Then, and only then, did I find myself unable to give it my approval. I wanted to approve it if I could, for Mr. Wilson, the Democratic party and the country. Yet I felt that party politics should have no part or lot in the disposition of a document involving the destiny of nations and the peace of the world. Yet I knew its rejection would thrust it inevitably into the arena of the next campaign, thus belittling its vast importance and forcing its ultimate fate, by the count of ballots cast by voters knowing little and caring less about the consequence of their decision. And thus it was finally disposed of.

My analysis of Part XIII confirmed my first impressions of its character. Such a scheme has no place in a great peace treaty, a reflection which might well be carried to the entire scheme of the League. My complete views are in the *Congressional Record* and it is sufficient here to say this part sought to provide for the well-being of organized labor the world over by recognizing them as a distinct class, wherever found, and entitled to especial consideration. Hence it created an international nation, if I may use that word, composed of the organized units of labor; gave them a written constitution, a permanent administrative government and a legislature empowered to enact laws or covenants and recommend their adoption by member countries. It gave it also a large inquisitorial authority, made special provision for the determination of all questions or disputes arising under or about Part XIII. The members of the League assumed the burden of financing its activities without asserting any control over expenditures.

It would have been quite as proper and more in accord with justice and fair play to have devised similar bodies for the benefit of farmers, physicians, merchants, manufacturers, lawyers, engineers and radio broadcasters everywhere, thus giving all classes at least an equal chance in the race for class competition and class supremacy. I shall be greatly mistaken if the historian of the future does not put his finger upon Part XIII as the last expression of demagogery in international affairs and as made to order for the intrigues of international communism. If peace were possible only by the creation of a world class, endowed with especial powers of government and legislation, a state of war is much to be preferred; since such an institution, composed of labor, or of any other special class, carries the seeds of both national and international disintegration.

Only three Senators saw fit to discuss this part of the Treaty. Senator Fall, of New Mexico, and I attacked it on principle, fundamentally and in detail. Senator LaFollette assailed it because it failed to do full and adequate justice to the sacred cause of labor. Its dangers and defects were freely discussed in the cloakrooms, yet I am satisfied that if that part of the treaty constituted its only defect, the Senate would have tumbled over itself in its eagerness to accept it. We did, however, succeed in carrying a reservation applying to it.

Because of my strictures upon Part XIII I was the recipient of special attention from Gompers and all of his associates except Mr. Furuseth of the Seaman's Union, who also opposed Part XIII. I was arraigned as an aristocrat, the "enemy" of the laboring man, a traitor to the country and a pariah among my countrymen. The usual expletives, personal and otherwise, were showered down upon me through the mails.

Another part of the treaty where Mr. Wilson was outmanoeuvred by the slick Lloyd-George and the blustering Clemenceau lay in the imposition of reparations and indemnities upon the vanquished wholly indefinite as to amount, based on ability to pay as estimated and determined by the victors. Statesmanship may have been present at the Conference but the only skill it displayed there lay in becoming invisible and remaining so.

Early in 1920, I was approached by Senator Peter Gerry, of Rhode Island, who informed me that he, in collaboration with two other Democratic Senators, had prepared a reservation to the treaty which he intended offering the next morning. He proceeded to read it to me; it committed the government of the United States to the effort to secure for Ireland a hearing before the Executive Council of the League. If effective, it would become a reservation binding upon the country and, in case of our failure to accomplish its object, it might impair or avoid our ratification of the treaty. That, however, did not concern me; he (Gerry) was very anxious that I should not oppose his reservation, saying that if I could so assure him, it probably would be accepted without debate.

I asked him if his purpose was not to placate the Irish vote; very frankly he said yes, and that it was needed to offset the effect of the Lodge Resolution of the preceding summer. I told him that the practice on both sides of the chamber of making a world treaty

the football of Irish politics in America was disquieting and distaste-
ful; that I would oppose it, though without much hope of accom-
plishing its defeat. I endeavored to convince him that his purpose
was too transparent to succeed, even if his reservation might be
adopted, but he was obdurate about it and left me in an ill humor.

That afternoon Senator Lodge crossed the aisle and, seating himself beside me, asked if I knew what Senator Gerry had in mind. I
replied that I did, whereupon he asked me if I intended opposing it.
I countered by asking him if he intended opposing it openly. He
said he thought it should not be adopted and that he would vote
against it. I said to him, "Senator, I will oppose the reservation both
with voice and vote, but my opposition will count for little compared
with yours. I am in the minority, even in my own party. You now
are the leader of the majority and chairman of the Foreign Relations
Committee; therefore you are, or should be, the most powerful and
influential member of the Senate. If you will merely say that it is
unwise, or impolitic, or improper to pass the Gerry reservation, it
will be defeated. On the other hand, if you sit quiet, merely recording
your vote with the negative, nothing that I can say or do will affect
the result."

The only encouragement I received was that he would content
himself with voting against it. The next morning Senator Gerry
offered his reservation; it went over for a day, when he called it up.
At once I offered an amendment, including Korea, the Island of Yap,
the Philippines, Guam, etc., in its purposes. A Republican Senator,
Nelson of Minnesota, asked what object I sought to accomplish by
my amendment. My reply was that I wanted to ascertain whether
or not we had any Korean or Yap voters in the United States; that my
curiosity would be satisfied with the fate of the amendment; that
the only object of the original reservation was to tickle the Irish
vote, hence we might as well please the Koreans if there were any, by
making equal provision for them in the reservation. I say with grief,
but without disappointment, that I had no support from the floor.
When I yielded it, my amendment was rejected, and the Gerry reservation was adopted by a majority of two, Lodge voting in the negative.
He could have killed it by one word of disapproval.

Thus do statesmen and moulders of public opinion in America dis-
port themselves. I could not refrain from remarking to the chamber
when the vote had been recorded, that if there was any man or
woman in the United States who was deluded by the thought that
the Senate could pass on any public matter, great or small, without
dragging into it petty partisan politics, let him or her read the *Congressional Record* in the morning and be undeceived. The thought

occurred to me that I might be subjected to censure for my expressed views, and it was but little that I cared. But they took it, lying down.

This record has gone into the jockeying in the Senate over the handling of the treaty and its Siamese twin, the League of Nations, rather fully because our country now is suffering from the effects of the provisions of these documents, even though the United States did not ratify and was not a member of the League. The League was established just the same and became nothing better than a debating society, and its illegitimate child, the International Labor Congress, still functions with an ever larger Communist membership, and with a substantial part of its expenses paid by our taxpayers.

These notes by Senator Thomas show that he had a remarkable clarity of vision and great courage to give voice to unpalatable predictions which, after thirty to forty years' time, are borne out by the now dangerous, unrestrained power of labor unions, and the equally dangerous growth of the farm co-operatives, the latter spawned in a culture medium purged of antitrust and taxation laws.

Senator Thomas's talk with President Wilson, given at his request about ten days before he took his Western trip in 1920, to "pep up" the country in favor of his League, should be of interest.

I presented myself at the White House the next morning. Mr. Wilson came down the main staircase with a paper in his hand. After greetings were exchanged, he said, "Senator, before leaving Washington I want to discuss with the friends of the treaty a plan which I think will expedite ratification."

I interrupted at once, telling him that before he made me his confidant, he should know that in my then state of mind I would vote against the treaty, and not for it. He seemed surprised and told me my statement distressed him greatly. I replied that it gave me no pleasure to distress him, but that was better than to deceive him. He put his paper in his pocket and asked if it could be possible that I opposed the League for the reasons so frequently given by the irreconcilables. I told him I thought some of their reasons were sound ones; that I had others as good, if not better than theirs; because they concerned not only economic features but those of Part XIII as well.

"Part XIII?" inquired Mr. Wilson. He thought a moment and then said, "Why that is the labor part, isn't it? I thought everybody was perfectly satisfied with that." I told him his assumption was largely justified because Senators shrank from criticizing it lest they offend organized labor, but that I had occasion to know that most of them entertained, privately, the same opinion that I had, and that I intended to present my objections to the Senate very soon. He then asked me to state them to him. I did so. I directed his attention especially, however, to Articles 408 to 417 inclusive, the last two clauses of Article 396, Articles 422 and 423. The last one, I told him, in my judgment contravened beyond all doubt the constitutional provision that the judicial power should be vested in the Supreme Court and such other courts as the Congress, from time to time, should establish.

He thought I magnified unduly these objections, but in the discussion of them I became convinced that he was not familiar with the meaning and purpose of Part XIII, but that he accepted it as it was, and as an aid to the securing of his beloved League. This was the more remarkable in that Part XIII was made, in express terms, an integral part of the League.

He then asked me if I seriously entertained the view that the scheme of the League was beyond our constitutional powers; I replied without hesitation that I did and, if permitted, I would give him my reasons for it; reasons I had not yet expressed publicly and which, as far as I knew, had not yet been advanced by anyone. (Some of them afterwards, in 1920, were very clearly and exhaustively set forth by Judge Charles Kern, of Lexington, Kentucky, in the columns of the *North American Review*.) The President asked me to do so, whereupon I said in substance:

"The treaty-making power of the Federal government cannot be so enlarged as to include, under the guise of a treaty, something beyond and above it. A treaty is a contract or agreement between two or more signatory nations, affecting them alone, adjusting controversies and claims, establishing commercial relations, providing methods for the adjustment of future differences, forming alliances for offense or defense, etc. Our authority in these matters, unlike that of other nations, proceeds from and is limited by the Constitution.

"Your League is not a contract or agreement in any sense of the term. It is a political entity, a quasi government equipped with independent authority, exercising limited executive and legislative functions, established at some central point or capital, charged with certain duties and equipped with some method of enforcing its mandates, armed in some degree with the powers of the purse and the sword. If we have authority to participate with other nations in the creation of such a political organization, and then to invest it with power, that authority must be found elsewhere than in the treaty-making power. It must be one exercisable only by the Congress with the Executive's approval. I am unable to find this power anywhere, and it is inevitable that if we have authority to create one such entity, we may create others when our needs or our sense of expediency may require it.

"In order to function, moreover, such a body must needs be endowed with some degree of sovereignty. From what sources is this sovereignty derived? You, Mr. President, answered that question when you said, in one of your addresses, that each member nation, by joining the League, transferred a small part of its own sovereignty to the new organism. That must be true. But upon what argument can the American government justify its delegation or surrender of any of the national sovereignty, however insignificant, to an alien power?

"The people have made us the custodians of its sovereignty as long as we represent them. They require of us an oath to uphold the Constitution. We cannot fulfil our oath if we may transfer any part of our sovereignty elsewhere. We cannot recapture that which we transfer; it took a long civil war to settle that problem. And it is evident that if the President and the Senate may surrender a part, however small, they may surrender a larger part, or the whole of it, if so minded. To my mind it is equally plain that if we can create a new and independent organism, and endow it with a part, or the whole of the national sovereignty, we may delegate it as well to a nation heretofore existing. We could give it all, or a part of it, to Great Britain, France, or Japan by the simple process of treaty making. No man of common sense will say that we have the power to do this; but, on the other hand, no man of common sense can escape this consequence once he admits that we can dispose of any part of the national sovereignty to any power of any sort, at any time, under any circumstances whatsoever."

The President made no direct reply. He smiled, patronizingly, I thought, then rose and said, "Senator, if I can have an hour's talk with you on these matters I am very sure I can convince you that your objections are untenable. May I do so?" I assured him that I was anxious to be convinced; that if he could do this I would be under lasting obligations; that I would come at any hour of any day that he might designate. He said he certainly would do so before leaving Washington. But he never did.

Before taking my leave I asked if I might apprise him of the condition of affairs on the Hill. He said, certainly. I then told him that owing to my well-known attitude concerning the treaty I had peculiar means of ascertaining the views of individual Senators. Because of this I was certain that the treaty would never be ratified without reservations. Hence, that situation being definite, I thought it should be dealt with by the Executive who, instead of breasting the irresistible current, should confer with the mild reservationists; place himself, if possible, at their head, and, by such means, secure their assents to reservations as little unpalatable as possible. He then could accomplish his ultimate purpose and, at the same time, enjoy credit for the achievement.

The President curtly replied that other Senators gave him different information. This prompted the last word that I ever exchanged with Mr. Wilson. I said, "Mr. President, any Senator who tells you that the treaty can or will be ratified unconditionally either doesn't know the real situation or he is deceiving you!" I am sure he was impressed but little with my constitutional objections to the League, because he once said to me that whenever a Congressman began raising constitutional objections to a measure he at once suspected that man had something up his sleeve!"

In 1919 and 1920, bimetallism reared its head once more, largely owing to the scarcity of silver during the war. England, in connection with currency problems in India, had prevailed upon the Congress to release to her some $250,000,000 in coined silver dollars from the Treasury. These were for her use in providing India with an adequate circulating medium. Under the act, this silver was to be returned after the war and again be coined in silver dollars. During the emergency, and for a few years after the war, the open market price for silver reached a ratio as low as 13½ to 1 and remained there for some time. This was a price for silver of about $1.55 per ounce.

Mr. Moreton Frewen, an Englishman of culture and means; a globe trotter; an informed and trenchant writer and an earnest student of economic problems, was the most intelligent and persistent advocate of bimetallism of his generation. He believed in it thoroughly and was a vocal champion for it for over fifty years.

In pursuit of data, informative of the uses of silver as currency, Frewen traveled to China, India, The Straits Settlements, Mexico, and South America many times. The columns of many British papers and magazines have always been open to him. In writing he is always sure of his facts and hews to his line with no regard for consequences either to himself or to others. He has flayed Indian policies and rulers without mercy, challenged the wisdom of British hostility to silver, analyzed its effects upon Indian prosperity and that of the world, and frequently jeopardized his own business and social status by his courageous and unanswerable criticisms of the men and the influences responsible for the establishment of the gold standard.

Immediately after the war, while silver was selling freely at a price in excess of the ratio of 16 to 1, Frewen thought it opportune to push for some action favorable to bimetallism. He prepared and published a vigorous article on the subject in the *Nineteenth Century Magazine* and then came to America, confident of securing the selection of an International Commission for pushing it through the initiative of the United States. Senator Thomas introduced in the Senate a resolution to that end, and supported it in a very carefully prepared speech which commanded the interest of the Senate during its delivery. But this interest proved to be wholly academic. The press did not respond, the Senate Committee on Banking and Currency would not report the resolution, even adversely, and Mr. Frewen returned to England, a disappointed man, finally discouraged and disheartened. Senator Thomas concluded that the cause was dead— this was the golden opportunity and it had failed.

Mr. Bryan, who owes everything mental, material, and

political to his espousal of free coinage, remained entirely
aloof from this rebirth of the cause. Perhaps it was just
as well—he had long ago boxed the political compass in
the effort to satisfy his unappeasable hunger for political
notoriety.

## CHAPTER TWENTY-EIGHT

CHARLES S. THOMAS
Private Citizen

ELECTION year 1920 was a year of political turmoil. The defeat of the Wilson treaty and League had split the Democrats wide open and, at the same time, had given the Republicans a new lease on life. Because of dissatisfactions with the Wilson administration, the Republicans had captured and organized the Senate in 1918; they now proposed to make a rout of it in 1920. President Wilson suffered a stroke in the summer while making a speaking tour in the West in behalf of his precious League, but he still was occupying the White House as Chief Executive. He was bedridden and totally incapacitated to discharge the duties of the Presidency, yet he refused to step out gracefully and permit Vice-President Marshall to take over. He quarreled with his Cabinet, brutally dismissing his Secretary of State, Lansing, because he had dared, in an emergency, to call for a Cabinet meeting. All this set the stage for a Republican landslide in November, 1920.

Senator Thomas was tired; he had worked prodigiously and unremittingly on three important Senate committees during the war; the strain had been great and he was in a frame of mind to step down and leave the future to younger men, even though reluctant to admit it was time to retire. He once said, in respect to Senator Teller, who served six terms, that just after his re-election, for the first three years of the new term, he would state that he had a thankless job—it wasn't worth having, even on a

silver platter; the fourth year he wished his party would
let him alone; the fifth year, if the party wanted him so
damned bad, they would have to draft him; the sixth year,
well, then he began to want it like hell! In a lesser degree
Senator Thomas was somewhat like that.

His family all urged him to retire while at the height
of his career. He was seventy-one years old in 1920 and
the war years had taken a lot out of him. He was inclined to accede to the wishes of his family until one
summer day the war horse heard the "charge" blown on
the bugle. This one summer day he had a message from
Dewey C. Bailey, mayor of Denver, asking him for an
interview. He set a time and Bailey met him at his home,
and the two of them conferred. Bailey called his attention to the discord prevalent in Democratic ranks, and
told him that he was the one Democrat who could resolve
the party problems by standing forth as an avowed candidate. He called to his attention the local strife among
the Republicans—they were so certain it would be a
Republican year that the woods were full of candidates,
eager to serve the public, and backbiting each other.
Bailey wanted to be governor and he cast a most enticing
lure—his control of the city machine, which he promised
to deliver solid for Senator Thomas as senator and for
himself as governor. He spiced his talk with the clichés
he knew would set the hook in his fish—party duties
and party regularity. So Senator Thomas ran again, Bailey
failed to deliver, and he was beaten badly by Hon. Sam
Nicholson, the Republican candidate.

At the expiration of his term in March, 1921,* he
decided to remain in Washington for a few years. During
his Senate incumbency his law firm in Denver had broken
up and he did not feel up to organizing a new one. He
still had quite a few clients and these returned to him
when he was free again to accept retainers—chiefly Mr.

* See Plates XLIII, XLIV, and XLV in the Appendix.

A. E. Humphreys, who had been a highly successful oil "wildcatter," and the big Midwest oil group operating in Wyoming.

One day in his Washington office, soon after his retirement, he was waited upon by a group of three Korean gentlemen. They told him they wished to retain him to represent their organization—Koreans for Freedom, or some such title, made up of expatriate Koreans all over the world—at the Disarmament Conference to be held that year in Washington. They wanted him to present a petition in behalf of the restoration of sovereignty to Korea by the Japanese.

He listened to them carefully and then told them they would be wasting both time and money in any such procedure; that the petition might be received but that its fate most surely would be, at best, its "assignment for study," or some such disposition leading to its deposit in a dusty and soon-to-be-forgotten pigeonhole.

They informed him they knew this as well as he did; that they had ample finances, contributed monthly by expatriate Koreans; that their policy was to offer petitions of this nature at every international conference possible. They insisted that he accept the retainer and make the presentation.

"Why do you come to me for this?" he asked them. "I am a retired Senator and, as such, no longer do I possess the influence and standing that you should have for your project."

They told him they wanted him because he was a friend of Korea and already, on the floor of the Senate, he had demanded a reservation to the Treaty of Peace with Germany in behalf of Korean independence.

He protested—told them he had offered his amendment to the reservation for Ireland and brought in Korea to expose to the American public the petty partisan politics of the members of the Senate; that he had had no hope it would get favorable consideration from the Senate when he offered it.

Nevertheless, they told him, "You did this for Korea in a public forum; it was broadcast to the world; printed in the *Congressional Record;* it accomplished a great deal for Korea." Again they begged him to accept their retainer.

So he did so; presented their petition to the Disarmament Conference in due course, and saw it suffer the very fate he had predicted for it. His clients were more than satisfied and grateful, and they paid him a large fee cheerfully.

In 1926 the British announced they would put India on a gold bullion standard. The Silver Producers Association of the United States retained him to make a trip to London to explore, so far as he might be able, and to report what effect this action would have on the free markets for silver. Not only was this a profitable assignment but it was a most interesting experience. His outstanding services in the Senate were even better known to the British authorities than they were in America, and were more appreciated. High government officials, Bank of England executives and the heads of private banking firms of that country made him cordially welcome and did everything possible to further his mission and make of it a success.

Late in 1928, Senator Thomas closed his office in Washington—an office he shared with Hon. Clyde Dawson—and returned to Denver to live out the rest of his life. While it is certain that he missed the give and take of political life, he enjoyed the companionship of his friends, all of whom let him use space in their offices. There they would go in and exchange reminiscences with him. He had a great fund of stories covering the frontier days of the West and, in the right mood, he could talk for hours of those times, telling stories about well-known figures—stories both of great humor and stories of pathos.

His gift of narrative was superb and his memory could recall a great wealth of detail and circumstance—even dates. Actually he enjoyed his retirement until the 1929 crash came, followed by the era of Franklin D. Roosevelt.

In the spring of 1932, I asked him one day who he thought finally might be the nominee of the Democratic party for president. He replied, "I'm very much afraid it will be Franklin Roosevelt. He has been first in the field and has been breaking his neck to get it."

I asked him why he was "afraid" it would fall to Roosevelt. He then gave me an appraisal of Roosevelt that was to prove 100 per cent accurate. He knew him well and had had frequent contact with him when he was in the Senate and Roosevelt was Assistant Secretary of the Navy.

He told me that Roosevelt was brilliant, but only superficially so; a good and persuasive speaker; an opportunist purely and simply; and shrewd and clever at political gambits. He designated him as shallow in his thinking and without steadfastness in his relations with friends and associates who might dare to differ with him. Where just plain expediency demanded, he tossed them to the wolves. In this respect he referred to his treatment of Al Smith and Jimmy Walker. The latter, he said, of course deserved to be dumped, but the reason for it was not his desserts but because he had become a political liability to Governor Roosevelt. He went on to say that he was a member of the bar, but a very insignificant one; he had had fine schooling, but was ignorant of the fundamentals of economics and, in fiscal matters, would be a dangerous man as Chief Executive of the nation. Politics, he said, was the role at which Roosevelt was in his element; he was a "natural" at that, able and willing to intrigue and adopt any policy at all to his purposes; he could be on both sides of a question without embarrassment; he could and would play on the emotions of the classes able to furnish the largest numbers of votes at the polls, with complete disregard of the right and wrong of it. He was, unfortunately, crippled by polio, but he was energetic nevertheless, where politics was concerned. At this point he recalled a saying of Goethe: "There is nothing more terrible than energetic ignorance." In short, he told me that F. D. Roosevelt was about as well fitted to be Chief Executive of the nation as any five-year-old child.

Roosevelt, as we know, received the nomination. He was in Denver on his campaign tour and, while there, he sent word to Senator Thomas that he would like to see him and talk about the campaign. Senator Thomas sent word back to him as follows: "Thank the nominee for his courtesy, but tell him I see no point in an interview with him as I do not intend to support him."

When Roosevelt devalued the dollar by raising the price of gold, and decreed that citizens must turn over to the Treasury all gold they might be possessed of at the old, long-standing price, Senator Thomas wrote a letter to Roosevelt, telling him that he had a nest egg of some $250 in gold coin; that he was refusing to part with it and, if that was a crime, he could make the most of it. He said, further, that he was an old man and he felt he might just as well finish out his days in a Federal prison as to let himself be made a party to a rape of the public.

The Attorney General wrote him the sum was too insignificant for official notice to be taken of it.

## CHAPTER TWENTY-NINE

THE LAST FEW MONTHS

I USED TO talk with him and try to get him to quit worrying about the course of the New Deal wrecking crews; I urged him to watch the passing show (about which he was powerless to do anything), to exercise his strong sense of humor and of the ridiculous, and to try thus to get some fun out of it. He would reply that my counsel was sound, but that he was unable to stop his worry about the future of his "children," living in an increasingly bad orgy of public debt, public spending, profligacy, economic inanity, and a fiscal policy dredged up from the extreme end of the limit of ignorance and patterned faithfully on the historic drunken sailor. I pointed out that his "children" all were over forty years of age; that if now they were unable to take care of themselves they never would be, and worry would do nothing for them.

He said to this, "That is only too true, of course. It seems to me a shame that a man should live to my age solely to find that he is twice the jackass he thought he was! No man can ever live sufficiently long to avoid the making of new mistakes!"

One day I asked him how he felt about the Senate, after eight years of service there, as compared to what he fancied it to be before he had been successful in attaining membership in it. He thought about the matter for some few minutes and then spoke about as follows:

"The personnel of the Congress, and especially of the Senate, seems to have deteriorated under the operation of the primary method of selection. If this it not entirely true, then the primary method of selection has begotten a sense of dependence upon it which is hardly consistent with the due and untrammeled discharge of legislative duty by the representatives. For the latter strives only to retain the favor of his constituency, and that seems easier by liberal grants of money and sensational attacks upon public officials, than by functioning as national legislators which, as heretofore stated, inevitably leads to the subordination of the general welfare to the local interest. The modern tendency synchronizes with the retirement of the convention and the substitution of Senatorial electors for legislative appointments. Both Houses are reaching dead levels of mediocrity which must be reflected in inferior legislation, class groupings, and the death of all initiative. Perhaps it would have come in any event; we are witnessing now the groveling of Senators and Representatives to retain the favor of a President by passing at his call legislation that is most harmful to the economy. It is evident, the world over, that parliaments and legislative bodies are losing prestige by revealing the weaknesses of Democracy. The latter seems to display an impotence in governmental capacity in proportion to its expansion of authority. Its power is diffused as it is acquired, and the swing of the pendulum toward power, associated with a central responsibility, is apparent even in America. This swing seems to follow the deflation in money values: the franc has fallen ever since the war ended, and even the French are discussing the expediency of a dictatorship; Spain, tiring of Democracy founded upon universal suffrage, and following the example of Italy, has thrown itself with enthusiasm into the arms of a dictator.

"The new system also parallels the decadence of the sense of official trusteeship. Until recently, a controlling sense of duty to the public, especially in the collection and disposition of the public revenues, was practically universal, and the notion of utilizing the treasury in the political interest of the lawmaker was exceptional. The change began with the pension system. Its growth was not overrapid until the primary became the instrument for the selection of candidates, since which time billions of dollars have been appropriated by the Congress and legislatures on purposes which are wholly foreign to the objects and principles of taxation. These 'grabs' are made to placate groups, or sections, or movements, which, in turn, are expected to support the political ambitions of those who make them possible, and they are just as dishonest as, perhaps more so than, the defalcations of an administrative officer. But the practice has become too common to provoke adverse comment, or to trouble the conscience of the official.

"Practically every Senator still in office when Senator Newberry's case was disposed of, and all congressmen of either party who have been conspicuous in denouncing Senator Fall and Edward L. Doheny, have advocated and supported the soldiers' bonus bill which misappropriates four billion dollars of public money; they have advocated and supported the Haugen-McNary Bill for marketing agricultural products. Each of these is as offensive to public morals and official decency as anything so far developed in the oil inquiries. The first has diverted, with similar legislation sure to follow, more money from the Treasury than all the oil reserves of the country are or ever will be worth. Yet it provokes little indignation and scarcely any comment. The only motive behind it is the soldier vote for which, both parties, desiring, have rivaled each other in their advocacy. This augurs ill for the future, for more nations decay and disappear through the extravagance and corruption of their rulers than by wars and conquest.

"There were giants in the Congress before the primary took over, particularly in the Senate. Most of them then, even though endowed with man's natural selfishness in personal matters, still had a driving sense of public responsibility and the most of them would have died before surrendering their convictions to a blustering executive, or to groups of soldiers and labor unions. There are no giants in the Congress today (1934) and there never will be again. Mediocrity is now the order of the day."

Another day he returned to this same subject, recalling the battle in the Senate over the Irish reservation to the League of Nations. He referred to the actions of the Senate and observed that the motives of the Senators on this matter did not commend themselves to the judgment of candid men; that the Senate on that day (March 18, 1920) made a record as humiliating as it was unexpected.

He then went on to say, "It is futile, of course, for me to mourn over the decadence in our public men, but it is something that truly grieves me, and it is also something that most of the world is indifferent to, even if aware of it. This appalling indifference contributes to its prevalence and makes it all possible. The world does not long remember events of importance in the rush of the new which absorbs the public interest to the exclusion of the old; even the individual is not likely to cherish in his memory many major events of his life, but usually he retains flashing and unrelated vignettes of little happenings and these often return vividly to his consciousness until he dies. You, my son, will find this to be true, as also it is true of me.

"The memory of my election as governor has become dim with the years; so also my accession to the Senate; but the small, incongruous and commonplace scenes of everyday life remain clear and sharp. A little towheaded girl, crying inconsolably over the body of her little dog, killed out in the dusty street; you, a small boy, pridefully showing me your first pair of pants; a remembered vision of a lovely, curly head with long-lashed, closed eyelids, breathing gently, asleep in the half light of a shaded lamp; a crippled old crone, painfully sorting a pile of discarded trash; the unrestrained joy of your little girl when first she finds she can walk alone; the headlong fall of a wild duck, arrested in flight by your shotgun charge and, when retrieving it, your childish remorse over killing it; these, and a hundred such memories always remain. This is good, for they help us forget ourselves at such times and make our hearts and our thoughts more charitable."

In April, 1934, he began to fail markedly. Finally, about three weeks before the end, he had to take to his bed and, to his utter disgust, he had to have a trained nurse to minister to his needs. Life no longer had any lure for him; he hated the New Deal and all its actors and proponents in Washington; he despised the lawmakers who so eagerly aided and abetted the rape of the nation; and he wanted to die. He refused to eat, sinking quite fast day after day until, one night, he failed to wake up when morning came. He was eighty-four years and five months of age. The state of Colorado lost one of its giants when he passed away but I do not think its people realize what has been lost to them, even to this day.

L'ENVOI

THE DROP CURTAIN at the Tabor Grand Opera House in Denver carried a painted scene showing an old, broken-down structure, classic in style, overgrown with wild vegetation and returning to the oblivion from which it came. It bore a quotation from Kingsley:

> So fleet the works of men, back to their earth again;
> Ancient and holy things fade like a dream.

Fame, also, is fleeting. It either is lost completely with time, or it suffers change; it even gets inflated out of all proportion to that which originally gave it substance.

The writer of these few high lights of mining reminiscence also had, in his youth, experience in Leadville, Creede, the California Mother Lode, and at Goldfield. His father was one of the pioneers in Leadville—lived there from 1870 to 1884. In 1935 he thought it of interest to take his wife and twelve-year-old daughter and a friend of hers of the same age to Leadville to see the city where her grandfather built his fame and some of his fortune, particularly his political fortune.

Room reservations at the Hotel Vendome were duly spoken for, though at that stage of the depression this was only a gesture, and my party was loaded into an automobile and taken to Leadville. The Vendome Hotel was built in the early eighties. At the time the French architect, Mansard, was quite in vogue and, while he had nothing to do with plans for the Vendome, his type of roof was adopted for it. For the rest the structure was Victorian and early Pullman.

The hotel could boast of many celebrated and distinguished guests in the eighties and nineties—General Grant, Mme Modjeska, Mark Twain, and Jenny Lind, to name a few. Among them also was Oscar Wilde, who stayed there for quite a spell on a lecture tour. His lectures were well attended and very successful. His subsequent troubles with the law in England did nothing to dim the lustre and glory of the Vendome, in having "hosted" his stay in Leadville—quite the contrary. This city was tolerant. Tabor also had a suite of rooms in the Vendome with his Baby Doe. Tabor had built the Clarendon Hotel as his own when he built his Leadville Opera House (now the Elks' Opera House), and he maintained a suite in each hotel for several years.

When we went there in 1935 the hotel was under a new management and it had been refurbished a bit. This consisted mostly of a new coat of paint over some dozen or fifteen earlier coats of paint on the woodwork; some repapering of the walls done over at least a dozen other paperings; and some new counterpanes for the old-fashioned brass and iron bedsteads. There was an elevator—a little cage operated by a steel cable passing down through the bonnet and floor of the cage. The management provided a colored factotum who was bellboy, porter, and elevator boy, all in one.

Mrs. Thomas and the two girls, together with the luggage, were turned over to this factotum while I took the car for servicing and parking for the night. The little party squeezed into the small elevator for a trip to the second floor. The upward journey was slow enough for a little conversation so Mrs. Thomas asked the colored boy if he knew where Oscar Wilde's room was and said she would like to see it, especially if it was still furnished just as it was when he occupied it.

"No, ma'am. I don't know nuthin' 'bout it," said this
party, showing the whites of his eyes, surprisedly.

He took them into the rooms of the corner suite overlooking Harrison Avenue. He was asked for some ice
and said he would get it as soon as he could go across
the street to the restaurant—"We ain't got no ice in
dishyer hotel."

The girls were just getting settled in when a peremptory rap sounded on the door. Mrs. Thomas opened it,
to be confronted by the hotel manager and the colored
boy. The manager turned to the boy and said, "Is this
the woman?"

Wide-eyed and looking very scared, the boy answered,
"Yaas, suh. She's de one."

"Well! This boy tells me you are asking to be shown
to a man's room here. I want you to know, Madam,
that this is a respectable hostelry, and no such carryings-
on will be permitted."

"But you don't understand! My husband's father was
one of the pioneers here—you must have heard of him;
Senator Charles S. Thomas. We brought our daughter
here to see Leadville and to learn something of its past.
Oscar Wilde was here on a lecture tour, and we only
want to see the room he had and also the rooms that
Tabor had."

Turning again to the bellboy, he said, "You sure this
is the woman?"

"Yaas, suh. She's she." He stuck to it, looking from
one to the other.

"Well, Madam, I want to tell you we don't allow
women in this hotel to go to men's rooms. Mr. Wilde is
not registered here, nor have we any reservation for him!
As for Senator Thomas—I never heard of him!"

Just then I appeared, was introduced, and succeeded
in convincing the manager that no immoral purpose really
was being thwarted by him. He unbent enough to tell

us that he was now occupying the Tabor suite and would be glad to show it to us.

He did. It was all done over in atrocious fashion, with great, awkward, overstuffed furniture, many heavy lamps. It was crowded with the gimcracks sold to tourists in Europe. Mrs. Thomas made him her friend for life by remarking, "Ah, I can see that *you* are a man of the world; a great and discerning traveler!" He puffed up so at that that we almost had to open the windows. The rooms couldn't possibly have been in worse taste if they had still retained the old Tabor decor.

The manager stuck to his ignorance of Oscar Wilde. He didn't know Oscar, now or in the past; he could not tell us what rooms he had had fifty years before. He didn't even show us a room where Washington had slept! Such is fame.

On a motor trip I had to make through Nevada in 1950, I had occasion to pass through Goldfield. Except for the topographical landmarks, there remained only one man-made structure that was recognizable—the Goldfield Hotel. There it was—six stories high, of red brick; completely empty, its windows staring vacantly out over the desert. I found Sun Dog Street, where Tex Rickard had his home; where he had worked so hard to get a lawn going; where he had planted trees. The home and the grass and the trees all were gone; almost all of the other houses and buildings in town were gone. I doubt that more than fifty people were still there in that place which had had over twenty-five thousand people in it forty-five years ago.

"So fleet the works of men——"

MINING TERMS

ARRASTRA. A Mexican device for amalgamating gold and silver with mercury for its recovery. It is a crude grinding mill, composed of a round basin, paved with hard, flat rocks. In the center is a post, free to revolve. A crossarm, about three feet up the post, has at each end a large rock chained to it so they can be dragged over the bottom paving. At the top of the post is a longer crossarm, the ends of which can be hitched to mules to furnish power for revolving the post. Ore, with water and mercury, is put in the basin, the mules go to work walking round and round. At the end of the operation the ore pulp is removed and washed to recover the amalgam.

BACK. The roof of an underground working.

BAR. In placer mining, a sand bar in a stream.

BONANZA. A Spanish word, meaning "fair weather." Used by miners to designate a rich ore body.

BORRASCA. A Spanish word meaning "tempest, storm." Used by miners as the antonym of bonanza.

BREAST. The term for the unbroken face of an underground working.

CROSSCUT. A tunnel, underground, at right angles to the course of a vein.

DRIFT. A tunnel, underground, following a vein.

GALLERY. Any horizontal underground passage.

GOB. Waste rock, underground.

LODE. Often used synonymously with vein. More exactly it is a series of parallel and interlocking veins inside of well-defined walls.

MINER'S INCH. A water measurement developed by the Forty-niners. It is equal to 11¼ gallons per minute.

POKE. A buckskin bag used by miners for carrying gold dust.

Rocker. A device for washing gold gravels. It has greater capacity than a pan. It is a long box, set on rockers at each end. The top is provided with a sloping board with slats nailed across it, and a hopper at the upper end. A long stick fastened upright at the end of the box is used to rock it back and forth as gravel and water are fed into the hopper. The agitation causes the gold to settle where it is caught by the slats, which are called "riffles."

Shaft. A vertical (sometimes inclined) opening in the ground from the surface, for reaching underground workings.

Stope. A working, off a drift or crosscut, from which ore is mined.

Tailings. The waste product from rockers, arrastras, mills, etc. The material that is fed to these devices is termed "heads."

Whim. A crude hoisting device. It consists of a revolving post, with a drum at the bottom and set upright. A long crossarm at the top, to which a mule is hitched, turns it. The hoisting rope is led to the drum. As the mule walks around, the drum winds up, or spools, the rope.

Winze. A shaft which is sunk from an underground working.

APPENDIX

(Duplicate)

NEVADA GOLDFIELD REDUCTION COMPANY

GOLDFIELD, NEVADA, Sept. 13, 1906.

BOUGHT OF Frances Mohawk Mining & Leasing Co.

LOT	SACKS CAR	MOISTURE PER CENT	COPPER PER CENT.	LEAD PER CENT.	SILVER OZS.	GOLD OZS.	ZINC PER CENT	GROSS	MOISTURE	SACKS	TARE	NET
			ASSAY PER TON						WEIGHT			
40	9 Sacks	6.5	——	——	9.1	101.15	——	666¼	43.8	5	Sample to owner 2½	616.2

FIGURED
{
Gold   at 100% of $20.00
Silver at 95 per cent of 65¢   per ounce   Value, per Ton, ... $2028.61
Lead   per ounce
                                    per unit   Total Value, " 616.2 lbs., $ 625.01
Copper   per unit
}

CHARGES
{
Freight
Treatment
Sampling   @ $127.85 per ton   Charges, $ 42.27
Guard
Risk and Insurance   Net . $ 582.74
Sacking
}

J. A. Somers
Auditor.

Superintendent.

Plate XVIII

(Triplicate)

NEVADA GOLDFIELD REDUCTION COMPANY

GOLDFIELD, NEVADA Jan. 12, 1907.

BOUGHT OF Frances Mohawk Mining & Leasing Co.

LOT	SACKS CAR	MOISTURE PER CENT	COPPER PER CENT	LEAD PER CENT	SILVER Ozs.	GOLD Ozs.	ZINC PER CENT	GROSS	MOISTURE	SACKS	TARE	NET
					ASSAY PER TON					WEIGHT		
491	No. P. 30041	5.8	-	-	-	17.04	-	122000	4863	-	37800	79317

FIGURED			
Gold at 98%	per cent of $20.00	per ounce	Value per Ton, - - - $ 336.54
Silver at		per ounce	
Lead		per unit	Total Value, 79317 lbs, $ 13346.67
Copper		per unit	

CHARGES

@ $ 33.36 per ton

Freight figured on wet weight
Treatment " " dry "

Charges, $ 1377.59

Net - $ 11969.08

Walter Fowler
Vice President.

Auditor.

Nevada Goldfield Reduction Company

Goldfield, Nevada. Dec.3,06.

BOUGHT OF Frances Mohawk Mining & LeasingCo.

| LOT | SACKS CAR | MOISTURE PER CENT | ASSAY PER TON | | | | | | WEIGHT | | | | |
			COPPER PER CENT	LEAD PER CENT	SILVER Ozs.	GOLD Ozs.	ZINC PER CENT	GROSS	MOISTURE	SACKS	TARE.	NET
292	I.C. 19648	6.60	-----	-----	-----	18.9	-----	107280	5174	-----	28880	73226

FIGURED

Gold 98¼ per cent of $ 20.00 per ounce Value, per Ton, . . . $ 373.27

Silver at per ounce

Lead per unit Total Value, 73226

Copper per unit

CHARGES

@ $34.83 Freight figured on wet weight
Treatment " " dry "

Charges, $ 1336.87 lbs., $ 13666.53

Net - $ 12329.66

[signature]
Vice President

[signature]
Auditor

Plate XX

(Duplicate)

NEVADA GOLDFIELD REDUCTION COMPANY

GOLDFIELD, NEVADA, Sept. 18, 1906.

BOUGHT OF Frances Mohawk Mining & Leasing Co.,

LOT	SACKS CAR	MOISTURE PER CENT	COPPER PER CENT	LEAD PER CENT	SILVER OZS.	GOLD OZS.	ZINC PER CENT	GROSS	MOISTURE	SACKS	TARE	NET
				ASSAY PER TON						WEIGHT		
36	U.P. 55657	7.8	---	---	2.75	25.46	---	132700	7230	---	40000	85470

FIGURED

Gold at 98% of $20.00   Value, per Ton, ... $ 504.55

Silver at 95 per cent of 65¢   per ounce

Lead   per unit   Total Value, "85470   lbs., $ 21561.08

Copper   per unit

CHARGES

Freight
Treatment
Sampling   @ $47.53 per ton   Charges, $ 3203.01
Guard
Sacking   Net - $ 19358.07
Risk and Insurance

Superintendent.

Auditor.

(Triplicate)

NEVADA GOLDFIELD REDUCTION COMPANY

GOLDFIELD, NEVADA, Sept. 27, 1906.

BOUGHT OF **Frances Mohawk Mining & Leasing Co.**

LOT	CARS CAR	MOISTURE PER CENT	ASSAY PER TON							WEIGHT				
			COPPER PER CENT	LEAD PER CENT	SILVER OZS.	GOLD OZS.	ZINC PER CENT	GROSS	MOISTURE	SACKS	TARE	NET		
48	PC&StLR 878611	7	——	——	2.00	16.95	——	116000	5915	——	31500	78585		

FIGURED {
Gold at 98% per cent of $20.00   Value, per Ton, . . . $336.00
Silver at 95 " " " 65¢   per ounce
Lead   per unit   Total Value, 78585   lbs., $13203.28
Copper   per unit
}

CHARGES { @ $35.62 per ton }

Charges, $ 1504.94

Net · $ 11697.34

Joseph R. Forster,
Vice President.

J. A. Levine,
Auditor.

Plate XXII

A. R. Talbot — W. J. Bryan — T. S. Allen

Talbot, Bryan & Allen,
Attorneys and Counselors at Law.
Suite 330 Mc Murty Block.

Lincoln, Neb. April 16 – '96

My Dear Mr Thomas,

I am greatly obliged to you for getting our plank into your platform. Am glad you succeeded in electing O'Donnell. I know Hallett & Seldomridge. They are sound. I don't suppose your delegation is committed to any candidate. If we succeed in getting a 16 to 1 plank at Chicago our delegation may present my name. Whether it goes farther than a compliment will depend upon the feeling of other states. I am not saying this to the public

Plate XXIII

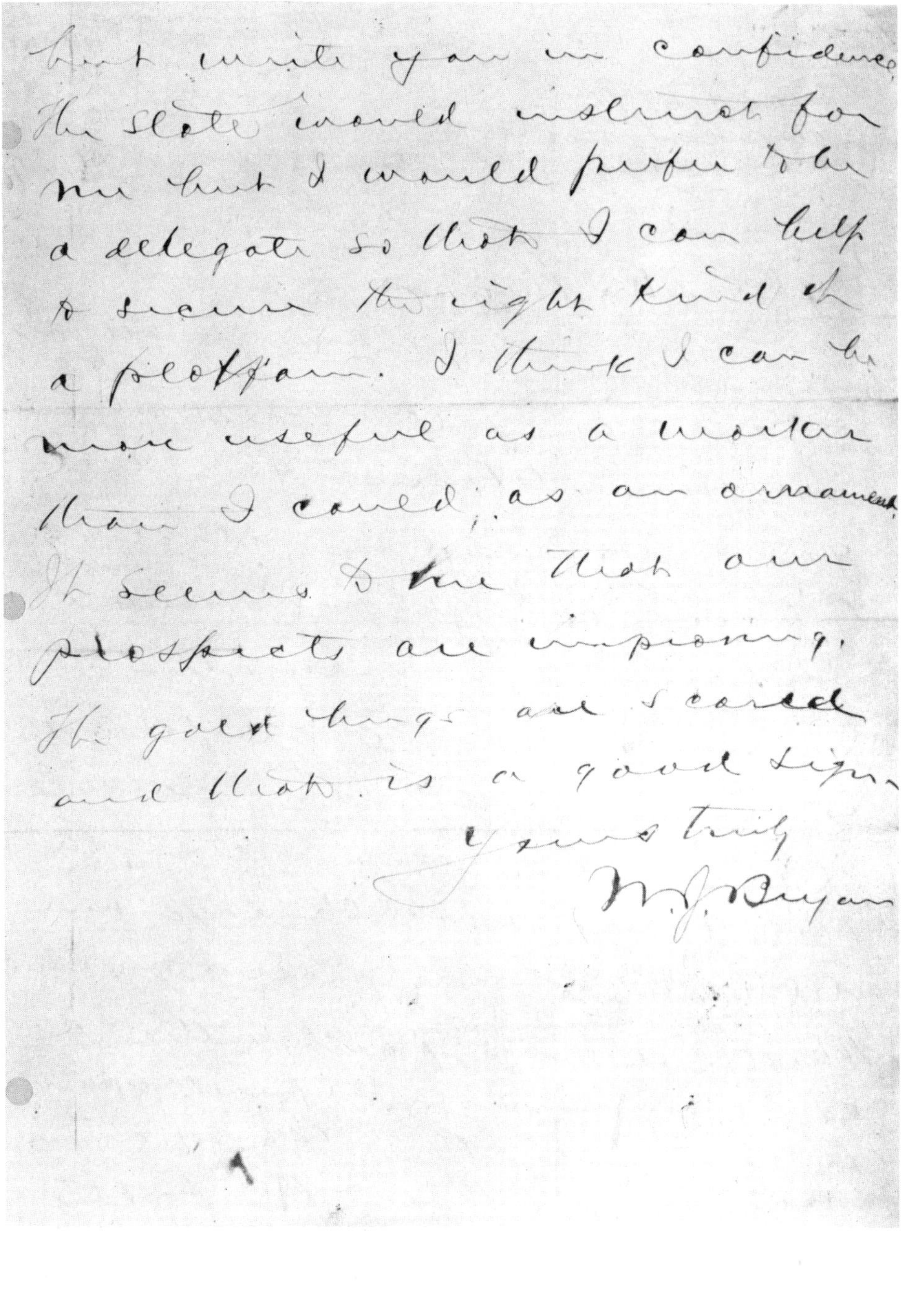

but write you in confidence.
The state would instruct for
me but I would prefer to be
a delegate so that I can help
to secure the right kind of
a platform. I think I can be
more useful as a worker
than I could; as an ornament.
It seems to me that our
prospects are improving.
The gold bugs are scared
and that is a good sign.
Yours truly
W. J. Bryan

Plate XXIV

THE BURRO

✦ ✦ ✦

And by the way, I believe that every intelligent reader of the MINING FINANCIAL NEWS who knows his Nevada and her burros will concede that Sam C. Dunham, nearly ten years ago, said the last word in regard to the peculiar characteristics and vocal accomplishments of what the Sun's minstrel reminds us was once known as the "Washoe canary." It was during the political campaign of 1902 that Sam printed in the Tonopah Miner his first tribute to the burro. It will be remembered by those who took an interest in Nye county politics during that campaign that the unique spectacle was presented in Tonopah of the county central committees of the Republican and Labor parties effecting a "fusion" to take the offices away from the Democrats, who had held them by divine right with only sporadic interruptions ever since the county was organized. This unprecedented action on the part of the Labor party, which was about as logical as would have been the "fusion" of the Nigger Republican Club with the Democratic party, naturally caused great consternation among the Democrats of Nye county. Sam was then editor of the Tonopah Miner, which was "on the fence," and inasmuch as the county printing, which was worth five or six thousand dollars a year, would go to the newspaper that supported the successful candidates, it was a very delicate matter to decide where to jump.

✦ ✦ ✦

It was while he was deciding which way to "flop" that Sam wrote his famous political editorial entitled "The Burro." This is it:

" 'Sabe V. el burro?' As we walked down the middle of Main street this morning, keeping away from friends and endeavoring to solve by inspiration the political problem in Nye, so that we might write a leader defining our 'political position,' we met a 6-foot prospector steering a 3-foot burro in the general direction of Gold Mountain. (For the information of our numerous Eastern readers, we will explain that a burro is what is known in classical language as an "ass." It is a beast of burden. It performs with patient forbearance on the desert the function the dog performs with cold indifference on the Yukon, the mule with malevolence in the Middle West, and the automobile with fatal results in the effete East.)

"The burro wet met this morning bore in his countenance the patience of centuries and on his back an elaborate camp outfit, consisting of a sack of flour, a slab of bacon, cooking utensils, a roll of blankets, a tent, etc. The dust was deep and his burden almost greater than he could bear, and he was proceeding with due deliberation and caution.

"The prospector, who seemed to be in a hurry to get somewhere, ever and anon prodded his beast of burden with a pick-handle. The only visible effect of this persistent prodding was a slight elevation of the burden, due to the concurrent effort of the rear end of the burro to overtake the front end, which was moving along in the even tenor of its way. If there was any change of expression in that patient face, we didn't see it.

✦ ✦ ✦

"As we watched the trio—the prodder, the burro and the burden—pass slowly up the street, the prodder still prodding and loudly traducing the proddee's ancestry, we thought, How like some human asses we have known is this overburdened beast, and how aptly he illustrates the inability of his human prototype to grasp a great opportunity—to do the right thing at the right time in the right place. Oh! what an opportunity was there, our countrymen! By simply extending one hind leg and vitalizing it as a progressive American mule can always be depended on to do on similar occasions, and planting its extremity in the right place—depositing his ballot, as it were—he could have given his persecutor a cramp that all the Jamaica ginger in Nye county couldn't alleviate.

"And speaking of burros reminds us that we have up in our exclusive end of town a baby burro. We interviewed it yesterday. It was born just two days ago, but it looks two thousand years old. What a sad, solemn little face! In its wonderful eyes the pathos of twenty centuries of persecution, insufficient nourishment and bad jokes! As we stood and contemplated this melancholy waif of the desert, we took off our hat, for we suddenly realized we were in the presence of a representative of the purest race in the world. A naturalist who is sojourning here and classifying specimens told us the other day that the Nye county ass is the same old ass of Bible times —that the burros we see around town devouring old shoes and gunnysacks and Nevada newspapers, and drinking our expensive water from our back doorstep, are the same in every respect— ears, appetite and all—as the ass that came out of the ark.

✦ ✦ ✦

"What representative of the human race can show so pure a strain of blood? Even the Jew has changed his physique and his physiognomy, if we may base our judgment on the pictures in Judge, and his complexion is slowly but surely bleaching out. But the ass, by proudly holding aloof from the common herd and avoiding miscegenation and mesalliances, as the French would say, has come down to us pure and undefiled. We have it on the authority of an eminent philologist that even his language is unchanged—that while seeking a scanty subsistence on the western slope of Jim Butler's mountain he sings the same old song, in the same old way and in the same heartbreaking key, that he sang two thousand years ago to the humble fishermen on the shores of Galilee in far-off Palestine.

"And speaking of Palestine reminds us of a picture we saw nearly forty years ago, when we went to Sunday school for the last time, before we came out into the world and our heart grew hardened—before we came to Tonopah. It was a scene in a desert. In the picture were four figures—a man, an ass, a Woman and a Little Child. They were journeying down into Egypt, the man leading the ass, the Woman riding and carrying in her arms with infinite tenderness the Little Child. As we stood and looked at the baby burro yesterday, we thought that perhaps the patience and the meekness and the sadness we saw in its solemn little face had come down through the centuries from its ancestors that bore down into Egypt the Burden and the Consolation of the World."

✦ ✦ ✦

from the Mining Financial News, New York, N.Y. (1907)

Plate XXV

THE BURRO

Later, the same year, in the Christmas number of the Tonopah Miner, Dunham paid a metrical tribute to the burro under the title of "The Nye County Ass." I reproduce it here:

"The Ass that roams yon barren hill
  In search of sustenance
Is not what carping critics call
  A subject for romance.

The housewives in this arid town
  Whose water he has spilled,
We're very sure, from what they say,
  Would like to see him killed.

The prejudice of these, and all
  Who're wakened from their sleep
At midnight by his mournful song,
  Is permanent and deep.

But he who burns the midnight oil
  And barters night for day,
Is never wakened from his sleep
  By harsh, nocturnal bray.

And such a one, with prejudice
  Against nor beast nor class,
Would crave to be allowed to speak
  A good word for the Ass.

The Ass has been so vilified—
  So persecuted, too—
That we're inclined to spare the space
  And give the cuss his due.

Look at the picture here displayed;
  Inspect it with all care—
Gaze in that solemn little face,
  And read the story there:

The pathos of two thousand years
  Of ancient jokes and low,
Of insufficient nourishment
  And hereditary woe!

Go take your Bible from the shelf—
  Or come and borrow ours—
And turn to where it tells about
  The great diluvian showers.

Examine well the pictures there,
  And you will quick remark
That Asses just like these of ours
  Took passage in the ark.

Of all the races on the earth—
  Or man, or fowl, or beast—
We've every reason to believe
  The Ass has changed the least.

And when it comes to pedigree,
  Since Adam's slip and fall
We are convinced the Ass can show
  The purest one of all.

Ours is the same old, patient Ass—
  Ears, appetite and all—
That scaled the Heights of Lebanon
  And browsed by Zion's wall.

His gentle voice, from time remote,
  Has undergone no change,
And when we hear it in the night
  It has the same old range.

The song he sings on yonder hill,
  So loud—and sad—and slow,
Was heard in far-off Palestine
  Two thousand years ago.

It is the same heart-breaking song,
  Pitched in the same sad key,
That woke the humble fishermen
  On storm-tossed Galilee.

The shepherds heard the sad refrain
  That wondrous winter night
When far athwart the Eastern sky
  God flashed the World's New Light.

And now we make a plea to all
  To cease their loud complaints
Against the songs of long ago
  Which satisfied the saints.

The Ass has borne your burdens here
  So patiently and long,
That you should bear as patiently
  The burden of his song.

So when you meet a patient Ass,
  O'erburdened on the road,
No matter whether man or beast,
  Help lighten up his load."

✦   ✦   ✦

Plate XXVI

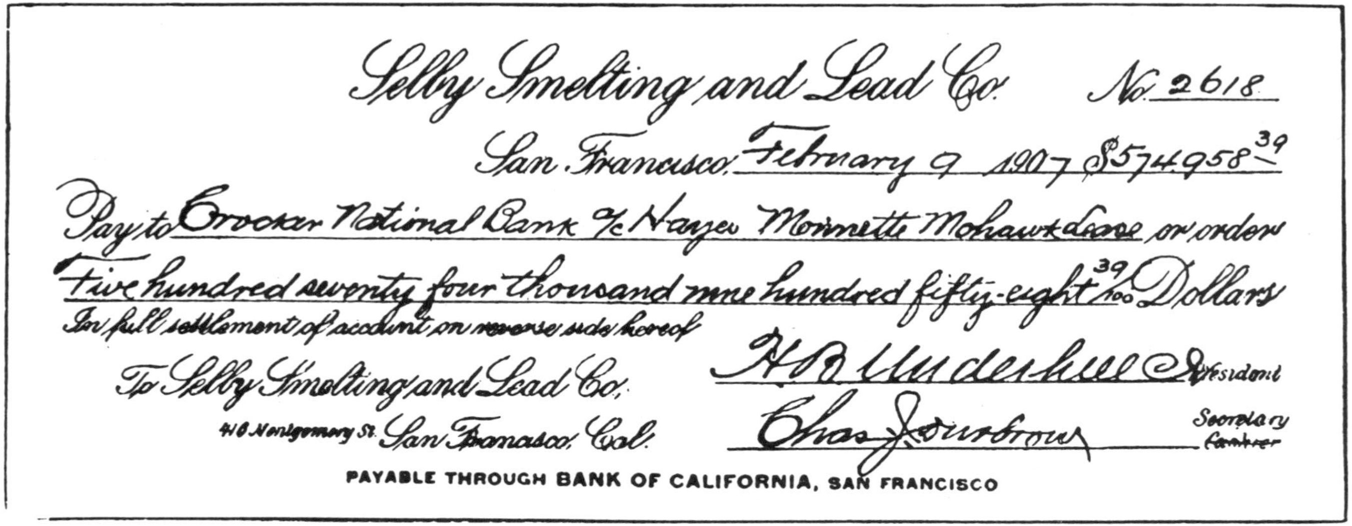

Selby Smelting and Lead Co. No. 2618

San Francisco, February 9 1907 $574958 39/100

Pay to Crocker National Bank % Hayes Monnette Mohawk Lease or order

Five hundred seventy four thousand nine hundred fifty-eight 39/100 Dollars

In full settlement of account on reverse side hereof

To Selby Smelting and Lead Co.,

418 Montgomery St. San Francisco, Cal.

H. R. Underhill Jr. President

Chas. J. Ourbrow Secretary / Cashier

PAYABLE THROUGH BANK OF CALIFORNIA, SAN FRANCISCO

The $574,958.39 check above was given by the Smelter at San Francisco in settlement for 47 tons of ore shipped from the Hayes-Monnette lease on the Mohawk mine at Goldfield, Nev., The ore carried 609.61 ounces of gold and 75.38 ounces of silver to the ton. The Mohawk property is part of Goldfield Cons. properties at Goldfield.

Plate XXVII

Jumbo Mining Company of Goldfield, Nevada

COLUMBIA POSTOFFICE

JUMBO, NEV., *Dec 1* 190 6

Shipment Francis Mohawk Lease.
Carlaalor

WE HAVE ASSAYED YOUR SAMPLES WITH THE FOLLOWING RESULTS PER TON OF 2,000 LBS.

NO.	MARKED	GOLD OZ.	SILVER OZ.	COPPER PER CT.	LEAD PER CT.	PER CT.	PER CT.	TOTAL VALUE
	Francis 105000#	16.20						319.95
	" 169750#	8.54						166.53
	" 120740#	11.56						225.42
	" 121764#	32.73						674.60
	" 152220#	41.06						821.20

Gold at _____ per oz.
Silver at _____ per oz. Charges $ _____
Copper at _____ per unit
Lead at _____ per unit

C. S. Thomas Jr.

OFFICE OF

Jumbo Mining Company of Goldfield, Nevada

COLUMBIA POSTOFFICE

JUMBO, NEV., *12/7* 190 6

Mohawk

WE HAVE ASSAYED YOUR SAMPLES WITH THE FOLLOWING RESULTS PER TON OF 2,000 LBS.

NO.	MARKED	GOLD OZ.	SILVER OZ.	COPPER PER CT.	LEAD PER CT.	PER CT.	PER CT.	TOTAL VALUE
26	Thomas 176	19.86						$ 397.20
27		160.56						3211.20
28		16.20						334.00
29		38.44						768.80
30		17.82						356.40
31		10.40						208.00

Gold at _____ per oz.
Silver at _____ per oz. Charges $ _____
Copper at _____ per unit
Lead at _____ per unit

H. G. Harbaugh

Plate XXVIII

(Triplicate)

Nevada Goldfield Reduction Company

Goldfield, Nevada   Jan. 5, 1907.

BOUGHT OF   Frances Mohawk Mining & Leasing Company.

LOT	SACKS CAR	ASSAY PER TON						WEIGHT				
		MOISTURE PER CENT	COPPER PER CENT	LEAD PER CENT	SILVER OZS.	GOLD OZS.	ZINC PER CENT	GROSS	MOISTURE	SACKS	TARE	NET
504	Wagons 2	1.25	—	—	—	189.10	—	28630	250	—	6560	19820
495	Wagons 4	1.58	—	—	—	300.69	—	21420	293	147	—	20980

FIGURED

Gold 100 per cent of $20.00   Value per Ton, — — $ 4929.62
Silver at   per ounce
Lead   per unit   Total Value,   40800   lbs, $ 100564.38
Copper   per unit

CHARGES

@ $160.28 per ton

Charges, $ 3369.80
Net — $ 97294.58

Vice President.

Auditor.

Plate XXIX

VON SCHULZ & LOW
ASSAY OFFICE AND CHEMICAL LABORATORY.

1746 CHAMPA STREET.   TELEPHONE 1562.   P. O. BOX 1537.

MARK OF SAMPLE	ASSAYED FOR
As below.	Chas. S. Thomas, Jr.

	PER TON OF 2,000 LBS.		PER CENT LEAD	PER CENT COPPER WET	PER CENT ZINC	PER CENT SILICA	PER CENT IRON	PER CENT MANGANESE	PER CENT LIME	PER CENT
	OZS. GOLD	OZS. SILVER								
# 126.	109.46	-------								
# 127.	6.40	-------								

IN REFERRING TO THIS CERTIFICATE PLEASE GIVE DATE BELOW.

DENVER, COLO.,   NOV 6 1908   190___

CHARGES, $_____

Von Schulz & Low

A. VON SCHULZ   A. H. LOW

VON SCHULZ & LOW
ASSAY OFFICE AND CHEMICAL LABORATORY.

1746 CHAMPA STREET.   TELEPHONE 1562.   P. O. BOX 1537.

MARK OF SAMPLE	ASSAYED FOR
As below.	Chas. S. Thomas, Jr.

	PER TON OF 2,000 LBS.		PER CENT LEAD	PER CENT COPPER WET	PER CENT ZINC	PER CENT SILICA	PER CENT IRON	PER CENT MANGANESE	PER CENT LIME	PER CENT
	OZS. GOLD	OZS. SILVER								
# 128.	14.32	-------								
# 129.	32.31	-------								
# 130.	41.02	-------								
# 131.	28.96	-------								
# 132.	238.24	-------								
# 133.	29.06	-------								

IN REFERRING TO THIS CERTIFICATE PLEASE GIVE DATE BELOW.

DENVER, COLO.,   NOV 6 1908   190___

CHARGES, $_____

Von Schulz & Low

MOHAWK MINE - JUMBO 500-LEVEL - 1908

Plate XXX

RED TOP MINING COMPANY

No. 51 *Dec 9* 190 6

Description *Ashrode 1st*
Raise N. of Engine
750 Level Frances

Gold Value $ *1136 ⁰⁰* *568.⁴⁰*

Silver Value $

RED TOP MINING COMPANY

No. 31 *Dec 8* 190 6

Description *Hays Monnette*
East drift from winze. 4'

Gold Value $ *1042 ⁰⁰* *5²⁰*

Silver Value $

RED TOP MINING COMPANY

No. 79 *Dec 6* 190 6

Description *Hays Monnette*
2nd level East drift
from Winze. 2'.

Gold Value $ *768 ⁸⁰* *35⁴⁰*

Silver Value $ *15*

RED TOP MINING COMPANY

No. 78 *Dec 6* 190 6

Description *Hays Monnette*
2nd Level Winze. S drift
back 4'

Gold Value $ *334 ⁰⁰* *16 ⁷⁰*

Silver Value $

RED TOP MINING COMPANY

No. 27 *Dec 6* 190 6

Description *Frances Mohawk*
Ashrode Streak on
1st Level
160 ⁵⁶ g.

Gold Value $ *3211 ²⁰*

Silver Value $

THE WRITER'S SAMPLE TABS — FALL 1906

Plate XXXI

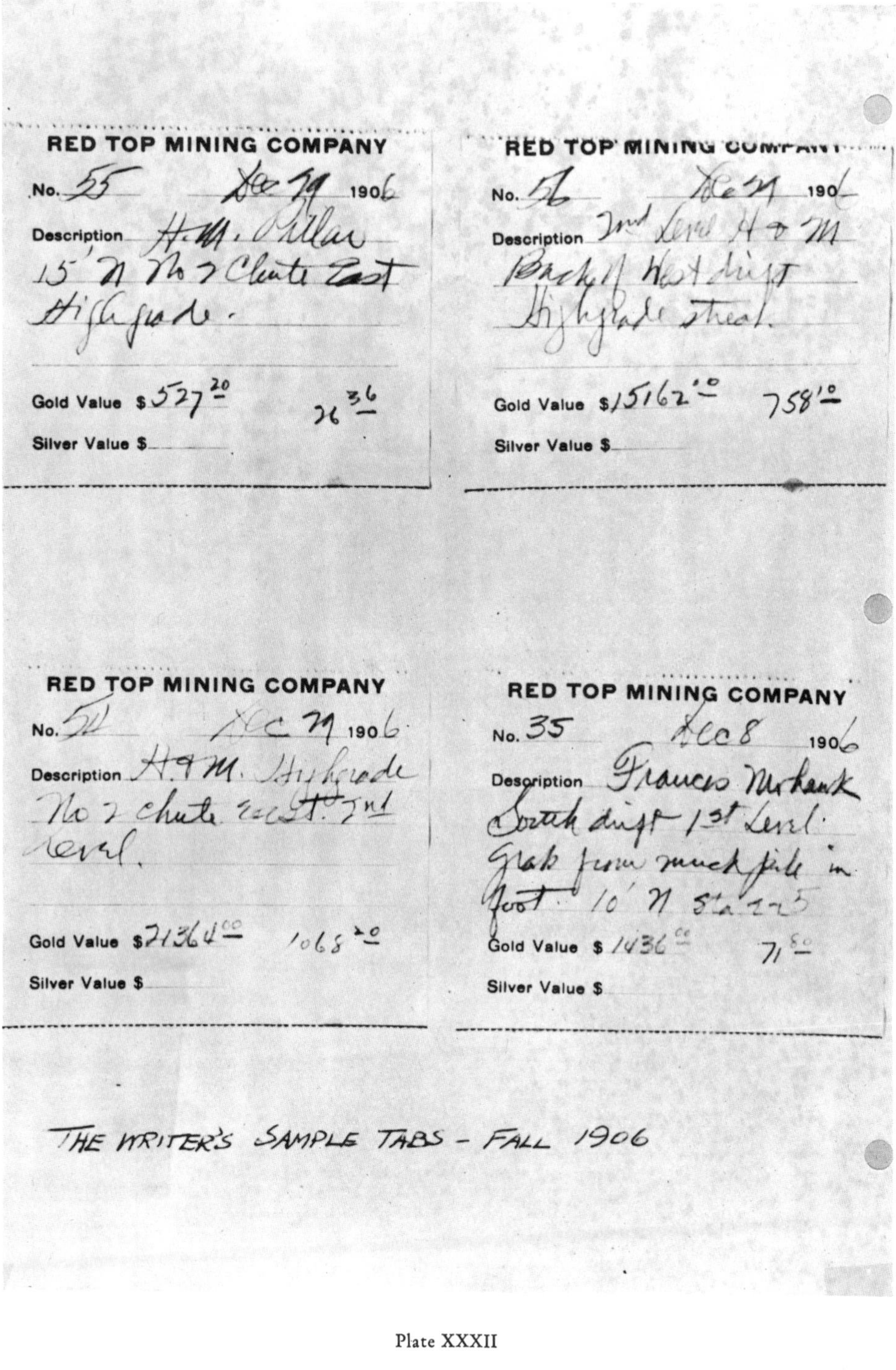

RED TOP MINING COMPANY

No. 55   Dec 29 1906

Description H. M. Pillar
15' N No 7 Chute East
Highgrade.

Gold Value $527 20   26 36

Silver Value $

RED TOP MINING COMPANY

No. 56   Dec 29 190

Description 2nd Level H & M
Back of West drift
Highgrade streak.

Gold Value $15162 00   758 10

Silver Value $

RED TOP MINING COMPANY

No. 54   Dec 29 1906

Description H & M. Highgrade
No 7 chute east & 2nd
level.

Gold Value $7364 00   1068 20

Silver Value $

RED TOP MINING COMPANY

No. 35   Dec 8 1906

Description Frances Mohawk
South drift 1st Level.
Grab from muck pile in
foot 10' N Sta 225

Gold Value $ 1436 00   71 80

Silver Value $

THE WRITER'S SAMPLE TABS - FALL 1906

Plate XXXII

WOMENS STOCK EXCHANGE THROWN INTO SHOCKING ROW BY DISSENSIONS OF LADY MEMBERS

The "only women's stock exchange in the world" is struggling to down its emotions in its quarters in the Citizens' National bank building.

The lady who calls out the "puts" or puts out the "calls"—or what it is—is sticking up her nose at the lady president; the lady treasurer is insulted because some one asked to see her books, and the man stock expert, who was imported from Boston, has fallen a victim to the demon Rum.

Now isn't that enough to kick a hole through the middle of Wall street?

But how easy it is for women to solve a problem!

They got together yesterday afternoon and snubbed the "other" faction of ladies, and confidentially elected a new president. They have decided to keep the new president's name a secret.

All the ladies who elected her are sworn not to divulge even a whisper.

Undismayed by its previous harrowing experiences, the "only women's stock exchange in the world" is now ready to plunge back into the ranks of troubled finance.

Bubbling Beginning.

This epic really begins with last July, when the exchange was organized.

Mrs. Mary Milligan burst breezily in from Goldfield and fired her women friends with militant spirit. Why let men monopolize the stock market! Why? she demanded. Answer: The only women's stock exchange in the world.

They had wafers and tea and cut flowers and potted palms, and a young lady who sang about "Happy Days", at the formal opening.

Mrs. Milligan separated herself from $300, and was made president and manager; Mrs. Anna L. Briggs, the woman real estate operator, was made secretary and treasurer, and Mrs. Clara

Shortridge Foltz was elected attorney.

They got into perplexity right away, because when they wanted to sell "seats" on the exchange for $100 each they met with skepticism. The women said that $100 was too much to pay for any kind of a seat. There wasn't anything to show for your money.

"What we ought to have," said the lady managers, "is some stock or something so we can have certificates."

Stocks and Seats.

They arranged to give stock as a "premium" with every seat purchased—somewhat on the order of trading stamps.

George Ade says that when a woman wants to make a home run she doesn't bother about whether she hit the ball or not—she just makes the home run.

So they issued $500,000 worth of stock. To their dismay, however, Mrs. Foltz told them that if they had such a lot of stock they had to have assets.

They had an amazing lot of worry about assets for a while, until finally Mrs. Foltz kindly donated some oil land that wasn't needed in the family, and Mrs. Briggs gave them a city lot somewhere in the suburbs. They they had assets and everything.

Including quarrels.

They became angry with Mrs. Milligan, in spite of the fact that she got it up. So she got sore and quit the job and took back her $300, which was the first disaster.

"There is no use," said the ladies, ruefully, when Mrs. Milligan had gone. "We have simply got to have a man around—just at first."

A Man from Boston.

They looked around very carefully, and at length one of them, in a glow of enthusiasm, announced that she had discovered a young man from Boston. He was a perfect gentleman and sym-

from the Los Angeles Times, Los Angeles, California (1907)

Plate XXXIII

pathetic and kind, and showed them all about stocks. They scratched Mrs. Milligan's name off the stationery, and the man from Boston was installed as the "caller" as well as manager.

Whenever stocks were reduced to 49 cents excited femininity surged about this one lone man.

But one day when they came in he appeared sick. His eyes were glazed and his face was flushed, and his beautiful Bostonese accent was somewhat muddled.

Sympathetic ladies prescribed for him, but he didn't seem to rally, and at length they had to call in another man. He pronounced the illness to be that ailment scientifically known as a Brannigan, otherwise a souse, or a bun. In fact, the man from Boston was afloat on a wonderful jag.

They scornfully bade the man begone. Second disaster.

She Convinces.

After trying various other expedients—and men—Mrs. A. B. Hays appeared on the scene. Mrs. Hays knew all about mines. She heard their little troubles with a superior smile. Easy for her!

"Ladies," said Mrs. Hayes, with a confident air that convinced. "Ladies, you have been doing this all wrong."

They believed her.

They tried to remember some of the things she said about it when they next saw their husbands. It was the most professional sounding thing—

Mrs. Hays said they ought never to have given stock away as premiums with the seats on the exchange like trading stamps. She said it wasn't dignified.

She said they ought to reap a RICH REVENUE from the sale of seats on the exchange.

All the ladies thought that would be a beautiful way to do. The only trouble was that all the ladies hadn't been paying cash for their seats. In fact, the exchange had been selling its seats on the installment plan; so they didn't get much real money. Some of those buying seats are Salvation Army women.

Mrs. Hayes said the first thing that always is to be done is to investigate the books.

'Nother complication.

Mrs. Briggs, the secretary, felt insulted at this suggestion. She said it wasn't treating her like a lady. There was a meeting over it, and Mrs. Briggs wept, and they all decided that Mrs. Hays' ideas were making too many people's feeling get hurt; they decided that

they would rather have the trading stamps, anyhow, because you have so little to show for it when you just have a seat in the exchange.

Besides, they found out that they would have to give back the oil lands and the city lots if they did as she said.

Mrs. Hays was furious at their fickleness and said she wouldn't have anything more to do with it.

Woman Caller.

In the meantime, after the mortifying failure of the man from Boston, they decided that men are a hard lot anyhow, and they appointed a woman to be caller of the exchange.

Mrs. K. L. Lane, who owns the largest picture hat on the exchange, was unanimously chosen to be caller, and bravely accepted. If there is anything trying it's writing on a blackboard with a lot of women looking at the back of your own gown, especially raising your arms that way.

Although her manner of calling the stocks was simply sweet, Mrs. Lane also had a little trouble.

Mrs. Lane took sides with Mrs. Hays, and it was worse than a church row.

One faction had indignation meetings around a table in the stock room, and the other faction locked the door of the stenographer's office, across the hall, and also had indignation meetings.

That was the situation yesterday when they had a little secret meeting and elected Mrs. M. E. Hamilton president and resolved not to tell a living soul about it—especially the few on the the other side.

That Secret.

Mrs. Hamilton was much annoyed when the secret got out.

"Why," she said, severely, "there must be a mistake about this. It was to be kept a secret for AT LEAST two weeks about my election. We didn't want ANYBODY to know it. This positively must not appear in the paper."

Mrs. Earl D. Gray, the new secretary, opened her eyes very wide in what is technically known as the "baby stare."

"Why," she said, "where did you hear such things. Oh," (stamping her very small foot) "these reporters make me so a-n-g-r-y. Somebody has been telling the awfulest fibs."

At this point Mrs. Briggs, the retiring secretary and treasurer, slipped an arm about her successor's waist and gave her a gentle squeeze of warning.

"There, dear," she said, with a withering glance at the newspaper men, "what they say can't make the slightest difference in the world. The women's stock exchange shall be a success despite everything." — Los Angeles

Deadly Altercation With a Rifle and Revolver for Weapons.

MAN WITH THE REVOLVER WINS BY QUICKER ACTION

Special to The Tribune.

WINNEMUCCA, June 11.—As the outcome of a quarrel over a mining claim, a fatal shooting affray, in which Jack Bell met death at the hands of Martin Lorenzo, occurred about noon yesterday near the De-Long ranch on Happy creek, in the Jackson mountain country.

Lorenzo and Bell, it seems, both claimed title to a mining claim, originally located by the former and re-located by Bell, the latter claiming that the work had not been performed according to law. Several times they had quarreled and the feeling between them became so bitter that Lorenzo, who was working on the DeLong ranch, quit his job and was going to leave for Boyd Basin to avoid further trouble.

The men met in the hills yesterday near the DeLong ranch, and Bell was shot to death by Lorenzo. William DeLong was the only witness of the shooting, and he was some distance away when the affray occurred. DeLong says that he met Bell shortly before noon yesterday, the latter being on horseback and armed with a rifle, in the canyon a short distance from the ranch. As Bell passed DeLong, Lorenzo was coming toward them, but some distance away at the time. Bell asked DeLong if the man approaching them was Lorenzo, and upon DeLong replying that it was, Bell shouted back: "Well, I'm going over and have it out with him." Bell rode up to Lorenzo and some angry words passed between them. Bell brought his rifle to his shoulder and drew a bead on Lorenzo, but just as he pulled the trigger the latter shoved the muzzle of the gun aside, drew his revolver and fired, the bullet striking Bell in the abdomen. Bell's horse swerved and he fell from the saddle. As Bell lay on the ground, writhing in mortal agony, Lorenzo fired two more bullets into his dying adversary's body and completed his bloody work.

Bell is said to have formerly lived in Cedarville, Cal., and to have a wife and child in Lovelock, but this latter report can not be verified.

Plate XXXIV

THE WESTERN UNION TELEGRAPH COMPANY.
INCORPORATED
24,000 OFFICES IN AMERICA.   CABLE SERVICE TO ALL THE WORLD.

This Company TRANSMITS and DELIVERS messages only on conditions limiting its liability, which have been assented to by the sender of the following message
Errors can be guarded against only by repeating a message back to the sending station for comparison, and the Company will not hold itself liable for errors or delays
in transmission or delivery of Unrepeated Messages, beyond the amount of tolls paid thereon, nor in any case where the claim is not presented in writing within sixty
days after the message is filed with the Company for transmission.
This is an UNREPEATED MESSAGE, and is delivered by request of the sender, under the conditions named above.
ROBERT C. CLOWRY, President and General Manager.

103

RECEIVED at

544. Xn. By. O. 36 Paid, x

Mq. Chicago August 23 1906

L. M. Sullivan Trust Co.

Goldfield Nev.

You offered five thousand dog good next day sold same and received your
hair raising telegram cancelling am and have been ready to wire
deposit and deman stock. Better dig peacefully wire and
will forward deposit.

Henry Anchester.

11:30Am

MONEY TRANSFERRED BY TELEGRAPH.   **CABLE OFFICE.**

Form No. 200.
THE WESTERN UNION TELEGRAPH COMPANY.
INCORPORATED
23,000 OFFICES IN AMERICA.   CABLE SERVICE TO ALL THE WORLD.
ROBERT C. CLOWRY, President and General Manager.

Receiver's No.	Time Filed	Check

SEND the following message subject to the terms
on back hereof, which are hereby agreed to.

Aug. 23, 1906.

Henry Anchester,

Pabst Bldg.,

Milwaukee, Wis.

Come out here and repeat to my face the message you

sent over the wires. I will pay your expenses coming. You won't

need any going back.

LARRY SULLIVAN.

☞ READ THE NOTICE AND AGREEMENT ON BACK. ☜

Plate XXXV

Ownership of $16,000 in Gold Determined; Court Declares It Stolen.

Goldfield Miners and Assayer Are Told Their Conduct Was Un-American in Not Seeking to Defend Selves by Exposing Thieves.

"God forbid that the time will ever come when there will not be sufficient heroic honesty to stamp out dishonesty, and especially such disgraceful dishonesty that the testimony in this case has proved to have existed.

"Mr. Clerk, enter a verdict in favor of the plaintiff as owner and possessor of the property. Gentlemen of the jury, you are excused until 2 o'clock this afternoon."

This was the dramatic ending of the suit of the Goldfield-Mohawk Mining company in the federal court shortly before 11 o'clock today. Judge Lewis delivered a scathing denouncement of the high graders who have been operating in Goldfield, Nev. The suit was brought to determine the ownership of a large shipment of ore from the Mohawk mine. Judge Lewis directed a verdict in favor of the company.

George Richardson and Frank Cochrane of Goldfield, Nev., were the defendants and the ore was worth $16,000.

Judge Lewis had evidently paid close attention to every bit of testimony. He had written down "points which I thought at the time would be used in the arguments," as he put it, and he discourse he delivered made the ears of the listeners tingle.

EXPERT TESTIMONY.

"Experts, men who have studied the questions at schools provided from the funds of the people; experts who have given their lives to their work; experts upon whose judgment great sums of money are invested, have told us on the stand that not more than 5 per cent of this ore could be classed as ore that did not belong to the Mohawk company, and not one word of testimony has been offered to controvert their testimony," Judge Lewis said.

"The usual tests have positively proved th: this ore belonged to the Mohawk company.

"Everyone knew that ore was being stolen from the Mohawk company.

"There was no doubt that the stealing was going on, yet we do not find any effort being made to find the thief.

"Whenever there is gathered together a body of honest American citizens and the imputation is made that there is a thief among them, the natural impulse of these American citizens is to demand an investigation and to aid in this investigation to discover who the thief is.

"Yet we do not find any action of this kind here.

MUCH ORE STOLEN.

"Mr. Cochrane took the stand. He said he was an assayer and that he had an office in Goldfield, yet he was unable to state on the stand the name of a single customer who came to his place of business. We also learned that the ore was shipped to Pueblo under a fictitious name."

Then came the dramatic climax and the order for the verdict for the plaintiff.

Harry Bryant and S. H. White of Pueblo represented the Mohawk company. After the verdict was ordered, Mr. Bryant said: "The Mohawk company had over $1,000,000 in high grade ore stolen from it within four months. Two hundred thousand dollars more of it was recovered in Reno and San Francisco. The high graders' assay offices did a great business.

"In this case thirty-four sacks were stolen, hauled eighty miles and shipped to Pueblo. This should eternally settle this case."

Attorneys J. H. Maupin and D. B. Ellis represented the defendants.

from the Denver Post, Denver, Colorado (1907)

Plate XXXVI

The Unique and Adobe Concert Halls

Are Unfair Houses

We request all Union men not to patronize these halls

The unfair girl workers are:

TESSIE ALFRED	KITTIE LA BELLE
LITTLE FAY	MAZIE
SKIDOO BABE	FAY

Signed by

THE CONCERT HALL GIRLS

IN CONSIDERATION of my being employed by the ....

.... company for such time as my services shall be satisfactory,
and at the wages heretofore fixed by said company, and subject to the rules and regulations fixed by said
company, and by the Goldfield Mine Operators' Association relating to the employment of men in and
around the mines of Goldfield Mining District, I hereby covenant and agree with said company that I am
not now and will not be during the time I am working for said company a member of Goldfield Miners'
Union Number 220 of the Western Federation of Miners or of any other union in Goldfield or elsewhere,
that is directly or indirectly affiliated with or has any connection of any kind, nature or description with
said the Western Federation of Miners.

Witness my hand and seal at Goldfield, Esmeralda County, Nevada, this ....

day of .... 190........ .

.... [Seal]

Agreement required of miners after strike of November, 1907

THE MONTHLY POEM

Not having at hand anything in the shape of
classic verse that seemed to us sufficiently local
and appropriate for this Christmas number of
"Gossip", we threw our pen into the breach and
filled the gap:

THE MINER'S CHRISTMAS

The wind blew shrill; the miner woke
And struck a match to get a smoke.
The door unhinged let in the blast
That chilled his marrow as it past.
And sharply smote the sand and sleet
Upon his large protruding feet.
Cold were those feet; he tucked them in
And drew his knees up to his chin,
"Don't it beat Hell!" he said in pain,
Then laid him down to sleep again.

Plate XXXVIII

BUCKHORN MINES

To Employes:

The following wage scale will be in effect on and after Nov. 1, 1909.

All to be eight hour shifts-- Time and one-half for overtime.

PER SHIFT		PER SHIFT	
Laborers -	$3.00	Carpenters	$4.00
Muckers -	3.25	Mechanics -	4.00
Miners -	3.50	Engineers -	4.00
Machinemen	3.75	Timbermen -	3.75
Machine Helpers -	3.50	Pumpmen -	3.50
Shaftmen -	4.00	Teamsters -	3.25

Board will be $1.00 per day for the present. We have no desire to make any profit from the boarding house, and will reduce price of board if possible to do so.

This is a low-grade mine and must be operated economically if at all and any interference in the way of attempts to change wage scale by Labor Unions or individuals will be considered unfriendly to the Buckhorn Mines. If you do not like the wage scale you will please not request work.

FRED. J. SIEBERT
General Manager

Plate XXXIX

How a Bunch of Goldfield Sports Raked In the Shekels At a Quiet Little Game in Ely

One thing stands out in the whirl of Ely's New Year festivities, and that is the slashing poker game played at the Capital up to an early hour yesterday morning between A. D. Meyers, the Goldfield capitalist, M. F. Rickard, "Little Tex" and J. A. Fesler. It was a spectacular tournament. When it ended, Meyers had lost $7,600; Rickard won $16,600, and Fesler had lost $9,000, says the White Pine News.

The three were together on Monday night, taking in the sights of the camp and enjoying the New Year's cheer which flowed freely from nearly a score of fountains.

Towards morning they dropped into the Capital, and to while away the time, started a game of draw poker with a $50 limit. All three began with $500 worth of chips. The Goldfield millionaire soon grew restive under the limit. He wanted it raised. To accommodate him, it was advanced to $100. This satisfied him for only a short time, and then he remarked that the game could be made more interesting with a higher limit. As he spoke he glanced significantly at the ceiling. Rickard and Fesler understood.

"Very well," said Tex, "let it be the roof."

From that moment the play grew skyrockety. The hands were played with a vim and daring which took the breath away from the onlookers.

The Aultman street resorts were crowded even at that hour in the morning with merry-makers, and the news that a spectacular poker game was in progress soon spread through the street. The crowd flocked to the scene. The place, usually crowded, was jammed to the doors, but there were only a few who actually gained points of advantage from which they could watch the ebbs and flows of the battle with cards.

The largest pot of the tournament was played for toward morning. It contained $10,000 in cash and chips. Meyers opened it, and both Rickard and Fesler stayed.

Myers drew one card, and Rickard drew one. Fesler drew three. Meyers then bet $100, Rickard raised him as much, and Fesler saw the raise; Meyers then boosted the raise and Rickard again went him better. There was then about $1,000 in the pot.

Fesler, after again glancing at his hand and pondering for a moment, dropped out of the game, leaving the other two to fight it out.

Raise followed raise until there was $10,000 in the pot. The end came when Rickard raised Meyers $1,000. The millionaire grew thoughtful, and reviewed the cards in his hand. Plainly he saw it was no time for bluffing, and that his wealth would not help him in that emergency. After quietly lighting a fresh cigar and drawing two or three puffs, he spread his cards on the table. He was beaten.

The breathless onlookers craned their necks to see what he had. It wasn't much—except from the viewpoint of a millionaire. He had ace up.

"Little Tex," seeing that the pot was his, was not so willing to gratify the curiosity of the spectators. He put his hand back into the pack and shuffled the cards. What he held will only be known to himself until he chooses to tell it. Fesler, having dropped out before the end of the play, also returned his hand to the deck without showing it.

If Meyers' aces up were strong enough to carry off the $10,000 on a show-down, he was at least spared the pain of knowing that he had been "bluffed out."

The game ended soon after, but that was only the beginning of events for the spectators. The winners and the loser, who was as cheerful as a cricket, then began to spend the poker money; that is, Rickard did, and Meyers and Fesler drew upon a "bundle" which they had in reserve. Until an early hour yesterday morning the crowd that had witnessed the game was not allowed to spend a cent.

from the Goldfield News, Goldfield, Nevada (1907)

Plate XL

A QUIET LITTLE GAME OF STUD POKER AT LIDA

Accused of first degree murder in causing the death of David Wright at Lida late last fall, Harry Wiseman was placed on trial yesterday in the district court.

A jury was completed shortly before 6 o'clock last evening, after both the defense and the state had exercised numerous challenges and dozens of men on the panel had been closely examined, particularly with reference to their ideas regarding the infliction of death in cases of this character. The jury as finally selected consists of George B. Holleran, J. D. Griffon, Samuel Petaors, J. J. Noone, William Boykin, Gobe Lewis, J. B. Cottle, L. V. Stanton, Eugene Perretti, G. B. Lallo, Jake R. Martin and John Boesch.

This trial will detailize the tragic events at Lida on October 2 last, when four men were shot, one of them fatally. The affair was strictly a saloon row, wherein bullets rained in a bar room and dropped four men within a twinkling. Only one leaden messenger proved mortal, the one received by Wright, and it is for the latter's death that Wiseman must answer. He is accused of murder in the first degree and should he be found guilty as charged, the penalty would be death.

This morning Judge O'Brien will pronounce sentence upon Williams, the Indian, found guilty of the same kind of a crime and who will probably receive the death penalty.

During the afternoon of October 2, Wiseman, proprietor of the Northern at Lida, is said to have walked up to the Mohawk saloon in the same town, conducted by William Seeman, and seeing a party playing poker, drew his gun while standing in the door way, at the same time saying, "I guess this will get me into the game."

"Well, I guess it won't, too," is said to have been the response of Seeman. Wiseman fired several shots at Seeman, it is alleged, but none took effect in his body. However, one bullet struck Harry Stoyer, another J. E. Hibbs, and another David Wright. Then Seeman opened fire, it is claimed, and landed a bullet into Wiseman's jaw and another in his shoulder, from the effects of which wounds he was in the hospital for months. Wright failed to survive and on November 1, or nearly a month after the shooting, he passed away.

The contention of the state is that Wiseman precipitated the trouble and did the first shooting and that in getting a bullet or two, he received only what was coming to him. The district attorney brands the shooting of Wright as plain murder without provocation. The defense, it is understood, will advance the plea that the trouble was general and that it cannot be proven that Wiseman fired first, also that the question as to whether Wright really died from the result of the bullet wound, or of chronic Bright's disease, will be raised. A. W. Liechti and George Springmeyer represent Wiseman, while District Attorney Swallow and his assistant, J. Emmett Walsh, are prosecuting.

Wiseman is a comparatively young man. In court yesterday, he was quite pale and his forehead was liberally sprinkled with pimples. He is of slight build and wears a small, dark-brown mustache, faultlessly curled. His dark grey checked suit was adorned yesterday with a white carnation and sprig of fern.

The case will be resumed at 10 o'clock this morning and promises, before the day shall have passed, to produce some highly interesting testimony regarding gun men in the old camp south of Goldfield.

Notice to the Public.

Thomas B. O'Brien is no longer a member of Nevada Miners Union No. 1.   HENRY FALKEY, Secy.
WM. CUNNINGHAM, Prest.

from the Goldfield News, Goldfield, Nevada (1907)

Plate XLI

Grand Raffle!!!

Chances 1c to $10.00 (real money!)

Panamint Joe, the Moses of Prospectors, is cashing in, fairly pronto. He's short to the house, and must sell his outfit.

Want a Horse?

A nice roan horse, sound as a ring:
Nine years old, ten in the Spring:
One eye is gone, one is of glass——
Three lame feet, and a tail at his ass.
His head bulges out, his butt curves in——
Damn' fine horse——for the fix he is in!

Also a jackass, old as Methuselah; can smell gold like a bloodhound can smell a nigger. Pack outfit, worn out when Lincoln was President, thrown in.

See John Browning *the Cock-Eyed Trainer of Jumping Fleas* at the Bank Saloon

Plate XLII

Goldfield Turns Out in Masse To Gaze on the Work of Tex Rickard in Cutting His Lawn

The man was coatless, hatless and breathless as he hurried along the road, raising a cloud of dust that could be seen a block away.

"Where are you going?" asked an acquaintance whom he met as he took a short cut through a back alley.

"Come on," said the other, "I'll tell you as we go along—y'know Tex Rickard is going to cut his lawn today? Well, he is, an' I'm goin' out to see it."

When they arrived within two blocks of Sundog avenue they heard a whirr-r-r-r of wheels that sounded like a machine shop in full operation.

"What the blazes is that?" asked one.

"Ding-busted if I know—come on, or we'll miss it."

As they turned the corner they saw a delegation coming from Bellevue street, and heading in the direction of the corner of Crook and Franklin. At the corner itself, a throng of perhaps 500 people was gathered, watching with interest something that was going on in the yard.

From the yard there came the strange noise they heard, and upon edging through the crowd they saw a man in a pair of blue overalls, pushing a queer looking contraption over an oval shaped piece of lawn about the size of a doormat. He was performing the work with infinite pains, trimming each separate blade of grass to precisely the same height as the other, and prolonging the operation for the edification of the audience.

"Is that Tex?" asked someone in the crowd.

Work of the Gardener.

"No," answered the man who knew, which personage you will always find in a crowd, "that isn't Tex. Tex doesn't want to come out, he's up in the attic, hiding, because the crowd has called for a speech several times. That's his under gardener—the head gardener went to Los Angeles a few days ago to take a course in horticulture, with the idea of beating that man Burbank, and when he comes back he is going to undertake a series of experiments, with the hope of raising lemons on the Joshua palms.

"What will they do with the lemons?" the man who wanted to know.

"Well," said the man who knows, "the primary intention is to provide lemons enough to supply the Northern, so that the growing tendency of the population of Goldfield for lemonades may be gratified; the secondary one is to use the surplus to wrap in tissue paper, pack in scented boxes and mail to the ginks who leave Goldfield in a huff, and spend their spare time on the outside, knocking the camp."

"Fine business," said the other.

"See that delegation of skirts over there?" asked the man who knows. "That's the Goldfield Woman's club. They have attended to watch the man cut the grass and to extend to Tex the thanks of the community for growing a patch of grass. After it is all over, they will hold a meeting and give prizes for the best essay on the growth of grass in Goldfield, and for the best answer to the question as to the size of the wheat crop in Goldfield during the coming autumn."

Future of the Crop.

"What is Tex going to do with the grass that is cut?" asked the seeker after information.

"Well, his present intention," answered the man who knows, "is to pile it in a corner and let the wild bulls and bears bid for it. He may, however, send a pound of it to the Jamestown exposition for the purpose of showing the enterprise of Goldfield citiens."

"Don't you think it would be a better idea to let the lambs have it for fodder? They'll probably need it after the bulls and bears get through with them," said the other.

"By the way, what is that delegation of athletic looking young ladies over there?" he continued.

"Oh, that's the new Goldfield Golf club. They have a lease on the lawn for ten years, and expect to start a $10,000 clubhouse in a few days. They intend bringing a few Scotchmen over to teach them the fine points of the game."

"Do you think any of the eligible young men of the town will join?"

"Well, to tell you the truth, I hardly think so—they're too busy with high-balls to bother with golf balls."

About this time Tex was pulled out of the attic by a bunch who found him hiding under a bed, and forced to introduce some of the notable personages who were present.

Among the latter people, who were far too modest to give their names, was included the gentleman who first raised a radish in Goldfield; the first lady who raised a sweet pea; the gentleman who grew five leaves on a poplar tree; the man who said he saw a fence post sprouting in a locality so far away that no one would take the trouble to find out whether it was true; the man who found a potato-bug on a sage brush; and finally the first lady who discovered a caterpillar crawling along on one of the fronds of a morning-glory vine.

Just before the touching exercises were concluded, a boy on a bicycle, in the livery of the Western Union, came browsing up the road, stopping occasionally to sit down and rest, while he smoked a cigarette, but finally dismounting at the outskirts of the crowd. He pushed through, whistling the latest Goldfield version of a popular song, "Everybody rustles but the messenger boy," and stopped at the side of the lawn. "Telegram for Tex Rickard," he shouted.

Tex took the telegram and read it, while a serious expression spread over his face. The telegram was as follows:

> Oyster Bay, Aug. 9, 1907.
> Mr. Tex Rickard, Care Northern Saloon, Goldfield, Nevada.
> Hear you are cutting your grass. Congratulations. You are eligible for president of the U. S. Can you spare a bale to add to my harvest?
> THEODORE ROOSEVELT.

The crowd voted by acclamation to send the president a sample in a candy box, which is all Goldfield can spare.

Amid the stirring strains of the Goldfield band, each of which organization was crowned with a wreath of the grass, the immense throng joined in singing the Goldfield anthem in praise of Pan, the god god of the woods and green things, the chorus of which is as follows:

"We may all have lawns in our own
   back yards,
  In the sweet bye-and-bye
We may all cheer the landscape with
   bright green swards
  If we only try.
We yet may see great lofty trees,
Or fields of wheat bend in the breeze.
They depend, of course, such things
   as these,
  On just you and I."

from the Goldfield News, Goldfield, Nevada (1907)

Plate XLIII

SIGHS FOR THE GOOD OLD DAYS

WHEN PROSPECTORS WERE PIONEERS

OF "SHANNAHAN'S SHEBEEN"

The following verses were handed to the editor by Mr. J. J. Reilly of Wonder, who ran across them some time ago, and as they refer to one of Nevada's Bonanza Kings of early days, Mr. Reilly felt they were worth preserving. The human side in them appealed strongly to him as an old mining man and will no doubt recall instances in the lives of other men from this state. The name of the author has been forgotten.

"THE MORNIN'S MORNIN."

This is the tale that Cassidy told,
In his halls a-sheen with purple and gold.
Told as he sprawled in an easy chair,
Chewing cigars at a dollar the pair ;
Told with a sigh and perchance a tear,
As the rough soul showed through the
|cracked veneer ;
For a Greuze and Millet were hung on high
With a rude little print in a frame between,
A picture of Shanahan's old Shebeen.

"I'm drinkin' my mornin's mornin'
But it doesn't taste the same,
Though the glass is of finest crystal,
And the liquor slips down like crame ;
And my Cockney footman brings it,
On a sort of silver plate—
Sherry and bitters it is, Sir,
For whiskey is out of date."

"In me brand new brownstone mansion,
Fift' Av'noo over the way,
The cathedral around the corner
And the Lord Archbishop to tay,—
Sure, I ought to be stiff with grandeur,
But my tastes are mighty mean
And I'd rather a mornin's mornin'
At Shanahan's old Shebeen."

"Oh well do I mind the shanty,
The rocks and the fields beyant,
The dirt floor yellow with sawdust,
And the walls on a three-inch slant.
(There's a twelve-story flat on the site now,
Twas meself that builded the same ;
And they called it the 'Montmorincy,'
Though I wanted the good old name.)

from the Goldfield News, Goldfield, Nevada (1907)

Plate XLIV

My dinner pail under my oxther,
Before the whistle blew,
I'd banish the drames from me eyelids
With a boggin—maybe two.
And oh twas illigant whiskey,
It's like I have never seen,
Since I went for me mornin's mornin'
To Shanahan's old Shebeen."

"I disremember the makers,
I could not tell you the brand ;
But it smiled like golden sunlight
And it looked and tasted grand.
When my throat was caked with mortar
Or my head was cracked wid a blast,
One drink of Shanahan's dew drops
And all me trouble was past.
That's why as I squat on the cushions
Wid divil a thing to do ;
In a mornin' coat lined wid velvet
An' champagne lunch at two ;
The memory comes like banshee,
Myself and my wealth between ;
And I kens for a mornin's mornin'
At Shanahan's old Shebeen."

"In a mornin' coat lined with velvet—
And my old coat used to do
Alike for mornin' and evenin'
(And sometimes I slept in it too.)
An' twas divil a sup of sherry
That Shanahan kept, no fear ;
If you couldn't afford good whiskey,
He'd take you on trust for beer."

"The dacintist bunch I knew there,
McCarthy (sinanther since)
An' Murphy, they mixed the mortar.
(Sure the Pope has made him a prince.)
You should see an avic o' Sundays,
Wid faces scraped and clean,
Whin the boys stood a mornin's mornin'
Round Shanahan's old Shebeen."

"Whist, here comes His Grace's carriage ;
Twill be lunch time by and by,
An' I darsen't drink another,
Though my throat is powerful dry ;
For I've to meet the Archbishop ;
I'm a tarrier now no more,
But Ohone, those were the fine times then,
                                        |lad,
And the talk of them makes me sore.
And whisper, theres times I tell you,
When I'd swap this easy chair,
And the velvet coat, and the footman,
With his sassenach nose in the air,
And the Lord Archbishop himself, too,
For a drink of the days that ha' been,
In Shanahan's old Shebeen."

Plate XLV

HON. CHARLES S. THOMAS.

Mr. SMOOT. Mr. President, I would like to have the Senate turn from a little levity to something that I think Senators would like to give a moment's attention to.

Mr. President, within a few moments there will be a great change in the membership of the Senate. Many of our close friends on both sides of this Chamber will retire.

I shall take but a few minutes of the Senate's time to express my appreciation of the unselfish, patriotic, and most valuable public services of Senator CHARLES S. THOMAS, of Colorado.

His retirement from the Senate is a distinct loss to the Senate and the Nation. During the full term of his service in the Senate he has never resorted in a single instance to demagoguery. He has never dodged a vote nor cast one contrary to what he believed to be for the best interests of his country. I respect him for his sterling manhood and honor him for his unquestioned honesty. No more courageous man ever served in this body. I honor and love him for his undoubted Americanism and skilled statesmanship. May the Great Master protect this great American and so arrange that his last days will be his happiest ones. [Applause.]

Mr. KENYON. Mr. President, I want to add just a word to the fitting and appropriate remarks of the Senator from Utah concerning the distinguished Senator from Colorado [Mr. THOMAS]. There is always a tinge of sadness when a session is drawing to a close and we are compelled to part with some of our fellow Members, and I think after we leave this body one thing we will look backward to above everything else will be the comradeship of the Senate, for while there is bitterness at times, yet underneath it all there is a wonderful spirit of comradeship.

If one in meditative moments were to have any worries about the future of this country, it would be because of the lack of courage that is displayed in public life, the local representation as distinguished from the broad national representation, and year by year as I have been in this body my admiration has

from the Congressional Record, Washington, D.C. (1907)

Plate XLVI

grown for the men who, while representing their States, have the courage to put above that representation for the entire Nation; that courage has been possessed by the Senator from Colorado to a remarkable degree. His service here is an inspiration, and it will be an incentive to younger men to follow him and fight as courageously as he has fought for some of the things in which he thoroughly believed. Though we might at times differ from him, we all admire his courage and his ability.

Many good men are leaving this body. Comparisons are probably odious. We will miss them all. Mr. President, I have said privately, as I now say publicly, that in my judgment the opinion of the people in the days to come will place the Senator from Colorado and his work side by side with the names of those who have been recognized in the past as the great Senators in this body. As he leaves, he goes with the good will of all. The Treasury of the United States loses one of its most vigorous defenders, the Senate one of its most valued Members, and the country one of the ablest Senators who ever sat in this body. [Applause.]

Mr. THOMAS. Mr. President, it is very difficult to express in apt or appropriate phrase the depth of appreciation and gratitude which this largely undeserved and wholly unexpected tribute has created within my bosom. I thank the Senators who have seen fit to so kindly emphasize my generally unsuccessful and unsatisfactory service in this body, and to assure them, and all of my colleagues, that I am more than repaid for all I have essayed as a member of this Chamber by the good will, the appreciation, the respect, and the friendship of my colleagues, irrespective of party lines.

Before one enters this illustrious body as a Member he is prone to entertain opinions and impressions of its members, gathered from expressions in the public press or from a general course of public opinion which have been frequently misdirected and more frequently erroneous. My personal experience confirms the view that there is in public life neither here nor elsewhere any body of men, taken by and large, whose standards are higher, whose capacity for service is greater, whose patriotism is purer, than the Members of this greatest deliberative body in the world. While we differ materially upon matters both of principle and of procedure, we make progress by respecting the convictions of each other, and at the close of our service we perceive in retrospect that succeeding Senates have striven to serve the country according to their own ideals, their standards of duty, and the pressing problems of their time.

Plate XLVII

This at least has been my experience. The eight years which I have spent as a Senator of the United States, covering a period of greatest stress and crisis in all the Nation's history, have been a fruitful source of education, of development, and courage, courage for the future, an abiding confidence in the destiny of America, and of renewed devotion to the principles of American Government.

Senators and brethren, one and all, I thank you from the bottom of my heart for this too extravagant tribute to my services, and beg to assure you that to the end of my life I will remember this as the proudest moment in a long course of years crowded with duties and responsibilities.

Mr. MYERS subsequently said: Mr. President, I am sorry that there shall be lost to membership in this body all of the Senators who are retiring to-day; I have particular regard and most kindly feelings for all of them; but I wish to say a word of one Senator especially, and that is the distinguished Senator from Colorado [Mr. THOMAS]. I understand that a while ago a very high and fitting tribute was paid to the distinguished Senator from Colorado by the able Senator from Iowa [Mr. KENYON] and also by the Senator from Utah [Mr. SMOOT]. I am sorry I missed the pleasure of hearing those tributes. However, I am not content that the session should end without adding an humble word of my own, expressive of my admiration and esteem for the distinguished Senator from Colorado [Mr. THOMAS]. His career in this body has been and is an inspiration to me. I have not always been in accord with him; I have not always voted as he voted; but his fearlessness, his courage, his statesmanship, his high ideals, his superb Americanism have always elicited my very warmest and unqualified admiration. To my mind, he stands as a striking type of the very highest degree of Americanism, and of upright, courageous statesmanship. I feel that I have been greatly strengthened and benefited by my association here with him and I shall always hold in mind his official career, as an example worthy of emulation in conscientious devotion to duty. He carries with him my warmest affection and highest esteem and my admiration for him shall never diminish.

Plate XLVIII

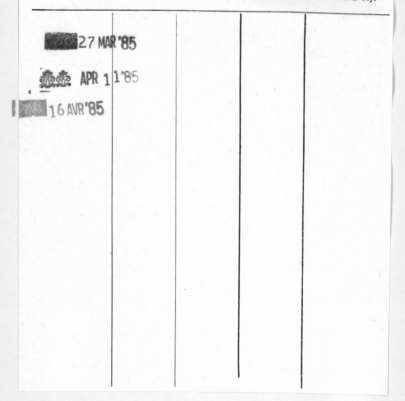